Teaching Adults
Fourth Edition

OLDHAM COLLEGE

Teaching Adults
Fourth Edition

Alan Rogers
Naomi Horrocks

 Open University Press

Open University Press
McGraw-Hill Education
McGraw-Hill House
Shoppenhangers Road
Maidenhead
Berkshire
England
SL6 2QL

email: enquiries@openup.co.uk
world wide web: www.openup.co.uk

and Two Penn Plaza, New York, NY 10121-2289, USA

First published 1986
Reprinted 1988, 1989, 1991, 1992, 1993, 1994
Second edition 1996
Reprinted 1998, 1999, 2000, 2001
Third edition 2002
Reprinted 2003, 2004, 2005, 2007 (twice)
First published in this fourth edition 2010

A catalogue record of this book is available from the British Library

ISBN-13: 978-0-33-523539-1
ISBN-10: 0-33-523539-5

Library of Congress Cataloging-in-Publication Data
CIP data applied for

Typeset by Graphicraft Limited, Hong Kong
Printed in the UK by Bell and Bain Ltd., Glasgow

*Fictitious names of companies, products, people, characters and/or data
that may be used herein (in case studies or in examples) are not intended
to represent any real individual, company, product or event.*

Mixed Sources
Product group from well-managed
forests and other controlled sources
www.fsc.org Cert no. TT-COC-002769
© 1996 Forest Stewardship Council

The McGraw·Hill Companies

Contents

Foreword: Using the Map for the Road Ahead

Imagine that you are on a mountain side. The path behind and ahead of you changes all the time, sometimes going up steeply, sometimes going down, sometimes more gently undulating. The area is combed with paths, all occupied by individuals and groups of climbers. You have in your hand a map but it is a bit unreliable, for it was drawn by people who passed along this path some time before and the paths keep changing as more and more people use them. Then your path and the path of some others coincide; for the next section of the road, some of the other walkers coalesce into a group and you meet up with them and for a short time travel together, exchanging experiences and insights. Then their path and yours separate and the group disperses, all along different tracks.

That is teaching adults. For a relatively short time, you have met up with one or a group of adults, and for a time you will travel together, sharing insights and experiences. And this book is something of a map. Reading and using this book is only a part of your journey; there were journeys for you before and there will be journeys afterwards. But for a time you and your student learners can try to follow the map; then you will separate, though some may stay within hailing distance for a time.

The aim of this book is to help you in the relationships within the learning group. Learning to teach adults is a matter of increasing your understanding not only of your subject but of yourself and of the learning group and in this way to improve your practices. This book will help you to explore (again) your attitudes towards the student learners in your group.

Looked at in this way, you can see that you do not need to motivate the participants in your travelling group to walk the walk – i.e. to learn; indeed, they do not need to learn how to learn for they are already learning all the time with enthusiasm and commitment, mostly through informal learning. But much of this learning will be unconscious, resulting in tacit funds of knowledge and skills, and even when they are conscious of it, as in a new job with its 'I'm on a steep learning curve', they may not regard that as 'learning'. For them, influenced by what has been called 'the empire of education', 'learning' may be seen as the same as 'being taught'.

But your student learners may well need to learn how to *study* (which is only one form of learning). And they may well need to be motivated to learn *what you wish them to learn*. For in today's world, increasingly in adult education, there are adult student learners who do not wish to be there (we heard very recently of a large police training programme where the majority had been 'required' to be there when they wished to be back in their own locations – which made hard work for the training team!).

The argument of this book is that if we can identify and understand something of this informal learning and use it in our teaching of adults, if we can help the participants to become more conscious of their existing funds of knowledge and skills and draw on them, then our task of helping adults to learn something will become more effective. This is not, of course, easy; it will be much easier for us to regard the group as a whole as uniformly ignorant and needing our standardised inputs. That will make us feel good, superior, needed. But it is not teaching *adults*, people who are our equals; this is not horizontal but vertical learning. So that part of our journey at this stage is to re-examine ourselves, our attitudes towards the people we meet and work with for a time, our commitment to them, the confidence we bring to the task.

And then we need to re-examine our adult students. They too are in the middle of a journey; they too each have a past journey and will have their own future journeys, sometimes together, sometimes apart. Each of them brings his or her own experiences, their own insights and concerns, which they need to contribute to the common task. They, like us, will have a goal, the next staging post or milestone of their journey. What they learn while with us – both what they learn formally and what they learn informally through the programme – will literally 'inform' their future journeys.

And this means that, whatever may be the formal circumstances in your adult learning context, the measures of success you choose for your group will be your own measures; they do not need to be only the formal assessments of the programme. And each of the participants will have their own intentions, their own different measures of success. Passing the examination or test (if there is one) and obtaining the certificate may well be important for some members of the group; but for others, the chief gain may well be 'walking tall', increased curiosity about the way ahead, increased confidence to travel on – though for the one or two over-confident, it may perhaps be a reining in of expectations through wider horizons and better perspectives of the risks in front of them. This book provides an opportunity for you to look again at the goal(s) you have set before yourself as well as the route to get there; and also to look at the paths and destinations the student learners have set before themselves.

Reading a map is not like reading a book. A map is consulted from time to time; it is explored, not in sequence. It is used again and again. So that reaching the end of this book will not be the end even of one stage of your journey; for we hope that as you and your learning group travel together, you will wish to consult various bits of this map as and when issues arise; that you will find in it matters which help you; and that you will re-write those bits of the book when your own experiences of teaching adults show that your path is different from what is outlined here. This is not the final word on 'teaching adults'; rather, it is a guide book with all the fallibility which one person has when trying to teach others who are already knowledgeable and experienced but who wish to have an opportunity for some critical reflection on what they are already doing or are planning to do. And that applies not only to those we are teaching but also to ourselves. Becoming professional in teaching adults is not only to reflect critically on who we are and what we are doing (that is the easy bit) but to change, to grow and to develop – that is really hard. We hope we are contributing to this process.

Very recently, one of the authors met a doctor who is in general practice who said that he had been recommended to read this book during an early training session but that it did not make as much sense then as he hoped. But in the last few weeks, he had picked it up again and found it quite different. As he said, every now and again, he realised that it was explaining to him something which had happened to him, that it made sense of some experience which he had had. Throughout the conversation, the words 'ring true' occurred. He said that the book threw light on his experience and his experience confirmed from time to time parts of the book.

And that is how we ourselves see this book. Aimed at all those who in our sense of the word 'teach adults' – that is 'help an adult to learn' something, whether individually or in groups, whether in non-formal or formal classes such as 'mature students' in educational institutions or distance learning programmes – its main purpose is to throw light on what we would like to call this 'relationship of explanation'. It will, we hope, be of value to all those who use it during their pre-service training as they plan for their teaching. But it will be of greatest value to all those who come to it after some time of teaching. It will help to make conscious the large amount of learning the reader will already have done unconsciously; it will help you to make sense of your experiences. It will throw light on those experiences, while at the same time those experiences will confirm or challenge much that this book says. The relationship between the contents of this book and the reader's experience will, we hope, be symbiotic.

Alan Rogers
Naomi Horrocks
October 2009

Before You Start

We are assuming that, as a reader of this book, you are a practising teacher of adults, or that you are responsible for organising programmes for adults, or that you hope at some time to teach adults. Whichever of these is true of you, you bring with you a good deal of experience and expectation. The best way of relating to the material that follows would be for you to make it concrete for yourself, to apply it to some immediate situation; for this book is not intended to be a theoretical discussion but a practical examination of some of the principles of teaching adults.

Face to face

You may therefore find it helpful, before you go any further, to choose an example of a learning programme that you have taught, are going to teach, or would like to teach to adults, for which you have been or are responsible, or have attended as a student participant – any situation, in fact, in which you can envisage yourself in a position of teacher in relation to a group of real or imaginary students. It will, we think, help if you write it out here before you start. You might care to answer the following questions briefly:

Activity

- What is the subject of the learning programme?
- How long is the programme and how often will the group meet?
- Who and how many are the student learners?
- Where and at what time will the group meet?

You can use this information and build on it as you read this book. The Activities are designed to help you reflect on your role as teacher. As you progress, these thoughts can be developed into a case study or reflection on your role as a teacher.

Chapter 1

Teaching Adults Today – the Context
Why are we teaching . . . ?

This introductory chapter argues that teaching adults in its multiple manifestations has come to be more central to the educational mission of today rather than marginal. But those who teach need to be aware of this context and the ways in which it influences the purpose of what they do.

From certainty to uncertainty

In the 1980s, when the first edition of this book was being prepared on the basis of training programmes for mostly part-time tutors, we were all very certain about adult education. We knew that adult learning was different from the learning of children; and we asserted this difference strongly, perhaps because adult education was a marginal activity in both the educational world and the political world and we felt the need for reassurance. Today, now that adult education (in the form of 'lifelong learning') has moved more to the centre of the stage in both of these arenas, now that more of those who teach adults are full-timers working in institutions of some sort or another, now that there is a vastly increased literature on adult learning, we are paradoxically much less certain about the distinction.

From deficit to diversity and back again

There are several reasons for this change of mood over the intervening period. One is the strength of the postmodernist thinking which held the field for a time but which is no longer so prominent. Another is the growing appreciation of the significance to education of anthropological concepts rather than the sociological concepts of the 1970s onwards which characterised much of this period but are again apparently on the wane. This change of climate has been outlined by several writers (e.g. Paulston 1996) in the following terms (for a fuller discussion, see Rogers 2004: 13–68):

- From the 1940s to the later 1960s, education in many Western societies was dominated by an *orthodox* set of ideologies – i.e. there is one right form of education, and the main aim is to provide this education for all persons as part of the modernisation project. The implication for adults was that adult education was seen as largely remedial, making up the *deficit* of education not received in earlier years, whether this was basic schooling or more advanced education. In the UK, much Workers Education Association (WEA) education, university extramural education and community education (e.g. Lovett 1982; Griffin 1987) was seen as providing a 'second chance' to adults who for one reason or another had not been able to take advantage of the 'accepted' educational provision up to and including university-level education.
- From the later 1960s, education was dominated by a *heterodox* set of ideologies. Education was seen as one of the contributory factors creating rather than remedying inequality. Those who were 'excluded' were seen to be oppressed, *disadvantaged*, not just in deficit. What was needed was a new kind of education, different from the schooling model. The implication for adults was that educational opportunities should be provided not just for personal gain but to address issues of inequality (racial, gender, religious, etc.), to lead to individual empowerment and/or social transformation. Adult education was a form of education specifically for adults, not just an adapted repetition of the schooling of earlier years.
- From the later 1980s, however, education became dominated by a *heterogeneous* set of ideologies. *Diversity* was the keynote, not deficit or disadvantage. And the aim of education was to promote difference and the understanding and acceptance of difference. The implication for adults was that education was not something which was confined to the early years and of one kind only. Rather, there were many different kinds of education needed by and available to people of all ages and kinds. Explorations of women's ways of knowing were one major part of this emphasis on difference. Thus, instead of trying to help our students to conform to the norm (the orthodox approach) or to overcome 'oppression' (the disadvantaged approach), some adult educators were seeking for every student to create their own learning in their own way, to 'celebrate the other' rather than to colonise the other.

All three strands have of course existed side by side and have been intermingled in various combinations. Today, in the first years of the

21st century, with an economistic view of education, the orthodox now seems to predominate: individualised learning rather than collaborative learning; formal courses rather than informal; standardised approaches, curricula, methodologies, modes of assessment and certification characterise official educational policies; the only right way to teach literacy, for example, is synthetic phonics. And the individual right to this uniform education has in large part been replaced by the national interest – a skilled and competitive workforce and a united nation. It takes much for adult educators to stand up against these trends, to assert the role of education to challenge and transform society, the right of different groups to have different forms of education.

And, since we and our readers are all part of this changing scene, it is inevitable that the tone of this book should be different from the tone of the first edition. There is (we hope) less certainty, more awareness that most of what is said about teaching adults is highly contextualised, contested and contingent, more reflexivity about the role of adult educators. The text stresses some of the differences to be found in the now very wide literature on adult learning and education, including the needs of those who now teach in more formal settings than we used to do.

The purposes of adult education

Earlier editions of this book have been accused in some reviews of omitting the socio-political dimensions of adult education. This was deliberate, for several reasons. First, it was recognised that the readers would come from a variety of different contexts, and it would be an impossible task to try to sum up all of those contexts (this has in fact proved to be true; the book has been translated into several different languages and is used as far apart as China, India and Greece). Secondly, it was not clear that readers of the book would be interested in the authors' personal picture of what was happening in the field of adult education in the UK – for every history, every attempt to describe what has occurred over the past half a century or more, is an individual construct, a personal painting of scenery for the stage on which actions are occurring. But more important than this, the book was not intended to be about *adult education* as a socio-cultural phenomenon. Rather, it was (and still is) intended to help all those, in whatever ideological context they may be, to embark on *helping adults to learn* in their own context – put very simply, to encourage teachers of adults to investigate their own context and to design programmes appropriate to their own and their students' ideologies.

But we can here summarise our views on such matters (for a fuller discussion, see Rogers 1992). In summary form, we see in Western societies three main forms of education for adults:

- what is often called vocational education (the word 'occupational' may be preferable, for the discourse of 'vocational' education is normally taken as applying to paid work, whereas many adults are engaged in occupations which may not be remunerated in the formal sense) – learning programmes aimed at increasing effectiveness in the workplace, wherever that may be;
- social role and socially transformative education – learning programmes aimed at changing society; and
- personal growth education – learning programmes aimed at individual development and fulfilment.

We see these three strands forming something of a plait, so that over the past hundred years or more, different strands come out on top and the other strands are underneath. At some times and in some contexts, personal growth predominated in adult education, with social trans-formation next and occupational education as less important; this was the period of 'the great liberal tradition', for example (Wiltshire 1976). At other times, social transformation predominated (e.g. access programmes; social inclusion; the works of Freire and others), with personal growth next, and occupational development again the least privileged. Now in the first part of the 21st century education is once more largely dominated by economic concerns. Government investment in adult education is focused on vocational or occupational programmes and social inclusion (citizenship), and the 'skills agenda' is the dominant discourse in both government-assisted programmes and the privatised and market-oriented provision for career advancement. Aiming primarily at economic growth and social inclusion, we would argue that there is a current lack of vision at government and other provider level about the socially transformative and individualisation purposes of education.

The same picture may be drawn another way. It can be argued that adult education is designed to enrich the lives of 'the people', as well as to enrich the state of which they are members. Individualised, competi-tive, normative forms of education will, it is thought, lead to increased economic benefits. Others may suggest that adult education is aimed at helping some persons to escape from their existing (marginal and/or necessitous) way of life into what is seen as a more centrally located or richer one. Social inclusion, conformist learning will lead to integration into the 'mainstream' and social harmony. While yet a third purpose of adult education can be seen as being to help change society in the search for greater justice, equality and understanding. As it has been expressed, we, as teachers of adults, need to decide whether the education we pro-vide for adults is to help them to reconcile themselves to their lot in the slums (make them happier), to help *some* of them to escape from the slums, or to help those who live in the slums to change those slums in their own ways (Rogers 2006).

These are not just matters of academic debate. They reflect our own personal agendas, the reasons why we are in adult education at all. We all will find within ourselves our own motivations which inevitably will influence the way we teach, and the way we relate to our student learners and to those who employ us. Today, in the UK as in much of Western society, under the influence of what is often called post-welfare 'neo-liberalism' (Welton 1995; Youngman 2000), occupational education is clearly privileged, although some elements of personal growth and some very minor elements of social transformation still survive. Most contemporary adult education is dominated by instrumental concerns rather than empowerment, social transformation or personal fulfilment. Each of us needs to determine how far this scenario is true for us and what our relations to it are: we know where we stand in this scenario.

Activity 1.1

Where do you stand in this scenario? Will your teaching:

- enrich the lives of the students or the state of which they are members?
- improve the life chances of your students?

From (adult) education to (lifelong) learning

The discourse of adult education of the 1950s and 1960s came to be replaced by 'continuing education' which emerged as the major discourse in the 1980s. Continuing education was seen as opening formal education to wider groups and extending its range and validity into later life rather than cutting it off in the first two or three decades of life. Courses for adults became more institutionalised (more like 'schooling') while at the same time distance and open learning 'modes of delivery' took formalised courses off campus. There was an epistemological lurch into the discourses of formal education which took over much of adult education. A useful picture here is that of the athletics match against the marathon. In the marathon, anyone can enter (self-selection); it is collaborative (each entrant helps and encourages the other participants); and the goals are set by the individual entrant (to finish, or just to complete the first 13 miles or so, to race against another competitor or against one's own time in an earlier marathon, etc.), so that all can 'win' in their own terms. In an athletics match, on the other hand, only a few who have prequalified can enter, selected by others; it is competitive, not collaborative; it is run on a special track, not on normal roads; and only the first three (hierarchically) can 'win' – the rest 'fail'. The main part of adult education up to the late 1980s was much like the marathon, but under the onslaught of continuing education, that form of adult education is fast disappearing today from our society, although its influence can still be felt in some parts of the educational world.

The concept of 'lifelong learning' came along to redress this formalised approach. The revolution in thinking cannot be overstressed: 'Within a generation we have moved from a world where most people could still expect to undertake little or no education or training after adolescence, to one where such education is a condition of economic survival for most if not all. [This has] overturned the notion that education and training are solely a preparation for, and separate from, life and work' (Jarvis 2001a: 25).

Lifelong learning as seen in its early stages sought to change the focus away from the competitive to the situated, away from institutionalised education to 'lifeworld learning', away from 'teaching' to 'learning'. It tried to refocus agency onto the individual learner rather than the providing institution – it suggests that more of the control of one's own learning programme lies with the learner. Perhaps the most valuable element in lifelong learning is its emphasis that all learning is *embedded learning* – it takes place in and from a specific context for quite specific purposes and returns to affect and shape that context. And it sees 'adult education' (to use what is now something of an outdated terminology) as the encouragement and maximisation of learning more than the provision of courses.

But much of the current discourse of lifelong learning has moved away from these issues. For one thing, as we shall see, the concepts of education and learning (which are not the same thing) tend to get confused (see pp. 129–30). Secondly, most of the recent discussions of lifelong learning are economic in nature, accredited vocational training or professional development of a new kind, and more of the adult learning settings are work-related. There have been some attempts to reconcile lifelong learning with social transformation education but they find it hard to make their voices heard, except perhaps in the new social movements (Mayo 1997; Foley 1999). And the personal growth (liberal) element in lifelong education seems at the moment to be mainly confined to what is somewhat patronisingly called 'third age learning' (Jarvis 2001b), although recently revived interest in 'informal learning' seems to mark a new interest in a wider adult learning agenda (DIUS 2008; Hager and

Halliday 2009). But these elements are still there and we do not doubt that they will grow stronger over the years to come. The plait still exists and it is constantly changing as power changes.

For underlying all forms of education, including and perhaps especially adult education, lies the question of power. Discourses are created and perpetuated by special interest groups who seek to use them as an instrument of hegemony to control the value systems of other people. We need to ask, in all the teaching of adults we do, whose interests are being served? For lifelong education does not come without a price tag, and it serves the interests of particular sections of society. In any society, some forms of knowledge are privileged above others (Barr 1999), and this leads us to question whether the adult education we are engaged in reflects rather than challenges these dominant concepts.

Activity 1.2

In what ways are the interests of

- the individual students
- any particular section of society
- someone or something else
- being served by your teaching?

Why lifelong learning now?

Which leads to the question as to why the discourse of lifelong learning has suddenly become more powerful, taken up by governments, firms and educational institutions who previously had no sympathy with adult education *per se* – something which adult education practitioners have been urging on power-brokers for many decades. A number of different ideas have been put forward to explain this. Some suggest that it is wholly or largely related to the information and communication revolution which has created an entirely new environment for the education and training of adults. Others feel that in part at least the reason is money. It is clear that in some areas, private training providers became aware that profits can be made from some forms of lifelong education, and this trend has been followed by a number of educational institutions that have sought to increase their funding by making provision for adults in the form of continuing professional development. Governments seek to reduce their responsibilities by encouraging private providers of learning programmes. Increased commercialisation in society has brought about the consumerisation of education; participants are now customers or clients. This would seem to be the reason why the practice of lifelong education is dominated to a large extent by the vocational strand of the plait; and why the personal (liberal) and the socially transformative strands have become weaker. Again, major changes have come about in 'civil society' (like lifelong learning, a term of many colours). The older social movements (e.g. trade unions) are being replaced with new, less coherent social movements (e.g. environmental pressure groups); the role of government *vis-à-vis* both commercial interests and civil society has changed and is still changing. Yet others see as a factor the demographic challenges of the past few decades when (for a time) a decline in the numbers of school attenders and a significant number of immigrants needing special educational provision led to an increase in a range of pluriform provision for adults, later to be replaced as the school-going population increased leading yet again to a decline in adult education.

But perhaps the main reason for the predominance of the lifelong learning/education discourse today is that the formal systems of education, finding that various forms of adult education were growing in strength and social purposefulness, have co-opted adult education by re-designating it as lifelong education. They have expanded their empires. 'Formal education . . . [is] extending into work-based learning for adults as well as into adult and community education'; more outside groups have a vested interest in the outcomes of adult learning programmes. In addition, there is what we wish to call 'the educationalisation of everyday practices': for example, parenting, citizenship and healthy living are being taught formally. Formal education systems are asserting their claim to be the standard by which the effectiveness of all educational activities (including what all of us do in teaching adults) may be judged. With growing concern about quality assurance, accountability and 'maintenance of standards' which has led to repeated restructuring and a large number of different awarding bodies, 'Learning has become synonymous with the achievement of quantifiable targets, leading to new meanings of 'participation in learning' and 'non-learners' (Ecclestone 2005: 1, 4, 7). But some adult educators have never had any great love for what has been called 'the arrogance of the learned', the 'I-know-what-you-should-learn' attitude of so many educators – even though they themselves have benefited personally from their institutions and programmes and certificates. Which is why, throughout this edition of the book, we have retained from time to time the term 'adult education' rather than the uncertainties of 'lifelong learning/education'.

Before we look at some of the implications of all of this for those of us who are engaged in face-to-face teaching of adults, we want very briefly to look at two current developments within the field of adult education which seem to us to be particularly significant.

The first is the application of ethnography to adult learning programmes. The argument is simple: those who teach adults on the whole believe that those who come to our learning programmes bring with them a wide range of existing knowledge, experience, insights and skills which are important for the new learning. They are not ignorant, unskilful, inexperienced; even so-called 'illiterates' have experience of literacy and engage in literacy tasks. But (as we shall see in more detail in Chapter 6) much of this knowledge and experience is unconscious, 'tacit knowledge', so the traditional ways of finding out about this existing knowledge and experience (i.e. asking the student learners) are not always adequate. Therefore the use of ethnographic approaches to learning is increasing. Whereas Action Research suggests the cycle of activity is one of 'plan–do–observe–reflect' (see http://ear.findingavoice.org/intro/index.html for a good introduction to action research), ethnographic enquiry in adult learning programmes suggests the cycle is one of 'observe–reflect–plan–do/teach'. (The best introduction to the use of ethnography in adult learning programmes is Brice Heath and Street 2008; for discussions of this approach, see Nirantar 2007 and Gebre et al 2009; for excellent case studies, see Prinsloo and Breier 1997; Mahiri 2004.) The use of ethnographic approaches to teaching adults informs the whole of this book.

Secondly, there is increasing interest in what are often called 'the non-cognitive benefits' of participation in adult learning programmes, what are sometimes described as 'soft learning outcomes' such as increased confidence, changed values, and social skills in terms of relationships, respect, tolerance, etc. The range of such learning achievements is very wide – so wide that some have seen the term 'non-cognitive' as a hindrance in describing them and have used other terms such as 'wider benefits' or 'self-regulated learning'. Increasingly, however, these learning achievements are moving from the periphery to centre stage; increasingly, they are coming to be included among the goals and objectives of the adult learning programme; and increasingly ways are being sought how to measure such outcomes (Campbell 2007). One of the best introductions comes from the UK 'Wider Benefits of Learning Project' (which should of course be called 'the wider benefits of *participation*', for such benefits come from participation in the programme even if the programme content is not learned; many adult literacy participants, for example, who attend but do not learn literacy still gain enormously from their participation in the programme). (For further discussion, see Campbell 2007; Duckworth et al 2009; Schuller and Watson 2009.) Again, these issues underlie our discussions below of goals and evaluation (Chapters 7 and 12).

What are the implications of all of this social, political and conceptual context for the readers of this book? Is it just an interesting sideshow? We suggest that it is very important. We all need to ask ourselves what we are doing when we seek to teach adults:

- how far our programmes are persuading our students into accepting a norm set by ourselves or our institutions or our context (reducing deficit);
- how far we are helping the students to reflect critically on their own situation and to overcome the oppression inherent in the context leading to a more equitable society (challenging disadvantage);
- how far we are encouraging our students to become different from each other and from us, while at the same time becoming more appreciative of these differences (increasing diversity); and
- how far we are measuring our achievements in terms of the narrow learning objectives or the wider benefits of participation in the learning programme.

We teachers are, we feel, at the forefront of promoting uniformity, transforming society, or increasing and welcoming diversity. These are questions which we should be posing to ourselves throughout our teaching of adults.

Exploring the context of your teaching

Such considerations are often influenced for us by the organisation with whom we work; and we need to be conscious of that context, for it will affect much of what we do when teaching adults.

People engage in teaching adults in many different contexts and for many different purposes.

Sometimes the *context* is formal, within the walls of one of our educational institutions. At other times the teaching takes place through an organisation specifically set up to help adults learn, like an industrial training agency or professional body. Or again it may be within one of a host of informal situations: community and voluntary associations, social movements and women's groups, sports agencies, churches, museums, record offices and libraries, or among members of the rescue and caring professions. We notice the way in which bodies such as the RSPB help adults to learn about birds, how the BBC through its *SpringWatch* programmes encourage much learning about natural history.

The *formats and settings* are many. People teach adults formally or informally in prisons and church halls, in colleges and private houses, in sports and leisure centres and in factories, in shops and offices, in community buildings and military bases, in schools and specialist adult education centres, in health clinics and on university campuses, in training centres and temporary caravans. They teach during the day, in the evening, at weekends and while on holiday. They can teach face to face or by distance learning methods or a blend of the two (blended learning).

Sometimes the *process* is a direct one – a structured course on management or computers, or retraining in new techniques of construction, an extension course for farmers, a woodwork class or church confirmation group, a diploma or degree programme. Sometimes it is less direct – a residents' group fighting a planning proposal, a choir rehearsing, a health group striving to use a controlled diet, a group of people setting up a cooperative, a reading circle, a drama group putting on a performance.

And it is undertaken for a variety of *purposes* – to lead to qualifications, or changed personal attitudes, or the development of the community, or new skills for work purposes or for hobbies, or the improvement of basic skills, or to open doors to further learning or the increase of confidence – or just for fun.

Activity 1.3

Consider the following and add your thoughts to your case study:

- *setting*: would you say that it is formal or informal?
- what is its *format* and *context*?
- *process*: would you say that it is direct or indirect?
- what is its *purpose*? What do you hope the student learners will get out of your course?

The field we operate in, the teaching of adults, is thus a vast one with a myriad of different expressions, confusing because unlike schooling and college education, it seems to lack structure and form. Anywhere where two or three people are gathered together to learn something on a systematic basis under supervision, someone is found teaching adults.

It may be helpful to distinguish between three main adult education sectors (Figure 1.1):

- *formal* – courses and classes run by schools, colleges, universities and other statutory and non-statutory agencies making up the educational system;
- *'extra-formal'* (or sometimes called 'non-formal education') – courses and classes run by formal agencies *outside* the educational

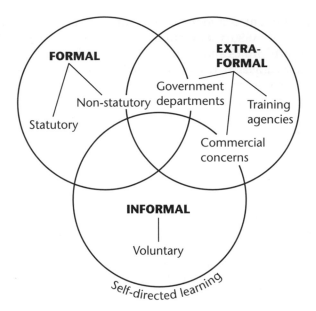

Figure 1.1 The sectors of education for adults (you may find it helpful to locate the learning programme(s) you are involved in on this figure, if you can)

system, for example other government departments, industrial training agencies, trade unions and commercial concerns (what are sometimes called today 'learning providers');
- *informal* – educational activities[1] engaged in by voluntary agencies and informal groups.

(For a possible taxonomy of adult education, see Appendix to this Chapter.)

The categories partly overlap, since informal learning programmes may be provided by formal agencies, and many informal bodies run very formal learning programmes.

There are in addition non-taught *self-programming groups of adults*, study circles without a face-to-face teacher such as reading groups, natural and local history societies. There is also the area of *self-directed learning*. The latter comprises educational opportunities for individuals provided by bodies like broadcasting organisations, correspondence agencies and publishers. Web-based and distance education are forms of self-directed

---

1   To make things very clear, we distinguish 'informal education' from 'informal learning'; see Chapter 6.

learning. One of the most extensive modes of systematic adult learning are those journals and magazines that mount programmes of study in subjects like cooking, dressmaking, do-it-yourself, woodworking, photography, computing, health and beauty, and gardening, all of which attract large audiences. Languages are often learned from CDs. Self-directed learning opportunities are also provided by numerous cultural organisations offering musical and dramatic events, public lectures, exhibitions, visits to places of environmental and historic interest and the like – activities that an adult may choose to take up on their own (or with their family) in order to follow a special interest and to achieve a particular accomplishment, whether related to their job or not (Tough 1979; Brookfield 1985).

Because of the nature of this book on 'teaching adults', our focus is on the face-to-face contexts within which many adults are being helped to learn. While from time to time we comment upon some of the implications of our discussions for on-line learning, individual or in e-groups, our main aim is to help those who teach to teach more effectively, to reflect on and develop further their own strategies on the basis of a wider understanding of some of the issues involved.

Three main parties

There are, then, three main parties to the adult learning experience – the organiser or providing agency, the teacher, and the potential student participants. In some contexts, there may be several other possible stake-holders, intermediate agencies, such as bodies who act as a servicing intermediary between providers and student participants and sometimes between providers and employers for their workforces (as in the Learning Partnerships or the former Learning and Skills Councils, some funding bodies such as the EU or former government bodies, organisations that act as brokers between clients and providers, contracting agencies), all of whom may set clear or less than clear guidelines for the development of adult learning programmes. But the three key players are the organisers/providers, the teacher and the participants.

And, as we have seen, a number of different ideologies lie behind the various forms of teaching adults, and these affect the ways we as teachers of adults react. The most important of these relate (a) to the objectives of the learning programme, and (b) to the involvement or non-involvement of the student participants in the planning process. Some programmes, especially those in the training field, are offered with clearly identified and specific pre-set objectives, a more or less standardised level of achievement. Others are offered with more open-ended goals, such as

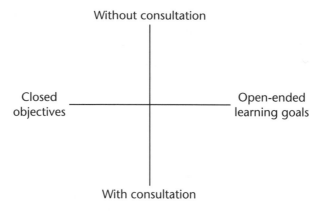

Figure 1.2 Organisation of adult learning programmes

personal growth (see Chapter 7). Most programmes lie somewhere between these two extremes. Equally, some programmes are organised with and some without consultation with the prospective participants; again, each teaching–learning activity lies somewhere along the continuum formed by these two opposites (Figure 1.2). The determination of both of these matters is a question of policy on the part of the providing agency.

Activity 1.4

You may wish to plot where on Figure 1.2 your own learning programme comes. Try to think about why your programme fits in where it does on the grid and consider how this affects the way you plan your programme. You may not be entirely happy with where your programme sits. For example, you may want to have more open-ended learning goals than your programme allows. Can you think of ways that you might incorporate this within your programme?

Such issues reflect the distinction that needs to be drawn in most cases between the *providers* (organisations, institutions or individuals who plan the programme and outline the various parts of it) and the *teachers*. Where there are other stakeholders, the relationship between teacher and provider will be more complex; on the other hand, in some parts of the non-formal sector (e.g. the churches), teachers and providers may be one and the same person. And in all cases, the teacher is a planner of the learning situation as much as an instructor. But despite these caveats, the interests of provider/organiser and teacher are in many respects different, and it is well to bear this distinction in mind.

In most cases, then, the construction of an adult learning programme is seen to be a matter for negotiation between provider and teacher; but in the end it is the *student participant* who will respond to the learning opportunity on offer, who will determine whether to take up the programme or not. And it is to this that we turn in the next chapter.

Further reading

Coben, D. (1998) *Radical Heroes: Gramsci, Freire and the Politics of Adult Education.* London: Garland.

Duke, C. (2008) Trapped in a Local History: why did extramural fail to engage in the era of engagement? *Ad-Lib Journal for Continuing Liberal Adult Education,* 36: 3–19.

Fieldhouse, R. (1996) *A History of Modern British Adult Education.* Leicester: NIACE.

Schuller, T. and Watson, D. (2009) *Learning Through Life.* Leicester: NIACE.

Stephens, M.D. (1990) *Adult Education.* London: Cassell.

Tennant, M. (2006) *Psychology and Adult Learning.* London: Routledge (especially Chapter 9, pp. 122–135).

Youngman, F. (2000) *The Political Economy of Adult Education.* London: Zed.

Appendix

Providers*	Qualification courses	Non-qualification courses	Personal growth and community development courses	Basic/access courses
Formal: statutory bodies, educational				
• general programmes open to adults, e.g. schools/colleges/universities • special provision for adults, e.g. extramural/Open University/ advanced continuing education/ industrial training bodies/adult literacy agencies/technical training and validating bodies	School-leaving certificates Diplomas Degrees Higher degrees	Short courses, e.g. Management training Information technology Updating skills and knowledge	Non-vocational 'liberal' adult education, e.g. History Landscape and gardens Local history	Return to study, e.g. Literacy Numeracy English language Access to HE Return to work courses
Extra-formal: courses provided by central or locally administered public bodies and other agencies outside the formal educational system				
• training agencies/government departments/ agencies/museums and libraries • trade unions/firms and businesses/ professional associations/mass media	Certificates and other awards, e.g. vocational qualifications	Short courses, e.g. On-the job training Health and safety New regulation training General updating	Community programmes, e.g. Health (smoking/alcohol/ pregnancy/family planning) Healthy eating Sports and hobbies Cultural	Return to study – first steps, e.g. Literacy Numeracy English language Return to work
Informal: voluntary bodies				
• primarily educational, e.g. WEA/adult literacy agencies/private colleges/ correspondence courses • primarily non-educational, e.g. aid and welfare organizations/religious bodies/community groups/ unemployed workers' groups/ self-help groups	Certificates Diplomas Certificates	Leisure Crafts Do-it-yourself/art Women's programmes Retirement courses	Community programmes Women's programmes Unemployed Retirement courses Residents' programmes/ planning/weight-watchers Relationship guidance Parenting Prisoner release programmes	Literacy Numeracy English language First steps programmes as above

*Many programmes are provided by partnerships between organisations in different categories.

Chapter 2

A Contract to Learn
How do we come to be here . . . ?

It has on occasion been suggested that the most important thing which adults bring to their learning programme is their experience. In this chapter, we suggest that equally important are the expectations and the agendas which adult student learners bring and that these are in large part created by the information about the learning programme which is supplied to the prospective participants.

Adults come to all learning programmes with a range of expectations about the programme and its outcomes. And these expectations are created by the interface between their past experience and the publicity material they have received about the programme.

Adult teachers/tutors today may have less responsibility for the recruitment of their student learners than in the past, although many are still required to produce some publicity material. But even if the teacher is asked to teach a group of student learners with whom they have had no contact beforehand, the fact that the student learners have already developed their own expectations about the course means two things for those of us who teach adults – that we must recognise and explore what others have said in our name, and that we all have to be careful in writing and presenting our course outline to these student learners.

For the student learners' expectations about the learning programme will have been created as much by what the teacher has to say as by what the providing agency has to say. All three parties are involved in the creation of such expectations (Figure 2.1). It is factors like this which mark the education of adults off from other sectors of education. Apart from other matters, teaching adults is different from other educational programmes not only because the organisation of learning is different, but because the relationship between the teacher and the student participants is different.

Adult participation is voluntary and purposeful

Two characteristics are common to virtually all forms of teaching adults. The first is that *the participants are almost always voluntary learners*. Those

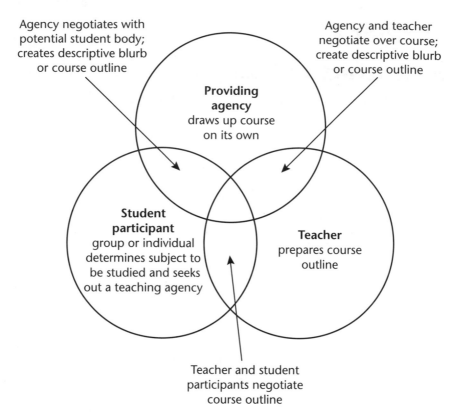

Agency negotiates with
potential student body;
creates descriptive blurb
or course outline

Agency and teacher
negotiate over course;
create descriptive blurb
or course outline

**Providing
agency**
draws up course
on its own

**Student
participant**
group or individual
determines subject to
be studied and seeks
out a teaching agency

Teacher
prepares course
outline

Teacher and student
participants negotiate
course outline

Figure 2.1 Drawing up the learning programme: you may wish to consider
the various interactions which went into the making of your programme

who come as student participants to the programmes being offered come
out of choice, and the teachers who come face to face with them are
confronted by people who in most cases have selected their teachers
rather than the other way about. There are, it is true, an increasing number
of forms of adult learning in which the freedom of the participant is
somewhat circumscribed (see pp. 79–80). Programmes of industrial training
or staff development provided in the workplace, for example, are at times
less than fully voluntary. Pressures may be exerted on some people to
attend learning programmes when they would rather be somewhere else.
So it is necessary to keep some qualification in mind when we speak of
the voluntary nature of the adult student. Nevertheless the adult nature
of the participants means that they are attending programmes of education because they have decided for one reason or another to be there and
not to be elsewhere.

Secondly, *they have come with an agenda*, an intention, in most cases to
achieve a learning goal. Again, we need to bear in mind some qualification

to this general statement. Some will have come more for social reasons than for the immediate learning, while others may not always know clearly what they want, or may want one thing and in fact find achievement in something different. Those who are there because they have been told to come may have less clear intentions than the others. Nevertheless, they each come for a purpose – and if they don't get it, sooner or later they will stop coming. There are, it is true, cases of adults staying in learning programmes from which they are getting little for long periods out of politeness or a sense of loyalty, but in the end they too will usually withdraw.

Two conclusions follow:

- The provider and the teacher in programmes for adults need to *attract* participants into their programmes. The key word in all the many varied fields of adult learning programmes is 'offer'. The providing agency offers a learning opportunity, and the participants determine whether to accept the offer.
- This means that a *bargain* has been struck. A (usually unspoken) agreement is concluded between the provider/teacher and the student learner: that the one will offer the learning opportunity and that the other will work to achieve some goal or other. This is true not only of those cases where the programme has been negotiated between the provider (and/or the teacher) and the potential participants, where the terms of the engagement may be set out in some detail. It is also true when the organisers devise the programme without such negotiation (see pp. 13–4). The terms of the bargain may not be set out in full, but an agreement is there nonetheless.

A contract to learn

These differences do not negate the proposition that an agreement has been struck between teacher/provider and learner. It takes a different form for each type of teaching–learning programme. But what will not be in doubt is the willingness of the teacher-agent to set up the learning environment and programme, and the agreement of the participant to engage in a series of activities in order to achieve certain outcomes. A contract[1] between the student learner on the one side and the provider and/or the teacher on the other side exists, however vague it may be.

---

1 The phrase 'learning contract' has been used to describe a particular form of educational encounter, but we are using the word 'contract' here in a more informal sense as applying to all forms of teaching adults.

Providing agency and the contract to learn

The provider establishes the parameters to the learning opportunity – the context, including the rest of the programme within which the course is set; the subject; the format (location, number of meetings, time and duration of each meeting); the modes of publicity. They may do all of this on their own, or in association with the teacher, and/or after discussion with a prospective student group. Where a professional association, residents' group, local society or similar body exists, it is possible to discuss in advance what they want to learn and in what way, and a number of adult teaching bodies discuss programmes with firms and other potential 'customers'. But on other occasions such opportunities, even where they exist, are not taken. The organisers determine by themselves or in discussion with their teachers what they think the potential student participants should learn and how. Certificated programmes are governed by the regulations of the institution or authority which provides or accredits them, such as the length of terms or course contents. Access courses are run in accordance with the requirements of the approved curriculum rather than the requirements of the student learners; basic skills programmes are bound to some extent by government regulations; more advanced continuing education and continuing professional development (CPD) programmes are frequently standardised. The framework within which each adult learning opportunity stands has come to exert a major influence on the provision, to the detriment of the other partners, the teacher and/or the participants.

The teacher and the contract to learn

There are occasions when the teacher is excluded from the discussion. The organisers build up a course outline and then find someone to teach 'their' programme. This is especially true of certificated programmes. In these cases, the teachers take over a programme already created and fit their work to that. But it is often also true of more open adult learning programmes. If, for example, we are asked to take a ten-meeting course for beginners on upholstery or an introduction to Excel, the parameters have already been set, irrespective of whether we feel that ten meetings constitute an appropriate length of time for beginners to master anything meaningful about upholstery or Excel, or not.

On other occasions the teacher is a party to the construction of the learning opportunity. This is often our first task – to determine what is to be taught, how much can be covered and at what level, how it should be taught, to whom and to what purpose. Again, like the organiser, we may do it on our own, or in association with the providing agency, or in consultation with prospective learners.

The programme devised by the teacher is constructed for the student participants. The contract to learn is made with them; it is not between the teacher and the providing agency (a different contract is usually in force there). The organisers will of course be keen to see what we have in mind to teach; in most cases they will be able to offer advice based on practical experience on matters of both publicity and course content. It is thus worth our while to discuss the outline with the providing agency. But the contract of learning is not directly made with that body. Nor is it made for other teachers, examining boards, professional associations, local education committees, educational institutions or academic colleagues. The contract is made directly with the potential student participants; it is the first point of contact between teacher and learner.

In most cases, we are required to draw up the agreement before we meet the potential student participants, even before we know who the learners will be. This problem is often a severe one. One answer that has sometimes been proposed, and which is probably the worst of all possible worlds, is to do no planning at all – to wait until we meet the student learners for the first time. But normally this is impractical. We need to establish the subject areas of the programme just to call together the prospective participants. Where a group already exists, it is possible for us to meet them and to determine the outlines of the programme of learning jointly; but even here our expertise as teacher or group leader and our experience in this type of programme are called upon to indicate the realistic limits of what can be achieved in any given length of time, and to set out practical proposals for a programme of work. The task of planning the learning programme normally falls to the teacher, however much we may negotiate with the potential student participants in the process.

But we are not completely free in drawing up our proposals. First, we are limited by the context within which we are teaching. Providing and funding agencies will normally have a substantial input into the development of any adult learning programme. The format of the programme has frequently been set already – by custom, by the organising institution or by negotiation with the learners – and this may impose restrictions on what can be done. Many aspects may already have been fixed for us when planning our programme:

- the *length of the programme* (frequently determined by traditional school or university terms, although courses other than the 'one-term/semester' or '20-meeting' variety are growing, determined by the time the learners have available, the time needed to master some skill or branch of study, or costs);

- its *frequency of meeting* (often weekly, although more flexible formats are becoming more common);
- the *duration of the class meeting* (usually one and a half or two hours, but again more flexible arrangements are appearing, especially weekend and day-release courses);
- the *location* of the course/programme.

The participants may have some say in the timing of the programme and its location, although this seems to be becoming rarer as continuing and lifelong education become more institutionalised.

Activity 2.1

You might care to indicate with your own learning programme which areas of planning were undertaken by yourself, were 'given' to you or were agreed jointly with the planner; and whether the student determined any of them:

	Teacher	Planner	Jointly	Students
Length of programme				
Frequency of meeting				
Duration of session				
Timing of meeting				
Location of course/programme				

It may be that your programme includes other modes of teaching such as blended learning, virtual learning or self-directed learning. If this is the case, how does this affect your course planning?

Secondly, we are limited by our views of the prospective students. Consciously or unconsciously, we make a range of decisions about who they will be, how much they already know about the subject, what they want to learn, how much work they will expect to do and what sort of activities they will be prepared or be able to engage in. To a large extent, we tend to rely on stereotypes of adult student learners – and we may be wrong in all of this. They may not be willing to play games, hand in written work, bring specimens for classwork, even read set texts. They may not be able because of their life circumstances to undertake some of the work we plan for them. But in our planning, we make assumptions on all these matters. The programme we draw up is not a question of what we as teachers alone want. Using our experience, we produce a balance between what we have to offer and what we believe the student participants may or may not be looking for, or what they may or may not be willing and able to do.

The student learner and the contract to learn

The potential learner is fully participant in the contract-making process. Although the terms of the offer are initially drawn up by the provider and/or the teacher, the readers are nevertheless active in interpreting what they read. They are the third party to the contract. They do not passively accept or reject what is on offer, but interpret the material presented to them in the light of their existing knowledge and experience, and their intentions. They assess, often unconsciously, the language in which the programme is set out. They weigh up the context in which the learning programme is being provided – this, as they see it, will control the course or at least give it its orientation. They will bear in mind the building in which it is located, the title of the body that has organised it, what they know about the teacher, and so on. And they will decide on the basis of what they see and what they assume whether the programme will meet their intentions or not.

Potential students have to work with what they are given. In some cases they can deduce from the material provided something about the nature of the programme. But more often, in interpreting the contract, they have to fall back on other experience and knowledge, such as what they know about the institution providing the programme.

The population at large seems to have fairly fixed expectations of what each of the main providing bodies offers in the way of adult programmes. For example, learning programmes organised by statutory agencies and their constituent centres are often (rightly or wrongly) judged to be more directive and practical in nature, while those provided by voluntary bodies are seen to be more participatory and with a measure of social concern lacking in local authority programmes. Programmes offered by voluntary agencies will, it is thought, be informal rather than formal in teaching–learning styles. Those organised by industrial, commercial and other training bodies are considered more intensive and exclusively vocational (even narrow) in content. In the UK, programmes offered by further education colleges are in general felt to be more technical and those offered by universities more academic. WEA-type classes are frequently assumed to be introductory in level and more socially purposive, while university programmes are believed to be more advanced, appealing to those who already have some educational attainments.

None of this is strictly true, but these views influence behaviour. Thus, some people attend learning programmes offered by an advanced training institution because of their expectations of what will happen to them and of how useful the programme will be, whereas they will not go near a similar class offered by a voluntary body, such as the Workers Education Association (WEA) – and vice versa. However much one may wish to change the image of the body concerned, it is difficult to do so.

Adult participants thus choose the institution which they deem will best serve their purposes, their agendas. For adults come to learning opportunities and programmes with a goal in mind, to fulfil a desire or intention. They will often search for the programme which best fits their plans and their conditions (the internet is making this easier for many). When presented with a programme brochure, they do not simplistically accept what is printed but make their own meanings out of it – and decide on the basis of what they create whether to join the programme or not.

Making and interpreting the contract

As we have suggested, such an agreement is based on a series of assumptions made by both teacher and adult participant even before the two have met. Neither teachers nor learners start with a blank sheet. The teachers begin with a set of ideas about who the students will be and what they will be teaching. The participants have some idea of what they want and what they are going to get.

Most of these assumptions are unspoken, even when a process of consultation with prospective student participants has been engaged in or when the learning programme is set out in detail. On both sides there are hidden presuppositions about the process on which they are embarking. These presuppositions may not be valid, but to a large extent they determine the effectiveness of the learning process.

The assumptions of the potential participant are created in part by calling into play views developed over many years and also, and particularly, by interpreting the information given about the programme on offer. This latter varies widely. In educational institutions such as universities and further education institutions, the information is usually included in the institutional brochure and increasingly on their website, and it conforms to the format dictated by that institution. In general, adult education programme publicity at its minimum gives some indication of the subject (usually a title), format (frequency of meeting and length of time involved), location and timing, and the institution or organisation under whose umbrella the programme is being provided. There is sometimes a 'blurb' containing information about the content of the programme of study. The following examples[2] reveal something of the range of information offered to potential student participants.

---

2   Most of the examples come from programmes on offer in the years 2008–09.

From a local authority leisure and learning programme consisting of four sectors (accredited courses, pathways to learning, leisure courses, and sports):

	Venue	Start date	Times	No. of weeks	Full fee	Benefits fee
Piano beginners	Adult Ed venue	22/09/08	09.30–11.00	12	£76	£38
Lipreading	Voluntary setting	26/09/08	12.00–14.00	30	free	free
Flower painting	Community setting	26/09/08	10.00–12.00	10	£84	£42
Children's care, learning and development	High School	04/11/08	18.30–21.30	35	£458	£122
Digital photography	High School	15/09/08	19.00–21.00	6	£50	£25

From a field studies centre (run by a commercial concern):

Grass identification in spring (1)

- Centre: private venue. Tutor: name given
- Dates: Friday 18 April–Sunday 20 April 2008
- Res: £220; Non-Res: £165
- Level: Intermediate/Improvers
- Professional development course
- Course accredited by a university

Winter wildfowl

- Centre: private venue. Tutor: name given
- Dates: Friday 22 February–Sunday 24 February 2008
- Res: £185; Non-Res: £130
- Level: Open to everyone

Sometimes more detail is provided. From a university open studies programme:

Wildlife and Habitat Conservation

10 credits at level 1

Wildlife and Habitat Conservation

What are the threats to wildlife in the UK and what steps can be taken to conserve it? This module introduces you to the methods concerned with conservation action and the organisations involved in that work. **Click Here for Course Outline**

Day/Time: Wednesdays 7–9pm
Venue: University
Tutor: name given
Course Director: name given
Start Date: 8 October 2008
End Date: 17 December 2008
Fee: £197

Field trips: Sunday 26 October 2008   Sunday 14 December 2008

Application Form   Click Here To Apply Online

Deadline for applications: Monday 15 September 2008

From a commercial agency describing itself as 'The World Leader in Vendor-Independent Training for IT Professionals':

FrontPage 2000 Website Development: Hands-On

You Will Learn To: (7 items)

Course Benefits

Who Should Attend

Course 207 Content

Hands-On: Throughout this course, extensive hands-on exercises guide you through the design and creation of a fully functional website. Exercises, performed under the guidance of an expert instructor [not named] include: (8 items)

Yours FREE To Take Home: a CD of Web-related software to aid site creation

4-Day Courses, Tuesday to Friday in LONDON [dates given]

This course helps you to prepare for Microsoft professional certification exam(s)

Such information, even the briefest, immediately creates a set of expectations. For example, the implication of

| Monday | Still Life | 2.15–4.15 p.m. | 17.9.08. to 26.11.08 | Tutor: MS 10 weeks | £84 |

in an adult and community education service programme is clear. A series of two-hour meetings will be held on each Monday afternoon for a set number of weeks in a suitable (designated) building, open to anyone of either sex who wishes to attend (however inexperienced they may be) and who pays the relevant fee. A series of activities will be undertaken, the intended outcome of which will be a person more able to create and/ or appreciate still-life paintings. The context will indicate whether there is formal assessment and accreditation. All this and more can be read into those few words viewed in the context of the rest of the brochure.

Balancing publicity and the contract to learn

As we can see, the information provided for potential participants about the contract on offer is often very limited. It is argued by some providers that this is due to the lack of resources available to many adult education agencies, but frequently it is because organisers do not see the necessity of giving more detail. In these cases, the material produced is primarily issued as publicity for the programme rather than as a description of the learning agreement. Its main aim is to persuade the readers to join the learning programme.

This desire to attract participants into our programmes often leads providers to feel that they dare not provide too detailed information about what is involved in their programmes in case it 'puts people off'. The publicity aspect predominates, and the search for striking phrases sometimes outweighs the informative content ('Whose Afraid of Virgins and Wolves?' for a course on myths and legends, for example).

But some planners argue that there is no need for more than a list of titles with dates and times of meeting and cost:

| Thursday | 7.30 p.m. | Beehive Construction | Starting 21 September | £80 |

The potential learners do not need to know the name of the teacher. It is enough (so the argument goes) for them to know that if they turn up on Thursday evenings in the place and at the time specified, pay the stated fee and do the work (unspecified), they will be taught how to make a beehive.

But such a list will only appeal to those who already know a good deal about the subject – to those, for example, who know that 'still life' refers to paintings. It provides no indication of the level of work intended, of the demands to be made upon the learners, of the entry requirements for each course, and so on. The organiser tends to assume that all these pieces of information are already known by the reader. But they may not be. Is the beehive construction course intended for the expert-carpenter-but-novice-apiarist or for the expert-apiarist-but-novice-woodworker – or for both?

The omission of details reveals much about the assumptions of the organisers. Some tend to rely on the reputation of the providing agency for the credibility of what they offer. They base their constructed learning programmes on their experience of previous student participants. The fact that the programme is run by such-and-such university, local authority, college, voluntary body or training organisation is to them enough indication and guarantee of the kind and quality of the learning programmes offered.

But whether it is enough to persuade new participants to join in these programmes must be doubted. Potential student participants need to have enough information if they are to formulate in their own minds whether to accept the proffered contract of learning: what the learning programme is all about, what is expected of them and what they themselves might expect to gain from the experience. Simple lists of titles, unless backed up by other information, will frequently lead to a good deal of uncertainty even on the part of those participants who do come, and it will take some time once the learning programme has commenced to resolve this uncertainty. This is, we think, the main reason why adult education programmes tend to appeal to already existing students rather than to newcomers who do not have the experience to interpret the information presented to them.

The parts to the contract

Teaching adults is in some ways similar to publishing a book – it calls for a title, an author, a brief summary of or introduction to the contents – and of course the cost! The information needed to attract potential students into our programmes and to set out for them the terms of the learning contract is much the same: a title, a statement of the format of the programme, a note of the teacher and of the cost of the learning programme, and some description of the content of the learning programme – an indication of the 'market' at which the programme is aimed and the intended outcomes of the experience.

As with some books, the *title* is on occasion chosen more for its euphony or intended striking qualities than for the light it throws on the subject matter. This may be adequate for those student learners who come back year after year to the same sort of programme and who have grown accustomed to the stylistic habits of the organiser, but it does not always help to draw new people into our programmes. 'Men under Masters', without any further elaboration, is not exactly indicative that a study of local history in a nineteenth-century industrial town is intended.

Few publishers would think of issuing a book without the name of the author; but many organisers issue adult learning programmes without the name of the *teacher*. Those who are considering whether or not to accept the learning contract on offer have the right to know who the teachers are and what expertise and experience they possess. On other occasions, a name without further information is provided. It is assumed that the institution will guarantee the individual's expertise as both authority and teacher, or that these persons will be well known to potential participants either as 'a good teacher' or as an expert because of their other activities. In these cases, recruitment of students is largely confined to those who know of the teacher and their immediate circle. At other times, the teachers will be endorsed by the qualifications or position they hold or by the experience they can bring to the task.

More frequently, there is a *description* of the subject matter of the learning programme. This is often short and uninformative. We expect the learners to have some idea about the subject they want to learn before they come to our programmes. A full description of the course may not be possible or desirable, but the prospective participant is entitled to know something of what the programme of work will be about, what sort of learning activities are expected to take place, what the purpose of the exercise is, at what level and for how long the programme will continue, who the learning programme is intended for and what sort of activity they may expect to be engaged in. For example:

Management for the 21st Century

B . . . F . . . , MBA, IPFA, DMA, MBIM. Six lectures commencing 3 October 2008, 7–9 p.m. Fee: £415 [location given].

The course will explore the range of techniques, skills and behavioural styles available to the modern manager including decision-making techniques; leadership and motivation; communications; personnel and the management of change. It is intended to meet participants' needs as far as possible and will use discussion groups, practical exercises and consciousness-raising techniques.

Course texts: J.A.F. Stoner and R.E. Freeman, *Management* (1991);
F. Luthans, *Organizational Behavior* (1992); R.D. Donnelly, *The Role of the Manager* (1993).

Selecting the participants

At times such blurbs spell out the target group or level of commitment, experience or ability that the programme calls for from the participants, particularly any pre-requirements set by the teacher. A school-leaving certificate course provided for adults, such as 'GCSE Biology', makes this clear, as do those programmes which contain specific reference to such levels. From a community college brochure 2000–1:

Title	Prerequisite	Suitable for	Start date	Day and time	No of sessions	Course fee
Introduction to Excel	None	Anyone	9 May	Wed 4–7	1	Free
Excel workshop	Basic Excel skills	Excel users	16 May	Wed 4–7	1	Free

At times, the title is the giveaway: 'Italian Beginners', 'Computing for the Terrified', 'Bookkeeping – OCR Computerised Acc (Sage)' or 'Drug Therapy Update for GPs'. Or this is done in the descriptive blurb: 'This introductory course . . .' or 'This advanced language course . . .'. However, even then we leave it to the readers to decide for themselves whether the levels *they* have in mind are the same as ours.

At other times more indirect methods are employed – the selective use of language, for example – to indicate the level of the programme and to select the participants. A one-day 'PowerPoint Workshop' will appeal only to those who know what PowerPoint means. Courses entitled 'Assertiveness for Women: Never Say Yes When You Mean No', 'The First Five Years: Mother and Child Relationships', 'Return to Study', 'Book-keeping for Small Businesses' and 'Law for the Householder' all select their own audience and indicate the level by the choice of words.

Language may be used in the description even more pointedly to select some and to exclude others. The inclusion of specialist names and the presence of long or technical terms will normally put off anyone not already acquainted with the subject. Carefully chosen language is sometimes deliberately employed in this way to exclude some persons (Figure 2.2).

But often the language used in titles and descriptions is careless and inconsistent. For example, courses entitled 'Peace as an Ecumenical Imperative' and 'The Methodology of Consumerism' may well put off precisely those for whom they are intended. On occasion, the blurb can

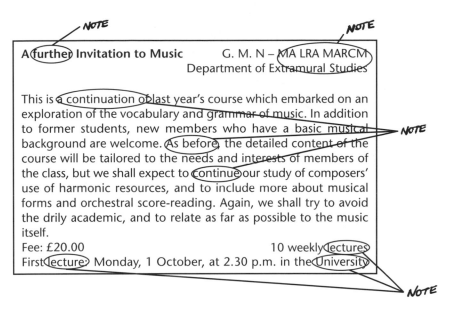

Figure 2.2 A learning contract designed to deter the novice from attending

contradict itself. The course on child psychology which states that it is designed to appeal to mothers of young children who have no prior knowledge of child development will nevertheless discourage precisely this same group by sprinkling the blurb with names like Skinner, Laing, Bruner, Maslow and Piaget, as if the teacher wished, even before the classes have started, to show how much they know. Such unthinking internal contradictions occur time and again in the programmes offered to adults.

Understandings and misunderstandings

The prospective learners are, then, active participants in the process of creating the contract by interpreting what they read. Frequently those who prepare learning programmes for adults do little to help them. What may be in the mind of a minister when it is announced that there will be a study group for the next eight Thursday evenings in the church hall (or parsonage lounge) on 'The Letters of St Paul' may not be the same as the expectations that such an announcement will create in the minds of the hearers. Some of them will not come, feeling that they could not cope with the work required; others will attend out of loyalty to person or institution. A number will come in anticipation of getting something out of the programme, but will not be sure what it is they are expected to get. The

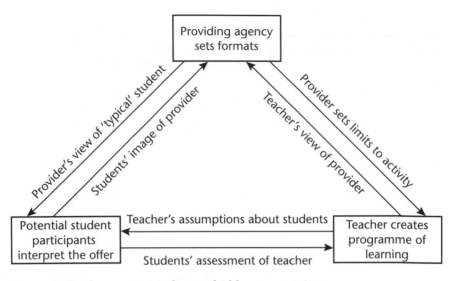

Figure 2.3 The contract to learn – hidden assumptions

organisers may well not have clarified for themselves whether the intended outcome will be a greater understanding of that part of the New Testament, or a greater liking of reading the Bible in general, or changed moral attitudes leading to changed patterns of behaviour. A contract exists but it is vague because much of it has been left unformulated.

Much then is presumed by all three active partners to the process of creating the contract to learn (Figure 2.3). There is a range of assumptions in the mind of the organiser – about the subject, about the purpose of the programme, about the student participants, about the teacher. There is a series of expectations and objectives in the mind of the teacher – about what the providing agency wishes, what the student participants want or are able to do, and what are the most important aspects of the subject being studied. Equally, the processes of publicising the programme and recruiting voluntary adult participants will arouse a set of expectations in the minds of the potential students. With so much unstated, to expect any real match between these three sets of assumptions is asking too much. The potential for uncertainty, for misunderstanding, for hindrances to learning and even for conflict, when the basic premises of all parties have been so ill-stated, is great. Effective learning calls for the contract to be set out more clearly and if possible agreed by all sides.

Once the group has met, the teacher and student learners can together explore the nature of the bargain they have made. It is useful for the teacher of any group of adults to try to discover at the start what sort of expectations each of the group members has drawn up in their own mind from the publicity material. We as teachers also need to spell out more fully our own expectations. This can be done through a course outline, presented to the student participants for discussion. Such a procedure enables us to test the assumptions we have made and to amend the proposed schedule of work (if possible) in the light of this reassessment. And it enables the participants to adjust their expectations if necessary and to decide whether to renew or cancel their commitment to the programme on offer in the light of their own intentions. And it is not a matter of doing this just at the beginning of the learning encounter – it will need to be revisited from time to time as the course develops.

This book as an example of a contract to learn

This book is itself an example of such a learning contract. It is intended for those who know or wish to know something about teaching adults. The agreement is that if you read it and experiment on the basis of it, then you will have an opportunity to reassess your teaching of adults and to examine possible alternative approaches. You can use the book entirely as you please, reading some bits and skipping others; you can use it to achieve your own purposes. It is a tool of your self-directed learning. In fact, this is its main aim, to become a resource for you to reflect critically on your teaching of adults. This is the contract this book offers and by which it should be judged.

The book first arose out of a number of courses conducted with various groups of teachers of adults in the UK and abroad. Some were full-time professional teachers of adults; others were part-timers. Several were people who do not see their primary role as educational (e.g. clergy and health visitors) but who have come to realise that they spend much of their time teaching adults. The illustrative material used in the book reflects its origins, and is drawn from a wide variety of settings.

The book follows the sequence of the courses taught over many years. We begin by trying to define what we mean by the terms 'adult' and 'education' (Chapter 3) and 'adult student' (Chapter 4). It then examines the concepts of learning (Chapter 5) and teaching (Chapter 6). The second section of the book concentrates on planning the learning programme, setting the goals and objectives of the learning programme (Chapter 7), forming and running the learning group (Chapter 8), exploring the roles of the teacher and the participants in the group (Chapter 9), and choosing the contents and methods used in teaching adults (Chapter 10). The final section deals with making the programme effective – discussing blocks to learning (Chapter 11) and the necessity for constant evaluation (Chapter 12). The book is rounded off with a plea for greater student

participation in all parts of what is really their own process of learning –
a plea which is even more relevant today than when it was first written
(Chapter 13).

The fact that this book has arisen directly out of teaching has caused
some problems in ordering the material. In teaching it is often necessary to
repeat what has gone before; in a book, such repetition needs to be avoided
as far as possible. We have tried to cut repetition down to a minimum.

Learning to teach

The book is based on the premise that as teachers of adults we have much
to learn about our craft. Initially, there was pressure to call the book some
variation on *Adults Learning* rather than *Teaching Adults* in order to stress
that adult learning programmes are student-centred, that teachers of
adults should be more concerned with what their students are doing than
with what teachers are doing. But while we agree with the basic concern
being expressed, we have resisted this pressure. Teaching is an activity
that calls for a range of attitudes, skills, knowledge and understanding
on the part of the teacher, and all of these need to be learned. This book is
about learning to teach. It provides a learning opportunity for the teacher
of adults – not just to discuss how adult learners learn but how the
teacher can so plan and act as to help them to learn more effectively.

We are conscious that to adopt this approach may seem to be too
directive. Some will feel that the book allows inadequate scope for choice
on the part of its readers, that it seems to be too concerned with 'right'
attitudes, 'right' practice, and not enough concerned with personal
growth. We hope this is not true, that its concentration on basic principles rather than specific methods will allow for the maximum individual
interpretation. But a book is by nature a partial tool of adult education. It
cannot establish that two-way learning process lying at the heart of all
good adult education. It can build on the experience of the reader only
to a limited extent.

Nevertheless, used as a tool it can do something. You can read its
various sections in any order you like, starting with the material which
is most relevant to your particular circumstances, your immediate concerns. For it is important that you, the reader, control your own learning.
You will need to relate the material discussed to your own experience
and use it to reflect critically on your experience. A number of activities
have been suggested to help you to do this, but you can ignore these and
devise your own means of active involvement with the subject matter in
these pages. However, without some activity relating the material to your
own situation, the discussions will remain remote from real life. Most of
the book will be concerned with matter with which you are familiar. It is

not trying to tell you anything new. Rather, it attempts to encourage you to make conscious what you are doing or planning to do, to explore it more fully for yourself and to systematise it.

Writing a contract of learning

Many teachers of adults assume that student participants choose to come to our programmes because they understand what it is we are offering them. We are on occasion surprised to find that they have something different in mind when they come. Frequently we put the blame onto them; we allege that they have not read the programme description carefully enough. But we as teachers rarely make enough effort to make the contract explicit. It would be a valuable exercise both for our own sakes and for the sake of the student participants to set it all out clearly: 'if you (who?) do this (what?) under my supervision (why?), you will learn . . . (what?)'.

The main medium for setting this out is the publicity notice. It may thus be a useful exercise for you to look at the description, if one exists, for the learning programme that you proposed for yourself on page xi; if one does not exist, you could try to write one now (see Activity 2.2). It then needs to be examined in the light of what we have been saying in this chapter. What does it say, not merely as a piece of publicity but as a learning contract? Whom will it attract as potential voluntary participants and whom will it deter? What image will they gain from it of the course or programme on offer? How much will they be able to deduce from the notice and how much from the context in which the programme is being offered? Will there be contradictions and confusions, or will blurb and context complement each other?

It will then be possible to proceed to a fuller version of our learning contract. In this, we will need to be much clearer about the objectives we wish to achieve and the steps to be taken in order to achieve them. The contract is not with our colleagues or our employing agency; it is with the potential student participants even if we have never seen them. The contract will need to address itself at least to the following items:

- What is the learning programme all about? What is its subject? What will it cover and at what level?
- What is the format of the programme? How long will it last? What are the frequency and duration of the meetings? What work will it call for between group meetings?
- Who is the programme for? What preliminary knowledge or experience is required? How will you make sure that the right

kinds of student participant get to know about the programme and are persuaded to join it?

- What will the programme of work be? What sort of learning do we expect to take place?
- What is the purpose of the exercise? In what ways will the learners be different at the end of the programme of work?

(If you are currently teaching a group of adult students, you could invite them to do the same exercise and see if there is any mismatch between their understanding of the learning contract and yours; at least you can get them to discuss the outline you have prepared in this way.)

Activity 2.2

By now you have built up a profile of your learning programme. Using this and the prompts below, set out a contract between you and your students.

- Basic information around timings, venue, duration and so on
- What preliminary knowledge or experience will students need?
- What sort of learning will take place?
- How will the students be different at the end of the programme?

Such a statement is not final. Once we have met the participants, once we and they have embarked on the process of learning together, we may find it necessary to renegotiate the contract, sometimes more than once as the programme progresses. This is part of the creative process of teaching adults. But the fact that the contract to learn has to be renegotiated in this way is not a reason to refuse to think about it from the start, to leave it until later. Because our students have chosen to study with us, to accept our package out of all those on offer, we need to make sure that both we and they are clear what that package is.

Our first task, then, as teachers of adults, will be either to draw up for our prospective student learners an outline of the programme or to interpret in more detail the outline prepared by others. The importance of this is that it will:

- help to determine who will come to and who will feel excluded from our programme;
- help the participants to decide whether our programme will meet what they see as their agendas or not; and
- help to create the expectations about the programme with which the student learners will first come, and which will to a large extent determine whether the programme is effective or not.

We need to be *very careful* when we draw up our learning programme outline.

Further reading

Chickering, A.W. (ed.) (1981) *The Modern American College: Responding to the New Realities of Diverse Students and a Changing Society.* San Francisco, CA: Jossey Bass.

Edwards, R., Sieminski, S. and Zeldin, D. (eds) (1993) *Adult Learners, Education and Training.* London: Routledge.

Thorpe, M., Edwards, R. and Hanson, A. (1993) *Culture and Processes of Adult Learning.* London: Routledge.

Tight, M. (ed.) (1983) *Adult Learning and Education*, vol. 2. Beckenham: Croom Helm.

Chapter 3

Perceptions of Adult Education
What do we mean by . . . ?

> The meaning we give to the terms we use reveals how we view the subject. This chapter discusses how people construct for themselves the concepts of 'adult', 'education' and 'adult education'. It suggests that inherent in all 'teaching' is a tension which determines much of what the teacher is able to do.

Teaching adults is often equated with adult education but the two may not be the same. Education in one of its meanings is the wider context within which our teaching takes place, so that adult (and now lifelong) education is the context for teaching adults. We therefore need to try to understand what we mean by adult education before concentrating more closely on teaching adults.

The search for understanding: adult education

There was a period when definitions of 'adult education' occupied much time and energy, at a time when those who were engaged in that activity sought to make it more mainstream, to get adult education onto the policy agenda, to obtain for it a place in the sun. Much ink was spilt on trying to determine what different people meant by the words 'adult', 'education' and 'adult education' and what distinguishes adult education from the other sectors of education, but all that this debate reveals is that there was much confusion. Despite the fact that, mainly in the form of continuing education and more recently lifelong education, adult education has become more important in the public eye, a good deal of uncertainty still remains as to what these terms mean. As Cross (1981), speaking of 'lifelong learning', said to her United States readers: 'It is quite possible that lifelong learning now outranks motherhood, apple pie and the flag as a universal good. Almost everyone is in favour of lifelong learning, despite mounting confusion over the meaning of the term'. But in spite of the problems, it is worth persevering with trying to understand the way we use the concepts that lie at the heart of what we want to do – to teach adults.

A number of different terms have been coined in an attempt to overcome some of the problems seen to be inherent in the expression 'adult education', each of them conveying some additional information or idea. It is important to remember that the different terms used represent different ideologies and that the meanings and value systems they indicate change over time:

- *'Continuing education'* – this term as used in much of the literature has changed its meaning from its emergence in the 1960s. At first, it stressed the unity of education, for children and for adults – 'from the cradle to the grave'; education (whatever that means) continues throughout life. Gradually however it came to have for many people a more limited meaning: educational programmes that are planned for adults who are returning to the formal educational system of schools and colleges, people who in America are called 'non-traditional students' and who form a major focus of interest in much adult education (Davies 1995). And even more narrowly, the term is often used to mean professional and vocationally oriented training programmes at advanced levels for adults who have already received a good deal of education. 'Continuing education' is thus increasingly seen in narrower, not wider terms, as institution-controlled learning programmes.
- *'Recurrent education'* is another such phrase. It embraces schooling as well as adult education, and stresses the provision of opportunities for individuals to enter, leave and re-enter the educational world at will. Many see in it calls for the reform of the formal schooling system to accommodate the needs of new groups of learners. Special concern has been shown by some of those who advocate 'recurrent education' for older-aged student participants, for whom a number of special learning programmes have emerged.
- *'Lifelong learning'* and the French term *education permanente* are also used, with slightly different meanings; but both tend to see education as built into the process of living rather than as separated into a range of special classroom and study activities. The most recent discussion of lifelong learning (*IFLL Report* 2009) sees it as a system of learning opportunities, formal and informal, excluding informal/incidental learning.
- *'Non-formal education'* describes all out-of-school education for any group of any age. It refers not merely to the format of this education but also to the contents, which are seen to be more life-related than the traditional school curriculum, and to the processes which are claimed to be more interactive and participatory than directive (see Rogers 2004).

Comparing adult education

For many years, there was a search for a definition that would embrace the very diverse educational cultures of (for example) Ireland, Indonesia and Indiana, so that the practice of adult education in all countries could be compared. Some people hoped that an overriding conceptual framework could be devised to cover what is one of the most culture-bound of all activities (ISCED 1975). As a result of this concern, international statements defining adult education became longer and increasingly involved in an attempt to suit all places and all conditions. The Organization for Economic Cooperation and Development (OECD), for example, indicated its belief that

> adult education refers to any learning activity or programme deliberately designed by a providing agent to satisfy any training need or interest that may be experienced at any stage in his or her life by a person that is over the statutory school-leaving age and whose principal activity is no longer in education. Its ambit thus spans non-vocational, vocational, general, formal and non-formal studies as well as education with a collective social purpose.
>
> (OECD 1977)

The United Nations Educational, Scientific and Cultural Organization (UNESCO), concerned for the so-called 'developing countries' as well as the West, had a wider view of the scope of adult education: 'organised programmes of education provided for the benefit of and adapted to the needs of persons not in the regular school and university system and generally older than 15 . . . organised and sustained instruction designed to communicate a combination of knowledge, skills and understanding valuable for all the activities of life' (UNESCO 1975a: 4). It included:

> the entire body of educational processes, whatever the content, level or method, whether formal or otherwise, whether they prolong or replace initial education in schools, colleges and universities, as well as apprenticeship, whereby persons regarded as adult by the society to which they belong develop their abilities, enrich their knowledge, improve their technical or professional qualifications, or turn them in a new direction and bring about changes in their attitudes or behaviour in the twofold perspective of full personal development and participation in balanced and independent social, economic and cultural development.
>
> (UNESCO 1976)

Perhaps the broadest definition of adult education was that of the (then) National Institute of Adult Education (now NIACE), England and Wales:

any kind of education for people who are old enough to work, vote, fight and marry and who have completed the cycle of continuous education commenced in childhood. They may want to make up for limited schooling, to pass examinations, to learn basic skills of trade and profession or to master new working processes. They may turn to it because they want to understand themselves and their world better and to act in the light of their understanding, or they may go to classes for the pleasure they can get from developing talents and skills – intellectual, aesthetic, physical or practical. They may not even 'go to classes'; they may find what they want from books or broadcasts or take guidance by post from a tutor they never meet. They may find education without a label by sharing in common pursuits with likeminded people.

(NIACE 1970: 10)

Post-initial education

The term 'post-initial education' for a time came to command a good deal of support as a description of adult education. It was implicit in the NIACE statement of 1970, and the term was used in the Nairobi Declaration (UNESCO 1976), while a number of reports relied heavily on the idea, if not the term itself. The UK Advisory Council for Adult and Continuing Education (ACACE) wrote that understanding the term 'adult education' would be assisted

if a major distinction was made between 'initial' and 'post-initial' education. This is a more basic distinction than such kinds of administrative divisions as 'compulsory' and 'post-compulsory'. The initial education stage would obviously include going to school, including nursery school, but it could go on full- or part-time into the mid-20s. After compulsory schooling, initial education takes a wide variety of forms: full-time study in sixth form, university, college, polytechnic, medical school, military academy and so on; part-time day-release; evening classes and correspondence courses; on-the-job training in the factory.

(ACACE 1979: 9–10)

All education after this is post-initial – that is, adult education. The Alexander Report for Scotland used the term 'initial education' to mean all educational experiences undertaken by a person prior to the time of taking up a first full-time career post (which may of course be long delayed). On this basis, initial education includes:

all school-based or compulsory education and also the education of those who go straight from school to university or college in pursuit of higher qualifications. In addition we regard those whose immediate post-school employment involves vocational day-release or sandwich courses or apprenticeship training schemes as still undergoing initial education. All educational experience which an individual undergoes subsequent to or additional to this initial education we term continuing education' [the phrase Alexander preferred to 'adult education'].

(Alexander 1975)

In Northern Ireland, (adult or) continuing education was seen in similar terms: 'Continuing education is regarded as any education which adults voluntarily undertake, excepting that which they pursue full-time or part-time directly following the period of their compulsory education' (NICCE 1980: 10). The report of the Adult Education Commission for the Republic of Ireland (Department of Education, Ireland 1984: 9) used a definition that was only slightly different: 'Adult education includes all systematic learning by adults which contributes to their development as individuals and as members of the community and of society apart from full-time instruction received by persons as part of their uninterrupted initial education and training'.

The post-initial idea thus implies that an individual engages in a preliminary period of initial education starting at the age of 3, 4, 5 or 6 in most countries, and ending at some age usually between 12 and 24 according to whether they leave school at the earliest possible moment or stay on at college, university or an institution offering professional studies. At the end of this period, all people of whatever age who 'return' to education after a gap are engaged in 'post-initial education' (Figure 3.1).

There are however several difficulties with such a definition. First, applying this concept to those countries where a considerable number of people receive no initial education at all, or where there is a high

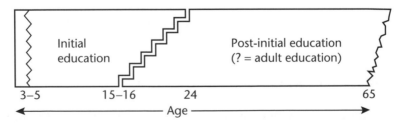

Figure 3.1 Initial and post-initial education in the lifespan of the population

withdrawal rate at various ages between 6 and 16, is not easy. Even in the West the distinction between the end of initial education and the beginning of adult education is not always straightforward, especially as new forms of initial education are emerging. Does adult education cover those many young people who nowadays leave initial education for a short period and then return to it in the form of day-release or block-release programmes, part-time courses, youth training schemes and other activities where they may join older persons in search of some means of qualifying themselves for a job? What about those compulsory training programmes that some people are required to take during their first years in post under their contract of employment (in the banks, for instance)? Are graduates who take further full-time training courses to make themselves more attractive to a prospective employer still in initial education or in post-initial education? What about the person who after leaving school does one or two years' accountancy or architecture (for example) and then goes to university or college for professional training? What about those people who continue their initial education through distance or open learning modes while working?

More important, from the teacher's point of view, is the decision as to what courses and programmes constitute 'post-initial' education. Is a training course or school-leaving certificate course (for example, in a college of further education) attended by both school-leavers *and* returning adults (a 'mixed economy' course) initial or post-initial education? This is a matter of considerable import to both provider and teacher.

Activity 3.1

Would you define the course you have taken as your case study (page xi, Before You Start) as:

- initial education; or
- post-initial education?

How did you come to your decision? Which factors did you consider when making your judgement? Do you think it is necessary to make a distinction between the two? How might the distinction affect the way you view your programme or course?

A definition of adult education which sees it in terms of post-initial education – that is, as part of the *structures* of a hierarchical educational system ranging from primary (or pre-primary) through secondary and third-level education, all of which comprise initial education and are followed sequentially by post-initial or adult education – would seem to be unsatisfactory. Perhaps this is the reason why lifelong learning has emerged as a non-sectoral and over-arching concept for all education.

Today, searches for definitions of adult, continuing and even lifelong education no longer feature so prominently in the publications on adult learning today, and the distinctiveness of teaching adults is less stressed. It is pointed out that much of what goes under the banner of 'adult education' is in fact applicable to most forms of teaching, that we are talking about 'good education' rather than the specifics of *adult* education. But for all that, we believe it is useful to consider the debate and for each of us to explore our own position within it.

A different way forward may be to try to examine the distinctiveness of education for adults as lying in its *process*. To understand this process, we need to look in more detail at the meanings given to the terms 'adult', 'education' and 'adult education'.

Adult

A wide range of concepts is invoked when we use the term 'adult'. The word can refer to a *stage* in the life cycle: each individual is first a child, then a youth, then an adult. It can refer to *status*, an acceptance by society that the person concerned has completed their novitiate and are (or should be) incorporated more fully into the community. It can refer to a social *subset*: adults as distinct from children. Or it can include a set of *ideals and values*: adulthood.

Many people tend to think of 'adult' in terms of age. But no single age can define an adult even within one society, let alone on a comparative basis, because legal and social liabilities come into play at different ages. We have only to think of voting, getting married, fighting for one's country, holding property, buying a drink or cigarettes, being sued, incurring sentences, obtaining credit, driving a vehicle, engaging in paid labour or attending various forms of entertainment – all of which have age-related restrictions applied to them – to see that we cannot say an individual becomes fully adult at any specific age. There are many who feel hesitant about using the legal school-leaving age, which varies from country to country, even in the West; and the legal age of majority is lower than the end of initial education for many people.

Some definitions are clearly inadequate. For example, in one study, an adult 'is defined as anyone either aged twenty-one or over, married, or the head of a household' (Johnstone and Rivera 1965: 26). Another asserts that 'The taking on of social roles characteristic of adulthood –

roles such as worker, spouse or partner, voter, and parent – differentiates adults from children better than chronological age does' (Merriam and Cafarella 1999: 393).

The problem of defining an adult – and a non-adult – is so great that at times those bodies with greatest experience of making such definitions give up. UNESCO (who have now adopted an international benchmark of all persons aged 15 and upwards) in 1976 determined that adults are those people whom their own society deems to be adult. An adult is both self-recognising and recognised by others. And this is important, for adulthood, like childhood, is for many people a social construct. While in part both of these concepts have a biological basis (physical growth and psychological development), the implications of these changes, how they are understood, and the social reactions to them are cultural. Both adults and children consist of an *experience* (being a child, being an adult). Both too are active in determining their own lives – even children, with their own folklore, language, laws and games, etc.

Adulthood seems in every culture to be contrasted with childhood. There are a number of issues relating to the way different cultures construct childhood. In some contexts, childhood is a very short period, in which case adulthood starts early. Among other groups, however, childhood is long, and adulthood therefore appears to be 'delayed'. For some, childhood is a period of innocence, for others it is an age in which self-centredness needs to be disciplined (socialisation), while yet others follow the adage of Shakespeare that there is nothing good nor bad but nature makes it so. In some contexts, it is believed that children need to be isolated from the real world, cherished, kept in dependence, while in other constructs the opposite is felt: children need to be integrated into the society of which they form a part, to be encouraged into independence. All are agreed that adults are different from (indeed, in most cultures the opposite of) children. They are the fulfilment of what is partial in children. Whereas children are 'growing up', adults are 'grown ups'; they have (in that sense) 'arrived'.

Characteristics of adulthood

One approach, then, is to identify those characteristics inherent within the specific cultural construct of adulthood. In every culture, there is a series of expectations about those who claim and who are recognised to be adults, though these will vary from individual to individual and from culture to culture. Characteristics such as far-sightedness, self-control, established and acceptable values, security, experience and autonomy are among the most common ones advanced, although not all of us would claim that to be an adult a person needs to possess all these traits.

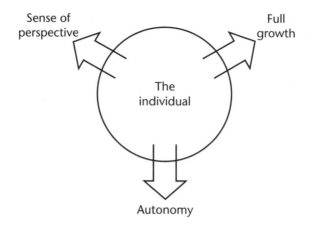

Figure 3.2 The (Western) concepts of the adult and aspiring adulthood

Maturity

Western humanist educators such as Houle and Carl Rogers have developed this theme most fully. Three main clusters of ideas seem to lie within their constructs of adulthood (Figure 3.2). First, the term is used in the sense of being *fully grown*. An overriding concept for many behind the word 'adult' is that of maturity. In the natural world, we speak of a mature tree or mature cheese as being fully developed. When applied to human beings, the word bears stronger overtones than it does in respect of the natural world. It represents the development of talents to a level of achievement; relatively fixed traits and interests, established patterns of behaviour. But human maturity is not just a state (though we can recognise the characteristics of a mature person) but also an ideal to be aimed at rather than achieved in full. Nevertheless it still includes the idea of the *full development* and utilisation of all the individual's talents; and the process of moving towards ever greater maturity is one acknowledged as being associated with adulthood.

Perspective

The other two clusters of ideas linked with adulthood may be seen most clearly by looking at the opposite construct, childishness. There are occasions when an older person in many cultures is regarded as behaving 'childishly', in a non-adult fashion. Such childishness may consist of the individual seeing themselves as either being more important than they are seen by others to be, or conversely as less important than they really are. The former throws a tantrum, acts petulantly, makes a fuss and is often said to be 'over-reacting'; such are frequently further infuriated by the accusation of childish behaviour. The latter withdraws, sulks or submits passively, normally accepting the charge of childishness with less hostility. In both cases 'adults' are expected to behave with a greater sense of perspective than is being shown, a perspective that will lead to sounder judgements about themselves and about others. We expect adults to have accumulated experience that, if drawn upon, will help them achieve a *more balanced* approach to life and to society, to be more developed in their thinking in relation to others.

Autonomy

Associated with this is a third element of adulthood, *responsibility*. One of the key concepts of being adult and not being childish is that of being responsible for oneself, for one's deeds and development. One study defines people as adults 'because they have assumed responsibility for managing their own lives' (cited in Merriam and Cafarella 1999: 393):

> To say that someone is an adult is to say that he [*sic*] is entitled, for example, to a wide-ranging freedom of life-style and to a full participation in the making of social decisions; and it is also to say that he is obliged, among other things, to be mindful of his own deepest interests and to carry a full share of the burdens involved in conducting society and transmitting its benefits. His adulthood consists in his full employment of such rights and his full subjection to such responsibilities.
>
> (Paterson 1979: 10)

Frequently the adult is responsible for others as well, but at the very least they are responsible for their own actions and reactions. The adult can decide not to be responsible in some respect or other, but this surrender of self-reference may be seen by others as a denial of adulthood. Adulthood, then, for many people implies some measure of autonomy, responsible decision-making, voluntariness rather than involuntariness. It is of course important that we do not assume that children do not have any autonomy. They do; and development can be seen as the widening of autonomy from a base which already exists. But in most cultures, adulthood is associated with a major level of autonomy and decision-making. This is not to deny the fullness of social interaction within one's community; but it is to stress that the ultimate responsibility which such interactions carry with them lie with the individual adult.

Adulthood, then, in each of these three aspects is seen by such writers as an ideal towards which each person is struggling – never fully attained but always more or less clearly set out before us. There is in each person, these humanists assert, a drive towards becoming more mature, more 'balanced' and more responsible.

Such views of autonomy are seen by some as being very Western, liberal and individual (Boud 1988). However such definitions may apply in Western cultures, they are felt by others not to be appropriate to other cultures. Hungry people have not developed anything like their full maturity or potential. Slum dwellers, slaves and refugees are certainly not independent but oppressed. And it is not easy to take a balanced view of life while under conflict or threat from natural disasters. And yet in these contexts there are still adults.

Other cultures therefore see adulthood in different terms, often the opposite to Western cultural values. In many groups in China, for example, adulthood is seen in terms of 'family continuity, socially prescribed roles, the acceptance of hierarchical relationships as supreme, compliance with authority [rather than autonomy and individual responsibility], a value on stability versus change . . . an identity that is externally ascribed, subordinated to the collective, seeks fulfilment through the performance of duty . . . highly malleable', characterised by 'a group-oriented way of thinking [rather than] an individual focus'. Studies of indigenous cultures suggest that many of these reveal a concept of adulthood (the ideal self) 'founded upon traditional tribal values, orientations and principles . . . environmental relationships, myths, visionary tradition, traditional arts, tribal community, and nature-centered spirituality' which are missing from Western constructs of adulthood (Pratt 1991: 302; see also Merriam and Cafarella 1999: 129–30, 334).

Adulthood and teaching

It can then be argued that these three characteristics – maturity, perspective and autonomy – are traits that mark off the socially accepted adult from the non-adult in some societies. Such an analysis can carry profound implications for us as teachers: they can help to establish both the aims and the curriculum of the teaching we provide for adults (Figure 3.3). Our programmes and courses, if they are to confirm and not deny the adulthood of our student participants, will seek:

- to promote *personal growth*, the identification and full exploitation of the talents of the individual;
- to encourage the development of a sense of *perspective*;
- to foster confidence, the power of choice and action, to increase *autonomy* rather than to deny it.

In such a perspective, if the content and the material of the learning programmes we conduct and the methods we employ in them do not

Adulthood	Childishness	Implication for the goals of teaching
Personal growth/ fully developed	Nascent talents, changing interests	Full development and exploitation of talents and interests
Perspective/mature judgements about others and self	Lack of perspective • over-important • too humble	Development of sense of perspective
Autonomy/self reference	Flight from responsibility	Development of confidence/ practice of responsibility and decision-making

Figure 3.3 The implications of different perceptions of adulthood for the teaching of adults

tend to help our student participants to become more mature, more balanced and more self-determining, then it can be argued that we are denying the adult nature of those we are teaching.

Activity 3.2

Do you consider that your course

- encourages the full development of each of the student participants?
- helps to develop their sense of perspective?
- helps to develop confidence, autonomy, self-direction?

What is it that you do that encourages and helps your students in these ways? Could you do more to develop their sense of perspective, autonomy or self-direction?

Diversity within unity

But such an approach, useful as it is for teachers of adults, lays stress on the similarities between adults by drawing a clear-cut distinction between adults and younger persons. It treats adults and children more as entities than as collections of different individuals and groups. And it hides the wide range of differences which exist among both children and adults.

In any society, there will be many different concepts of adulthood, not just one. And persons can use more than one concept of adulthood if it suits their particular ambitions and agendas. It has been suggested that those who live in some indigenous cultures '*simultaneously* use [both] indigenous value systems [and] the most appropriate concepts, technologies, and content of modern education' in seeking to develop their own idealised self (Merriam and Cafarella 1999: 130–1). Concepts of adulthood are changing all the time and are often mixed.

Thus, being an adult will change from group to group and over time. Studies of groups of women in India show how their concepts of adulthood altered as they met different situations in their lives: 'The pace of the transformation has been relatively "fast" or "slow" for different categories of women, depending on their socio-economic status, education and place of habitation' (Verma 1995: 161). Identifying such diversities may in the long run be more important than deciding who is and who is not an adult in any particular culture.

The importance of all this for us as teachers of adults would seem to be the necessity for us to ask – within our own cultural boundaries – how the concept of adulthood is constructed: how are adults in our society differentiated from children and adolescents? What do we and our student learners mean by the term 'adult'? What perceptions of 'adulthood' do they each bring with them? What are the goals and aspirations of 'adulthood'?

Education

The term 'education', like 'adult', is again used in several different senses. For some, it means a *system* of institutions which aims to provide learning opportunities, usually state-run and promulgating state-dominated ideologies. This is for others too narrow a sense, for they see 'education' as much wider than a system. For many of them (especially in the lifelong learning discourses) the meaning of 'education' has been extended to cover *all forms of learning*, whether inside or outside of any institution. Indeed, on occasion that is how the word is used in daily life. It is not uncommon to hear people say that an activity such as travel or going to a nightclub was an 'education'. What they mean is that they learned a lot from the experience. But this meaning is perhaps too wide to make real sense of what is happening, for education is not simply the same as learning, though it includes learning. A more reasonable position envisions education as a process of *assisted or guided learning*. This too may have a negative connotation in that it often (but not always) implies some form of manipulation which imposes particular views on others. But it is not necessary for us to accept such a negative view.

Those, then, who take education to mean 'assisted learning' point out that this means that what we are doing (teaching adults) is education, even if it occurs outside of any specifically 'educational' context. A parent or carer helping a child to learn cooking in a kitchen is educating that child. A person showing a friend or neighbour how to fill in a form is teaching that friend or neighbour. Teaching (it can be suggested) is not the same as instructing: someone preparing distance learning materials is 'teaching' as much as someone working in a classroom with a learning group. Both are 'helping others to learn'.

Learning throughout life

Such an approach depends on a distinction between assisted ('taught') learning and unassisted learning. As we shall see in more detail later (see Chapter 6), there is a view of learning which sees it as an activity in which we take part all the time in the course of everyday living, as the process by which we face, cope with and make sense of our experience. Throughout our lives, we face situations in our work, in our domestic settings and in our wider relationships that were not conceived of when we were at school or college, and they all call for new learning. Such continued learning is an informal natural process, performed as we interact with our socio-cultural context.

We learn as we enter new *social roles* – as wage earner, as householder, as spouse, parent and grandparent, as voter and member of a local community. What is more, society is constantly revising its interpretation of those roles; today's parents adopt postures towards their children and towards the rest of society often very different from the postures adopted by *their* parents. How we relate to other people is one area that calls for constant new learning.

We need to learn to meet the changing demands of our various *occupations*, whether heart surgeon, historian, handicraft expert or home-maker. All the tasks we engage in, whether they comprise paid employment or work in the home, call for new knowledge, new skills and new attitudes at various stages. There are some senior posts (e.g. in government and the churches, education and commerce) for which there is no form of initial education and which therefore have to be learned 'on the job'. Some occupations make constant calls for major readjustments and new learning, while others require fewer changes. Even those who are unemployed find themselves engaged in a series of situations that demand new learning.

As we change and grow older, there are corresponding changes in our personal interests, ambitions and desires. The need to learn as part of our individual development, for our *self-fulfilment*, is a major element in this lifelong learning. As some skills decline, new ones are learned; new interests replace earlier ones. Marbles give way to antiques, outdoor pursuits to less energetic ones.

And many of us feel the need to learn before we embark on new experiences. We read up before we travel; we look at magazines or manuals in preparation for a task we have set ourselves; we develop our study skills before starting a formal learning programme. We learn *in preparation* for further purposeful learning.

These four main areas are not of course entirely discrete. Learning in relation to our job may also be part of self-fulfilment and personal growth; so too may social role learning. But they do provide a general guide to the main groups of challenges which call for learning activities.

Learning and education

Most of this learning is done incidentally, from many new kinds of experience and perceptions: for example, from advertisements, news items, chance meetings and accidents. All of these provide us with learning opportunities (often unintended) which we may seize upon or pass over as we feel inclined. All leave marks on us, some more and some less permanent. This natural learning is part of the process of living.

But we would wish to argue that such incidental learning that occurs at random throughout life is not 'education'. Education for us includes learning, which is its essential ingredient, as flour is of bread. Nevertheless, flour on its own is not bread; learning on its own is not education. The OECD definition of adult education as 'learning opportunities for adults' is not adequate, for such learning opportunities exist in a haphazard fashion all around us, whereas education occurs at specific times. There are times when we are not engaged in education, even though we are learning; something more is needed to make learning into education.

Education is planned learning

One possible perspective, then, is that education can be seen as an artificial creation, unlike the natural learning processes. Harold Wiltshire draws a distinction between the two when he describes education as being:

> *planned processes of learning undertaken by intent*, the sort of thing that commonly (though not by any means always) goes on in classrooms and that involves some who are teachers and some who are taught . . . In much discussion of adult 'education', the word is used much more loosely. Thus in much French writing about '*education populaire*' it seems to be used so as to include the whole range and apparatus of leisure-time activities – cinemas, libraries, television and sports clubs – on the grounds that these exert an educative influence on people who use them and are

therefore aspects of education. Certainly there is a sense in which anything that happens to us, from getting drunk to listening to Beethoven, may be said to be 'quite an education'; and certainly we learn (living tissue can hardly help doing so) from our experiences, including those of our leisure. But such learning is unplanned and largely unintended: we do not go into either the pub or the concert-hall with a primary intention of learning. If we intend to learn we behave differently: we join a class or buy an instruction manual; we adopt the role of student and submit ourselves to a planned process of tuition.

(Wiltshire, in Rogers 1977: 136–7)

Education, then, can be seen to consist of planned learning opportunities, constructed and purposeful activities, wherever it takes place. Words like 'structured', 'development', 'cumulative', 'sequential' and 'progress' are associated with many people's concept of education. To take just one example, the UNESCO report on *Educational Radio and Television* (1975b) stated that 'educational' broadcasts are marked off from other programmes by the fact that:

- their purpose is to contribute to *systematic* growth;
- they form a *continuum* of provision;
- they are so planned that their effect is *cumulative.*

Some broadcasters in their desire to widen the scope of 'educational' programmes have doubted this definition, but it still seems to be a satisfactory one.

The aim of all this planning, preparation and review is to promote and to direct learning. Education may therefore be seen as the provision of organised conditions for learning to take place, a means of providing learner support and assistance. It is aimed at directing and maximising effective learning.

Education in this sense involves at least two parties. On the one hand, there is the agent (e.g. a formal educational institution such as a college or university, a firm or business, a voluntary organisation or church, a publisher, editor or correspondence course writer) or the teacher, or both. They plan the learning opportunity and assist the learning. They intend certain outcomes to spring from their planning, even though in the process they will themselves come to learn much. On the other hand, there are the student participants. They too usually intend certain outcomes from the activities in which they are engaged; they are motivated by a willingness to engage in a range of activities in order to achieve a particular learning goal. There is in education purpose and planning on both sides.

Much has been written in recent years about 'self-directed learning' (Brookfield 1985). In this process, the learner takes the initiative and plans their own structured learning process. But in most of these cases, there is some outside planner as well – someone who wrote the textbook or manual, who planned the sequence of articles in the magazines or journals used by the learner. There is still someone engaged in 'teaching' (helping the learner to learn). Self-directed learning may on many occasions take place outside the educational sector, but it has many of the characteristics of the intentional, planned, purposeful, and assisted learning that is education.

Characteristics of education

If we adopt this view of education as 'assisted learning', three character-istics may be identified as inherent within these planned and purposeful learning episodes (for more details, see pp. 133–8):

- The process is *sequential and cumulative*. It is not just a number of unrelated 'magazine' items, individual parts without any interconnection. Rather it builds up piece by piece, making rela-tionships between the diverse elements of the learning process.
- The process addresses itself in some form or other to *general principles*. It does not consist of the anecdotal, the one-off episode or miscellaneous facts, but draws from these some con-clusions that may be applicable elsewhere. Consumer education, for example, is not a matter of identifying an individual product or supplier of which particular consumers should be wary; rather, it uses those incidents in such a way that the consumers can make judgements for themselves in a wider range of instances. The result of taught learning is that the learner can apply the new skills, knowledge and understanding acquired in different situations.
- The process is also in some sense *complete*. However open-ended the teaching process may be, there is some 'rounding off' of the material dealt with, some form of fulfilment, of meeting the goals, so that the student participants do not feel left high and dry, incomplete and unsatisfied. Taught learning is of course never complete; it consists of opening doors, leading on to the next stages of the sequence. Nevertheless, each stage has some completeness in itself, some sense of achievement, even of satisfaction and pleasure – as with music, some sense of closure.

The elements of education

A useful way of seeing 'education', then, is as a planned learning opportunity which one party provides for or with another in relation to an agreed objective. Such opportunities can be created anywhere – in the home, at work or in community contexts – whenever guided learning takes place.

This would suggest that there are five main elements to education, which may be seen to be in close relationship to each other:

- the *teacher-agent* (TA), who may be at programme level the institution or organisation that provides the learning opportunity, and at learning group level the teacher/tutor;
- the *student participant* (SP), the individual or group who put themselves intentionally into the learning situation;
- the intended *goals and objectives* (GO), however loosely or closely defined;
- the sequence of events that will enable the student participants to learn, the steps towards the intended goals; that collection of *methods/content* (M/C) lying at the heart of the planned learning process; and
- the *context* within which the activity takes place.

The relationship between these elements may be illustrated as shown in Figure 3.4, although this representation is too static for what is one of the most dynamic of human situations. All elements of the planned learning opportunity undergo change, and each goal leads on to new developments and to new goals.

The role of the *teacher-agent*, whether organiser or teacher, in this process is crucial. It is the teacher-agent who sets up the learning situation, even though the student participants may come increasingly to take control of the learning process. The teacher-agent assesses the needs

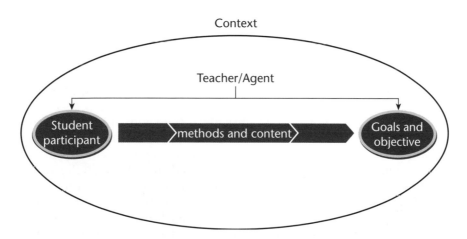

Figure 3.4 The educational process

Goal	Specific achievement, externally moderated	Personal growth, internally moderated
Teacher's role	Teacher introduces student to subject matter	Encounter between student, teacher and subject matter
Student's role	Student more passive	Student participant fully engaged
Content	Discipline of subject matter, limited choice	Open-endedness; subject matter less important than activities
Methods	Directive	Interactive

Figure 3.5 The impact of goals on the teaching–learning process: the continuum

and aspirations of the prospective learners, establishes the goals and constructs the programme of methods and contents, the course of action that will enable the participants to 'learn' their way towards the agreed goals. The teacher-agent is the planner – at least in the first instance.

The *student participants* are also active in the planning process. They intend to learn, to achieve their own goals. They, like the agent, have certain outcomes in mind; they come to the learning situation with a set of intentions (sometimes unformulated) and actively set about fulfilling these (see pp. 84–7).

The nature of the *goals* set in the planning process (see Chapter 7) will bring in its train a range of implications for the role of the teacher, as well as for the contents and methods used. A narrow objective, aiming at some specific competency or externally moderated achievement, will tend to lead to greater stress being laid on the part played by the teacher than on the learners' activities. On the other hand, a concentration on a wider objective such as the growth of the individual will lead to an emphasis more on learner-centred than teacher-centred processes (Figure 3.5).

The planning agent (teacher-provider), then, has in mind certain *expected outcomes* – the results that will flow from the learning undertaken. However, most of the student participants come with their own intentions, which may or may not be the same as those set out by the agent. They will seek to use the learning opportunity to achieve their own outcomes. Each of these sets of purposes influences the other. The teacher's planned outcomes help to shape the learners' expectations, and the learners' intentions and hopes should affect the formulation of the teacher's intentions.

Both sets of expected outcomes may well be different from the *effective outcomes* of the teaching process. Since those being taught consist of a mixed group of learners, each of whom responds to the learning programme in a different way, there will always be a series of unexpected outcomes. The teacher-agent needs to keep these differences in mind when planning the learning encounter (see Evaluation in Chapter 12).

We cannot easily separate *methods* from *content*; the two are closely related. But the nature of the goals we set helps to determine whether the emphasis of our programme of work lies more towards content or towards method. Programmes with narrowly prescribed objectives tend to concentrate more on content than on methods; an adult class leading to a certificate in English literature, for instance, or a course on new legislation relating to health and safety at work, define for themselves more or less precisely the content of the teaching–learning encounter. Those teachers who feel it necessary for the student participants to come face to face with a set amount of material will tend to use directive rather than participatory methods, for both teacher and taught expect a specified content to be 'covered'. On the other hand, programmes aimed more at personal growth, confidence building and assertiveness are likely to be less rigidly controlled. Their impulse lies more in the processes involved in the teaching–learning programme. In these cases, we may feel it more important to engage in participatory learning methods than to cover a set amount of material.

Whatever our decisions, which may well change as the course progresses and as we reassess the aspirations of the learners with their help, methods and content are integrally related in the planning of a teaching experience. They cannot be discussed apart, and neither is more important than the other.

And all of this takes place within a *context* – a context which helps to determine the nature of the teacher-agency and the power relationships involved; which largely determines who the student learners will be and who they will not be, who will be included and who will be excluded; a context which will certainly shape the goals of the programme; and a context which will determine what content is chosen (for all societies privilege some kinds of knowledge and demean others) and what kinds of methods are used. Learning and teaching do not take place in a vacuum but within a socio-cultural context which controls the values inherent in the process.

Education as encounter

Some would argue that what we have proposed is too mechanical a notion of teaching. Instead, they see education as an encounter without prior determination of the outcomes. They lay stress on the fact that each student participant reacts uniquely to the material they are meeting or are perceiving anew, and that in any case the outcomes may not reveal themselves until some time after the learning programme has ended. They emphasise the open-ended nature of the meeting of learner, teacher and material, and the unpredictability of learning. In fact, they urge, learning may not take place at all; and in the nature of the encounter, the teacher may learn as much as the student.

All of this is true; and certainly the outcomes of this encounter with adults cannot be prescribed. But a teaching–learning situation still calls for a *conscious decision* to create such an encounter. Even when that decision is accompanied by a desire for open-endedness, there is still a *purpose* behind the encounter. It calls for a process of *planning*, of selection of the experiences to be used as the basis for the learning. Equally, such a view of teaching as encounter calls for an *intention* on the part of the participants, a willingness to engage in the encounter. The outcomes of our teaching may be different from those we plan for or anticipate, but some element of planning is essential.

The dynamic relationship between all the elements within teaching is not confined to the initial planning of the learning programme. It becomes clearer as the process goes on. The teacher-agent is (or should be) active all the time, reassessing the student participants, evaluating progress made, amending and redefining the goals, reconstructing the methods and content and learning all the time with the participants. The student learners too are active, clarifying their intentions and changing their objectives. A course once set and never altered, directed towards unchanging goals, can only with difficulty be called 'education'; for to us education is a process of change in which teacher and learner join together in relation to a third element, a series of agreed but changing goals.

Education, training and indoctrination

Our definition of education as a planned and interactive learning opportunity is however not enough unless we also consider whether the term carries with it a value judgement or not. Are *all* planned learning situations 'education'? A terrorist organisation's programme of field training will be seen by most people as very different from a local conservation society's series of visits or a women's group's acting workshop, although all three may be motivated by a desire to change attitudes, and thus behaviour, and ultimately systems in society at large. So we are forced to ask whether, for education to be education, the goals must be 'good'.

The problem is an old one: how to define 'good' in this context (see, for example, Whitehead 1959). Clearly once again we are in the field of social constructs. 'Socially acceptable' may in some circumstances not be adequate to describe the good that education is intended to do, for many educators of adults wish to use their learning opportunities to encourage some form of change in society, and change is not always 'socially acceptable' (think, for example, of the early Western trade union and the later women's movements). Those of us who have been brought up to think in terms of traditional liberalism will conceive of the good that education can bring as increased individual freedom. Others may assume that an increased ability to generate wealth (either for oneself or for society at large) is the good that education should achieve, while yet others will talk of a sense of social responsibility, the rectification of social inequalities, the increase of cultural richness and harmony, or environmental concern and action.

Rather than pursue this line of thought here, perhaps a more useful approach is in terms of 'wide' and 'narrow' goals. In this sense all structured learning opportunities can be seen as lying along a continuum. At one end are those planned teaching–learning programmes with narrow goals, the aim of which is to demonstrate that there is a 'right' way to do something or other. These are largely in the skills area but not entirely so; they teach that there are 'right' ways of working things out and of learning. Choice is strictly limited and not encouraged. This is what we usually mean when we speak of *training*. At the other end are all those activities that set out to convince us that there is a 'right' way of thinking and feeling and behaving. Once again there is a limitation, even a denial, of choice; there is only one set of values and attitudes to hold. This is essentially *indoctrination*. Between these two extremes is that large area of education where the goals are wider: to demonstrate that there are different ways of thinking and doing, to encourage the development of choice and self-determination (Figure 3.6).

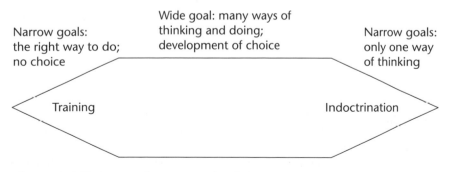

Figure 3.6 Training, education and indoctrination

Our question, then – whether we see the term 'education' as referring to *all* planned learning opportunities or only to those for which the goals are 'good' – may be a matter of personal choice. We can call all learning activities specifically created by one agency for another group of people 'education', in which case we can talk of using education for good or bad ends. Or we can define 'education' as consisting only of those programmes and courses with wide rather than narrow goals, thus cutting off training and indoctrination from the world of education. It is a question of personal definition.

On the whole this is more a matter of concern to the organiser of programmes than to the teacher. Nevertheless we as teachers have to decide for ourselves whether *our* goals are wide or narrow, whether we are engaged in education, training and/or indoctrination. Probably elements of all these will come into our teaching at different times, arising from our commitment to our students and to our subject.

Activity 3.3

Are the goals of your course wide or narrow? How would you define your course?

Does your course consist more of:

- training: the right way to do something?
- indoctrination: the right way to think?
- education: the increase of choice?

Adult education

Is adult education simply the addition of our definition of 'adult' to our definition of 'education'? Do we mean by the term 'adult education' the provision of planned learning opportunities for those persons whom society deems to be adults or does the phrase imply something more? Is there a distinction to be drawn between 'the education of adults' and 'adult education'?

Adult education as content

Some people have argued that the difference between these two concepts lies in terms of the *contents* of the programmes. Thus they see the 'education of adults' as referring to all forms of education for those over the age of 16 (or 18 or 20), irrespective of what is being studied. It thus includes some subjects (both skills and knowledge) better learned at a younger age (e.g. playing a musical instrument). On the other hand, they would restrict the term 'adult education' to those topics which can be learned or best learned *only* as adults, because they rely on experience (politics, say, or interpersonal relationships, or spirituality) or because they relate to adult roles (parenthood or management). Some have suggested that the key ingredient of *adult* education is that it is life-related, that it helps adults to address their own issues from 'real' situations. Such a definition would however exclude from 'adult education' a great deal that belongs to it. Literacy and basic skills, for example, typewriting, sports, languages, woodworking and computing are all better learned while young, but they feature in most programmes of recognisable adult education. And there are some subjects – art, for instance – which experience shows do not have age-related criteria for learning.

Activity 3.4

Do you consider your course subject or content

- especially appropriate for adults?
- more appropriate for younger persons?
- equally relevant to both groups?

Adult education as process

Because of this, others have suggested that the difference between what may properly be termed 'adult education' and the 'education of adults' lies less in *what* is being learned (although some subjects are especially appropriate to adults) than in the *approach* to adult learning. They draw a distinction between those programmes that teach adults as adults and those that teach them in ways more appropriate to younger learners. The 'education of adults' can then be seen to cover all forms of education (planned learning opportunities) for those over the age of 16 (or whatever), whether the student participants are treated as adults or whether they are treated as if they were younger learners – taught, that is, as if they were largely or completely ignorant of the subject being studied, without relevant experience, unable to be relied upon to control their own learning, having little or nothing to contribute to the learning process. 'Adult education', by contrast, consists of all those forms of education that treat the student participants as adults – capable, experienced, responsible, mature and balanced people. In this view, the essential difference of adult education from all other kinds of education lies in its power relationships, the equality of teacher and student participants – 'teaching on equal terms'.

We have suggested above that many in Western societies promote the view that all forms of teaching adults should respect and enhance the adulthood of those who have voluntarily become our students. This makes any approach to the education of adults that does not possess the characteristics of 'adult education' inappropriate. To deny the adult students' adulthood is not just to create unnecessary barriers to effective learning, to deprive ourselves of the most useful resource we have for the learning task; it is to insult them with our own arrogance.

An approach which seeks to promote an increased sense of 'adulthood', however, creates tensions for ourselves as teachers of adults. For one thing some of our students may express a wish to be taught in ways that deny their adulthood. They may want to go back to school, to surrender their autonomy in order to learn some new thing (this is discussed further in Chapter 11). At the same time, our concern for the subject matter to which we have submitted ourselves and to which we hope our students will submit themselves may pull against this concern for the adulthood of the student participants. The primacy of the goal of greater adulthood over all other goals is one of the main issues faced by those of us who teach adults.

Two patterns of education

This distinction between treating participants as adults ('adult education') and failing to do so (what we may call 'adult schooling') reflects a tension deep within education itself. The tension is felt in all sectors but is at its most acute in the teaching of adults. It reflects two contrasting attitudes towards the task in hand and to all elements of that task. The tension can be expressed in a series of polarities:

- between education as content and education as process;
- between education as 'teaching a subject' and education as 'teaching people';
- between education as preparing for life and education as a part of living;
- between education as discipline, conformity to an external standard, and education as liberation.

A useful (though in places overdrawn) summary of these two approaches can be seen in Figure 3.7. This distinction between two fundamentally different approaches to education has been pointed out by many writers,

'Conformist'	'Liberation'
Make student participant like teacher	*Make student participant independent of teacher*
1 There is an external reality to which student must adapt (subject discipline). Truth is known.	1 There is no externally 'right' way of knowing and behaving. Truth is not known.
2 Student can't be trusted to pursue own learning; teacher takes initiative.	2 Human beings have a natural potential for learning; student takes self-initiative.
3 Presentation = learning.	3 Most significant learning through doing.
4 Material exists on its own, independent of both teacher and student.	4 Significant learning takes place when subject matter is perceived by student as having relevance for their own purpose.
5 Teacher must help the transfer of knowledge to student: students cannot obtain knowledge by themselves.	5 Knowledge cannot be transferred; all knowledge is created by student for themselves.
6 Process of education is to accumulate brick upon brick of knowledge and skills – progression of subject is externally set.	6 There is no set sequence of learning; students engage with material in their own way and in their own sequence.
7 Constructive and creative citizens develop from passive learners.	7 Creativity in learning depends on active involvement; student participates responsibly in learning process.
8 Evaluation by teacher of student's progress is a necessary part of learning.	8 Learning is best achieved when self-criticism and self-evaluation are primary; evaluation by others is of secondary importance.
9 Cognitive learning can take place without affecting rest of person.	9 Learning that involves the whole person – feelings as well as intellect – is most pervasive and lasting.
10 Learning is a one-off experience and need not be repeated.	10 The most useful learning in the modern world is learning how to learn; a continuing openness to experience and an incorporation of the process of change into oneself are necessary goals of education.

Figure 3.7 Two approaches to teaching

from Houle (1961) with his statement that 'Education either functions as an instrument that is used to facilitate the younger generation into the logic of the present system, or it becomes the practice of freedom, the means by which women and men deal critically and actively with reality and discover how to participate in the transformation of their world', to Paulo Freire with his strongly asserted statement that education cannot be neutral: it either domesticates or it liberates the student participants.

Activity 3.5

When planning your course, would you say that your chosen teaching methods are closer to the conformist end or liberation end of the continuum? What are your reasons for placing your course at a particular point in the continuum? Are you satisfied that it sits in the 'right place'? If not, what could you do to change this?

The tension that is teaching

It would, however, be a mistake to suggest that one of these models is wholly correct and the other is wholly wrong. Rather, they represent a tension that is never resolved. This tension impinges on both the teacher and the student participant. Education with adults is both in part a preparation for life and in part an integral element in the process of living. It seeks both to help the student participants to change towards a predetermined goal and yet at the same time to help them to become more independent and to challenge that goal. It is both training and education, both discipline and free growth. In education the teacher helps the learner to become free, but within the limits of a field of study or expertise. We seek to bring the student participants into contact with the primary material and leave them free to use it for themselves.

The teachers too may find themselves torn – between the desire to help the students develop into something they have already indicated they want to become (a painter, a more confident person, a more efficient professional, a more skilled technician or trade union official, etc.) and the desire to respect and encourage the autonomy of the adult learner. We may be torn between the clear vision we have of our subject and our willingness to encourage our students to see it for themselves in different ways. The teacher is aware that there is such a thing as the 'bad' use of literature, bad dressmaking, bad gardening practice, bad history and so on; that there are standards, in fact. Although we may be conscious of the limitations of our own judgements, nevertheless we believe that there are criteria in our discipline to which we ourselves seek to conform and to which we hope our student participants will wish to conform. Yet we want our students to grow in independence, self-determination and self-appraisal.

And it is here that we need to recognise that we as teachers come from a particular cultural background; that we are created beings, built up through many different experiences. It is a culture which privileges certain kinds of knowledge and which discredits other kinds of knowledge (Barr 1999). The criteria we apply to ourselves and to our subject matter are all partial, contingent and contested, even within our own discipline. We are not neutral, not impartial; we are the product of our culture and at the same time we are the disseminators of the values of that culture. It cannot be otherwise – but if we can become aware of this and reflect critically on our situated value systems, we shall become much more open when we meet other cultural value systems among our student participants.

Nevertheless, we need to go ahead on the basis of our expertise, whatever that may be. And there will be times, in the ordering of the material that the student participants handle in order to move towards the agreed goals, when the discipline side predominates; times when the training aspect – the most effective way to do things – is most prominent, when the teacher's role is to point out the good and the bad (the process of evaluation, as we shall see, depends on *values* – see Chapter 12). Even here, however, the ideal is for the participants not just to accept the judgements of the teacher but to come to make their own judgements, to accept the discipline of the subject for themselves.

But education cannot consist of this alone. There are other times when the freedom, the self-determination of the student participant, the autonomy of the adult, has full play. They will create their own approaches, their own strategies, and our task is to encourage such individual initiatives rather than suppress them.

It is not just a question of getting the right balance between these two aspects of education. The tension is inherent within the whole process of planning for learning. The introduction of a purpose, a goal, as a third element into the relationship between the teacher-planner and the learner creates the tension. For this goal makes its own demands on both the teacher and the learner. It directs both the material and the methods used in the learning process. The teacher who has a goal is not totally free, any more than the learner who desires to achieve a goal can be completely free. Freedom in this respect comes from accepting discipline.

The purpose of the educational encounter can then be seen as being to achieve a series of mutually agreed objectives, and this purpose imposes a discipline on both the teacher and the taught. Both, but particularly the teacher, will feel the tension between the discipline that education is and the freedom that it seeks to promote. There is no right solution to the problem. We all have to live with both sides of the equation.

Further reading

Barr, J. (1999) *Liberating Knowledge: Research, Feminism and Adult Education.* Leicester: NIACE.

Boud, D. (1988) *Developing Student Autonomy in Learning.* London: Kogan Page.

Brookfield, S.D. (1983) *Adult Learners, Adult Education and the Community.* Buckingham: Open University Press.

Jarvis, P. (1995) *Adult and Continuing Education: Theory and Practice.* London: Routledge.

Wallis, J. (ed.) (1996) *Liberal Adult Education: The End of an Era?* Nottingham: Continuing Education Press.

Chapter 4

Adult Students
Who are they . . . ?

This chapter first discusses some approaches to developing a profile of the participants in our programmes, including the lifespan approach, and then lists some of the main characteristics of those who join adult learning programmes. It argues that adults, when they come to our learning programmes, construct themselves as 'students'.

Much attention has been given in recent writings on adult education to the adult student learner. Whole books have been devoted to the topic, and most general studies of adult education, based on the premise that all forms of teaching adults ought to be student-centred rather than teacher-centred, contain sections dealing with the specific characteristics of adult student learners.

Student profiles

One feature of this discussion has been the compilation of lists of characteristics of the adult student. The aim is to help teachers of adults to become more conscious of what they are doing when they draw up a profile of their students, to test out the items specified to see which do not apply to their particular group and to identify other characteristics particular to their teaching context. Most of these lists are limited in their application in that they are directed more towards the participants in part-time non-vocational, non-qualification adult education of a more or less academic orientation than towards those in basic education, practical skill-based courses, formally certificated courses or advanced professional development programmes.

In many of these descriptions, huge generalisations are often made about the adult student participant. It has been suggested, for example, that adult students are 'people well beyond schooldays, full of a mixture of regret, determination, guilt and ambition, but dogged by lack of confidence and self-belief, harassed by noise and diversions, facing problems of time and space to study, tiredness and opposition and mockery from spouses and friends'. (These descriptions have all come from a number of recent writings purporting to describe the general principles on which adult education is predicated.) But clearly these do not describe all (or even perhaps many) adult students: such 'outdated images of adult learners' contained in 'a strong contemporary image of the uncertain, under-confident adult returner who fears traditional forms of assessment' are clearly inappropriate in today's adult education (Ecclestone 2005: 6). Each such description needs to be drawn up with a proper regard to the group in question.

Drawing a profile

We all draw pictures of who our student participants are going to be. We do this as an integral part of the process of planning the programme and the course. Some of us can rely on past experience to help us, but new teachers of adults cannot do this. They may turn to other more experienced teachers to assist them, but even this is not always possible. And such a process is often unconscious. We rarely make explicit the views we hold about the prospective learners, their abilities and motivations, what we can and cannot expect from them. Even in those programmes where the goals are negotiated with the potential participants, the teacher-planner still makes several assumptions: for example, that they want to join in, that they are willing to entertain the notion of change and are capable of engaging in the processes put before them.

We thus fall into unquestioned presuppositions about our prospective student participants. We may on occasion assume that the learners are at the opposite extreme from our goals: that they possess no skills at all, if our goals relate to the acquisition of skills; that they are completely ignorant of the subject in hand, if our goals are knowledge-related; that they hold negative attitudes, if our goals are attitude change; that they have not yet begun to comprehend, if our goals are concerned with understanding; that they lack all forms of confidence, if our goal is confidence-building. None of this may be true. Indeed, it is most unlikely to be true. Those who come on a bird-watching course are likely to know something about the subject; those who attend car maintenance classes will invariably have had some experience of a car; those who wish to learn about women in literature are most likely to have done some reading in this field already and will have views (often strong views) on the subject; those adults who come to university degree programmes for 'mature' students often know more than their teachers allow for. So-called 'illiterate' students in fact have much experience of literacy; 'innumerate' learners already calculate often and efficiently. Unless we make conscious what we believe about our potential student participants, we are in danger of making false assumptions.

Testing the profile

Having compiled a list of apparent characteristics of our potential learners, it is necessary to test these at the earliest possible moment. In some forms of teaching adults – some distance learning, for example, or the educational programmes offered by the media, and the self-directed learning materials prepared by many agencies – the teacher-planners never meet the learners, so that the assumptions made cannot easily be assessed to see whether they are right or wrong. But in most other cases it will quickly become apparent whether we have judged correctly what the prospective student participants are able to do, what they are willing to do and what they want to do.

Sometimes we will get it all wrong, so that there is nothing to be done after the first meeting other than to redesign the whole learning package. As with most skills of teaching, we can improve with practice; but even after long experience, because every group of adult learners is different, we still need to test whether the presuppositions we have made about our student participants are correct or not, so that the programme of work can be revised or amplified as necessary.

Teachers are sometimes reluctant to do this in their first encounter with the student participants. It may be that they are hesitant to expose themselves from the start of their relationship with the learners, to give the impression that they are in any way uncertain. Or, having prepared some material for the first meeting, they may be anxious to give it. Such teachers sometimes justify this on the grounds that the participants who have turned up want to have something 'meaty' at the first session so as to judge better the content, level and pace of learning involved in the course. They argue that some prospective students would find a first meeting devoted to a general discussion an unsatisfying experience. Or the teacher accepts at face value the participants' assessment of their own knowledge or ignorance of the subject, their ability or inability to contribute anything useful towards setting the goals and constructing the programme of work. There are many reasons for not opening up to challenge the assumptions we have made about the participants.

Despite this, it might be better to spend at least part of an early meeting with any group of adult student participants listening rather than talking, assessing whether the views we have about their interests and abilities are right or not. The task will have to be done at some stage during the course, and it needs to be done as early as possible if we wish to avoid a lengthy gap between bringing together their expectations as learners and our expectations as teachers.

The range is wide

In order to test out these presuppositions, we need to undertake the process consciously rather than subconsciously. For many of us, it will be useful to write down our description of the potential student participants. But here we run into the biggest problem of all. Most of us teach in groups, and the wide range of those who join such groups, even small groups, may hinder us from making realistic judgements about what we can in general expect from our student learners.

Let us take one example as illustration. That which we call 'intelligence' today is rarely now seen as a fixed inherent ability that cannot be improved after the end of formal schooling, or a range of abilities that grow and decline along mathematical curves (see p. 99). Intelligence is now thought of in many circles as being 'plastic', context- and content-related, rising to peaks or falling into troughs throughout adulthood, largely governed by whether the activities engaged in and the environmental factors are culturally relevant, stimulating and encouraging or whether they are damaging and inhibiting. Particularly, the development of academic intelligence seems to be dependent more on the amount of educational experience one has received and on the subsequent use of formal learning skills in one's occupations than on any basic learning ability inherited or developed when young. Thus persons who have had a good deal of education and who have been engaged in tasks calling for considerable and regular amounts of new learning will be 'more intelligent' at 50 than they were at 25; conversely, those who have been employed in occupations that have not required them to engage in problem-solving and facing new challenges are likely not to have developed their intelligence to the same extent. In any group of adults engaged in a learning programme, the range of learning ability, even among people of roughly the same age and the same initial education, is certain to be considerably wider than in a comparable group of children.

Lifespan studies

Many adult educators use 'lifespan studies' for drawing their profile of adult student participants; for it is argued that if learning can be defined as a process of personal changes made in adapting to changed situations and experiences (see pp. 96–8), the study of different patterns of life is likely to throw light on such learning (Sugarman 1986).

From the 1970s to the 1990s, a number of general views of lifespan development emerged based on ideas about the major points of meaningful change that occur during adulthood. These were thought to give teachers a useful basis for the process of drawing a profile of their student participants. Today lifespan studies are fewer and less influential, although (surprisingly) the most recent authoritative statement (*IFLL Report* 2009) has reverted to an age-related division of the lifespan, talking in 25-year stages of divisions at 25 (for adults, 18–25), recognising that (in some Western societies among some of the population) young adulthood is extending for a longer period; at 50 years (25–50 being a period of career and raising a family with an 'acute time squeeze'); and 75 years (50–75 being characterised by alternative careers, new interests, new mix of paid and unpaid 'work' and new family structures). Beyond 75 years lie health and dependency issues and 'accelerated decline'! The turning points have been chosen on the grounds that (without being deterministic about exact dates) 'these are points where for large proportions of the population [of England?] physical, social and labour market factors come together in a different mix' (*IFLL Report* 2009: 83–100). (It is to be hoped that this part of this important report will be fully challenged).

However, almost all other studies avoid age-related criteria and refer to 'life changes'. The terms 'change' and 'development' are used in educational contexts in a variety of senses. A number of adult lifespan studies speak in terms of growth, the gradual and natural increase of maturity. Others speak of development – i.e. goal achievement (see Knox 1977). For some writers, the ultimate goal of adulthood is one of 'rational autonomy', moral maturity or critical reflection. On the other hand, some writers have rejected the concept of 'development' and replaced it with a view of *change* throughout adult life as a purposeless but still a successive process (see Giles 1981).

Lifespan developments and contexts

Most writers suggest that, unlike the child and the adolescent whose different stages are recognised (even if not universally agreed) as age-related, adults change and develop more by experience and by the exercise of competences than by age. There are of course physical changes that occur with increasing age, but these are not inextricably related to any specific age, and the changes that take place differ for each individual. There is in the West a strong emphasis on the physical elements in human make-up; thus ageing is frequently seen as a phenomenon to be resisted, something to be overcome rather than valued for the wisdom and status it brings – although this may now be changing. In other cultures, the spiritual is more predominant and this leads to different perspectives on ageing.

More recently, much of the emphasis in adult development studies is on the changes within the social and cultural context of the individual which call for new responses. This is a reaction to a tendency among some adult educators to see adults in too great an isolation from the social and physical environment in which they are located, to see society as static while the individual changes, to underestimate the effect of changes in social structures and values on the adult. But increasingly we see that we are dealing with a changing person in a changing world. Change, not stability, is the norm.

Among those changes are variations in perspectives, including the view of the ageing process itself. Because of their emphasis on the physical, Western societies have tended to see youth in positive terms while ageing is often constructed more negatively. In recent years, views in relation to older persons have, it is true, shown significant alteration, with growing positive attitudes towards older age groups, perhaps a result of the increasing number of these persons in society as a whole. In many developing countries, on the other hand, influenced by earlier Western cultural patterns, the reverse would seem to be happening; despite the increasing number of older persons, youth is increasingly being glorified and older age regarded with disfavour. Society is not only imposing identity on individuals but is constantly reinterpreting that identity.

Ages of man and woman

Most of us are acquainted with Shakespeare's 'seven ages of man': the infant, the schoolboy, the lover, the soldier, the justice, the 'lean and slipper'd pantaloon', and finally second childhood. Since Shakespeare's time there have been many attempts to better this description of adult changes. Some are very general: Whitehead's successive phases of romance, precision and rationalisation; or Egan's romantic stage, philosophic stage, and eirenic or fulfilled stage – these all display the 'plateau effect' of Shakespeare: growth, maturity and decline. The use of the term 'Third Age' for example perpetuates the construct of a three-stage life consisting of growth, performance and 'completion' or withdrawal.

Cognitive development

A growing field of study lies within adult cognitive development, especially the application to adults of Piaget's work on children. Several have added extra stages beyond the 'performing' stage. A number of these are very elaborate, some having no less than nine additional sequential and hierarchical stages. A sequence is proposed by which adults pass from the performing stage of Piaget into problem-solving and finally to problem-identification and creation. One study talks about five levels of consciousness which adults pass through, while others suggest a total of seven stages: 'to think reflectively does not emerge fully formed but develops in a sequential fashion, with earlier stages building on prior stages and laying the foundation for subsequent stages' (King and Kitchener 1994: 152). But although sequential, none of these stages is exclusive; a number of these authors suggest that adults can operate simultaneously on several levels. A few speak about 'transpersonal development' as the goal of adulthood: transcendental absorption into the Universal Consciousness.

Dominant concerns

Among the more influential group of lifespan theories are those that see changes during the adult phase of life in terms of dominant concerns. These are frequently age-related. Havighurst (1952), for instance, suggested that the individual passes through eight main phases. After childhood and adolescence comes adulthood, a 'developmental period in about as complete a sense as childhood and adolescence are developmental periods'. From 18 to 30, adults are focusing on their life; there is a concern for self-image, experimentation, jobs and love affairs. Education tends to be used for occupational advancement. From 30 to 40 is a period of stability and relatively less introspection, less self-doubt. The job is now most important, with child-rearing a close second. From 40 to 50 is a period of self-exertion and assertion, the peak of the life cycle. Public and civic activities are more important than participation in educational programmes. There is a turning out towards society from oneself, the family and the job; action is the means of dealing with the world, and this brings the first consciousness of physical deterioration.

From 50 to 60, adults begin to change roles. Educational involvement is for expressive rather than instrumental purposes. There is increasing physical deterioration (sight and hearing), and larger amounts of energy have to be exerted to avoid losing ground. 'Thought' rather than 'action' is the means of dealing with the world, and short-term rather than long-term achievements are sought. The adult spends the years between 60 and 70 deciding whether and how to disengage, and from 70 onwards is the period of making the most of disengagement. Healthy adults are not too preoccupied with the past, are self-accepting and relatively content with the outcomes of their life, but this period is often characterised by poor health, reduced means and dependence on others.

Havighurst's views, as set out above, are frequently cited by adult educators, for he relates such changes directly to educational activities. But these are too simplistic, too rigidly tied to ages, and they are based on Western male-dominated concepts of a successful work career; they have great dangers of becoming prescriptive. In any case, major changes in social and occupational structures have rendered such a neat analysis suspect.

These considerations led to other sequential approaches without tying each stage too closely to ages. Neugarten (1977) spoke of adulthood as representing a 'movement from an active, combative, outer-world orientation to . . . an adaptive, conforming inner-world orientation'. Three stages were identified: a period of expressiveness, expansiveness and extroversion, of autonomy and competence (up to about the age of 30); an intermediate period of reorientation; and a third stage of change from active to passive modes of relating to the environment with greater introversion. More recently, others see adulthood as repeated and successive stages of performance which are relatively stable, followed by periods of transition away from these more or less stable states through 'structure building' processes which may include disorientation and reorientation. Some relate these stages to different ages (Levinson 1979), but the view holds even if such ages are removed.

Tensions

Erikson (1965), on the other hand, saw the stages of human development in terms of tensions. There is, he argued, the general and continuing tension between 'the inner wishes . . . and the demands to conform to other people's standards and requirements', which all people experience and which leads to compromises if the adult is 'to maintain the integrity of his [sic] personality'. In addition there are a series of developmental tensions: in puberty and adolescence, there is the tension between identity and role confusion; in young adulthood, intimacy versus isolation; in adulthood, generativity versus stagnation; and in 'maturity', the integrity of the self versus despair. The educational implications of each stage are delineated: initial education for the child and adolescent, vocational education for the young adult, social and community education for the adult, and philosophical and creative education for the mature. Others speak of incongruence. The individual has

> 'two problems; maintaining inner harmony with himself [sic] and with the environment. Incongruence is developed within the person (intra-self) and between the person and other-than-self experiences (self/other) . . . The research of life-cycle psychologists supports the notion that younger [adults] manifest more intra-self and self/other incongruence than older, more mature [people].
> (Boshier 1989: 147–50)

Time perspectives

Lifespan changes may also be seen in terms of how time is viewed. Some writers have suggested that the child sees the future as far away; for the adolescent, the future is rosy; for the adult, time is finite; while the mature adult feels that time is running out. Friedmann (1977) elaborated this version of the 'plateau' theory of lifespan changes, being particularly conscious that successive stages do not easily correlate with ages. He thus overlapped some stages:

- The *entry stage* (say, 18–25): orientation is to the future – the future will be better than the present; change is good.
- *Career development* (say, 20–50): orientation is increasingly more to the present than to the future; away from interest in promotion towards an interest in the intrinsic value of work, together with participation and achievement in non-work areas.
- *Plateau* (say, 35–55): the main time focus moves to a feeling that time is running out; there is increasing neuroticism, especially among the lower socio-economic groups who cope less well than professionals and managers.
- After 55 comes a period of decline.

Gender and class factors

More recently it has been recognised that these schemata are too closely tied to datable stages, and attempts have been made to break away from this. As these examples show, it is recognised that there is considerable gender and class bias in such analyses, deriving from the origin of most of the studies – among reasonably successful American white professionals, those who on the whole predominate in continuing education programmes in the USA. The gender bias is surprising; all of these theories relate to male careers despite the fact that women predominate in many forms of adult education. The women's movement has been seeking to redress the balance.

A major strand has been the exploration of women's development in adulthood which sees one of the key themes emerging as the transition from identity (the self) into intimacy (empathy), moving from the acceptance of other's knowledge to the creation of one's own knowledge (Belenky et al 1986; Code 1991). Similarly, it is likely that the lifespan stages and expectations of blacks are different from those listed above.

The class bias has received less attention. Almost all the above descriptions rely upon doubtful assumptions concerning the social and educational background of the participants – the educated, the professionally employed and the ambitious. One attempt to redress this balance towards the working class suggests that:

> there is a rough sequence in a working life which the intellectual is too apt to forget. After the first period of school and pure technical training, the worker, for the ten years from 15 to 25, is

pitchforked into practical life – finding and holding a job after marriage and founding a home on small resources . . . between 25 and 35, as the worker approaches a more responsible job, education should broaden his [sic] ideas of the nature of authority, of the social and human implications of any new job, of the deeper purposes of society. Once this broadening process has been started, it may well lead on into history, literature and art . . . It means at 21 bread and butter and the wage packet. At 30 it may include ideas of status, leisure, civic responsibility; and at 40 and thereafter it may deepen into a concept of the good life.

(Hunter quoted in Stephens and Roderick 1971: 195)

The importance of context

These studies show how context has come to dominate more contemporary explorations of adult development. The conflicts and contradictions inherent in any lifeworld are part of the creative forces which make for the continuing change in the individual. Lifespan studies today have gradually been replaced with dialectic and with life histories. A number of different approaches can be seen. For example, some Western thinkers, perhaps drawing on the thinking of Habermas (see pp. 117–9), have elaborated this into the continuous interaction of a person's work, relationship to others and perceptions of self. Others are drawing heavily on the work of Bourdieu and his concept of *habitus* and on Foucault (see p. 116).

Roles, crisis points and cycles

It is significant how important work is in almost all Western lifespan studies. Adult learners are seen generally as workers. Attempts to draw up an alternative lifespan sequence to that of the male professional still assume a working life. But the New Work Order, changing patterns of careers in almost all sectors and long-term unemployment on a large scale together with changes in attitudes to work and retirement, have thrown doubt on much current thinking.

These changes and the patronising air that surrounds efforts to define working-class life stages, as well as an awareness of other changes (especially in marital relationships) have led to a number of different approaches, some of which concentrate on the pattern of family life and/or lifestyles. Some focus on the changing *roles* of the adult which form a unique pageant of life (Hughes and Graham 1990) or on the *crisis points* that occur in the life of most adults of a particular generation (Sheehy 1976), whether male or female, working class or middle class, black or white – although reactions to these new roles and crisis points vary considerably according to experience and the culture of the individual. The most common roles and crisis points identified usually relate to the first job, marriage, parenthood, the departure of children from the home, bereavement (especially the loss of parents and spouse), separation and divorce, loss of a job or other role, retirement and (less sequential and more occasional) moving house. Such events have been divided into individual and social, but the distinction cannot always be maintained. These are seen both as events with a specific time frame and also as a process. Among these writers, a common crisis point is seen to occur somewhere about the age of 40 in both males and females.

Others suggest that linear, normative, predictable and at times prescriptive stages are no longer appropriate and replace such stages with a concentration on social forces as the major source of personal change and development. Hudson (1991: 43) sees 'life as a complex, pluralistic, multivariate flow, with ongoing cycles in nature, societies and people. Families, corporations and nations are all part of a larger, often chaotic flow that can be influenced and shaped but not completely controlled . . . adult development [is] adaptation to change – change within themselves and within their environment'. Within these *cycles*, basic themes such as love, achievement and the search for meaning are played and replayed throughout adult life. Responding to these themes, to changing commitments and to altered circumstances in one's life is what adult development is all about.

Summary

The search for universally applicable stages of adulthood is revealing ever more divergence and less agreement. From our point of view as teachers, it is wise to remember that adults age, and that with ageing:

- Physical and some psychological changes occur, to a greater extent for some people than for others and in different ways.
- Roles change, all calling for new learning, and there may on occasion be difficulties as well as excitement and challenge in adapting to new roles or to new perceptions of roles.
- Various crisis points are passed, sometimes easily, sometimes with difficulty.

But we also need to note two further points. First, individuals are (with very rare exceptions) single entities; body, mind (and spirit) interact with the context to make a single person in a constant process of creation. It is whole persons who change, grow and develop, each unique yet sharing a common humanity.

Secondly no individual is an island. The adult 'develops in a continuously ongoing reciprocal process of interaction with his or her environment'. It is now much more widely recognised that the culture we inhabit tends to create our thinking and thus our development. We need therefore to explore in each lifeworld 'how the world about us defines who and what we ought to be' (Merriam and Cafarella 1999: 118). The way our culture defines 'work' and 'others' and even our own 'self' will be enormously influential in our development throughout adulthood. A Chinese approach is very different from Western approaches, as we have already seen (see p. 48).

But what has not been recognised is that those who write about lifespan development are themselves the creatures of cultural climates, mainly American (e.g. Carl Rogers 1974). It is highly significant that many of these thinkers now claim that the highest goal of adulthood, the aim of personal development, is the construction of one's own knowledge. King and Kitchener assert that in the final two stages of adult cognitive development, knowledge is no longer a given but will be constructed by the person via critical reflection. Belenky and her colleagues aver that the fifth and final perspective which women have on knowing is the construction of knowledge. Others suggest that the most advanced thinking comes not with certainty from the provision of answers but rather the uncertainty of posing questions, not the elimination but the toleration of contradiction. The move from a deficit approach (the need to receive other persons' knowledge) through the disadvantage approach in which the individual explores their relationship with others, and into the diversity approach in which each adult creates for themselves a truly unique knowledge of self, of others and of their world may reveal not only the cultural climate of the past half a century (see Chapter 1) but also how individual interpretations of development during adulthood over the past generation have themselves been constructed.

The implications for the teacher of adults of this multiplicity of views on adult development (and a number of others have not been listed here) can be summarised briefly. The mixed group that most of us face will not only possess a wide range of ability. It will also contain persons of different ages and at different stages of development, experiencing different roles and different interpretations of those roles, and also facing different crises points. And each of them will react in different ways to the very varied changes they are experiencing in their own life: 'Adults address and solve life events and dilemmas at different rates and times' (Hughes and Graham 1990: 8). The most important characteristic of any group of adult student participants is that they will be very diverse.

Activity 4.1

How do you (or would you) find out about your students and what they may already know about the subject of your course? Would you include in this process ways in which they may like to learn? What are the benefits and risks of this approach in the early stages of a course?

General characteristics of adult student learners

Does this mean that we can say nothing about those we are teaching? We think not. Despite the wide variations that exist between the members of our learning group, it would still seem to be possible to identify some characteristics of the participants in adult learning programmes which appear to apply to most of the group and which will affect the way we teach them. We have selected seven such characteristics, although cultural settings will modify these to some extent. What follows is our list; you may find it helpful to decide for yourself how far each of the categories is appropriate in your own circumstances and to make up your own list:

- the student participants define themselves as adults;
- they are in the middle of a process of growth, not at the start of a process;
- they bring with them a package of experience, knowledge and values;
- they come to education with aspirations and intentions;
- they bring expectations about the learning process;
- they have competing interests;
- they already have their own patterns of learning.

They all have a self-image as 'adult'

In Chapter 3, we saw that in Western cultures the construct of adulthood represents an ideal, never fully achieved. The concept seems to imply movement, progress towards the fulfilment of the individual's potential, the development of balanced judgements about themselves and others, and increasing independence. Our student participants are people who are becoming more mature, and the way we teach them can either encourage or discourage this development in self-fulfilment, perspective and autonomy.

The most visible way in which adult learners exercise their adulthood in relation to our programme of work is by voluntarily choosing to come to learning programmes. We need to stress this, for some participants in continuing and lifelong education programmes may be seen as compulsory students, sent there by their employers or other agencies against their will (see pp. 17–8). But even in such cases, these adult student participants have decided for themselves that they will comply with such directives rather than incur whatever consequences would follow from their decision not to do so. They are not like children in this sense of 'compulsion'; for whatever reason, they have chosen to attend.

Malcolm Knowles (1990) suggested that adulthood is attained at the point at which individuals perceive themselves to be essentially self-directing (although this may not for many persons be a single point in time). He believed that there is a natural process of maturation leading organically towards autonomy, but that this is limited by what the social culture permits. In many societies the local culture does not encourage the development of autonomy in some groups of people (women, for instance, especially married women, in many parts of the world). Thus, self-directedness is often partial; it may not extend to all parts of life (including education). Knowles pointed to the gap or tension that exists in these cases between the drive and the ability to be self-directing. Some people will feel more strongly than others this urge to take control of their own lives, to be involved increasingly in the decision-making processes affecting their life choices. But he claimed that it is there in virtually all adults nonetheless. His 'andragogy', to be effective, needs to build upon and foster this process of maturation into self-direction. A situation that reverses the trend, treating the developing adult as a child to be directed what to do and what not to do, will find itself faced on most occasions with major blocks to learning. Our programme needs to adapt itself to this increasing sense of self-determination if it is to maximise learning.

Knowles' views have been challenged as failing to take sufficient notice of the differences between adults and their contexts, for being prescriptive, a set of normative humanistic values (Hanson 1996). For example, some adults, re-entering education after some time away from school, expect to be treated as children. The expectations of 'being taught' are sometimes strong, and if these expectations are not met in some way or other, once again learning is hindered. However, experience suggests that even the most docile group of adult students, happy for much of the time to be directed as if they were in school, will at the right time rebel against their teachers when the affront to their adulthood or challenge to their experience become too great. It can be a great help to provoke such a situation when we feel the time is right to break up the more formal atmosphere and secure greater participation by the students in their own learning process.

They are all engaged in a continuing process of growth

Our adult student participants have not stopped growing or developing. They are not at a static period in their lives, a plateau between the growth stages of youth and the declining stage of old age; they are still people on the move. Whatever our view about the way adults develop, the key issue is that growth and change are occurring in all aspects of our student participant's life – in the physical arena, in the intellectual sphere, in the emotions, in the world of relationships, in the patterns of cultural interests. This is true of all participants in all types of adult learning – they are all on a journey. The pace and direction of these changes vary from person to person, but that it is happening cannot be doubted.

The teacher needs to take these patterns of change seriously. The people we are trying to help are not passive individuals – they are actively engaged in a dynamic process. And they are in the middle of this process, not at the start. They may be at the start of a new stage of the process, but this stage will draw upon past changes and will in turn contribute to the whole programme of development and growth. It is a process that, although continual, is not continuous. It seems to proceed in spurts, triggered off by new experiences (such as the adult learning programme itself) or new perceptions.

We are partially aware of this process of change within ourselves. Indeed, learning about teaching adults itself forms part of the changing pattern of our lives. But we are sometimes reluctant to accept that such a process occurs within the student participants – that they are in the midst of a series of changes when they come to us. It is not practicable for us to know all our student participants intimately enough to assess accurately the position each of them has reached, the way by which they have got there and the different directions they are going in. But we can be aware that the process is in every case continuing. Sensitivity to this fact, and to the fact that the educational experience we offer forms part of a number of ongoing change processes, helps a great deal in creating our responses to the varying demands the students make upon us.

They all bring a package of knowledge, experience and values

Each of the learners brings a range of experience and knowledge more or less relevant to the task in hand. New students are not new people. Through informal (and where appropriate, formal) learning, they have built up funds of knowledge (Moll et al 1992; Eraut 2000) and a wide range of skills; they possess a set of values, established prejudices and attitudes in which they have a great deal of emotional investment. These are based on their past experience. Knowles suggests that, for children, experience is something that happens to them; for adults, experience serves to determine who they are, to create their sense of self-identity. When this experience is devalued or ignored (e.g. by the teacher), this implies a rejection of the person, not just the experience.

This is true in all fields of teaching adults, even in the formal technical and higher educational programmes, but it becomes particularly important for the adult teacher in those contexts where personal growth forms the major objective of the educational programme. The tensions and concerns of both the learner and the teacher in these contexts have been particularly well described by John Wood in his 'Poem for Everyman' (1974):

Poem for Everyman

I will present you
Parts
of
my
self
slowly
if you are patient and tender.
I will open drawers
that mostly stay closed
and bring out places and people and things,
sounds and smells, loves and frustrations, hopes and sadnesses,
bits and pieces of three decades of life
that have been grabbed off
in chunks
and found lying in my hands;
they have eaten
their way into my memory
carved their way into my
heart
altogether – you or I will never see them –
they are me.
If you regard them lightly
deny that they are important
or worse, judge them
I will quietly, slowly
begin to wrap them up,
in small pieces of velvet,
like worn silver and gold jewelry,
tuck them away
in a small wooden chest of drawers
and close.

But such sentiments are not and never have been characteristic of all adult student participants. Far from being reticent, some are confident, and a few positively push their views and experiences at the group and at the teacher. But it is perhaps true of more adults in learning situations than we are aware of. The teacher of adults needs to be sensitive to the situation whenever it arises, and it often occurs in the most unlikely of settings and in every class, whether it is a closed group brought together for a specific training purpose, an open-recruitment general interest course, a highly structured formal class or a community education or development group.

Implications for teaching adults

What are the implications of students' prior experience, knowledge and values for our approach to teaching?

First, this 'package' determines what meanings are created by the learner. The student participants see all new material they encounter through the lens of their existing experience and knowledge (just as the teacher does), and this may distort the messages. Each participant will test all that they learn against their own experience to see if it 'rings true' or not. Constant feedback from the participants is essential if the teacher is to remain alive to exactly what they are learning.

Secondly, in those cases where the student participants do not believe that they possess any relevant experience or knowledge, where they insist that they 'know nothing at all about the subject', it is possible to help them to become aware that they do in fact possess relevant material (see p. 268). For unless the new learning is related to this existing reservoir of experience and knowledge, it cannot be fully absorbed into the person; it will sit uneasily with the rest of the individual's make-up, it will be compartmentalised from the rest of their being and will thus not fully affect their attitudes and behaviour. It is not a difficult skill for the teacher to acquire to explore with the participants something of what they already know about the matter in hand. Words and phrases relating to the subject of the course, collected from the participants and listed on a flipchart or otherwise, can demonstrate to them that they are able to contribute towards the programme of learning. It is usually only necessary for the teacher to make a beginning; once the process has commenced, the participants will normally be able to continue the exploration for themselves and find new ways of relating the content of the course to different parts of their own experience and knowledge. The start of the process is the most difficult step for some of the student participants to take, but it is an essential one before deep and permanent learning can take place.

Thirdly, not all of this set of values, experience and knowledge is correct or helpful to the required learning. Experience of teaching adults reveals that there is often as much unlearning to be done as new learning, and because of the emotional investment in the existing patterns of experience and knowledge, the unlearning process is one of the more difficult tasks facing the teachers of adults (see Chapter 11).

Fourth, this experience and knowledge (some of it unique to the individual participant and therefore new to the teacher and other participants) is a major resource for learning and can be harnessed into the work of the group. Much new material can be drawn out from the student participants rather than be presented by the teacher. Theoretically, we should all start from where the learners themselves are; but since we usually teach in groups this is not often possible except where the contract to learn has ensured that a more or less homogeneous group has been created. But the utilisation of the varied experience and knowledge of all the members of the group is essential, not only to ensure effective learning at a personal level; it will help to bind together the group and make all of its members richer.

Activity 4.2

Given that the most important characteristic of any group of adult student learners is that they will be diverse, how you do think this will affect your teaching? What will be the most important considerations for you and your programme of learning?

They usually come to education with their own intentions

It is often argued that adults come to education because of a sense of need. Being adults, it is said, they come with an intention to do something about changing their world. Unlike children, adults have the opportunity and the means to implement their learning immediately rather than wait until 'they are grown up'. They can use education to change their personal lifeworlds. Adults (so it is argued) come to achieve specific tasks in order to make their lives better.

We shall discuss the question of needs in adult learning in Chapter 5 (see pp. 106–11), but here we must note one or two points. First, it is not always strictly true that the members of our classes are motivated by needs. Some job-related programmes, for instance, contain participants who have little or no sense of need. Perhaps it is more useful to talk of all adult student participants as having a set of 'intentions', an agenda which for many of them can imply the meeting of a felt need or aspiration (see Chapter 2).

Secondly, for those who do come out of a want or need, it is on occasion a confused area. Sometimes the participant is imbued with a vague sense of unease and dissatisfaction. The reason for attending that they give to others and even on occasion to themselves is not always the true reason. Sometimes the reason is not related to learning at all but more towards social contact, or getting out of the house, or to please some third person (some research suggests that there is a high correlation between attending some forms of adult education and problems within the marriage relationship, to take but one example). But even when this sense of need is related to learning, there is at times an uncertainty as to what it is that they should be learning. R.D. Laing has expressed something of this in his poem 'Knots' (from the 1972 book of the same title):

> *Knots*
>
> There is something I don't know
> that I am supposed to know.
> I don't know *what* it is I don't know
> and yet am supposed to know,
> and I feel I look stupid
> if I seem both not to know it
> and not know *what* it is I don't know.
> Therefore I pretend I know it.
> This is nerve-racking
> since I don't know what I must pretend to know.
> Therefore I pretend to know everything.
> I feel you know what I am supposed to know
> but you can't tell me what it is
> because you don't know that I don't know what it is.
> You may know what I don't know, but not
> that I don't know it,
> and I can't tell you. So you will have to tell me everything.

Thus, at one end of the continuum of student intentions is the satisfying of some vague and ill-articulated sense of need. At the other end are those who are present out of an intention to undertake a particular learning task – for example, to learn a language or to acquire mastery over a computer program for job or leisure fulfilment; to understand the development processes of very young children to help them cope at home; or to come to a knowledge of one of the systems of government to enable them to play a more effective role in their local community. In the course of their own continuing development, some will find that they need a specific skill or knowledge set or understanding to enable them to fit more easily into some existing or new situation. Even those who come to adult education classes in search of a qualification rather than new learning may be there for different motives. For some, it is the necessary preliminary to securing promotion or access to more education; for others, it is part of their pursuit of self-affirmation, a need to achieve a publicly recognised validation. A number come to seek reassurance, personal confirmation of their ability to achieve the goal, an increase in confidence. There is a wide range of such wants and intentions.

Such purposes are often concrete and meaningful to the participants' immediate concerns, though on occasion the learning is intended for longer term future application. But others may not be so concrete. It has been suggested that some adults seek learning for *symbolic reasons* (i.e. they want to be seen as educated); some for *opportunity reasons* (i.e. the results of the learning programme will open doors to them not necessarily directly related to the learning programme, including access to further learning opportunities); and some for *practical reasons* (i.e. they want to use the new learning itself). But in each case the participant has a relatively clearly identified outcome from the learning programme.

Houle has represented this as a continuum of adult intentions (Houle 1961). At one end are those who come to achieve a particular piece of learning related to their present pattern of life (the *instrumental-* or *goal-oriented*), who wish to use education to achieve some external objective such as a certificate or job promotion or to solve an immediate problem facing them. For them the learning activity tends to come to an end once the objective (often separate from the learning process) has been achieved. At the other end are those who come for social and/or personal reasons or out of some general or indeterminate desire (the *process-* or *activity-oriented*). They like the atmosphere of the learning group, they find in the circumstances of the learning a meaning for themselves independent of the content or of the announced purpose of the activity. They attend because they get something out of the process apart from the subject matter involved. These people frequently seek the continuance of the activity even though the content of the learning may well change. They may pass from one learning programme to another, searching for satisfaction in the processes involved, a process sometimes called 'the revolving door'. In the middle are those who come to learn a 'subject' (the *subject-* or *learning-oriented*). They desire the knowledge or skill for its own sake. They pursue the subject out of interest. These people will

Orientation	Intentions	Learning process	Continuation at end of programme?
Goal-oriented	Achievement of some end product; problem-solving/attainment	Learning mostly in specific areas	Process ceases on 'successful' completion of course
Learning-oriented	Interest in subject	Learning in all parts of subject matter area	Continued learning in same or related subject area
Activity-oriented	Social or personal growth needs, may be indeterminate	Find satisfaction in activities	A new activity or situation activity is sought

Figure 4.1 Orientations of learning

frequently pass on to another educational programme in the same or related subject area, or continue to pursue the subject even without the assistance of a formal programme of learning. For them it is a matter of interest, adding to the richness of their way of life (the subject-oriented). Often no clear-cut distinction can be drawn between these different groups (see Figure 4.1).

The implications for the teacher of the different intentions of each of these three orientations are considerable: the responses of each kind of learner to the demands of the learning programme will vary. Those participants who are motivated to attend courses out of some sense of internal need may on occasion exhibit anxiety, sometimes mixed with hesitation and uncertainty: for the concept of need is threatening, demeaning both to oneself and to others. Such anxiety can be useful – it can promote learning provided it is not too great (see p. 116). A gentle encouragement to focus it upon particular learning objectives often brings about greater readiness to learn. The development of a sharper consciousness of the nature of the learning task and of the relevance of the material to the immediate concerns of the participant is an essential preliminary to the use of the learning programme to satisfy such objectives. On the other hand, those whose motivation is to achieve some external goal (to pass an examination, for instance) will often reveal great keenness. Here, too, the clearer the awareness of purpose and of the relevance of the task to meet this purpose, the greater the motivation to learn.

Activity 4.3

Is your course goal-oriented, learning-oriented or activity-oriented? It may
be a mixture of more than one. How might this affect the way you plan
your programme?

They bring certain expectations about education itself

As we have already seen (Chapter 2), adult student participants come
with a range of expectations about the learning process, a series of
attitudes towards education in general. Using their experience over many
years, they now construct themselves as 'students', putting themselves
into a position in relation to 'their teacher'. Their focus in coming to our
programmes is 'learning'.

In taking the identity of 'student', they are laying aside whatever they
bring in the way of their sense of adulthood, their existing funds of
knowledge and their experience that they feel are not relevant to the
goal of learning. (Their judgement in this may be wrong; what they strip
away as being irrelevant to their new role of 'being educated' may in fact
be highly relevant.) But this identity is not a fixed entity; it is a process of
change. Stuart Hall reminds us that 'identities are about questions
of using the resources of history, language and culture in the process of
becoming rather than being; not 'who we are' or 'where we come from'
so much as what we might become, how we have been represented and
how that bears on how we might represent ourselves' (Hall 1997: 4). In
other words, each adult student has come to engage with how they are
seen by the tutor and by the other students and to 're-construct' themselves according to some goal they already possess (Rogers 2003).

As Hall says, this construct is in part based on 'history', on their experience of schooling and of any education since leaving school. Recent
studies show that there are significant numbers of people in adult education today who have substantial prior educational experience but this
was from many years ago – they may be re-engaging with formal education after a very long break indeed. The conception of what education is
and what it is for varies widely. Some people enjoyed their years in
school; others did not. A number of our student participants assume that
adult education will be like school. They expect to be taught everything
by a teacher who 'knows everything'; they expect to be put back *in statu
pupillari*, which is what education and learning imply for them. On the
other hand, some are more willing to engage directly with the material
being handled. For some of them, the joy of the adult class is that it is

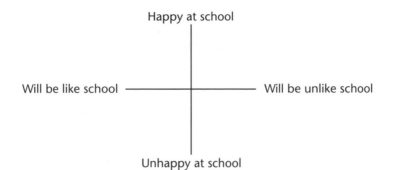

Figure 4.2 Student expectations of adult education

unlike school. Even for many of those who enjoyed their schooldays, the value of adult education is often that the contents and the methods employed are different from those experienced in the formal education system (Figure 4.2).

These expectations have different results on the attitudes of the participants. Some tend towards conformism, while others seek for a measure of independent learning. Some look for a more formal structure as a support for themselves, feeling more at home with 'being taught'. They may feel that their ability to learn has declined since they were last in education (and this may be true; on occasion we may have to spend some time with our student participants boosting their confidence and strengthening their skills of formal learning). Some of those who have had experience of education over a longer time may look for a less formal structure or become impatient, wishing to push on faster; they feel able to deal with the material easily.

In particular, both kinds of student participant bring with them a set of *self-horizons* relating to the sort of material they can or cannot master. Most of us believe that there is some subject or other that we can never learn, that is just not compatible with our range of inherent abilities and interests. It is odd that so many voluntary adult students still find themselves in classes containing a good deal of material that from the start they are adamant they will never be able to learn. Students attend courses in religion and yet say they cannot cope with 'theology'; students join art classes with a firm belief that they can never learn to draw. Learning in some parts of these fields is not for them; they confine themselves to the role of 'looker-on', as presumably they were at times in school. They may plead age, using this as an excuse to avoid identifying other causes of failing. By contrast, there will be those who see the entering of new areas as a challenge, difficult but not beyond the learning resources they can call upon.

We need to explore these constructs, about schooling and learning, about being a 'student' and what is expected in education, from an early stage in the learning programme. The worst thing we can do is treat all the participants alike, teaching one course to them all, adopting a one-size-fits-all approach. The problem of the teacher of adults, faced with a mixed group of student participants, encouraging those with low self-horizons and keeping the more self-reliant satisfied with their own progress, is one of constantly making choices between alternatives, of balancing the needs of one sub-group with those of another while maintaining loyalty to the subject matter of the course and the group as a whole.

They all have competing interests

Apart from those adults who for a relatively short period engage in full-time courses, adult students are part-time. Education for many of these is a matter of secondary interest; it is not their prime concern. Even for full-time adult students, their education is constantly overshadowed by the 'realities' of life: their job or lack of job, their family situation, their social life, other competing concerns. Some may come to our programmes with relief, to get away from other pressures. Others may come with reluctance, squeezing in learning time against the pressure of what they may feel to be 'more important' activities.

The adults who come to join us in the learning enterprise come from a complete social environment. They all have relationships such as parents, partners, workmates and friends, as well as being students. Adult learners should not be divorced from their background if their learning is to be relevant and thus effective. We need to take seriously the whole of the context within which our student participants live and where they use the new learning they have acquired. Students in other parts of the educational world may be taken out of their life situation to concentrate on their learning, but adult learners often continue to live within their lifeworld and to apply what they learn in that world.

Against that background, there are factors supporting as well as some detrimental to the learning endeavours. Not all of the competing concerns that the participants bring with them to our programmes are hindrances. Indeed, periods of intensive study can hardly be carried through without the identification of support networks around the adult learner, and it is to the advantage of both teacher and student participant to encourage the full exploitation of these supporting factors. This is particularly true where the class is a separate activity, not backed up by other studies as it is at school or college. A short course, taken part-time and on its own, will often assume in the life of many student participants rather less significance than it has for the teacher. We must not be surprised if our students' attention is at times distracted towards more urgent problems.

They all possess individual patterns of learning

Adults are engaged in a continuing process of lifelong learning, and they have already acquired ways of coping with this. They often fail to see this as 'learning' in the educational sense, but it exists all the same. Over the years, each of our adult student participants has developed their own strategies and patterns of learning which they have found help them to learn most easily, most quickly and most effectively (see Chapter 6). Learning changes are not brought about without effort, and the process can be painful. It takes an investment of time and emotions and, once done, no one wants to do it again. We all thus seek ways to ease the pain, shorten the time taken to master the necessary new material, and make the gains acquired more permanent. Experience has taught us what strategies we can adopt to achieve these ends.

Each of us learns in our own way, according to our particular aptitudes and experience. Some handle figures more easily than others. Some have fostered different methods for memorising facts (addresses, telephone numbers, etc.). Languages particularly throw up differences of approach in this respect. Some learners need a text, finding it hard to react to spoken words, while others respond easily to oral tuition. Both are valid methods of learning languages, and we should not try to force any learner into adopting a particular style because we prefer it to any other. We must remember that our student participants all have their own ways of learning which may differ from our ways of learning, and opportunities to exercise these have to be created if new learning is to take place.

The pace of learning of each student participant also varies. In general, in those areas where the participants can call upon a good deal of experience – social relationships and roles, for instance – they tend to learn a good deal faster than young people, provided that the new material does not conflict with existing knowledge. But where they have less experience on which to fasten the new material – languages, for example, or computer studies – especially if it calls for extensive memorising, they tend to learn more slowly and have greater difficulty in mastering the material than their younger counterparts.

Such matters are central to our concerns as teachers. There is a wide range of learning styles within any group of adult learners, and we need to devise methods that give each of the participants full scope for exercising their own particular learning method, and as far as possible not impose our own upon them.

Implications for the teacher of adults

We can see, then, that teachers of adults, especially those who teach in groups, are faced with a difficult task from the start. Unless the group is narrowly conceived (as in some forms of industrial training or adults in university courses), our student participants will consist of a wide variety of people all bringing their own advantages and disadvantages to the learning situation:

- Some see themselves as more adult than others; some are still searching in education for autonomy, others are more willing to accept dependency for the purpose of learning.
- All are growing and developing, but in different directions and at a different pace.
- Some bring a good deal of experience and knowledge in different parts of the subject matter, others bring less; and there are varying degrees of willingness to use this material to help the learning process.
- They have a wide range of intentions, some specific, some more general and related to the subject matter under discussion, and others unknown even to themselves.
- They are all at different points in the continuum between those who require to be taught everything and those who wish to find out everything for themselves; and they each have some belief in what they can and cannot do in the way of learning.
- They all have competing interests, often of greater importance to them than their learning.
- They have all by now acquired ways of learning which vary considerably the one from the other.

It is easy to view all of this in negative terms, to see most of what we have discussed as hindrances to learning. The pressure from competing interests, the worry and anxiety students have, especially about their learning abilities, based as these often are on misconceptions as to what education involves, the problem of coping with unlearning and the attack on the personality that this can at times imply – all of these may seem to make the task of the teacher of adults particularly difficult. We must not be surprised if some of the student participants do not move as fast as we would wish them to; if they have difficulty in grasping some of the material that *we* find so easy and have so carefully constructed for them; if they show a lack of responsiveness to all our promptings to engage more wholeheartedly with the subject matter of the programme. We must not be put off if some of the learners require us to demonstrate or lecture when we would rather that they practise for themselves or discuss.

But there are many aspects of this discussion that give cause for hope. Within the group is a well of resources that we can use. Some of these can be quickly identified: the wealth of knowledge, skills and experience gathered together in one room; the fact that all the student participants, whether they know it or not, are already engaged in some form of learning; the awareness, however dim, of purpose and need; the greater use of reasoning powers, and the fact that adult students, when provoked, 'accept' the teacher's word less readily (those of us who prefer to demonstrate and to lecture, to perform rather than to watch, to listen to our own voice rather than to the voice of the learners, will not see this as a resource); the desire of many of the learners to apply what they learn one day to their lives the very next day, and the fact that (unlike younger students) they are in a position to do so. All these factors can be seen as combining to form a powerful aid to learning.

We need to try to identify both those factors that prevent us from being fully effective in the teaching–learning process and those resources that can be brought into play in order to overcome the obstacles. In adult education, our students are not there just to be taught; they are our greatest resource in the learning process.

Activity 4.4

It is important as you read this chapter, that you relate it to your own experience. You may find it helpful to look at the assumptions you made about the potential student participants for the course you have chosen as your own case study, what characteristics they will bring with them to the programme. It may be possible for you, if you actually run a course, to test this against the group that materialises, so you can assess how accurate your first thoughts were.

A second exercise at this stage is to set out for yourself the range of helps and hindrances that you think your students will bring with them to the programme of study. Most of us do this without being fully conscious of it. To make it a deliberate process will help to bring into focus those whom we hope to help to learn.

Further reading

Boyd, D. and Bee, H. (2008) *Lifespan Development*. New York: Pearson.
Code, L. (1991) *What Can She Know? Feminist Theory and the Construction of Knowledge*. Ithaca, NY: Cornell University Press.

Cross, K.P. (1981) *Adults as Learners: Increasing Participation and Facilitating Learning*. San Francisco, CA: Jossey Bass.

Knowles, M.S. (1990) *The Adult Learner: A Neglected Species*. Houston, TX: Gulf.

Rogers, J. (2001) *Adults Learning*, 4th edn. Buckingham: Open University Press.

Tuijnman, A. and van der Kamp, M. (eds) (1992) *Learning Across the Lifespan: Theories, Research, Policies*. Oxford: Pergamon.

Chapter 5

The Nature of Learning
What is it . . . ?

It is now agreed that 'learning' is the interaction of the learner, the context, the kind of learning task and the processes involved. This chapter looks at the various theories of learning which have been constructed around these four themes.

Before we start on this complex area of discussion, we do need to note one thing. Many of those who talk and write about adult or continuing education/lifelong learning use the words 'learning/learn' in a very special sense. They talk about adults who have done no 'learning' since leaving school, about encouraging adults 'back into learning', of motivating adults 'to learn', implying that there are times when such an adult is not involved in learning (see p. 129). This is the way government and other bodies use these words at the moment.

That is not the way we are using the words 'learn/learning'. We see learning as something that every person does throughout the whole of their lives; as we shall see, every adult is already motivated to learn and is engaged in learning. They may not be learning what we want them to learn but they are learning, both desirable and undesirable ways of thinking, doing and acting. We shall see in the next chapter the distinction between formal and informal learning. We are here talking about learning, both informal and formal; what the government and other adult education writers mentioned above are talking about is planned and systematic learning, i.e. what others might call 'studying', not learning in general. This distinction is vital in all forms of teaching adults. *The adults who come to our learning programmes and those who do not come are both already learning in many other fields.*

Our task here, then, is to try to understand what 'learning' in this wider generic sense is all about. Some readers may be tempted to give this chapter a miss. They would argue that learning theories are both disputed and irrelevant to their task of teaching. But that would be a pity. For theory and practice do need to go together. Academics need to be challenged by teachers to explain what are the practical implications of their theories. And we practitioners will be more effective in our work if we understand more clearly what is happening when we teach.

Nevertheless, this is a complex and contested area, and to summarise it in such a short space runs the danger of oversimplification. There are, we think, two main reasons why the area is so complex. First, some theories concentrate on asking *why* we learn, what it is that drives us to learn, while others try to explain *how* we learn, what the processes involved are. For example, some humanists tell us that learning springs from our inner drives (the why), but this does not tell us how we learn. Those who urge critical reflection on experience tell us how we learn but not why. These are two quite different questions.

Secondly, as we shall see, it is now generally agreed that learning involves the interaction of several factors – including the individual learner, the context of learning, the learning task itself and the processes involved. Most learning theorists concentrate on one or at best the interaction of two such factors – and that leaves room for others to come along and tell them that their theory is deficient! So we get another theory.

In this chapter, we will outline briefly the main sets of learning theories before turning in the next chapter to a different approach which is emerging (see Phillips and Soltis 2003).

Activity 5.1

You will find it helpful to think about and note an example of a recent learning task **you** engaged in. Try to think of an example outside of a formal classroom (e.g. learning to swim or to handle a new mobile phone). Make a note of it; we shall ask you to refer to it throughout this chapter.

Learning and change

In common parlance, the word 'learning' carries at least two meanings. There is a general one of some kind of change, often in knowledge but also in behaviour. 'I met Mrs X today and learned that she has just left her job.' 'Today, a new bus timetable was introduced. A spokesman for the council said that he believed the public would soon learn to use the new routes.' But there is also a more intense sense of the verb 'to learn' meaning to memorise, to learn by heart: 'I can never learn telephone numbers'.

We may leave on one side the meaning of the word as 'memorising' and concentrate instead on 'learning as change'. To say that 'learning is change' is too simple. First, not all change is learning. Changes brought about by ageing or other physical processes can hardly be described as 'learning changes', though they may in their turn bring about learning changes. Secondly, some forms of learning are confirmation of existing patterns of knowledge and behaviour. But since the knowledge is more strongly held, the skills consolidated, or the behaviour more intensely engaged in after the learning, it can perhaps be said that this kind of learning is still change but that it is more reinforcement than alteration of patterns of knowledge and behaviour.

What we mean here by 'learning' are those more or less permanent changes and reinforcements brought about voluntarily in one's patterns of acting, thinking and/or feeling during the course of living within our particular environment.

Areas of change (learning domains)

There have been several attempts to describe the different areas of learning change.

The traditional distinction has of course been between learning knowledge and learning skills; but others have elaborated on this. Several point to the need to include attitudes as a third area. In the field of learning objectives, knowledge, skills and attitudes (KSA) is a well-worn path. More recently, Knud Illeris (2002) has spoken about the third dimension of learning, the emotions. Kurt Lewin (1935) suggested that learning changes occur in skills, in cognitive patterns (knowledge and understanding), in motivation and interest, and in ideology (fundamental beliefs). Gagné (1972, 1975) identified five 'domains':

- *motor skills* which require practice;
- *verbal information* – facts, principles and generalisations which when organised into larger entities become knowledge;
- *intellectual skills* – the 'discriminations, concepts and rules' that help in using knowledge;
- *cognitive strategies* – the way the individual learns, remembers and thinks, the self-managed skills needed to define and solve problems;
- and *attitudes*.

Learning then takes place in a number of different spheres. We may categorise these using the mnemonic KUSAB:

- We learn new information that is largely memorised and converted into usable *knowledge* ('I know').
- Knowledge may however be held uncomprehendingly. So that learning new *understandings* (organising and reorganising knowledge to create new patterns of relationships) is a different area of learning ('I see').
- We may learn new *skills* or develop existing skills further – not just physical skills, our ability to do certain things, but also skills of thinking, of coping and solving problems ('I can').

- We may possess skills but not feel willing to use them. So that the changing of *attitudes* (including beliefs and values) is a distinct sphere of learning ('I want to').
- Finally, learning to apply our newly-learned material to what we do and how we live, changed ways of *behaving*, is a separate area of learning ('I do').

The way these five domains of learning relate to each other is complex. Changes in attitude rely to a large extent on changes in knowledge and understanding, and behavioural changes can hardly take place without accompanying changes in other areas. But these relationships are idio-syncratic and uncertain. When new knowledge (e.g. 'smoking can damage your health') meets contrary behaviour (the habit of smoking), one of a number of different reactions may occur. The information may be decried, ignored or rejected ('It's all very exaggerated', or 'I know but I don't care'); the new knowledge may be accepted but rationalised away by other knowledge ('I agree, but less than 30 per cent of smokers die of cancer caused by smoking and I'll be one of the lucky ones', or 'It's more dangerous to cross the roads than to smoke'); or the new knowledge can lead to changes in behaviour. How any individual reacts to learning changes in any one domain seems to depend on personality and situational factors.

Four elements in learning

It is now increasingly agreed (Merriam and Cafarella 1999: 399–403) that learning springs from the interaction between the individual, the learn-ing processes and the socio-cultural context within which the learning is set. These three elements form part of the learning equation. But there is a fourth element, the *task* or the content/subject matter of the learning. It will we think be helpful if we can organise our discussion of adult learning theories round these four elements:

- learning theories focusing on who is doing the learning;
- learning theories focusing on the context;
- learning theories focusing on the kind of learning task being undertaken;
- learning theories focusing on the processes involved.

Activity 5.2

Look at your chosen learning task and try to see why **you** were involved, what part was played by the **context**, what kind of learning **task** was involved and what kinds of **processes** you used.

Learner-based theories

This is the largest area of discussion among educators, especially those concerned with student-centred learning. All writers agree that learners change over time, some adopting a *growth* model (linear and natural change) and others a *developmental* model (diverse and more purposeful change) (see pp. 96–7). Many suggest that all persons change in the same way – in the same direction and at much the same pace – but others think that this hides individual differences.

Intelligence and the brain

Before discussing these theories, we need to look first at one key area of research, on intelligence. Most writers now accept that, although there are some genetic areas of the brain with learning predispositions (especially those relating to language), the brain is not a 'hard-wired' engine already designed and unchangeable, simply functioning. The concept of a basic intelligence which after initial growth remains the same and can be measured (an IQ) has been challenged on many grounds (see p. 70), especially by the ideas of crystalline and fluid intelligence (Cattell 1987) and of multiple intelligences (Gardner 1993). A few have gone further, denying the existence of the mind as a finite entity in favour of a dynamic, ever-changing flux with unknown potential, and claiming that those who speak of fixed measures like intelligence, aptitude and personality traits for what may be temporary stabilised states are perpetuating myths and creating blocks to a 'truer' perception of the personality as fluid and active in its own quest.

More recently, the view that each of us is 'growing our own brains' has gained acceptability. The brain is thought to change each time we use it. We are able to develop some parts of it by stimulation and use, while other parts may remain underdeveloped or become atrophied. Each of us has a 'hand-knitted' brain (see Field and Leicester 2000: 65–74).

Behaviourist theories

One group of learning theories which concentrate on the learner suggests that the main aim of learning is to adapt our behaviour to survive. Stimuli from outside the individual provoke responses, and these responses can be directed towards achieving desired behavioural changes. Society (or the teacher) can control this process by selecting the stimuli and reinforcing the approved responses. Learning is thus brought about by an association between the desired responses and the reinforcement (rewards and punishments) through a system of success and failure indicators. Such responses become more complex as the learner grows, in a linear process.

These theories tend to suggest that the learner is relatively passive. Although a variety of responses is offered, only the 'right' (i.e. personally or socially satisfying) response is rewarded while other responses are discouraged. Feedback, the return from the learner to the source of the stimulus or to society around, is separate from and follows after the learning process.

Despite the many attacks on it, this remains a strongly held view, for it seems self-evident that much learning is initiated by external stimuli which call forth responses, and that society confirms or denies the validity of those responses. Behaviourist theories distinguish sharply between right and wrong; they assume that knowledge is truth, independent of both teacher and learner, that it is the same for all learners and can be known.

Stimulus–response is not seen as applicable only to low-level learning; it also applies at more advanced levels. Nor is it confined to skill learning; it forms the basis for cognitive and affective learning as well. Indeed, the general validity of the theory may be seen in the fact that it underlies most of the other approaches to learning. Cognitive theories which stress the inherent demands of the subject matter still rely on an assumption that responses are called out by different stimuli. And some humanist theories urge that stimuli arise from our life context, although our responses will vary, dependent on our individual experiences and personalities; we learn at an early stage of life by a system of approvals and disapprovals whether our patterns of behaviour are socially acceptable or not.

Cognitive theories

In reaction to these approaches, a number of theories emerged that directed attention to the activity of the learner in creating the response and to the nature of knowledge itself. These form a distinct group. They point to the active engagement of the mind in processing data, the instruments of perception, the emergence of insights, the development of memory, etc. The concept of intelligence as learning capability underpins these theories, not as a fixed capacity but one which continues to develop throughout life provided it is used and stimulated, so that one could be significantly more intelligent (or indeed less, if intelligence is not used) at age 50 than at age 30.

In order to learn, understanding is necessary. The material needs to be marshalled into meaningful units and then mastered. Thus the focus is on how the content of learning is structured, building up from easy to more difficult knowledge and skills, and on the practice of intellectual exercises. Although the learner is seen to be active rather than passive, the activity is controlled by the inherent structure of knowledge itself which the teacher-agent sequences. Words like 'must', 'necessary' and 'discipline' which occur in connection with this view of learning reveal that learners are faced with something bigger than they are, something to which they need to adapt themselves. The world of knowledge lies outside of themselves. As Piaget suggests, growth is linear, the development of the ability to cope with increasingly complex knowledge. Such views are not confined to the acquisition of knowledge or the development of new understandings; they apply to learning skills and attitudes as well.

Hierarchies of learning

Both behaviourist and cognitive learning theories posit that learning advances as more and more learning takes place; there are higher levels of learning which not all learners attain to. These levels are now being extended from childhood into the adult field.

Bloom (1964) suggested that learning takes place not only in the cognitive field but also in the affective, and that a series of steps common to all learners in the cognitive domain parallel those in the affective. Thus cognitive learning consists of the recall and recognition of *knowledge*; *comprehension*, understanding the material, exploring it actively; the *application* of the comprehended knowledge in concrete situations; exploring each new situation by *analysis* of its constituted parts and *synthesis* into new concepts; and finally *evaluation* in which the learners assess the value of the new knowledge in relation to the realisation of their goals. On the affective side, there is a similar progression: *receiving* stimuli, developing awareness, being willing to receive, eventually using selective attention; *responding* willingly, the emergence of a sense of satisfaction with the response; *valuing* the concepts and the processes they are engaged in, expressing preferences and eventually commitment; then *conceptualising*, attaching concepts to each of the values identified; and finally *organising* these values into a system that comes to characterise each individual. Gagné (1972) also drew up a progression of learning from simple 'signal' learning through stimulus–response, chaining, verbal association, multiple discrimination, concept learning and principle learning, to complex 'problem-solving'.

Personality theories

In yet another reaction against such hierarchies, 'personality' theories of learning emerged. Most of these depend on the distribution of personality types along a continuum of one kind or another – between the extrovert and the introvert, for instance, or between those who see the 'locus of control' as within themselves and those who see it as outside of themselves

('I was ill because I ate stale meat' as against 'the food in that restaurant made me ill'), or between the fatalist and the self-confident.

Those who locate people on such external–internal scales sometimes suggest that people at one end have a general expectancy that positive reinforcements are not under their control. They may lack self-confidence, possess feelings of inferiority, even expect failure and rely more on luck, fate, chance or God. Such people may feel that what they don't know is so vast and what they do know is so small that they may be discouraged from attempting to master new fields. At the opposite extreme, it is suggested, are those who believe that reinforcement is contingent on their own behaviour. These are usually thought to be more independent individuals, resisting manipulation; they will act, pay attention and (if they feel it necessary to the achievement of some goal) remember. They draw upon the information and other resources provided by their environment, select activities in which they have already been successful, and feel confident that what they already know will help them to master further skills and knowledge. Most people are thought to occupy midpoints between these two extremes or to display characteristics of both of these types at different times and in different circumstances.

Learning, then, according to these theories, depends not only on one's perception of the subject but also on one's perception of self. One example of this is the metaphor of 'learning maps' (Rogers 1993). This view argues that people draw a 'map' in their head with themselves at the centre, and place every experience, concept and activity on the map at a chosen distance from their self-centre. Those who like cooking and feel themselves to be good at it, for example, will locate 'cooking' close to the self-centre, whereas they may well put 'computers' or 'astronomy' closer to the periphery because they feel less at ease with these subjects or because these subjects seem to be distant from their main preoccupations. These are not of course fixed maps – they are constantly changing as events (experience) thrust new material onto them or bring some items closer to the self-centre than before. Learning, it is suggested, is easiest among those subjects which are close to the self-centre; and this implies that teaching includes a process of helping each participant to redraw their personalised map so as to bring the subject closer to the self-centre. So long as learners feel that any subject is far away, 'not for me', they will experience great difficulties in learning that subject.

A different continuum is that between those who are 'high achievement-oriented' (not just ambitious: this group embraces those who seek to play chess or breed pigeons better than their neighbours) and those who are anxious about failure. The former experience an 'approach motivation', a drive towards engaging in some activity or other, while the latter experience an 'avoidance motivation' (McClelland et al 1953). Success encourages the former and failure does not put them off easily, it can become a challenge; whereas both success (generally regarded as a 'flash in a pan' that will not necessarily be repeated) and failure alike encourage the latter to withdraw.

Various learning theories have been built on these analyses of personality types. We have seen that Houle (1961) drew up a series of different orientations of some learners (see pp. 86–7). But the danger with such schemes is that of assigning individuals to particular categories. Designations of this kind can become a hindrance to learning, if they are thought to prescribe the way in which people will behave; they will certainly determine the way we view other people. There is some value in knowing that such factors are at work, but they are not determinants, only explanations of what is happening.

On the other hand, the importance of attitudes (especially confidence) in the learning process and the relationship of attitudes to knowledge form the major contribution of personality theories. Learning is not just a matter for the head. McClintock (1972) described four kinds of learning behavioural modification, functional learning (the satisfaction of basic needs), the development of consistency (the reduction of inner tensions), and information processing – and suggested that the way in which knowledge (K), attitudes (A) and practice (P) relate to each other in each of these fields is different.

Activity 5.3

Ask yourself how you *felt* about your learning.

Humanist theories

It was as a reaction against the personality theories which seemed to reduce the control of the learner over their own learning and against the hierarchies of the behaviourists and cognitivists that the humanist theories of learning emerged. These are not so coherent as the other groups.

Humanist theories are associated with a move away from the certainties of empirical science, the universally valid conclusions of objective research, the stability and general applicability of scientific laws, the normally accepted values, into a world of living complexity, uncertainty, instability, the uniqueness of individual response and the conflicts of values. These theories stress that it is the learner's motivations and actions which largely create the learning situation. They emphasise the urges and drives of the learner towards (for example) increased autonomy and competence, the active search for meaning, the fulfilment of goals which individuals set for themselves – in short, the impulse towards being more fully human and adult. Learning and goal setting are seen to be natural, calling into play the abilities that the learners have already developed and which they seek to enhance. Learning, then, is the satisfying of inner drives. Motivation for learning comes from within, the desire to fulfil one's potential, self-actualisation, individuation (intra-personal); and the material on which the learning drive fastens is extra-personal, the whole of life, the cultural and interpersonal relationships that form the social context.

These views reassert the agency of the learner. They emphasise that the other theories talk about the learners being controlled by the stimuli, by the teacher, by the subject matter or by their inherent personality. The humanist views learning as the willing *active* engagement of the learners with the world around them and with themselves. For many, it is part of a process of struggle in which the learners seek to take control of their own life processes. The material on which they exercise their learning drive is less important than the goals they have set themselves. The role of the teacher is to increase the range of experiences so that the student participants can use these new experiences to achieve new learning changes.

Experiential learning

There is general acceptance that experience forms the basis of learning. Since Dewey wrote *Experience and Education* (1938) outlining the conditions which govern learning from experience, it has been increasingly agreed that the experiences we have lead us into learning. Experiential learning can be applied to the other kinds of learning theories. Thus the kinds of responses provoked by stimuli are in large part determined by experience. In cognitive learning, judgement about the subject matter of learning is based on prior experience. Humanists suggest that at the heart of all learning is the urge to make sense of and control experience.

The problem with 'experiential learning' is that it means many things to different people. It can mean (a) *learning from current experience* – that is, one's day to day experiences lead to learning. The gap between one's current experience and one's past experience will (it is argued) create the impetus for learning. It can mean (b) engaging actively with one's context in order to learn effectively (*learning by doing*). It can mean (c) *using one's past experience* to challenge the present. It can mean (d) *creating experiences for student learners* so that they can 'experience' what they are learning about. It frequently means (e) *learning by reflecting critically on one's experience*. But the main use of the term refers to the way in which current experience creates the learning need and prior experience governs the learning changes made in response to current experience (Boud and Miller 1996; Fraser 1995).

Experiential learning is a key element in contemporary discussions of lifelong learning. For if learning is embedded in life, much of adult learning will be informal, not publicly recognised. The Accreditation of Prior Learning (APL), the recognition of this informal learning from experience by educational agencies, is one way in which such experiential learning can not only be utilised but be harnessed to enable the adult to proceed into further forms of lifelong education (Evans 2000).

One of the major implications of experiential learning is that the concepts of 'simple' and 'difficult' in learning cannot be absolute, inherent in the subject, as the cognitivists suggest. Instead such concepts are seen to be relative, determined by the experience of the learner. What is 'difficult' in learning terms to one person within one cultural context will be easier to another person in a context where greater meaning or value is attached to the knowledge item involved. This undermines for adult learners much of the 'easy-to-harder' progression of many educationalists.

Experiential learning has been critiqued by a number of writers. They point out that this set of concepts is confused, depending on whether one is looking at the way the individual learner relates to and uses their own experiences, whether one is creating new experiences to enhance and direct learning, whether one is examining the power relations within experience, or whether one is viewing the totality of experience in terms of the interaction of nature, organisations, cultures and the individual: all of 'these orientations have their blind spots' (Fenwick 2001: 2).

Motivation for learning, then, from a humanist point of view, can spring from inner drives and needs, or from interaction with experience.

Motivation and learning

Humanist views assert that people are already motivated to learn. As we have already noticed, to talk about persons not being motivated is to misunderstand the situation. They may not be motivated to *learn what we want them to learn*, but all adults are motivated to learn their own learning in their own way.

Motivation is usually defined as a drive directed towards meeting a need or achieving an intention, those factors that energise and direct behavioural patterns organised around a goal. It is frequently seen as a force within the individual that moves them to act in a certain way, as a drive towards a goal or a drive to avoid some consequence. Motivation in learning is that compulsion which keeps a person within the learning situation and encourages them to learn.

Not motivated	external	introjected: internalise extrinsic	identified: useful to achieve goals	intrinsic: learning for own sake	interested/valued: learning has meaning for self-identity

Figure 5.1 Continuum between extrinsic and intrinsic

Motivation is seen as being dependent on either *intrinsic* or *extrinsic* factors. Extrinsic factors consist of those external incentives or pressures such as attendance requirements, punishments and rewards, or examinations to which many learners in formal settings are subjected, or the influence of other persons or organisations. These, if internalised, create an intention to engage in the learning programme. Intrinsic factors consist of those inner pressures and/or rational decisions which create an inner compulsion for learning changes.

Much adult learning is dependent on intrinsic motivational factors, but not all of it is. It has been argued that intrinsic factors are stronger and more enduring than extrinsic ones. But even within intrinsic motivation, there is a hierarchy. For example, a desire to please some other person or loyalty to a group, which may keep a person within a learning programme even when bored, are seen as motives of a lower order than a desire to complete a particular task. But some have challenged the distinction between extrinsic and intrinsic, seeing this is a continuum (Prenzel et al 2001; see Figure 5.1).

There would seem to be three main groups of ideas behind a theory of how motivation is developed. The first says that motivation is an inner impulse based on needs or drives. The second says that motivation can be learned. And the third claims that motivation relates to goals set or accepted by oneself.

Activity 5.4

In relation to your chosen example of learning, ask yourself what your motive was for learning. Why did you feel you must do it?

Motivations as impulse

Needs

There is a large literature which suggests that all learning (certainly all purposeful learning) comes from a sense of need: 'Learning takes place when an individual feels a need, puts forth an effort to meet that need, and experiences satisfaction with the result of his [sic] effort' (Leagans 1971: 33–4). The distinction between 'felt' needs and 'externally assessed' needs is important. Many adult educators identify a 'need' as they see it and try to engender within the adult learner a 'felt' need as the basis for learning. The awakening of a sense of need has been identified by many writers as a precondition of effective learning.

But we have to tread carefully here. Not all purposeful learning comes from a sense of need; some, for example, comes from an increased interest or a desire to test some theory. Indeed, 'needs' is a dangerous concept. It can lead to an assumption that 'I know what you need to learn, even though you don't know what you need'. Its main effect will be to make the student learners feel bad about themselves. And thus it reduces learner agency; purposeful adult learning comes as much from learner intentions as from any sense of need (see pp. 84–7).

Many humanists however assert the primacy of needs in learning. Individuals vary in the composition and intensity of these needs. At their simplest instinctual level, they may be the avoidance of pain and the search for pleasure, or the Freudian drives related to life, death, sex and aggression, although such instincts can be modified by learning. One set of views suggests that many of these needs arise from the demands of lifespan development (see pp. 70–7). Others regard them as a search for the reduction of tension – for example, the inner conflicts between different parts of the self and different experiences (intra-resolution), or the conflicts between the self and the external social and physical environment (extra-resolution). The individual is seeking for harmony, for peace.

Some writers have talked about primary needs (viscerogenic, related to bodily functions) and secondary needs (psychogenic); the latter come into play only when primary needs are to a large extent met. On the other hand, there are those who have described this distinction in terms of needs (physical) and drives (psychological).

Maslow (1968) is recognised as the apostle of the 'needs' school of thought. He distinguished basic drives from temporary needs, and established a hierarchy which is often quoted (Figure 5.2). He argued that all people are driven through the first four stages of basic needs. As each lower need is in part met, the next higher level is triggered. Several levels of need can be in operation at the same time. The highest level of need – self-actualisation, a need to create, to appreciate, to know and to understand – may not be reached by some individuals on more than an occasional basis. (Maslow indicated in his teaching a further level above self-actualisation: 'self-transcendence', a need to express tangibly concern for others, but this hardly appears in his writings.)

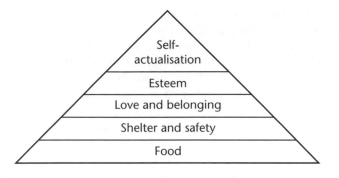

Figure 5.2 Maslow's hierarchy of needs

For the teacher, Maslow's work will be a reminder that within any group of adult learners, there will be a wide variety of needs, and within each participant there will be a different mixture of needs. This mixture will be constantly changing as the learning proceeds and as the individual's life situation changes. This is why predetermined and uniform learning outcomes can never be achieved in adult learning programmes. Each adult learner will take away from any learning situation what they require; learning is unique to each learner and uncertain.

But Maslow's hierarchy of needs fails us as adult educators precisely at the point we need it most. It offers us an analysis of the *preconditions* to the type of learning we are most interested in: the self-evident truth that the prior personal and social needs (food, security, personal relationships and a sense of esteem) must be satisfied, at least in part, before motivation for the more creative, evaluative and self-fulfilling kinds of learning will be aroused. But it also reminds us that some of our student participants come to our programmes from a desire for social relationships or to gain some sense of esteem, driven by needs that require to be met at least partially before further learning can take place.

Maslow also suggested (in what he called 'pre-potency') that if the lower levels of need are satisfied in part, the motivation to self-actualisation will be automatically triggered because it is inherent within each person. If it is not so triggered, this is because one of the lower levels of need has been inadequately met. This is by no means certain, and in any case, it does not explain the motivation towards the different forms of self-actualisation which occur. To explain this, we need to turn to other work on motivation, particularly that related to drives rather than needs.

Drives

Many writers stress the inherent drives within each individual – drives created partly by the cultural context and partly by the personality of the individual. They have been variously defined: drives towards autonomy and maturity, to make meaning out of experiences, to satisfy (emotional and intellectual) hunger, etc. Whether viewed as goal-seeking (based on specific self-set goals) or ideal-seeking (related to objectives set by the value system the learners have come to accept and hold), inner drives rather than outside imperatives impel the learner to seek out learning changes. As we have seen (p. 47), these can be seen as drives towards adulthood – autonomy, responsibility, self-direction – though the forms such concepts take are culturally bound, varying from society to society.

Such drives are often described in terms of a struggle, a desperate search for freedom. Habermas (see pp. 117–8) viewed human life as a quest for self-emancipation, a striving towards autonomy through self-formative processes. Freire (1972) identified three stages of learning: activities which are task-related; activities concerned with personal relationships; and what he calls 'conscientization', a concept that implies the transformation of the awareness of surrounding reality, the development of a concern for change, and a realistic assessment of the resources for and obstacles to such a process and of the conflicts it is bound to provoke, leading to action to transform the lifeworld (*praxis*). Learning is only learning when it leads to action.

A further group of humanist learning theories relate to the drive to make sense of experience, a search for meaning through *paradigm trans-formation* (see Taylor 1998). This view argues that the environment we live in is the result of our own creative processes; we build, name and manipulate the environment for ourselves. Learning is a process of rebuilding, renaming and remanipulating that environment, the modification and adaptation of those paradigms (i.e. accepted and usually unchallenged world pictures on which we build our lives) that underlie all our actions. Mezirow, the leading exponent of transformative learning, suggested that learning in childhood is laying down socially and individually constructed frameworks of meanings, a process of finding the keys, making sense of experience, forming perspectives. Learning in adulthood is a continuing process of reconstructing and transforming these meanings through challenging our assumptions, our frames of reference, in the course of active interaction with our environment (Mezirow et al 2000).

Learning, then, for many humanist writers is dependent on the innate drives of men and women towards autonomy or understanding in an attempt to control rather than be controlled, a search for liberation. Such views are widespread, although they are increasingly being challenged.

Learned motivation

There are however alternative views. One suggestion is that motivation is not inherent, like drives, but learned – the fruit of the reward and punishment systems that people have been exposed to. If this is true, then perhaps motivation may be altered by a new system of approvals and disapprovals, by specific activities accompanied by a change of the learning environment to emphasise achievement rather than failure. Exactly what the factors are that lead to motivation being learned is not clear. Stimulus–response theories may help here; success and pleasure in early educational experiences seem to play a part. It is pointed out, for example, that many of those who liked their schooling and were a success in educational environments return to participate in formal and non-formal educational activities, while those who see themselves as educational failures, although they may often use the lack of education to rationalise their lack of success, are only rarely motivated by this sense of deficit to return to education. Despite the fact that the issues remain unclear, the concept of learned motivation has much to commend it.

Goal-driven motivation

A third group of ideas centres round the view that motivation is related to the goals set and/or accepted by the learners for themselves. Motivation is not responsive but purposeful, an act of human agency. Different levels of motivation can be seen here. The internalisation of goals set by others (e.g. employers) is unlikely to lead to as high levels of motivation as those goals set by the learners themselves. It has been noted that motivation is highest among those who find the learning task itself satisfying, whereas those who have their sights set on goals which are external to the task (e.g. to pass an examination or to get a better job) tend to have a somewhat lower level of motivation. Motivation may also be related to the immediacy of the desired goal; the closer the goal the stronger the motivation.

The context of motivation

Motivation is clearly related to a number of factors: the inner needs and drives of the learner, the interaction between the individual and their experience, the learning which they have already done, and/or the goals they set for themselves. All of these arise from the life situation in which the learner is located. It is important for us to realise that motivation relates as much to the context as to the individual. All learning is located within a particular time and place; and we know that motivation is influenced as much by this setting as by internal drives and avoidances.

Herzberg's work (1972), although related to industrial activities, is of direct relevance to learning. While recognising that motivational factors will vary from individual to individual, he developed the concept of 'motivators' and 'hygiene' factors (demotivators). 'Motivators' are those factors which make the participants 'feel good' about their work – a sense of achievement, recognition, responsibility, advancement and personal growth. Most of these are internal factors. However, these feelings are not on the whole long-lasting, they need to be continually reinforced. But they spring directly from the work in hand. In contrast, the 'hygiene' factors that create a sense of dissatisfaction normally spring from external factors – from inappropriate direction or methods, inadequate working conditions, unsatisfactory relationships within the group and so on. These tend to be longer lasting in their nature.

These two sets of factors are not reciprocal, they operate independently. The encouragement of motivators and the reduction of hygiene factors are *both* necessary to achieve positive motivation. Removing the hygiene factors alone without increasing the influence of motivators will not help the task. Similarly, strengthening the motivators without removing the demotivators will not increase effectiveness.

Kurt Lewin (1947) has a similar approach with his 'force field'. He suggested that in every learning situation, there are forces which promote the learning changes and forces which inhibit the learning changes. He argued that it is necessary for the educator to identify these, to harness the one and to negate the other.

Motivational factors in learning, then, lie as much within the learning situation as within the individuals themselves. In this context, the teacher of adults plays a vital role. We need to be reminded of McGregor's (1960) Theory X and Theory Y (Figure 5.3). The teacher may assume that all student learners have an inherent dislike of work and will avoid it if they can (Theory X), that they wish to escape from responsibility, that they have a static range of abilities which nothing within the learning situation will improve, and that it is the function of the teacher to direct them to the work of learning. In this case, like all self-fulfilling prophecies, we teachers become a 'hygiene factor', a demotivator. Or we can assume that learning changes are natural to all human beings and certainly are the expressed desire of our student learners (Theory Y), that they are willing to accept responsibility for their own learning, that it is external factors such as the educational system itself or patterns of work in society rather than internal factors that are inhibiting the learners from exercising their imagination, creativity and ingenuity, and that all students are capable of breaking out of these inhibiting factors. In this case, the teacher will be a 'motivator' in the learning environment. Motivation depends as much on the attitudes of the teacher as on the attitudes of the student learners.

Theory X	Theory Y
The average human being has an inherent dislike of work and will avoid it if they can.	The expenditure of physical and mental effort in work is as natural as play and rest.
Because of this, most people need to be coerced, controlled, directed and threatened with punishment to get them to put in enough effort to contribute to organisational goals.	External control and threats of punishment are not the only means to encourage learners to make an effort to contribute to organisational goals. People will engage in self-direction and self-control to achieve objectives to which they are committed through the rewards which the achievement itself brings.
The average person prefers to be directed, wishes to avoid any responsibility, has relatively little ambition, and wants security above all.	The average person, under the right conditions, learns not only to accept but to seek responsibility. The capacity to exercise a fairly high degree of imagination, ingenuity and creativity in the solution of organisational problems is widely, not narrowly, distributed. In most societies, the intellectual potential of the average person is not fully utilised.

Figure 5.3 McGregor's Theory X and Theory Y

Critique of learner-based theories

As we have seen, there are many learning theories based on the individual learner – behavioural, cognitivist and humanist, and these tend to be concentrated on the inner drives or the interaction with context in experiential learning.

However, we need to critique such a picture. First, many learning theories are not easy to categorise. One of the most important writers of our time, Mezirow, has been classified as both cognitivist and humanist, whereas he would claim to be within the constructivist school of thought (see p. 145).

Secondly, they are seen as being normative; they do not allow for the diversity of human responses. They make sweeping generalisations about adult learning which cannot always be justified.

Thirdly, these approaches are decidedly Western. They are beginning to be challenged by other learner-based approaches, especially by some feminist thinkers and writers who claim that women's ways of knowing are different from those of men, based on the fact that women (in general) have experienced greater exclusion and 'voicelessness' than men. These theories suggest that women's learning passes through stages, from silence, to receiving other people's knowledge, to identifying knowledge for themselves, to what they call 'procedural knowledge' (working knowledge), to the highest form of knowing – constructing their own knowledge. Feminist epistemology is a major area of interest today (Belenky et al 1986; Code 1991; Ryan 2001), but at times it falls into making sweeping and universally applicable statements about matters which others would feel to be contingent and contested. The latter argue that women are not only different from men, but that there are as many differences among women as there are among men. To say that *all* women's learning is related to their higher levels of connectedness is to demean those women who do not conform to these criteria.

The one thing that seems to be clear from these learner-centred theories is that it is the whole person who is involved in learning. Individuals engaged in their own learning episodes use the whole of their being, including their perception of who they are, however that has been constructed. In this way, adult learners bring their individualised concept of being an adult as well as their experience and personality factors to their learning tasks. People differ – in learning as in everything else.

Context-based theories

Most of the learning theories centred on the learner tend to isolate the learner from their social context, 'virtually alone in . . . a world of objects he [*sic*] must array in time, space and causal relationships'. But increasingly there are others who suggest that learners draw their understandings and control of knowledge 'under the guidance of or in collaboration with more capable peers' (Bruner 1983: 138–9, 181), who suggest that there may be an element of 'teaching' (helping others to learn) in all learning: we learn with and through others.

The humanists suggest that the self-impelled learning process is called into play by the interaction between the person and the lifeworld, and in turn it calls upon the resources of this environment. But the social learning theorists go further than this (see Rotter 1982). They suggest that learning is created and controlled by active encounter between the person and the outside world more than by inner drives and urges. Behavioural theories thus find themselves being adapted and debated in new conceptual terms of highly individualised instead of generalised responses. Each learning is unique just as each learner is unique. All learning is contextualised, designed to meet a specific situation. The focus of learning lies outside the individual, although the processes by which each learner chooses which role models to adopt is a key element in these theories.

Activity 5.5

With reference to your own learning, ask yourself who helped you with your learning, and why.

Three main sets of context-based learning theories may be identified.

Human communications theory

In brief, human communications theory indicates that communication is a transaction, a series of two-way processes which involve a source (initiator), a transmission, a message and a receiver. There is inevitably interference and distortion in the transmission, and feedback is a necessary, though independent, part of the process in order to check whether what has been received is perceived as being equivalent to what has been sent. Interpretation is an essential element of the transaction, and in this the receiver is active, not passive. One example is Berne (1970), who combined communication theory with personality theory, building a view of learning on the difference within each person of 'parent' (P), 'adult' (A) and 'child' (C). He argued that communication between people may go seriously wrong if these attitudes become confused, if the lines get crossed, if for example one person speaking as 'adult' is responded to as 'child'.

But these theories go further than this. They argue that communication links people together into an organisation to achieve a common purpose. Communication is not just a one-way or two-way tool; it is a system or network of events. Learning is a process of change based on reactions to the continuous reception of messages which is the inevitable consequence of each person being part of a human communications network or society.

Social learning theory

Social learning theory stresses learning with others as well as from others. The interaction of the individual and the social environment starts with the members of the family and widens out from there, and much of the learning consists of imitation and the internalisation of value systems acquired from others. The need for direct human contact and the importance of peer group pressure in attitudinal development have become clearer. Like human communications theory, this is not just a stimulus–response theory. It emphasises the active engagement of the person with the environment, a dialectic with all the potential for conflict. Role learning and modelling are stressed, but it is recognised that such roles are socially and culturally constructed and are constantly changing and being reinterpreted. Vygotsky (1962, 1978) pointed out how much learning is based on the need to communicate and cooperate with others.

Situated learning

Lave and Wenger's (1991) study of situated learning, based on the apprenticeship model, suggests that we all learn by participating in activities with others as social beings. Such learning takes place when learners set themselves in what they call 'legitimate peripheral participation' situations (i.e. on the edge of 'communities of practice') where they learn the discourse, attitudes, values and practices necessary to allow them to enter into full fellowship with that community: 'Learners inevitably participate in communities of practitioners and . . . the mastery of knowledge and skill requires newcomers to move toward full participation in the sociocultural practices of a community' (1991: 29). The term 'scaffolding' has been used for the support and active cooperation of more expert peers, although it is an unsatisfactory term for what is an active rather than a passive support. Such learning can both free us and at the same time limit us to that social context.

These approaches have led to an interest in mentoring in education, the deliberate creation and assumption of role modelling from significant others by which learning of attitudes as well as knowledge and skills is promoted. It is argued that teachers' knowledge is heavily situated and sometimes difficult to explain in abstract terms. Working alongside mentors enables new and inexperienced teachers to see 'learning to teach as a process of learning to be, see and respond in increasingly informed ways while working in classrooms, i.e. to participate increasingly knowledgeably in the practices of teaching' (Edwards and Protheroe 2003: 229). While such approaches do not yet seem to be widely used in the training of teachers of adults, they have much to commend them; you may find it useful for your own development to find one or more (preferably more experienced) teacher(s) of adults and relate regularly with them.

Critical theory

The freedom suggested by situated learning theories is challenged by *critical theory* (Held 1980; Carr and Kemmis 1983; Giroux 1983). Each society and each part of each society privilege some kinds of knowledge and some kinds of behaviour, and these power relationships are passed on. When applied to education and training, critical theory focuses on the power relationships within every learning context. It explores the ways in which the values and assumptions of the powerful reach out to the less powerful through hegemony and the resistance which this process provokes. Learning is thus circumscribed by the socio-cultural context within which it takes place. Situated learning and mentoring may induct us into the existing power complex; they will rarely enhance our critical reflection on hegemony unless the community of practice itself is one of critically reflective practitioners. Learning in the critical theory sense is the process by which our discontent with the here and now, our search for transcendence, expresses itself in a quest for perfectibility, something beyond ourselves.

Total environment

Some modern learning theories have seen the engagement of the individual with the environment in a more holistic sense – the *total environment*, not just the social environment. The physical world which we inhabit, the built environment which we have made for ourselves, the mental world which we have created as well as the social environment are all elements with which we are bound in a perpetual engagement. Indeed, it goes further than this. Rather than experience being outside of ourselves, something which we can reflect critically on and from which we can learn, these views suggest that we are all made up by our experiences; that experience is us, so to speak: 'Cognition and environment become *simultaneously enacted* through experiential learning' (Fenwick 2001: 47).

Bourdieu's understanding of *habitus* is perhaps the most influential of these ideas. His view that every individual lives within a physical and social context which teaches him/her values and practices through direction and accident has led several to challenge him in terms of structuralism and entrapment; but if interpreted as a process in which every individual continually constructs and reconstructs their own sense of *habitus* through individual interpretations of the social and physical context leading to actions which in turn alter that environment, agency can be to some extent restored. A number of recent studies of learning (mainly formal) in relation to *habitus* are suggestive of the fruitful field this approach can open, both by exploring further its potentialities and challenging some of its assumptions (Corbett 2007; Benei 2008; Pahl 2008).

Such approaches lie within the humanist tradition. But they are a different school of theories. Learning is not seen by these writers as merely the satisfaction of urges, seeking rest and harmony, the diminishing of anxiety, the relief of tension, the enhancement of satisfaction, creating new and more useful knowledge or more satisfying meanings.

Rather, 'learning through living' is an inevitable part of our active engagement with our environment as a consequence of being a member of a common humanity. This may actually increase tension, a dialectic in which we seek to alter our environment as well as ourselves in the constant search for something better, some ideal, a struggle that will never end.

Knowledge-based theories

In discussions of learning, the influence exerted by different kinds of knowledge, the subject matter of the different learning tasks, is less frequently explored. We have seen in the cognitive learning theories views which are to some extent based on the content or subject matter of the learning. But the interaction of learner and context in learning is incomplete without considering the kind of knowing to be achieved in the learning. This is to argue that 'to learn' is not a intransitive verb. One is never *just* learning; one is always learning *something*.

The important element here is the conversion of information arising from experience into 'knowledge'. That there is a distinction, and a distinction implying preferences, can be seen from the words attributed to Einstein: 'Knowledge is experience, everything else is just information'. The distinction would seem to be that information becomes knowledge when we process it into a form by which knowing subjects actively use it – in other words, when we experience it: 'Knowledge is information-in-use, and it is the interaction of information with the human mind that gives it meaning and purpose . . . those insights and understandings that give meaning to information and data' (Sallis and Jones 2002: 8–9).

That there are different kinds of knowledge is well accepted. Knowing about, knowing how to do, knowing to live together, knowing myself (to be) are not all the same kinds of knowledge. Experiential knowing ('I know a [particular] building'), for instance, is different from theoretical knowing *about* buildings. To know someone is different from knowing *of* that person (Ryle 1949). Habermas (1978) identified three kinds of knowing[1] which form something of a hierarchy:

- *instrumental/technical knowing* – knowing how to manipulate the environment; the acquisition of skills and understanding needed to manage the world we live in (it is interesting that he places scientific learning on the lowest rung of his scale);

---

1 In his later writings, Habermas changed this analysis, but it remains a valid expression of different kinds of knowing.

- *communicative knowing* – knowing in the realm of interpersonal relations, knowing others, increasing social and cultural understanding;
- *emancipatory knowing* – self-understanding, awareness and transformation of cultural and personal presuppositions that are always with us and affect the way we act.

These different kinds of knowing (and therefore of learning) have different methods of investigation, of teaching, and of evaluation. It is likely that any learning activity will call upon all three kinds of learning in different proportions. Because learning is part of the wider interaction between the individual and their environment, it will involve a transformation of the relationship between the learner, the source or mediator of knowledge, and the knowledge itself.

Other content-based learning theories exist, distinguishing between different kinds of learning tasks involved in different subject matter. Perhaps the clearest distinction is that between *socialisation learning*, which concentrates upon the internalisation of the knowledge (instrumental, propositional and communicative) which others have, including their value systems, which is an essential part of being human within a human context, and *individuation learning* which concentrates on the creation of one's own knowledge which is an essential part of being an individual. The knowledge involved, the content of learning in each case, will be different and will clearly affect the learning processes. A similar distinction may be made between 'mechanical learning' and 'creative and critical learning'. Anisur Rahman links this distinction with that between education which increases choices and training which limits choices (see p. 127): 'Nor can one be "trained" except to perform tasks which are mechanical, not creative' (Rahman 1993: 222). Training, memorising, the transfer of knowledge may be suitable for mechanical learning but these are ineffective and dependency-making approaches, and therefore inappropriate to the development of creative adults.

Knowledge and power

Such views of knowing remind us that 'knowledge is socially created . . . some kinds of knowing have more power and legitimation' (Barr 1999: 117). In Western societies, scientific knowledge is normally ranked higher than practical knowledge. To give two examples, a diamond can be known as a carbon crystal, as a tool to cut glass, as a jewel of great investment value, as an ornament and no doubt in other ways. Such ways of knowing can be ranked, with scientific knowledge being deemed by many as above practical knowledge, with investment being superior to fashion. Again, the way that a soil chemist knows 'mud' (as a colloidal solution) will be different from that of the potter or brickmaker, and again different from that of a child using it to dam a stream. To say that a scientist's way of knowing is 'superior' to rather than simply 'different' from that of a child is to apply value systems to knowledge.

Because of the values attached to different kinds of knowledge, the control of knowledge and the public recognition and accreditation of some kinds of learning become matters which are structured into every society. There are gatekeepers to knowledge, of whom the teacher of adults is not by any means the least important. It is true that today, with information technology, the control of formal educators is being challenged or perhaps reassigned, but such changes are also being resisted. The conflict over knowledge is likely to grow further.

Thus, knowledge-based learning theories not only posit that different processes of learning are brought into play by different kinds of knowledge. They also carry with them socio-cultural implications in terms of power. They are not neutral, as the cognitive theories claim them to be.

Process-based theories

The final element in our equation of learning is that of the processes of learning.

Much writing tries to suggest that there is one over-arching way of learning which applies to all persons in all situations, with every kind of learning content, at all times.

Critical reflection on experience

The strongest claim in this respect is that made for *critical reflection on experience*. Freire (1972) and others have suggested that all learning is accomplished by *critically* analysing experience and acting on the basis of that analysis. Schön (1983) talks of learning as reflective practice. Others like Knowles have spoken of a learning cycle starting with experience, proceeding through reflection on experience and leading to action which in its turn becomes the concrete experience for further reflection and thus the next stage of the cycle (Figure 5.4a). Action is an essential part of the learning process, not a result of learning, not an add-on at the end, putting the new learning into application. Without action, learning has not effectively taken place.

Adapting the model

Such a cycle needs to be elaborated in three ways.

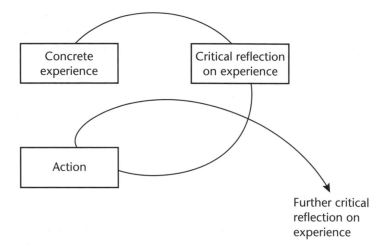

Figure 5.4a The learning cycle

Search and select

First, the process of *critical* reflection is complex. It involves making a judgement on experience, assessing it in the light of some standard drawn from other experience – either one's own or other people's. It means trying to determine how to explain the experience by using other criteria, assessing in what ways the experience could have been different. To give an example, farmers faced with a new pest or disease will ask their neighbours, 'What is it? We have never seen it before'; they thus reveal that they have first searched their own experience and are now actively seeking to access the experience of others in order to reflect critically on this new experience.

In learning through critical reflection on experience, then, there is an active *search* for new material. And then, drawing on our own and other persons' past experience, we *select* what we feel to be appropriate to judge the present experience by. Not all new knowledge is seen to be relevant; the new knowledge too is judged. This process is of course influenced by the social constructions around us.

The importance of new knowledge from outside the specific learning context cannot be exaggerated. It is against new knowledge, drawn from our earlier experience and the experience of others, however that is mediated to us, whether through teaching, speech, the written word, or observation, etc., that we measure the experience which forms the basis of learning, that we seek to make meaning. Without new knowledge, there can be no critical reflection.

Knowle's learning cycle thus needs to be adapted as shown in Figure 5.4b.

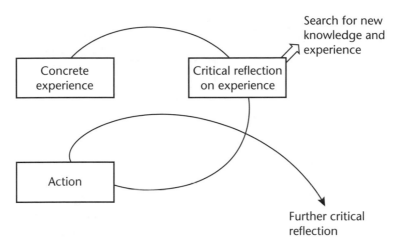

Figure 5.4b The learning cycle and the process of search and select

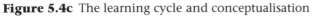
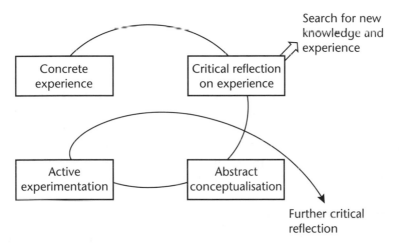

Figure 5.4c The learning cycle and conceptualisation

Conceptualisation

Secondly, as Kolb (1984) pointed out, critical reflection will lead in some cases to the development of generalisations ('abstract conceptualisation'). Critical reflection can be seen as asking questions about a specific experience in the light of other experience; abstract conceptualisation may be seen as going beyond the specific answers to general principles. Only in this way will the new insights generated by critical reflection become usable in other contexts. Hypotheses are formed which can be tested in new situations (Figure 5.4c).

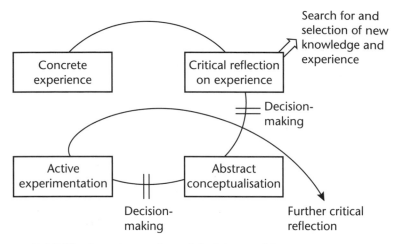

Figure 5.4d The learning cycle and decision-making

Decision-making

Thirdly, however, learning includes goals, purposes, intentions, choice and decision-making, and it is not at all clear where these elements fit into the learning cycle. Decisions are needed to determine which other forms of experience are to be used for critical reflection (selection). Decisions are certainly needed before translating some of the possible solutions and not others into active experimentation. And decision-making occurs at other points in the cycle. These have tended to be omitted from discussions of the learning cycle (see Figure 5.4d).

Preferred learning styles

Based on the learning cycle as adapted, Kolb (1976) identified four main learning styles. Each of the stages of the cycle calls for different learning approaches and appeals to different kinds of persons (Figure 5.5):

- learning through *concrete experience* – an engagement with direct experience (activists);
- learning through *critical reflection* – observing experience from different perspectives and judging experience by a variety of criteria (reflectors);
- learning through *abstract conceptualisation* – analysing experience to create new ideas, concepts and structures (theorists);
- learning through *active experimentation* – using these new ideas, testing theories out in practice (experimenters).

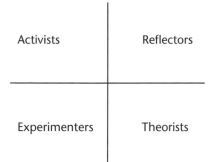

Figure 5.5 Learning styles based on the learning cycle

Activity 5.6

You may wish to ask yourself which learning styles you used to best effect during your chosen learning activity.

Some people suggest that there is a progression here: 'in the process of learning, one moves . . . from actor to observer, and from specific involvement to general analytical detachment' (Kolb 1984: 31). Jarvis (1987: 16) argues that 'all learning begins with experience'. Others however suggest that one may enter this cycle at any point, not always start with concrete experience. Thus one may start with a theory and move to trial and error (experimentation), using this as concrete experience which is then reflected on critically to revise or confirm the theory.

Kolb and others argue that every individual develops one or more *preferred learning styles* through experience (Figure 5.6). It is important to stress that we all tend to use all of these styles – we do not confine our learning efforts to one only. But we *prefer* to use one or perhaps two modes of learning above the others; we feel stronger at learning through some approaches rather than others. Based on the identification of such preferences, these writers have classified learners as 'divergers' (reflecting on concrete experience), 'assimilators' (constructing general principles from reflection), 'convergers' (applying concepts), and 'accommodators' (exploring new experiences) (Honey and Mumford 1992; Van der Kamp 1992).

Other kinds of learning styles have been proposed, such as the Learning Individual Programme (Rundle and Dunn 1999). But whichever is chosen, these views provide a useful reminder that individual learners feel most comfortable using their own learning strategies. Through a variety of learning activities engaged in over many years, adults have developed

We all have certain preferences in the way we learn.

Active learners
Some prefer to learn by doing something immediately. They don't bother to wait to listen to all the instructions, to read the manual first but get on with the job. They try to find out how things work. These people get impatient when someone tells them all about the task first. When they are asked a question, they give an immediate answer without waiting to work it out fully. They tend to be enthusiastic about new things; they like lots of new experiences ('I'll try anything once'). They are individualists in learning; and when they have finished one activity, they want to pass quickly to the next one. They want to see as many new things as possible; they like to meet lots of new people. They will often volunteer to take the lead in any activity. They like short-term goals and are usually bored by the slower work of implementing and consolidating a programme. They tend to believe what they are told.

Reflective learners
Some prefer to 'wait and see'. They sit back and watch others doing the task first, they listen to the talk of others. When they are asked a question, these people don't give the first answer that comes into their heads; they take time to think, they hesitate and are often uncertain. They want more information before they can give a real answer ('I want to sleep on it'). Before making a decision, they try to think through all the implications, both for themselves and for others. These people tend to like sharing their learning with others because this helps them to collect different opinions before they make up their minds.

Theorising learners
Some like to build systems, to get down to first principles. They don't want to deal with 'real cases' – these are thought to be too limited. Rather, they want to understand the whole. They speak in general rather than in concrete terms. They question the basic assumptions. They make rules out of all cases. They usually think problems through step by step. They try to make coherent pictures out of complex material; they often represent ideas in diagrams showing relationships ('What does it really mean? How does this fit with that?'). They try to be objective and detached. They are less sympathetic to human feelings, to other people's subjective judgements. These people want the world to be logical; they do not like too many different opinions.

Experimental learners
Some like to experiment, to apply their new insights. They come back from training courses full of enthusiasm and new ideas which they want to try out. Having been told something, these people do not believe it until they see it for themselves ('It may work for you but I want to see if it will work for me'). They try to find new and more effective ways of doing things. They take short cuts or devise new modes of working. They tend to be confident, energetic, impatient of what they see as too much talk. They like solving problems, and see new situations as a challenge from which they can learn a good deal. They like being shown how to do something but become frustrated if they are not allowed to do it for themselves very quickly.

(adapted from the works of Kolb 1976, 1984; Honey and Mumford 1992)

Figure 5.6 Table of preferred learning styles

a particular blend of learning styles which is stronger in its demand than any such blend in children. The preferred learning styles of children have not yet become established; by adulthood, these have become more crystallised (for a critique of the over-use of learning styles, see Adey et al 1999; Coffield et al 2004).

Critique of critical reflection on experience

There are real problems with critical reflection as *the* way in which adults learn. First, we need to remember that the development of understandings about learning styles was not intended to enable the teacher to put people into a particular category. Rather, this analysis helps to explain what is going on.

Secondly, we need to remember that once again this picture has been drawn on the basis of a limited range of research subjects, mainly white middle-class educated males with successful careers in Western cultures. Whether different styles may be found among black persons, among women, among other cultures (e.g. Muslim, Asiatic, Chinese or indigenous groups), among the less formally educated, is less clear. And whether such styles change with ageing or with life crises, or indeed if adults use different styles in different contexts or with different learning tasks, these are questions as yet unanswered. To suggest that all adults have a single set of preferred learning styles based on critical reflection on experience, styles which are used in all situations, is probably going beyond the evidence available.

But more importantly, most of the discussions of critical reflection (e.g. Brookfield 2000: 95) seem to concentrate on great crises in people's lives, on 'unexpected events' and 'critical episodes' which cause major disequilibrium 'between biography and [current or new] experience'. But there is more to adult learning than such events (e.g. the learning of languages). Our purposeful learning episodes are not all created by great upheavals. While critical reflection is undoubtedly a process by which we cope with major 'traumas', it also features along with many other strategies of learning in other learning episodes.

It is therefore unacceptable to suggest that critical reflection on experience leading to action is *the* way in which we learn. There are many different processes involved in learning. Critical reflection on experience would seem to be a key strategy in the process of creating meaning out of experience; it is certainly the main way in which 'critical learning' is developed. But there is more to learning than the search for meanings. The learning cycle, which still dominates much of the discussion about adult learning, has come under challenge as being too normative and prescriptive.

Constructivism

A second claimant to universal truth in relation to learning comes from constructivism. Cognitivist views tend to stress the interaction of the learner with a body of knowledge that lies outside of themselves, and therefore the key process is the transfer of information from an expert source to the learner. Constructivism is a response to this view. One of the most influential expressions of this group of theories is George Kelly's (1955) 'personal construct theory'.

> Current research has led to . . . a number of widely accepted principles . . . The most general one, characterizing all the current trends, is a well-nigh total commitment to the constructivist notion of the origin of human knowledge.
>
> This means that all knowledge which man [sic] has of the surrounding reality is the result of his own mental processes; in this sense, it is of his own construction. The constructivist view is a very different one from the traditional one which is often associated with teaching. Whether consciously or not, learning and teaching have traditionally been seen in terms of a direct transfer of information from the teacher to the learner. In denying the possibility of this kind of direct transfer, the constructivist theory opens up new challenges for teaching. If learning is an individual's active construction process in interaction with the physical and social environment, what kind of role can teaching play in such a process?
>
> (LEIF 1990: 14)

Learning is not something determined by external influences; each individual creates their own learning. We form personal constructs (units of meaning) from our ideas, feelings, memories and evaluations about events, places and people in our lives or from our cultural background (Bourdieu's *habitus*). In this way, we create a vision of the world and manipulate it rather than simply respond to stimuli or to external knowledge. The act of learning is then largely initiated by the learner, exploring and extending their own understanding, holding what has been called a 'learning conversation with themselves', making individualised perceptions of reality, meanings and knowledge.

This school of thought rejects the notion of knowledge existing outside of ourselves, an objective reality to be discovered by research. Rather, all knowledge is constructed – and therefore contingent, contested and provisional. Learning does not mean uncovering hidden truth but the construction of new perceptions. Those who search after truth are faced with choosing between various 'acts of knowing'. The focus thus switches from trying to establish the validity of the knowledge itself to the criteria by which we can judge the validity of the questions asked and the answers arrived at in each individual case – how can we determine which 'act of knowing' carries with it some experiential validity for ourselves in this particular situation?

This view has grown widely – and not just in adult education circles. For example, in management: 'Learning is not finding out what other people already know but solving our own problems for our own purposes by *questioning*, *thinking* and *testing* until the solution is part of our life' (Charles Handy, quoted in Ball 1991: 29, our italics). And in international development: 'Development . . . is not possible with somebody else's thinking and knowledge . . . Knowledge cannot be transferred . . . learning is always an act of self-search and discovery. In this search and discovery, one may be stimulated and assisted but cannot be taught' (Rahman 1993: 219, 222).

Such a view challenges the concept of learning based on the transfer of information. Indeed, Rahman (1993) asserts that 'transfer of information' is harmful: 'Those . . . who seek to transfer knowledge and skills serve mainly to disorient the capacity that is in every healthy individual to creatively search for and discover knowledge' (1993: 222). The distinction is between the 'input' model, in which knowledge, skills and understanding are 'given' or 'imparted' to the learners and the learner responds to these inputs from outside, and the 'action' model in which the learners are searching out the material they need, and making their own sense of their experience. It is not a matter of choosing between two equally effective strategies of promoting learning; the one is seen to be the enemy of the other.

Diversity of ways of learning

Like critical reflection, constructivism makes claims to universality in learning. But it would seem that there is a plurality of ways in which we learn. Weinrich, for example, lists four main processes: *reinforcement* through reward and punishment; *imitation* of role models; *identification*, 'a process which is more powerful than imitation, through which the [learner] incorporates and internalises the roles and values of the . . . significant [other]'; and *structuring*, in which the learners 'actively seek to structure the world, to make sense and order of the environment' (quoted in Henriques 1984: 19).

Others have suggested the following:

- the acquisition of information through listening, seeing, reading, etc.;
- the memorisation of data or processes;
- the changes inspired by watching others and then practising (imitation);

- the sudden and apparently unassisted insights which we all experience from time to time (*gestalt*);
- the learning that comes from the successful (i.e. the rewarded) completion of some task;
- haphazard experimentation and exploration (trying things out).

There is therefore no consensus about learning. Different theories are espoused with vigour (see, for example, websites devoted to the psychology of learning, two of which are cited in Further Reading to this chapter). For learning is a many-faceted activity which incorporates a number of different elements. Some learning may be brought about by the transfer of knowledge from A to B; some by reaction to external stimuli. Other learning may be brought about by drives and intentions (goals), transforming meaning perspectives or transforming social contexts; some by reflecting critically on experience.

This is not to say that all learning theories are 'right', though it may be that they are all valuable. It is to say that in our present state of knowledge and understanding we cannot say with certainty that any one theory is closer to expressing the 'truth' of reality than any other. To look for one over-arching learning theory may be to seek for warriors' dreams after the battle is over.

Therefore, instead of trying to establish one learning theory which covers all situations, perhaps we should be looking for more than one. Indeed, it may be that the learning we do on our own may be different from the learning we do in specially constructed learning programmes. This is the theme of the next chapter.

Further reading

Atherton, J.S. (2009) www.learningandteaching.info/learning/

Cranton, P. (1994) *Understanding and Promoting Transformative Learning*. San Francisco, CA: Jossey Bass.

Explorations in Learning & Instruction: The Theory Into Practice Database, http://tip.psychology.org/

Fenwick, T.J. (2001) *Experiential Learning: A Theoretical Critique*. Columbus, OH: ERIC.

Lave, J. and Wenger, E. (1991) *Situated Learning: Legitimate Peripheral Participation*. Cambridge: Cambridge University Press.

Merriam, S. and Cafarella, R. (2006) *Learning in Adulthood*. San Francisco, CA: Jossey Bass.

Mezirow, J. et al (2000) *Learning as Transformation*. San Francisco, CA: Jossey Bass.

Chapter 6

From Learning to Teaching
What does teaching add to learning . . . ?

This chapter looks at the learning processes we all use in our daily lives. It identifies two different ways of learning: the natural process of informal learning, and formalised learning. It argues that teaching adults should build on but at the same time go beyond the natural learning processes by helping the student learners to become more conscious of their own learning.

Learning and life

We have already seen (p. 95) that some people use language loosely. They talk about 'motivating people to learn' as if they are not already motivated to learn, or 'getting people to come into learning' as if they are not already learning. By this, they seem to mean persuading people to participate in certain learning activities, but their language implies that these people are not engaging in any learning outside of these activities. They use the word 'learners' to mean those who are engaged in particular activities, and describe those who are not engaged in these activities as 'non-learners'; they speak of 'people who have done no learning since leaving school'. 'Learning' and 'planned learning' thus get mixed up. Even experienced adult educators use the term 'lifelong learning' when they really mean 'lifelong education', or 'informal learning' when they mean 'informal education'. By using this discourse, they suggest that only their approved activities are 'real' learning. They do not appear to realise that 'lifelong learning' is simply that – learning which goes on for everybody more or less all the time (see Duke 2001).

The same tendency can be seen even in recent writings on informal learning – for informal learning has seen something of a rediscovery recently (e.g. Colley et al 2003; Hager and Halliday 2009). But even here, informal learning is often seen in 'educational' terms – that is, as the provision of learning opportunities outside of formal classrooms. One of the most recent and authoritative statements tries to get away from formal learning, seeing informal learning as:

structured or unstructured part time, non-vocational learning which does not lead to qualifications – or at least where qualifications are incidental to the learning. This kind of learning activity can take place anywhere – in a local college, community centre, pub or on the North Yorkshire moors. It embraces all kinds of activity ranging from family learning, sports and recreation to the arts, humanities and foreign languages.

(DIUS 2008)

But it is clear that this statement means by 'all kinds of activities' 'all kinds of *planned* activities intended to help people to learn something' which can be provided in a wide range of locations; and the same statement goes on to say that informal learning can be subject to a government policy of encouragement and promotion of informal learning by the provision of more 'learning opportunities which take place outside of formal educational contexts'. This envisioning of informal learning suggests that there are some people who are not in informal learning who should be.

We do therefore need to stress very clearly that our view of informal learning is very different. Informal learning is quite independent of all kinds of planned learning programmes such as employer-sponsored work-based learning or government-sponsored community-based learning programmes (we see these as 'non-formal learning programmes'). We see informal learning as a natural process, part of being alive. It is not dependent on 'the provision of informal learning opportunities' by others; it arises naturally in the course of everyday life. The most important thing that 'lifelong and lifewide learning' has reminded us is that learning takes place throughout our lives *in the course of our daily living*. Learning is going on all the time for all of us and is not confined to planned learning activities. *No one is not learning*. And it is vital that all of us who teach adults should understand and build on this natural learning process, not ignore or demean it. Everyone who comes into any of our programmes is already learning elsewhere; there is no such person as a 'non-learner' (see Rogers 1997).

Learning is part of living

Learning is embedded in living. It is closely related to the way in which individuals develop in relation to their lifeworld. We simply cannot avoid learning. And since the experience of living is continuous, so too learning is continuous. It occurs throughout life, from start to finish. Virtually everything we do, our attitudes and practices, have all been learned and are constantly being relearned.

This means that learning is individual. Although we may learn from and in association with others, it is not a collective activity: 'Each individual is processing the experience uniquely for personal use . . . In learning, the individual is the agent, even though the agent may be subject to the social pressures of the group' (Brookfield 1983: 1–4). Learning is affected and may even to some extent be controlled by society, the community, the family or other collectives, but the learning activity itself – introducing learning changes – is personal.

Learning is also active. It is not simply the passive receiving of knowledge and skills. There are many people who speak about learning as if it were something which a teacher *does to* a learner. They talk of the teacher 'imparting' knowledge or skills to the learners. Learning however is not someone giving information or skills to other persons. It is not filling up an empty pot with knowledge; it is not even watering a plant so that it grows naturally. Learning is a *positive action on the part of the learner*, calling in most cases for an act of the will.

Thus, learning is normally voluntary – we do it ourselves. It is rarely compulsory, even among children, although some experiential learning may be less than fully voluntary. And the distinction which anthropologists use between 'events' and 'practices' can also help us here (Brice Heath and Street 2008). In the course of daily living, we will all engage in many different 'learning events', individual learning activities which will take multiple forms. But seen over time, these everyday learning events will form 'learning practices' – that is, we will each create our own patterns of learning, our 'ways of learning'.

Learning, then, is natural, as natural as breathing. It is the continual process of adapting to the various changes we all face – in our socio-cultural contexts, in our social roles, in the daily tasks we perform, as well as in our personal growth and development: 'Learning, like breathing, is among the most basic of human activities. It is the process through which we become the human beings we are, and by which we internalize the external world and construct our experiences' (Jarvis et al 1998: vii). Just as breathing and eating can be seen as taking in air and food from the environment and extracting from them the (positive and negative) elements for our physical development, so learning is taking in experiences from the environment and extracting that which will (positively or negatively) contribute to our mental and physical development.

Thus an image often used for learning is that of hunger. Within every individual, it is suggested, there is a bundle of unsatisfied learning desires, although some people are more conscious of this hunger for learning than others. These may spring from inner drives, from half-finished earlier learning activities, or from our own changing interests and experiences. Some of these learning desires are very pressing, arising from or reinforced by urgent matters, tasks to be done. But most of them lie dormant, over-laid by more pressing concerns, awaiting either a suitable opportunity or an increased sense of need to bring them to life. A spoken or written word or a glimpse of something will arouse this unsatisfied curiosity, cause us to sit up and take notice when certain cues are heard or noticed, make us engage in selective perception (this is the 'I've always wanted to learn something about that' syndrome). For some people, these desires have been damaged or buried deep by other experiences, but they still exist and can in appropriate circumstances be awakened.

Intentional and unintentional learning

Learning, then, springs from two main causes. There are the more or less automatic responses to new information, perceptions or experiences that result in change, and there are more purposeful activities, the result of impulses which lead us to seek out or create new experiences aimed at achieving some kind of mastery. There is a difference in meaning between the use of the words 'to learn' in contexts such as: 'He burned his fingers. He learned not to do that again', and 'I had some trouble with the machine but I learned how to manage it'. The second implies both purpose and effort which the first lacks.

Much of our learning is incidental and unintended. A good deal is very casual: it comes from chance happenings (roadside posters, snatches of overheard conversation, newspaper reading or television watching, meeting people: 'adventitious learning [which] springs from accidental encounters with unintentional sources' (Lucas 1983: 2–3). We all seek to make meaning out of the experiences which occur in our lives. But be-yond this, there are occasions when we engage in some more structured process of mastering a situation – learning to deal with a new piece of equipment, for instance, or to adjust to new bus timetables or to cope with a new family situation. At certain times throughout their lives, all adults will bend their energies and attention to achieving some learning task directed towards a goal. Some of these occasions may call for formal methods of learning (learning to drive a car is probably the biggest pro-gramme of teaching adults in many countries), but we cope with most of them more informally. It is possible that unintentional and intentional learning shade into each other rather than being distinct.

At the same time, there are some 'sources of learning' that equally may be intentional or unintentional. Some simply respond to learning needs, often without appreciating that they are acting as sources of learning. Other sources intend learning to take place – through mass campaigns, advertisements, political persuasion, exhibitions, social propaganda, etc. – even though the target audience has no intention

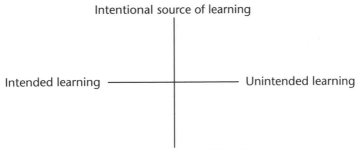

Figure 6.1 Learning matrix

of engaging in learning. Again, these too may shade into each other (Figure 6.1).

Activity 6.1

Stay with the example of your own learning that you used in Chapter 5 (p. 96) and try placing aspects of it in the matrix in Figure 6.1. Do they tend to cluster within one or more of the quadrants or are they spread throughout?

Learning episodes

Learning, then, goes on throughout life. But at times there are concentrated periods of learning, dumplings in the soup, so to speak. Some of these 'learning episodes' (as we may call them) come from external requirements: a task set for us by others, for example, or new legislation which calls for changes in our practices, or the need to repair a broken machine in the home or at work. Other such episodes are called for by some of the welcome or unwelcome changes that may come about in our personal circumstances. Many an adult has had to learn about new financial matters through divorce or separation. But the majority are undertaken voluntarily and often with some measure of enthusiasm and commitment, although some will be undertaken reluctantly, even perhaps with some anger. Emotions are always tied up in learning episodes. And such episodes are always purposeful – designed to achieve a particular goal which the learners set for themselves.

Learning episodes are therefore distinct from the incidental and unintended learning which characterises the majority of our learning experiences. And they are separate from (though they may at times draw upon) the more formalised learning programmes of education. They form a focus of attention today in the form of self-directed learning (see pp. 53–4)[1].

Learning objectives or 'clearing up messes'?

The fact that these learning episodes are intentional and purposeful, that the adult is active, struggling with their perceptions of reality rather than responsive to stimuli, suggests that they are directed by more or less clearly perceived learning objectives.

To some extent this is true. When we set out to learn to meet some new situation or to increase our expertise in some field of interest, there will be occasions when we will be able to focus our efforts on defined objectives, when we can see what it is that we are trying to achieve. We clear our mind of all that will block the way and set out to achieve the mastery we require of ourselves. When deciding to trace our family history, for example, or learn a new computer process, we can set for ourselves clear goals, and we can see whether we are making progress towards the achievement of these goals.

But in other cases, the situation is not so clear. Ackoff (1978), talking about managers, has pointed out that we are often in a more confused situation: we 'are not confronted with problems that are independent of each other but with dynamic situations that consist of complex systems of changing problems that interact with each other. I call such situations "messes". Problems are extracted from "messes" by analysis; they are to messes as atoms are to tables and chairs . . . [We] do not solve problems, [we] manage messes'.

This would seem to be particularly true of many learning episodes which we undertake throughout our lives – for example, moving house. Our task in these cases is not straightforward, simply meeting a need. Rather, it is to unravel a tangle, to sort out a mess. 'As adults, we learn things in an almost haphazard way, even if we do fit what we learn into some kind of framework' (Corder 2002: 9).

---

1 As Merriam and Cafarella indicate, natural learning episodes form one strand of the current interest in self-directed learning (1999: 288–317). But many discussants of self-directed learning concentrate on whether or not people show 'autonomous behaviour in learning situations' (1999: 310). The argument above reverses Knowles' approach that adults become more self-directed in learning as they progress. We are suggesting that all persons start with self-directed learning but that formalised learning interrupts and can even weaken this natural learning process.

In these circumstances, how and what we learn depends on how we define the situation we are facing. We analyse the issue, determine what the problem looks like so far as we can see it, and try to solve it. How we do that depends on how much and what kind of experience we bring to the 'mess'. That will determine the way we look at the problem and the language in which we express it. Learning is a haphazard process of trial and error, and we often get it wrong. As Schön (1983) puts it in regard to his chosen professionals: 'Problems must be constructed from the materials of problematic situations which are puzzling, troubling and uncertain . . . [We] are frequently embroiled in conflicts of values, goals, purposes and interests . . . the effective use of specialised knowledge to well-defined tasks depends on a prior structuring of situations that are complex and uncertain'.

Activity 6.2

How clear were the objectives of your learning activity? Did they stay the same or change as the learning progressed?

The importance of learning episodes to the teacher of adults

These self-structured and purposeful learning episodes will almost always invoke the assistance of some helper. They can thus be of considerable significance for teachers of adults – for our purpose is to create structured and purposeful learning episodes for our adult student participants. Since they are intended and purposeful, these learning episodes reveal more about the sort of learning opportunity that we can construct than does the more ubiquitous, haphazard and largely unintentional learning that springs from the constant interaction of the individual with the environment. The way adults learn purposefully on their own tells us much about the way they will learn in our programmes.

Some adult educators are hesitant about using these natural learning episodes as the basis for building a theory of adult learning. They point out that each of us engages with the environment in ways limited by our experience and existing learning abilities, and that this social environment itself controls our learning. They suggest that what is needed is to break free from the restraints of context. Nevertheless, these episodes show us something of the special features of life-embedded learning as distinct from the processes of the more decontextualised formal learning, and thus form a guide as we construct learning activities for those who come to our programmes.

Characteristics of learning episodes

Analysis suggests that there are three main characteristics relating to these learning episodes that are relevant to our discussion.

First, *they are episodic in character, not continuous*. They come in short bursts of relatively intensive activity, absorbing the attention, and they usually come to an end as soon as the immediate purpose has been felt to be achieved. There are some, particularly in the self-fulfilment area, that spring from long-term interests (gardening, for instance, or following trends in modern or classical music); but even within these patterns of persistent learning, there come more intensive short-term episodes of learning directed towards the achievement of some immediate goal. We cannot keep this sort of pressure up for long. We need to be motivated by an achievable purpose; and when that is over, there may come a rest or a slower pace of learning before the next episode occurs.

Secondly, *the goal is usually some concrete task or immediate issue that is felt to be important*. Intentional learning episodes are in general aimed at dealing with a particular issue. The situations they are designed to meet are concrete rather than theoretical, and they take place within a specific context, both immediate and cultural. Particularity is everything in learning episodes. We want to decorate *this* room in a way which will satisfy us and/or *those* whom we wish to please; we need to cope with *this* change in *this* family circle; we are trying to understand *this* new procedure in *this* work context, and so on. Even when the learning is part of a long-term and developing interest (chess, say, or cooking), the individual episode of learning is directed towards a particular goal to be achieved within this field.

There are several implications that flow from this:

- We do not on the whole *approach any situation academically*. To decorate a room, we rarely study design as such. To cope with a family matter, we do not take a course on interpersonal relations or psychology – although we might well consult books on the subject. We are not concerned so much with a subject as to resolve a one-off concrete situation.
- This means that the learning task is *rarely pursued in a systematic way*. It is not general learning, but limited to the task in hand. Few of us will pull down a textbook to cover the whole field. It is only with those who have had extensive experience of formal education, who have developed and maintained formalised learning skills, that a systematic exploration of a field of knowledge becomes at all common. This is a replication in private of the systems of learning that characterise formal education and is thus confined to relatively few, and to a few occasions in their

lives. They too also engage in more limited goal-oriented learning at other times. Most of us most of the time use only those parts of any subject that help us to meet our immediate task. We then stop – even if later we find that we have not quite finished the task.

- This form of learning is *rarely sequential*, starting with an introduction to the field of study and proceeding from A to Z in sequence. Nor do we start with the simple and move on to the more difficult. We tackle the problem with which we have to deal at the level at which it occurs in our lives. We cope with difficult language and terms from the start so long as these are of direct relevance to the learning process (e.g. learning for a planning application or a mortgage).

- The learners do not on the whole draw on *compartmentalised knowledge* such as was learned at school (e.g. history separated from geography or maths from physics). We bring *all* that we know from all sorts of fields to bear upon the particular instance. A more academic approach may occur on occasion, but even here there is often a particular need to be met that leads to the use of knowledge from different fields of study rather than a compartmentalised approach to knowledge.

- Such episodes are aimed at *immediate rather than future application*. There are, it is true, some learning episodes which are intended as a preparation before embarking on a course of action: religious preparation classes, prenatal groups, holiday language courses, pre retirement programmes, for example. But on the whole, most learning is achieved in the process of doing a particular task or meeting a specific situation, and therefore the material, as it is mastered, is applied at once. We set out to learn how to use a new washing machine by using it; we learn a new bus timetable as we use the service; we learn how to cope with a baby by coping with a baby.

Thirdly, since most of these learning episodes are directed towards specific goals, *there is relatively little interest in overall principles*. Few attempts are made by the learner to draw general conclusions from the particular instance being learned. Once the immediate situation is felt to have been resolved, the goal attained or the problem solved, the learner normally brings the process of investigation to a close, storing away the learning gained for another day. What is stored is the way to cope with the particular situation, not general principles. Learning to use a new washing machine will be concentrated on the specific model in hand, not on washing machines in general. The learning needed to cope with a new bus timetable will deal not with the entire transport system but with the one or two routes needed. Learning a new office routine will be confined to what is needed for the moment, not to wider applications. All of these may arouse in our minds wider issues of obsolescence and modern technology, or public and private transport provision, or the demands of innovations as a whole; but these will occur mainly as spasmodic thoughts and grumbles, usually quickly pushed away and forgotten. The efforts are centred on the immediate and the particular, not on the long term and the general.

Activity 6.3

Check this list against your own learning experience. How far was it 'episodic' or continuous; how far was it concrete or generalised: how far for immediate use or delayed use?

Two different kinds of learning

These characteristics enable us to establish a relationship between these purposeful learning episodes and the learning theories we discussed above. For running through most of that discussion is a distinction between two kinds of learning, although the way the difference is described varies. Carl Rogers for example suggested that 'the only learning which significantly influences behavior is self-discovered, self-appropriated learning . . . which has been personally appropriated and assimilated in experience', which he contrasted with 'information assimilation'. He contrasted 'the traditional pattern of schooling' with voluntary learning based on the concerns and experiences of the learners, critical reflection on knowledge, beliefs, values and behaviours of society, self-directed learning and the cyclic interaction of learning and action. He set the distinction out as shown in Figure 6.2.

Significant experiential learning	Traditional conventional learning
Personal involvement	Prescribed curriculum
Whole person	Similar for all students
Self-initiated	Lecturing
Pervasive	Standardised testing
Evaluated by learner	Instructor-evaluated
Essence is meaning	Essence is knowing and reproducing

Figure 6.2 Carl Rogers' (1983) distinctions between two kinds of learning

Activity 6.4

Tick those items in Figure 6.2 which appear to apply to your own learning programme.

Knowles, whose view of andragogy (the teaching of adults) has for a long time held the floor in adult education, contrasted this concept with pedagogy, 'the education of youth . . . the [two contrasting] models are probably most useful when seen not as dichotomous but rather as two ends of a spectrum' (Knowles 1980: 43). Constructivist learning (as we have seen) is similarly contrasted with 'the traditional view of learning which is often associated with teaching' (see pp. 126–7). Recent interest in 'natural' or 'informal learning' (Coffield 2000; Eraut 2000; Hager 2001; Hager and Halliday 2009) outside of schooling also highlights this distinction. It is the natural or informal learning that is most frequently used in the learning episodes, not schooled learning. The distinction between natural learning and taught learning is very widespread.

Informal and formalised learning

One of the clearest accounts of this distinction comes from language learning. Krashen (1982) and others have distinguished between the way a person acquires their first language (he calls this 'acquisition')[2] and the way they learn a second or subsequent language (which he calls 'learning')[3]. These form 'two distinct and independent ways' of learning – informal and formal.

---

2 We are not happy with the term 'acquisition' which seems to imply a deficit model by which a person lacks something which they acquire from the outside. But the term does indicate that the learner is active in learning. We hope our hesitations will lead to a search for a better term. 'Active learning' is not right, for formalised learning is also active. We have on occasions used the term 'natural learning' for this kind of learning, as we think that play is innate although its forms are socio-culturally constructed.

3 Again we have problems with this use of the term 'learning' on its own, for 'acquisition' is also learning. 'Taught learning', 'guided learning' or 'assisted learning' are all useful terms but they are not right, for some forms of formalised learning are not taught in a formal sense, and acquisition learning is assisted and guided in some way or another. 'Schooling' carries very negative connotations. 'Formalised learning' is nearer the mark. Other terms used for the distinction include 'explicit' and 'implicit' learning (Krashen 1982: 50).

'Acquisition learning' of initial language, the informal ways in which 'the language which every normal human brain acquires with seeming effortlessness' (Cenoz and Genesee 1998) is learned, is not really effortless. It is very active learning, initiated by the learner. It employs exploration and experimentation, trial and error, copying and mimicking, and practising. It proceeds by analogical thinking as well as by memorisation. Children play at language; they try out sounds and combinations of sounds, using some form of critical reflection to make their own assessment of what is right and what is wrong, seeking feedback from time to time. It is emotional, based on what *feels right* (hence the value of children's chanting). The initiative comes mainly from the learner, although encouragement may come from the environment and rewards may be sought by the learner in terms of pleasing significant others. 'Acquisition learning' is contextualised, highly specific, and it uses the ordinary lifeworld as its context. It is not normally structured or sequential, but works on what comes its way. Each episode ends when the particular task is done, and the recognition of the learning achieved is almost always *'post-hoc'*. But new episodes succeed each other continuously; the individual language learning project is never fully complete. Language in this sense is 'caught' rather than formally learned (Krashen 1982: 9–55).

Formal learning of a language, on the other hand, is based largely on memorisation, practice, external review and evaluation. It relies as much on the transfer of information as on experiential learning. The learning content is compartmentalised and irrelevancies are removed, as are many of the emotional elements. Such formalised learning has uniform pre-set goals for all the learners to achieve (which 'acquisition learning' does not have in the same sense), and the evaluation and rewards are set by others. It normally takes place in specially constructed contexts and is concerned with general (i.e. decontextualised) content, basic principles and rules (grammar) which enable the learner to find their way through various tasks. It uses specially prepared materials and specially created activities. It is highly structured and strictly sequenced, planned and externally assisted. It aims at the development of transferable skills.

It has been argued that such a distinction is somewhat overdrawn. There are almost always some formal elements in 'acquisition learning' of language; and there are often some informal elements in formal language learning. But on the whole the distinction between formal and informal learning is evident, not only in language learning but in other fields as well. For such a distinction is not confined to children, as Krashen points out, or to language learning. Both forms of learning continue into adult life. Most 'social role' learning such as parenting, club membership and citizenship (acculturation) is informal. When a new member of staff joins an organisation, for example, they learn not only the language of that body but also other things such as how to move through the buildings and how to relate to different persons in that organisation, all through informal learning (learning 'on the job'). Recent studies show that refugees in their new context do most of their learning by informal rather than by formalised learning. There are many occasions when adults employ informal learning rather than formalised learning, just as there are other occasions when they employ formalised learning processes. It is mostly in the form of learning new cultures that informal learning is used by adults. It is very interesting that today governments and other agencies are tending to use formal learning to supplement the informal learning in areas of parenting and citizenship (see p. 8) which every individual engages in; the informal learning does not cease when formal learning begins but the two do tend to get compartmentalised.

This distinction between 'acquisition learning' and formalised learning is similar to the distinctions which have been drawn between formal knowledge (i.e. formalised generalised principles) and informal knowledge (i.e. what works in particular contexts), and between explicit (precise and codifiable) knowledge and tacit (personal and intangible) knowledge (see Sallis and Jones 2002; Evans et al 2004). It is not, however, the same as the dichotomies drawn by Houle (1961) (see pp. 86–7) with his learning which 'functions as an instrument . . . to facilitate the [learner] into the logic of the present system' set against learning as 'the practice of freedom', or by Freire (1972) with his 'domesticating' as against 'liberating' education. For although 'acquisition learning' will normally be domesticating, in the sense that it will induct the learner into the culture in which they are located rather than opening windows, widening horizons, nevertheless at times some critically reflective processes are also involved, so that there will be potential elements of growth, development, liberation in 'acquisition learning'; while again formal learning can on occasion be liberating as well as normative and oppressive.

Sites and processes of learning

We need to distinguish between the processes of learning and the sites of learning. Resnick (1987) equated the two, suggesting that the learning that goes on inside formal settings (schools and colleges and other situations involving the use of textbooks, or in distance learning, etc.) is different from what she called 'out-of-school learning'. She suggested that in-school learning tends to be individualised, competitive, mainly mental, decontextualised, generalised and generalisable learning, while 'out-of-school' learning is collaborative, contextualised and situation-specific, and uses tools rather than minds alone. This is characteristic of most of the writings about formal and non-formal education (Rogers 2004).

It may be possible to identify two kinds of sites of learning, formal and informal. However, both informal learning and formalised learning can take place in both settings. It is probable that when many adults enter formal sites of learning, they tend to adopt formalised processes of learning which they associate from experience with those sites; much formal education encourages this. But they do not abandon informal learning, they learn much informally while engaged in formal learning. At the same time, those who have been extensively exposed to formal education may tend on occasion to use formalised learning in informal settings (in the home, the workplace, social settings, etc.), because they feel most comfortable with these processes once they have identified that what they are doing is learning. (This may help to account for the fact that most of those who participate in adult education programmes are persons who already have a good deal of experience in formal education.) But they still use informal learning processes. When adults engage in their own purposeful learning episodes, they choose those sites of learning which they feel are most appropriate to their intentions, and they choose those processes with which they are most comfortable.

There is thus a matrix, which is shown in Figure 6.3.

Activity 6.5

Using the matrix in Figure 6.3, assess how far you used informal learning processes and how far you used formalised processes in your own example of learning. Did it take place in institutional or non-institutional settings?

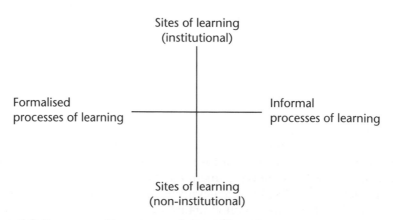

Figure 6.3 Processes of learning and sites of learning

Subconscious and conscious learning

Informal learning reverses some of the sequences we noted above. In informal learning, it is argued, people use tools first before they find out what uses these tools may have. We all learn both competency and understanding by 'doing' first; only after we have developed competency do we proceed to the making and transformation of meaning. Thus we start with a task which we find before us in our lifeworld and use everything that comes to hand: as Scribner (1988: 1) puts it, in learning, 'people strive to satisfy purposes that have meaning within their community, and in their activities they use tools, symbols and models that are culturally developed and transmitted'. In trying to fulfil this purpose/task, we draw upon our whole selves – our experience and self-concepts, including our concept of adulthood; we draw upon all the knowledge we possess and which we deem relevant in other fields as well, we draw on the whole environment. We use the experience and help of others.

And we do all of this more or less subconsciously, concentrating on the task rather than on the learning. Much informal learning is unconscious; and it leads to building up what are called unconscious 'funds of knowledge' (Moll et al 1992), 'tacit knowledge' (Eraut 2000) which we possess and use all the time in our daily practices but which we do not know we possess or are using. We learn as we meet life's daily encounters, as we go about life's daily tasks – and we are unconscious that we are learning. All we are conscious of are the encounters, the tasks.

The distinction, then, between informal learning and formalised learning seems to be close to the distinction drawn by Vygotsky (1962) between unconscious and conscious learning. But since consciousness is always present, the distinction may be redefined as whether the consciousness and the intention are towards the task or towards the learning; in other words, whether it is an activity concentrated on a *lifeworld task* or on a *learning task*. Because informal learning is related to an immediate task, it is 'subconscious' or 'unconscious' learning only in the sense that 'the learners are not usually aware of the fact that they are acquiring language but are only aware of the fact that they are using the language for communication' (Krashen 1982: 10). Vygotsky spoke of people 'learning to speak and then finding out what it means, of clumsily taking over the forms and tools of the culture and then learning how to use them appropriately' (cited in Cairns 2001: 20). In what Vygotsky (1962) called the 'zone of proximal development' – i.e. more formalised learning using the help of others – the learner 'gains consciousness and perspective'. It would thus appear that in formalised learning, the learner is conscious of *learning*; we may call it 'learning-conscious learning'. In informal learning, the learner is conscious of *the task* rather than of learning; we may call it 'task-conscious learning'.

There are of course occasions when task-conscious learning and learning-conscious learning (see Rogers 2003) are mixed. A parent showing a child how to cook, for example, will use a combination. Apprenticeships clearly involve informal and formalised learning. Induction into an office may often include both modes. Those who have become most accustomed to formalised learning within formal contexts may tend to use learning-conscious learning more frequently than those who have had less exposure to guided learning. But they will still use task-conscious informal learning.

Thus we can draw a series of situations in the form of a continuum of increasing consciousness of *learning*. At one end is incidental learning, obtaining knowledge more or less by accident (gossip or the media). Then there is task-fulfilment, without any consciousness of learning. There are the learning episodes which are more self-conscious of learning but are still heavily task-related (e.g. learning to set up home, to deal with a task at work, etc.). These are situations where people are known to speak of being 'on a steep learning curve' through some new role or other. They may be more structured but the objectives and evaluation lie in the performance of the task rather than in the learning. Then there are self-directed learning activities where the emphasis is more on learning than on the task (e.g. learning for travel). In these, some of the strategies employed will be formalised (e.g. the use of a textbook), and the growth of the consciousness of learning is more advanced. Distance and open learning contain much more formalised learning. Further towards the formalised end of the continuum lie those guided/assisted/taught learning programmes and activities which rely heavily on the control of others, where assessable learning is the key objective.

Activity 6.6

Ask yourself how far you were conscious of the *task* and of the *learning* in your own learning example.

There are, then, two more or less distinct kinds of learning, informal and formalised. They are not categories of learning but lie on a continuum. They are common to both adults and children. They occur in both formal and informal settings.

The uniqueness of adult learning

We can now try to answer the question as to whether there are forms of learning unique to adults and different from children's learning. This is an area which is becoming more contentious, partly because our understanding of children's learning processes and the processes themselves are changing rapidly under the influence of cultural and technological changes (Vosniadou 2001), and partly because we now understand that more than one learning process is involved.

Huge assumptions are often made about adults and their learning. For instance, it is suggested that adult learning consists of 'modifying, transferring, and reintegrating meanings, values, strategies and skills' rather than 'forming and accumulating as in childhood' (Brundage and Mackeracher 1980: 33). Mezirow also suggests that the unique element in adult learning is the *transformation of meanings* through experience, whereas children are *creating meanings* from their experiences. But this may be doubted, for children too are constantly transforming meanings as well as creating new ones. Much more research is needed before we can draw firm conclusions.

Adult learning strategies

Some studies have suggested that a range of strategies are used more commonly by adults than by younger learners. For example:

- Adults use *analogical thinking*, calling upon their existing knowledge and experience and the accumulated experience of others to see possible similarities that may indicate a solution. Through matching bits and pieces and creating relationships between them to identify where analogies may lie, they explore different ways of dealing with the learning situation. This learning relies upon the adaptation of knowledge and experience gained in spheres of activity *outside of the current issue*. It proceeds by being highly selective of the material felt to be relevant to the task in hand and trying out a number of possible solutions. When learning to mend a petrol lawnmower, for example, we may call upon half-forgotten experiences of motorcycles in earlier years. Such analogical thinking leads inevitably to *trial and error*; when learning to cope with new technology, we may engage in all kinds of experiments suggested by our own or other people's previous experiences in other spheres. While children may also use some analogical thinking, the range of knowledge and experience they have to draw upon is very limited.
- Adults often tend to rely on the creation of *meaningful wholes* in order to master new material. They create patterns focused on key issues. These structured shapes and relationships summoned up by cues enable the adult to incorporate the new material into existing patterns of knowing and behaving.

- Most adults *rely less on memory and rote learning* to retain what has been learned. Along with some of the sensory-motor skills, the process of ageing is often accompanied by a decline in both the ability to remember (especially short-term) and the ability to concentrate – a frequent cause of concern.
- Although adults share with younger people the ability and need to learn by *imitation*, and will often quickly grasp something demonstrated to them, in general they will not retain it without constant use as easily as their younger counterparts. Some adults will however seek to move quickly from imitation (conformism) to experimentation (independence), though others will be content to remain conformist in their learning.

But none of these is exclusive to adults. Children use analogical thinking, trial and error, as well as imitation. They may make less use of creating meaningful wholes (although they clearly search for meaning), and they may use memorisation more easily, but like adults they use whatever processes they feel most comfortable with.

Adult experience and learning

At the centre of almost all the discussions of this issue stands the adult experience. Merriam and Cafarella (1999) claim that there are four ways in which experience is related to adult learning which are different from children's use of experience:

- experience used as a resource for learning;
- learning through the drive to make sense of experience;
- experience used to transform meanings rather than to accumulate new knowledge and skills;
- experience acting as a barrier to learning.

But it can be argued that none of these is unique to adults. Children too use their experience all the time as a resource for learning (indeed much child learning consists of building on existing experience to widen experience). Children too possess a drive to make sense of experience and this promotes much of their learning. Adults accumulate *new* knowledge and skills as well as transform meanings, while children are constantly revising and transforming their earlier created meanings. Children too on occasion find their existing experience a barrier to learning. Thus it may be that the difference between adult experiential learning and children's experiential learning is a matter of degree. That adults have a greater range of experience (their own and others') to draw upon than children is self-apparent, but this does not necessarily mean that the processes of adult learning are any different from those of children, only that the mixture of processes may be different.

On the other hand, because adults are part of that culturally constructed complex defined as 'adulthood', their experience is qualitatively different from that of being a child. Adult experiences of legal processes, of family relationships and civic roles, of money and its acquisition, for example, are not only more extensive than those of children, they are qualitatively different: 'An adult's sexual or social experiences are of a kind that mark him [sic] off from the world of children. The same can be said of his experiences of a job, or politics, or war' (Kidd 1973: 46). A child learns through the experience of what it means to be a child, an adult through their construct of adulthood.

Adult development and learning

An examination of this issue (Brookfield 2000: 89–101) is suggestive. In summary, it proposes that there are several ways in which adults' learning may be significantly different from that of children. One is *the consciousness of learning*: adults can 'become self-consciously aware of their learning styles'; and 'learning to learn, while evident at earlier ages, is most fully realized in adults and is an important developmental process' (what Brookfield calls 'epistemic cognition' – 2000: 94). The second is *the ability to hold both the contextualised and the decontextualised in harness*. Adults can recognise that specific sites of action may make nonsense of general rules and theories ('dialectical thinking'); they can break the rules when a specific situation demands it ('practical logic'); they can 'act thinkingly', through critical reflection bringing decontextualised principles into their immediate and contextualised situation. These (it is argued) are the products of developmental processes, a stage beyond Piaget into 'post-formal operations'; younger persons cannot so act until they have gained enough and different experience.

From learning to teaching

We have argued here that both adults and children use informal learning and formalised learning. Adult learning may be distinguished from children's learning in terms of the different purposes of the learning and the greater and the different quality of the experience (constructed as either childhood or adulthood) brought to the learning. This then raises the question: how far is the *teaching* of adults different from the teaching of children (see Hanson 1996; Lovell 1980; Rogers 2003)? What is the role of the teacher in relation to the natural learning process, as revealed in both informal learning and in learning episodes?

Building on learning

Most teachers of adults operate in a more 'formalised' setting in the sense that it is a conscious *learning* activity rather than a task-oriented activity. Both formalised and informal learning are accessible in this setting. But the difference between informal learning and formalised learning appears to be clear. The formalised (educational) approach is that we learn first, then practise, and then use/perform. Informal learning reverses the order: we (try to) do, using our experience and the experience/help of others, and thus learn. Is the one then incompatible with the other?

It would seem that in their own learning episodes, most adults use informal learning more frequently and more effectively than formalised learning. It is the more natural process, as natural as breathing. If in everyday life 'acquisition is central and [formalised] learning more peripheral, then the goal of our pedagogy should be to encourage acquisition' (Krashen 1982: 20; see also Bruner 1966). But this does not happen often: as we have seen, much formalised learning (teaching) ignores or demeans informal learning rather than builds on it.

We want to suggest that, just as breathing can be improved (e.g. for singing, swimming or boxing), so informal learning can too, with the help of formalised learning, be made more effective. This would seem to be the main purpose of the teacher of adults – to *enhance* the student participants' natural learning and to harness it to purposeful ends. And just as enhancing breathing means making the person for a time more conscious of their own breathing (a thing which we do unconsciously for the most part), so one of the tasks of the teacher is to help the learners to be more conscious of their own (often unconscious) learning, to help them to bring general principles to bear on specific tasks and/or to draw generalisations from the specific.

Building on informal learning

There are a number of ways in which the teacher can build on the informal learning of their student learners. They can:

- Help the participants to revise their attitudes towards the subject matter and their self-perception (see pp. 79–80). It is important to encourage the participants to build up their confidence in relation to the learning. Adults will tackle almost any new learning if their gaze is focused on a specific *task* they wish to perform; but as soon as the consciousness changes to focus on *learning*, a new set of confidences is brought into play, a new identity of being 'a student' is created. And without confidence in the ability to learn, there will be no learning.

- Help the student learners not only to identify and use their existing learning techniques but also to build these up and enhance them, to make them more efficient, becoming conscious of their own learning.
- Help the participants to move from a concern with the particular to explore the whole field rather than just one part of it. This will mean structuring the field for study in a way which informal learning does not.
- Help the participants to explore their own experience more fully and more systematically; and at the same time to increase the range of experience available to the participants, especially knowledge from different contexts. Some of this will be theoretical knowledge. It will mean encouraging the participants to learn in some areas of which they have no real experience except at second hand.
- Help the participants to draw general conclusions from their specific learning, to decontextualise it so as to make it usable in other contexts. This will mean starting with specific issues but then assisting the learner to move from the concrete to the more general, to draw out the principles underlying the particular instances, in order to make the learning more permanent, more available for later use, rather than being simply a one-off incident of learning. Unless they come to perceive the learned material from a decontextualised viewpoint, the learners will only be able to apply the learning to that specific instance.
- Urge that the process should not stop once the immediate task is completed but lead on to further purposeful learning.

Building on the learning episode

The characteristics of the natural 'learning episodes' listed above suggest some of the detailed ways in which these objectives can be met (see Figure 6.4):

- *Breaking learning tasks down.* If learning is episodic and not continuous, we should perhaps rely on short bursts of learning activity. Material is more easily mastered if it is broken down into manageable units, provided that each such unit is linked to other items of learning, not left to stand on its own.
- *Who determines relevance?* If the natural learning process is focused on concrete and immediate issues, the material of our programmes needs to be felt to be relevant to the present concerns of the student participants. The best way to determine the relevance of the

Characteristic	Implications
1 Episodic, not continuous	• Rely on short bursts of learning activity. • Break material into manageable units; but hook each one on to other items of learning.
2 Problem-centred, not curriculum oriented; immediate goals based on needs and intentions; concrete situation; immediate, not future application; short term	• Make relevant to students' needs for motivation. • Be aware of students' intentions. • Students to set goals. • Start where they are, not necessarily at the beginning. • Do activity now, not prepare for it in the future.
3 Informal learning:	• Be aware of different learning styles; build up conscious learning skills.
• analogical thinking; use of existing knowledge and experience • trial and error	• Relate new material to existing experience and knowledge. • Be sensitive to range and use of experience. • Discovery learning; students to be active, not passive recipients. • Need for reinforcement; build in feedback. • Need for practice.
• meaningful wholes	• Move from simplified wholes to more complex wholes. • Help students to build up units to create whole; select out essential units from non-essential.
• less memory; but imitation	• Rely on understanding for retention, not memory. • Use of demonstration.
4 Lack of interest in general principles	• Move from concrete to general, not from general to concrete; encourage questioning of general principles; build up relationships.
• stops when need is met	• Encourage further learning.

Figure 6.4 The learning episode and the implications for the teacher of adults

learning programme is to encourage the participants to determine much of the programme. Their learning intentions will help them to set goals, and their experience and issues should play a large part in shaping the learning activities.

• *Start where they are.* If their natural learning is focused on a specific issue (concrete experience), it will be necessary to start not with the logical introductory material appropriate to the academic study of any subject but with the area of greatest concern to the student participants. To start as it were in the middle of the manual or textbook and to move from there both backwards and forwards, rather than starting at Chapter 1 and moving inexorably to the last page, may be more appropriate to many adult learners.

- *To learn by doing.* If learning is more naturally done actively than by passively receiving other people's wisdom, then it will be useful to engage directly with the activity under discussion rather than try to learn about it first and to practise it subsequently. Learning by doing the task at once rather than preparing for doing it theoretically would seem to be more effective. One learns cake-making best by making cakes, not reading recipe books or watching demonstrations; one learns history best by creating one's own historical narrative rather than by listening to or reading other people's history; adults learn literacy, numeracy and basic skills best by engaging in real literacy and numeracy tasks using real materials rather than the artificial exercises of the textbooks.

- *A wide range of methods.* Since all the student participants are well experienced in undertaking (informal) learning tasks, and since they have each developed their own learning strategies, it follows that the teacher needs to use a wide range of teaching–learning methodologies. We can help the participants to become conscious of their preferred learning styles and devise activities that encourage them to use and develop these further. It is not of course always practicable to explore with every member of the learning group their own way of working. It is certainly not possible to devise a common learning programme that will incorporate all the different learning styles into one *omnium gatherum*. A range of activities needs to be developed which the student participants can try for themselves, using their own strategies to maximum advantage. The imposition of the teacher's particular learning style on all the student learners will often slow them down.

- *Learning to learn more effectively.* The reaction of each student learner will vary. Some will wish to strengthen those learning styles with which they feel less comfortable, which they feel are weaker. Some 'activists' may thus wish to develop their skills of critical reflection or abstract conceptualisation, for example. But others will seek to use their strongest style to maximise their learning. It is never safe to rely upon any one approach in adult education. But in building on preferred learning styles, attention needs to be given to the skills of learning as well as to the subject in hand – learning *how to learn* about history and cake-making and management as much as learning the subjects themselves.

- *Participating in planning*. If the participants are accustomed to organising, planning, implementing and evaluating their own learning episodes, then the teacher should not seek to do everything for them. Adult participants can be involved in every stage of planning, implementing and evaluating the teaching–learning process.
- *Using the participants' experience*. If adults tend to use analogical thinking as a strategy for learning, this suggests that the teacher needs to encourage the participants to relate the new material to their experience, to assist them to bring that experience into play and to make it available to the group as a whole. Students who discuss their own experience in class are rarely being irrelevant; they are almost always working on the new material, exploring it in relation to their existing knowledge.
- *Encouraging discovery methodologies*. If informal learning employs trial and error, the exploration of alternatives needs to be encouraged by participatory and discovery learning methods (see p. 253). The learners should be active, not passive recipients of instructions and information. Practice and reinforcement will form part of the learning programme. Constant feedback can be built into the programme so that both teacher and student learners are able to assess progress regularly. This takes time: adults need time for learning.
- *Using less memorisation and more meaningful wholes*. The decline in memory which many adults face as they grow older suggests that the teacher should rely more on understanding and the creation of meaningful wholes for retention, not memorising. Rote learning on its own is an inappropriate strategy for adults. The learners can be helped to create such wholes for themselves. Together teacher and learners will select out essential from non-essential material.
- *Using demonstration*. Since imitation is as important for adults as for younger learners, demonstration forms an essential part of helping adults to learn. Except in special circumstances (e.g. as a deliberate technique of learning), it is not wise to ask the participants to perform a task without the teacher having first worked through an example with the group.
- *From concrete to abstract rather than from theory to practice*. The lack of interest in general principles which appears in many learning episodes indicates that the teacher of adults may need to start with concrete issues and move to more general matters instead of

the academic process of stating theory first and illustrating this with practical examples. Starting with the relevant immediate concerns of the learners may not always mean starting with the simple and moving to the complex; rather it will mean moving from the particular to the general. The drawing of general conclusions from particular instances/case studies would seem to be a more natural form of adult learning. With many adults, theory tends to *arise from* experience rather than theory *leading to* practice.

- *Promoting continuance of learning.* If adults learn constantly throughout life, the participants need to be encouraged to link the teacher-led learning experience with further learning when the course finishes. Any dependency that the participants may develop, by which they come to feel that the learning process must come to an end when the class or group ceases, ought to be avoided. We should be seeking to encourage them to learn without our help, to make ourselves redundant as teachers. The teacher's main aim is to help the participants to use their natural learning processes to become more effective independent learners.

Is adult teaching different?

If adults and children both use informal learning and formalised learning, does this mean that the teaching of adults is no different from the teaching of children?

One answer lies in the accumulations of differences we have seen above as distinguishing adult learning from children's learning. Or we can remind ourselves that the accumulated experience of the adult learners is likely to be much greater and very different from that of children. Or that their purposes of learning will be more highly tuned and insistent than the purposes of younger persons. Or we can re-emphasise that adults are able to hold the specific contextualised task in balance with the more generalised knowledge and that this will influence the teaching–learning process. Or we may draw attention to the fact that the preferred learning styles of adults are likely to be much more strongly fixed than those of children. In these cases, the teacher of adults is likely to meet a much wider range of capacities and motivations among the learning group, and stronger participant determination of *how* they will learn.

Power

This leads to what seems to us to be the key determinant of the difference between teaching children and teaching adults, the different power relationships within the teaching–learning situation.

These different power relationships spring from the different self-identity of child and adult. In the Western constructions of childhood, as we have seen, children usually see themselves as incomplete, not yet arrived, dependent, in transition towards a better (normally more autonomous) life. Much of their conscious formalised learning is compulsory and tentative (forward-looking). The teaching of children allows for these perceptions. The perceptions of adults, however, are different. Much adult learning is voluntary. Adults therefore are often more able to exercise greater power over their learning than children are. Adults too are often able to put into immediate practice what they are learning rather than wait for some time before it can be implemented. Above all, they are able to challenge the sources of new knowledge more directly and openly than children do, for they bring to the learning encounter their own sense of adulthood. The hierarchical relationships which are implicit and sometimes explicit within the cultural construct of childhood have to a large extent been replaced in adulthood with more horizontal relationships between the learner and the source of learning.

Again we must not overpress this. For, on the one hand, there are areas where children too can exercise some power over their own learning, where they engage in voluntary learning. There are areas where children challenge authority, especially today when different learning methodologies and more self-directed exploratory processes are being encouraged among children (e.g. using new technologies). There are areas where children are able to put into practice immediately what they have learned.

On the other hand, some adult learning is not voluntary. Further, there are areas of adult learning where the adult agrees to accept a hierarchical relationship in order to achieve their learning goal. For if some adults put themselves into the position of being consciously a 'learner', many adults today will construct that role as denying adulthood: as Wiltshire suggested, 'they will adopt the role of student and submit to a planned process of tuition' (see p. 53). Many who come to our programmes set aside their informal learning (of which in any case they may be largely unconscious or they do not regard it as 'learning', since they see 'learning' as something which is done under tuition) and expect to experience formalised learning, which can make it difficult for us as teachers to make their unconscious learning more conscious. For there will be a clash between their self-image as adult and their self-image as student learner.

Nevertheless, there is a specific dynamic about teaching adults which is often revealed by a sense of greater equality between teacher and student learner, a greater measure of student learner control which is inherent in Western concepts of being adult. Teaching adults has been described as 'learning on equal terms'; the students have much to teach the teacher as well as the reverse. Unless the adult student participant is valued *as an adult*, formalised learning will deny both the agency of the learners and the informal learning they engage in. It is the self-image of the learner, especially the concept of adulthood, which is the unique feature of the adult learning equation, even though this sense of 'adulthood' will vary from person to person. Any teaching which denies to the student learners real power in the classroom denies their adulthood.

Further reading

Brookfield, S.D. (1986) *Understanding and Facilitating Adult Learning.* Milton Keynes: Open University Press.

Brookfield, S.D. (2000) Adult cognition as a dimension of lifelong learning, in J. Field and M. Leicester (eds) *Lifelong Learning: Education Across the Lifespan.* London: Taylor & Francis.

Daines, J., Daines, C. and Graham, B. (1993) *Adult Learning, Adult Teaching*, 3rd edn. Nottingham: Department of Adult Education, University of Nottingham.

Imel, S. (1998) *Teaching Critical Reflection: Trends and Issues Alert.* Columbus, OH: ERIC.

Petty, G. (2008) http://www.geoffpetty.com/activelearning.html

Rogers, A. (1997) Learning: can we change the discourse?, *Adults Learning*, 8(5): 116–17.

Schön, D.A. (1983) *The Reflective Practitioner: How Professionals Think in Action.* New York: Basic Books.

Pause for Thought

We have seen that teaching adults in any sphere is a process of providing an opportunity for others (singly or in groups) to engage for themselves in a more or less intensive bout of individual learning, and of encouraging them to bring about in themselves changes in knowledge, understanding, skills and attitudes – changes that can be reflected in changed behaviour. Such learning depends on the intentions of the learners, and on the range of knowledge and experience they already possess and which they bring with them to the learning task, as much as or even more than on their learning abilities. In coming to us, they bring a range of expectations about the learning task which are in large part created by us as we inform them about the learning programme and its goals.

We have seen that there are many different theories about learning. Most of them suggest that the individual is engaged in learning through a process of active interrelation with experience, new knowledge or their social or total environment. All these theories have something to teach us about what we are doing, they each contribute to the list of factors that will make for the effective teaching of adults. But none of them commands general acceptance.

Rather than suggest that any one of these groups of learning theories is 'right' and the others are 'wrong', we have directed attention to two things:

- The 'natural learning episode': those incidents in which adults throughout their lives engage in intentional, purposeful and structured learning, using their own preferred learning approaches in order to achieve a particular goal or solve a specific problem.
- The distinction between on the one hand 'acquisition or informal learning', that natural process which (like breathing) we engage in without thinking about it, where the primary consciousness is centred on a specific task rather than on learning, and on the other hand 'formalised learning', where we are more conscious of learning. We have referred to these as 'task-conscious learning' and 'learning-conscious learning'. Both forms of learning are used in the learning episode as each learner thinks fit. But when adults come to our learning programmes, they construct their identity as 'students', and thus they to a very large extent lay

aside their informal learning processes and instead adopt an approach based on 'formalised learning'. Again such constructs will vary from learner to learner, dependent on their experience and expectations.

We have suggested that these two features remind those of us who teach adults that our student participants are already experienced learners. We all need to study these natural learning processes, for they help us to understand more clearly how to structure the learning opportunities we create for adults. We have also suggested that our purpose as teachers of adults is to build upon this informal learning, but at the same time to go beyond it – to help the learners to make its results more permanent; to help them to draw out general principles so as to widen application; to strengthen the processes to lead on to further purposeful learning; to encourage them, in short, to become more conscious of, freer and more efficient in, their own learning. We can use the characteristics of these learning episodes as a basis for creating adult learning episodes for our student participants which will fulfil these aims. And this means increasing the use of informal learning in our planned learning programmes for adults rather than relying solely on formalised learning. This will be the theme of the rest of the book.

Chapter 7

Aims, Goals and Objectives
What is it all for . . . ?

This chapter discusses the process by which learning goals are set and
made more conscious, and suggests that widening the goals may lead
to more critical learning. Teaching adults involves planning a learning
programme. We have suggested that within this process, we should
build on the informal learning processes which all our student participants are using regularly in the course of their daily lives. Their purposes
are directed towards self-chosen lifeworld tasks. The purposes that lie
behind the planned learning programmes for adults are directed
towards learning. Adult student participants have life-related goals;
teachers of adults have learning-related goals. The key issue is to bring
these two sets of goals closer together.

Aims, goals and objectives in adult learning programmes

A good deal of obscurity is often thought to surround the subject of goals
and objectives in education. The matter is however relatively straightforward. Goals[1] are what we want to achieve in and through the planned
learning programme, its purpose, the reason why we engage in it at all.

Every teacher has goals. If we envisage education as the process of
building purposeful learning opportunities, then the goals are those
purposes that the learning is intended to bring about, the learning
changes that will result from the activity. Both teachers and programme
planners set out to construct situations in which the student participants
undertake certain activities in order to accomplish something: gaining
new knowledge, mastering a skill, coming to understand something,
behaving in a new way to meet new demands, changing or firming up
attitudes, growing in confidence and maturity. The goals are the *intended
outcomes* of the teaching–learning activities, whatever these might be.

---

1   Please note that the word 'goal' is used here in two main senses: in a general
    sense of 'purpose', it covers all the three main types of goals, aims, goals and
    objectives; and it is also used in a specific sense of (intermediate) goal. We
    believe the sense is clear in each case it is used.

More and more adult learning programmes today are being focused on 'learning outcomes'. Those called upon to develop learning programmes are being required to formulate and set forth such learning outcomes. Three main sets of learning outcomes have been identified by some agencies such as the OECD: 'academic achievement and cognitive skills; personal development (e.g. democratic values); and work-related skills and attitudes'. Such generic learning outcomes are then being broken down further into 'competencies', some of which have been identified as 'key competencies' (e.g. Rychen and Salganik 2001: 17) which can be assessed. There are then different levels of learning outcome.

The problem with expressing the goals of any adult learning programme in terms of 'learning outcomes' is that the purposes behind such outcomes are often not stated. The main aim of the sets of learning outcomes noted above are to encourage greater participation in the democratic processes of the country concerned or to help the learner to contribute more to the economy of the country. Such aims may or may not coincide with the aims that the learners have.

This approach omits much which would characterise many forms of adult learning programme. The concentration here is on the learner seen as citizen and worker; the aim of adult education to lead to social transformation, for example, is ignored or marginalised. And there is little room here for the learners to take the learning programme and use it to achieve their own goals.

It is very important for us to appreciate that the goals of the various stakeholders in any adult learning programme will almost certainly be different. The providers of the course (for instance, the college or other institution providing the programme) will often have different goals from those of the teachers of adults who again may well have different goals from those (multiple and often changing goals) of the student learners. You may care to consider in your own case what you feel at this stage are the goals of the providers of your course, what are your own goals and what may be some of the goals of those who come to your course.

Activity 7.1

In Chapters 5 and 6 we asked you to think about your own learning. Now go back to your teaching case study and consider:

- What are the main goals of the provider or institution of your course?
- What are your own goals? and
- What may be some of the goals of the participants on your course?

Should we have goals in adult education?

Some people, especially some of those engaged in forms of community education, would argue that such a model of education is too directive, that we should not set goals for the learners, that we should seek only to fulfil the varied goals the student participants set for themselves, or that we should provide an open-ended learning experience so that the student participants can each achieve what they want in the programme without undue interference from the teacher. They argue that the real benefits of education lies in the process rather than the product, that pre-set prescriptive goals can lead to a simplistic, mechanical and linear concept of progress. There is a good deal of truth in this. It provides a useful reminder of a number of points:

- Because a (usually implicit) contract to learn is involved in the process of teaching adults, the student participants have come to the programme bringing with them their own intentions, *their desired outcomes*. These goals may lie outside the learning programme (e.g. 'to get a job'), and the student learner may not know what kind of more immediate learning outcomes will help them to achieve their goal. These intentions and desires may well become clarified and indeed change as the learning programme proceeds. The changing objectives of the learners are a real force in the dynamic interaction of adult learning.
- These participant intentions will *vary widely* from each other. Each of the student participants will take from the learning situation what they want. It is a salutary lesson for the teacher of adults, especially those of us who have a message to give, that our carefully planned objectives may be set on one side by our students and that they may well go off with some other outcome than the one we have to 'sell'.
- Because the learning situation consists of a dynamic relationship and because at least four parties are involved in this encounter – teacher, learner, subject matter and context – the *real outcomes* of the process may well be different from both the teacher's planned and the students' desired outcomes. The teacher and the student participants should be aware of the possibility of unexpected outcomes, the unplanned results of the teaching–learning process.
- Sometimes the results of the learning activity are *long delayed* and do not appear during or immediately at the end of the class or course.
- Nevertheless, the fact that the goals of the learners may be different from those of the teacher and agent, and that the real outcomes

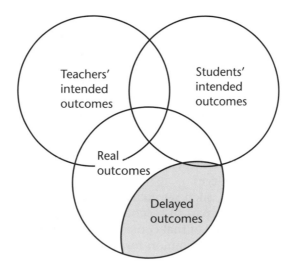

Figure 7.1

(both immediate and long-term) may be different from both of these (Figure 7.1) does not mean that the teacher should not set goals at all. Indeed, in planning any programme of learning, we cannot avoid having goals. Goal setting is an inevitable part of the process of planning learning opportunities for adults. They may be open-ended goals, very general in nature (personal growth, for instance, or 'providing an opportunity for the participants to reassess their own priorities in life'); or they may be more limited goals (to learn a set of keep fit exercises, say, or to gain an English degree). But they will exist all the same.

The student participants will normally be recruited into the learning programme on the basis of goals set by the teacher. For example:

Wildlife and Habitat Conservation

What are the threats to wildlife in the UK and what steps can be taken to conserve it?

The intended outcome of this adult learning programme is relatively clear. At the end of the course, the participants should be able to identify ways in which wildlife habitats can be conserved. What each participant will do with such learning outcomes will vary: some will wish to become activists in conservation, others just to understand more. Those who desire to attain such goals will join this programme of learning (although others, less specifically motivated, may also join).

Despite this selection process on the basis of the goals set by the teacher, there will usually be occasions when the participants – because they are adults, each with their own range of experience and their own agenda – challenge the teacher-set goals. In this lies part of the dynamism of the interaction between teacher and taught, so unlike the work done in most schools and colleges.

Even when accepted, such set goals leave room for a wide range of different options on the part of teacher and student alike. To take the example above, by the end of that course, the participants may be able to identify some of the most common forms of wildlife in these areas but may be in ignorance of others; or they may have begun to learn the processes of identification so that they can continue to explore and improve their skills when the course is over or during their own field-trips; or they may each have become expert in one particular field (orchids, say, or grasses), the rest being irrelevant to their concerns. These are matters that require a process of negotiation between the teacher and each of the student participants.

Defining the goals

Too often, as we saw in Chapter 2, the goals are left undefined. It is assumed that the potential student participants will understand what is implied when they read the learning programme blurb or course outline. But an adult class labelled 'Dressmaking' with no further indication of what is intended to be achieved will recruit students with a wide range of expectations. Even when the programme of learning has been negotiated with the student participants, the goals frequently remain vague. But since goals play such a large part in the learning process and since they are one of the keys to learner motivation, it is important that they are not left unstated, assumed or uncertain.

- The more clearly goals are defined, the more effective the recruitment is. Those who join the learning programme on the basis of clearly defined goals are more willing to engage in the learning activities and contribute fully to the work of the group.
- The more clearly goals are defined, the greater the learning that takes place. The student participant needs clear guidance as to the direction in which the learning programme is heading. If the

goals are left vague, the learner is uncertain what learning changes are intended.

- The more clearly goals are defined, the better the teacher can choose appropriate teaching–learning strategies, materials and methods. If the goals are left vague, the teacher too tends to flounder.
- The more clearly goals are defined, the easier it will be for the student participants and the teacher to evaluate progress, to assess how much and what kind of learning is going on. If the goals are left vague, neither party is sure if they are achieving anything or not.

Some people have suggested that all such learning goals should be SMART – that is specific, measurable, achievable, realistic and time-bound. But that can become too mechanical. It is precisely here that the issue we raised earlier (see pp. 134–5) on learning objectives being seen as 'clearing up messes' will be most important. In teaching adults, goals – while being clearly set out – must never become rigid, inflexible, pre-scriptive, controlling the situation. In association with the student learners, the teacher will need to try to determine just how the partici-pants are structuring the situation which has caused them to enter the adult educational programme, what sort of 'mess' they see and what kind of answer they will be seeking. Objectives may thus vary from one student learner to another – which does not make for an easy life for the adult teacher. It is easier if we can help them to come to a clear-cut commonly agreed learning objective, although that may not always be possible.

Levels of goals

We have already noted that there are different kinds of goals, different levels at which they may be identified. Some people have tried to describe these distinctions using different terms – *aims* being general, overall purposes, usually ultimate in nature; *goals* being the main purpose of the activity; and *objectives* being nearer still, those targets which, once achieved, contribute to the goals. Although this is seen by some as perhaps an unnecessary sophistication, arguing that the words are often used more interchangeably nevertheless the distinction has some value. For while we may specify clearly our goals at one level, we often leave the other levels unstated. Thus much of our work is based on unexplored goals that we have accepted for ourselves and we assume the student learners have also accepted merely because they are present in our classes and groups.

A useful way of describing these different levels is to use the analogy of a football match. The overall **aim** is to climb up the league and to win the championship at the end of the season. To achieve this aim, the **goal** is for the team to score more goals in this match than their opponents. To achieve this goal, the **objectives** would be to pass the ball to one of their own side. Each objective builds up until a goal is achieved. The multiple goals will (they hope) lead to the aim being fulfilled.

We need to examine each level of goals in more detail.

Overall goals (aims or ends)

Overall goals (aims) are those longer-term goals that inform as a whole the programme within which we teach. This is the purpose of the lower level 'learning outcomes'. They consist of those ideals (e.g. a more just and inclusive society, a richer quality of life, reduced poverty, greater professional efficiency, a more skilled or healthier workforce in a more competitive economy) to be aimed at, even if never fully realised, and which may be used to test our work by. In many cases, these are established by the organisation (if any) providing the programme or the setting in which it is placed – the local authority adult education agency, voluntary organisation or church, professional body, firm, development organisation, community association, university or training institution, for instance – and the public image it presents.

Thus behind every learning situation contrived by the teacher-agent is a set of assumptions about the nature of personality and society. We are vaguely conscious of the range of desired changes we would wish to help bring about in order to make our lives in particular and the world in general better. This is our value system which informs much of what we do, the purpose for which most of us engage in teaching adults at all. A teacher of gardening, for instance, can hardly teach the subject without a belief that gardens are a 'good thing' and that gardening practice and appreciation need to be improved and become more widely distributed throughout society. The same is true of most of the subjects we teach; we 'believe' in them in some sense or other and wish to promote them.

These aims are very rarely made explicit. They are assumptions that we imagine others (especially our students) share. But such assumptions may be challenged by adult student participants at any stage in the learning process, because their assumptions may be different from our own. We may believe that training for health and safety at work or a knowledge of certain religious writings is in itself a desirable thing, and assume that our students share these judgements. But we may be wrong. Sometimes the challenge is open: 'Why do we have to do these tasks, learn all this stuff?' Or it may be more polite, a withdrawal with the comment: 'I couldn't see the point of it all.'

Specific goals

What we have called 'specific goals' are the shorter-term goals we set, sometimes fully consciously, for our courses. Teachers have, in most forms of teaching adults at least, a fairly clear idea of the kind of changes in skills, knowledge, understanding and attitudes they may wish to encourage the student participants to bring about for themselves. Thus they may plan to offer the student participants the opportunity to become something they are not yet: a geologist or an electrician for example, or a more assertive person, a more effective teacher, a more efficient and happier worker, a more literate individual, a more critically reflective professional. The more clearly these specific goals are seen and the more closely they match the agenda of the student learners, the more effective will be the learning process. When the learners' intentions and those of the teacher are far apart is when a learning group is most ineffective.

This is the area where the tension that we have seen to exist within all education – between learning as discipline and learning as growth into freedom – is felt most keenly. Setting the goals out clearly will on occasion cause us a good deal of concern about being too directive in relation to our student participants. It is also in this area that the assumptions we ourselves make about the nature of knowledge and reality and the role of the teacher express themselves most fully. Making clear and precise our goals at this level will not only help us to construct a more effective learning experience for our students. It will also enable us as teachers to see how we work and what assumptions we make, and thus to test the validity of these assumptions for ourselves; and it will enable us more easily to renegotiate these goals with the student participants. Discussing goals is part of the process of making learning more conscious.

Immediate goals (objectives)

In order to achieve our specific goals, it is necessary to break down the task in hand into manageable units. Here lie the 'learning outcomes' in

terms of new knowledge, advanced skills, changed attitudes and values
– to learn how to handle wood, how to relax, to read old documents, to
use new machinery, to write notes, to read and discuss, to master new
concepts or to decide between various viewpoints – in short, to do all
the multitude of things that go to make up the learning activity. These
objectives lie within each teaching session or each learning exercise. For
the learning to be effective, it is necessary for the student participants
not only to see the desired learning change clearly but also to see the
relevance of the present task to the specific goal, the value of each learning outcome.

A hierarchy of goals

Setting goals is a more complicated exercise than this threefold division
might suggest. For it is important to remember that there are various
levels of goals that come between each of these three main tiers (aims,
goals and objectives). Nevertheless, the distinction between overall,
specific and immediate goals may be helpful as we plan our programme
of adult learning.

There is a relationship between these three levels. The 'lower levels'
are usually based on the assumptions and contribute towards the
attainment of the higher levels. On occasion, however, one level may
contradict the assumptions held at other levels. It is possible for teachers
of adults to engage in some forms of teaching because they believe
(overall goal) that the participants should be encouraged to become more
confident and self-reliant, and yet the immediate goals they set in each
teaching session deny the learners the opportunity for self-expression
and independence of thought and action.

One of the problems of taking any particular example is that there will
always be those teachers who say that such an example is a special case,
that the exercise doesn't work for their subject (e.g. music appreciation,
degree programmes, industrial training, adult literacy or flower arranging). But it is possible to ask three simple questions about any piece of
teaching you may be thinking of undertaking:

- *What* is the purpose of this piece of teaching? What are the learning outcomes? (*specific goal*)
- *Why* do I want such outcomes? (*overall goal*)
- *How* best can I help the students to achieve such outcomes?
  (*immediate goal*)

Activity 7.2 (see p. 159)

Most teachers of adults start setting their goals with the specific goals. An exercise based on your case study may help you to see this more clearly. Across the **middle** of Figure 7.2a put down in one sentence what you see as the specific goal of the course. It may well take the form of completing the sentence

'The purpose of the programme is/was to . . .'

Once you have done this, draw a short arrow upwards and try to answer the question 'Why?' Then ask 'Why?' again, and then again, if possible, until you reach into the area of your overall goals (to make people happy, to build a more just and equal society, to help people become effective workers, etc.) when the question 'Why?' no longer seems relevant and the answer is self-evident.

Then below the central statement, the specific goal, draw a short arrow downwards and try to answer the question 'How?' This too can be done several times until you have reached the smaller elements (immediate goals) of the learning activity.

It may be helpful to give you an example drawn from experience of one of us (Figure 7.2b).

We can note from our case study activity two general points about objectives. First, there is no single 'right' answer to any of the questions. Each of us might give a different response. For instance, in reply to the question, 'Why do I want the student participants to learn about local history?', some teachers will answer, 'Because the students have expressed a desire to learn about the history of their local community, and I see my role as helping them to do what they want to do, nothing more'. This is for them enough justification; whereas (as Figure 7.2b shows) the tutor in this case sees a social purpose in the task as well.

Secondly, most of the 'How?' questions lend themselves to a 'doing' response. This may be expressed as the teacher doing something (lecturing, talking, presenting, etc.) or as the student learners doing something (reading, practising, discussing, writing, visiting, asking, etc.). It is worth repeating that adult learning is most effective when the student participants are active, not passive, when they are doing the various activities that will lead to the attainment of the goals.

Overall goal

Overall goal	Why?
	Why?
	Why?
Specific goal	What?
	How?
	How?
	How?
Immediate goal(s)	How?

Figure 7.2a

Because I believe that strong local communities will benefit all their members

↑

Why?

To help build up stronger local communities as support groups for all of their members

↑

Why?

To help build up groups of people who are interested in and concerned for the amenities of their local communities

↑

Why?

The aim of this course is to help people to understand and (if they so wish) to practise the tasks of the local historian

How?

↓   ↓   ↓

By asking intelligent questions about the past of their own community	By coming to know about the range of source material available and searching for it	By developing the skills of analysis and interpretation of the sources and of writing up the results of their studies
How? ↓	How? ↓	How? ↓
By reading about the background to their history	By visiting record offices, libraries and museums	By discussing examples of local records in class
By reading other local histories	By visiting surviving monuments	By trying to read old handwriting under supervision (practice, exercises)
By looking around them and questioning what they see	By looking at other local histories to see the sources they have used	By practising writing up small parts of the work under supervision
By asking questions about the local community today	etc.	etc.

Figure 7.2b

Setting the goals

Lying behind every adult class and every adult course, in every context, is a set of objectives, an understanding of which can be arrived at by asking ourselves as teacher-planners *what* we are trying to do, *why* we want to do it, and *how* we plan to go about it. Two questions arise in relation to these goals:

- how does the teacher set them; and
- how do they relate to the students' goals?

But this implies a prior question: whether the provider or the teacher has the 'right' to set the goals. For it can be argued that goals and purposes of this kind can be seen as an act of manipulation, of aggression against the minds and personalities of our students.

By what right?

The main basis for the agent-teacher setting the goals is normally that our student learners have chosen us to provide them with help in learning. That is the way it operates in informal learning and as we have seen (pp. 79–80), most forms of lifelong learning for adults are voluntary – the participants have chosen to join our programmes. Constructing themselves as 'students', they have put themselves 'under' our instruction.

The basis for this decision is our perceived expertise. We are teachers precisely because we have some form of expertise. It may be a *direct* expertise; we may be a qualified joiner, cook, archaeologist or engineer. Or it may be an *oblique* expertise; we may have experience of groups, tools or methods of study without being an expert in all aspects of the subject under discussion. But whether direct or oblique, a recognition of expertise is essential if we are to acquire that measure of respect needed for the voluntary learner participants to accord us the role of teacher or group leader, to accept our creation of the learning opportunity, our guidance, our conduct of the class, our goals.

There will be those who object to such a statement, to the teacher adopting such a role. They may assert that our task as 'teacher' is to lay our experience and expertise at the disposal of the group of adults who may wish to learn with us, reminding us that we are a resource for the student participants. This is true, but such a role is common to *all* members of the learning group. In adult learning programmes, each person brings their experience and knowledge and shares these with all the others. The role of the agent and teacher, however, goes further than this. We are not just a member of the group like all the others. We have been given the role of director of the programme of work; we set out and generally oversee the activities (the *immediate* goals) through which the participants can move towards the more (*specific*) goal, and to do this we have to determine the nature of this specific goal, the purpose of the programme of learning, first. Even in courses leading to qualifications, where learning outcomes and assessment criteria are specified, the teacher will still have to set the goals for each session; the student learners as well as the agency expect this of the teacher.

How do we set the goals?

As teachers, we set out not only the 'specific' goals for the course, the purpose of the activity, but also the 'immediate' goals, the programme (schedule of learning) for the participants to follow. There are many different paths to tread, and from our experience and expertise we select those that seem most useful if the participants are to learn what they have indicated they want to learn.

The choice of these paths is revealed by the various answers we have given to the question 'How?' in the exercise above (Figure 7.2); and they may be set out in some form for the participants to see – in a *syllabus* or programme incorporating the ground to be covered and the methods to be employed. It is not an unchanging syllabus, a permanent programme of immediate goals, to be ticked off automatically in sequence. For as the intentions of the student participants become clearer or change during the learning process, so the programme will change. As the field is explored, as the subject is learned, as the varied experience of the student participants is harnessed to the learning task, so the range of enquiries and the activities to be pursued will develop. As time passes, so the world (even of dressmaking or keep fit) will change.

The immediate goals are expressed in the 'methods/content' part of the learning situation. Adult education is as much a process as a system or a set of structures. So the teacher (in negotiation with the student participants wherever possible) has to decide what the student learners need to *do* in order to achieve the specific goal. Do they need to watch? To practise? To listen? To read? To write? What *they* need to do will determine both the methods and the content of the programme of learning. If, for example, the goal is the performance of a skill – to learn how to use a set of tools, for instance – then the class participants need to watch a demonstration, to handle, practise and in the end use the tools meaningfully. If the goal is to understand, then they need to grapple with the various concepts that form part of the subject matter, play with them, rearrange and use them in writing and/or discussion. If the goal is the production of a community magazine, then they need to debate (the contents), to explore, to collect or create material, to write and draw, to discover information, to select. If the goal is to pass an examination, then they need to understand, to memorise, to practise writing under restricted conditions. The construction of the sequence of immediate objectives is part of the role of the teacher. It is our job to devise, modify and reconstruct the series of steps (the learning schedule) by which new skills, knowledge and understanding are acquired and developed. This is as true of literature and music, of computers and labour studies, of health and craft training, of bridge, fencing and flower arranging as it is of advanced engineering and accountancy updating courses.

Types of objective

This emphasis on activities, on 'doing', as part of the adult learning process, leads us to ask whether all goals and objectives can be expressed in behavioural terms or whether there are other kinds of objective. Bloom's (1956, 1964) taxonomy of learning objectives distinguished between cognitive (information and knowledge), affective (attitudes, values, feelings and emotions) and psycho-motor (physical and mental skills) objectives. Eisner (1985) suggested two types of learning objective: behavioural and expressive.

Behavioural objectives are the changes in behaviour arising from the learning which can be precisely stated and assessed: an ability to swim or to draw or to write a report. They are used particularly in learning skills (e.g. technical training) and are of especial value in helping the teacher and learners to assess the course arrangements and design and in measuring progress – the effectiveness of the curriculum in achieving these objectives. Indeed, some writers, influenced by Mager (1991), have claimed that all teaching–learning can be expressed in terms of *competencies*, so that the learning can be precisely evaluated. But this is hotly disputed by other educationalists.

Many behavioural objectives have been pre-set by the teacher, stating what the student learners are expected to *be able to do* at the end of the course. Brochures continue to proliferate with statements such as 'At the end of this course, you will be able to . . .' and there follows a list of activities which the participants should be able to undertake, the new skills/knowledge/understanding and/or attitudes which will be expressed in action when the programme has ended. But such a normative process is not really adequate. For the aim of any adult learning programme is to affect actual behaviour, not potential behaviour. It is not important what the student learners *can* do at the end of the course; what is important is what they *do* do afterwards. When, in an adult literacy programme, the participants at the end of the class show that they *can* read but after a short time it becomes clear that they are not actually reading, that programme should perhaps be regarded as a failure, not a success. More is therefore needed than just learning outcomes expressed in terms of competency objectives – some mobilisation of the student learners in order to carry out the learning into their daily lives. Some writers have suggested that the term 'behaviour' can refer to feeling, perceiving and thinking, but most people still draw a distinction between behavioural outcomes and affective outcomes.

Eisner's other kind of goals are *expressive objectives*. Whereas behavioural objectives are usually set by the teacher as 'predictive' goals and can be precisely stated, expressive objectives are more unpredictable in their results. The nature of much adult learning (e.g. increased awareness of self and context) cannot be prescribed. Each of the learners seeks to expand on, elaborate and make unique to themselves the skills, knowledge and understanding they acquire through the learning opportunity. They often do not know in which direction they will 'take off', and each of them will 'take off' in this sense in different directions.

Expressive objectives are therefore complex. They relate to attitudes, values, beliefs, aesthetics, appreciation, perspectives and insight. Behavioural objectives can tend to be simple and linear in nature; once the learners can complete one task, they can move to the next. Such objectives can be assessed by a series of increasingly advanced tests. But for adults particularly, many activities are not only unique to the learner concerned, they are unique to the occasions they are engaged in. Reading a text, for example, or sewing a piece of fabric, are not just simple skills. On each occasion the actions engaged in operate on several different levels at once. They may be done hesitantly or confidently; they may be done at an elementary level or at a more advanced level; they will be done for a particular purpose, unique to that occasion; and they may or may not achieve the desired result (Figure 7.3). These dimensions behind each learning activity form the expressive objectives of the adult student participant and accompany all behavioural objectives.

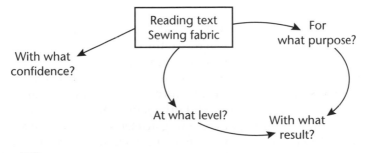

Figure 7.3

The value and limitations of behavioural objectives

This division of objectives into behavioural and expressive corresponds with the distinction that can be drawn between the *public* effects of our teaching (the way the learning will display itself in public) and the *private* effects (those internal changes in understanding, attitudes or skills of learning that contribute towards the overall development of the individual).

Behavioural objectives (the public face of learning) cannot encompass the whole of the learning process. There is much going on behind the behavioural changes, and a good deal of it we can never know. But 'this is not to say that we cannot recognize the existence of such forms of learning through observing alterations in behavior' (Brookfield 1986: 213). Indeed, it can be argued that we cannot see any part of these learning changes *unless* they result in some changed patterns of behaviour. 'Inner' learning will reveal itself through actions or expressed preferences. For example, learning in the appreciation of literature, music or art will reveal itself in a number of different ways, such as a desire to have more contact with the subject – reading different kinds of books, listening to different kinds of music, going to art galleries and exhibitions more frequently. Learning to understand the historical process may express itself in the range of concepts used in discussion and possibly in other activities such as visits to historic places. Learning new attitudes towards other people or coming to understand some scientific process will equally reveal itself in changed practices and behaviour. The explicit aim of most forms of professional development programmes is to change practices – to bring about greater efficiency or cost-effective processes, to use more up-to-date equipment or ways of operating, for example.

Different outcomes

While remembering that such objectives cannot describe all that is going on, it can thus be argued that all inner learning changes can be outwardly expressed in terms of some behavioural changes. Such observable changes will however be different for each individual adult learner and cannot be prescribed. The activities that will reveal the deeper levels of learning will take a wide variety of forms. One person may express their new under-standing of local history and the new attitudes this understanding has brought with it by joining a local history society; another may become an ardent conservationist, while still others may prefer to work on their own, reading more, writing or collecting artefacts, visiting historic sites, etc. All will display in their lives the learning changes that have sprung from the common achieved objectives, the acquiring of more knowledge of and insight into the history of their local community. In music appreciation, the outcome may be not just going to more concerts or buying more records but listening with discrimination, and this will express itself in decisions about the kinds of music preferred and discussed as well as in other ways. 'True, we can only assess [learning changes] by observing people's behaviour, but we cannot specify what this behaviour will be – beyond describing, in abstract terms, the principles to which the behaviour must conform' (Tennant 2006: 102). One of the tasks of the teacher is to try to determine with the student participants some of the many different ways in which the inner (private) learning changes may express themselves in (public) actions – in other words, what the participants wish to do with their new learning. And these desired purposes will become part of the objectives for the course, not as pre-set uniform and unchangeable goals but as some of the multiple expressions of the inner learning changes.

To help the student participants to achieve their own behavioural objectives, they need to be provided with opportunities to engage in these activities under supervision *during* the course. They do not need to wait until the course is over before they begin to practise their new competencies or to express their new learning. The tasks involved need to be seen to be realistic, useful and purposeful, not meaningless exercises. They should not, except in a few circumstances, be activities that will never be tried again outside the class. For example, to develop the ability to write an essay is perhaps a relatively rarely appropriate objective (except of course in examination courses where this is one of the key objectives), for writing essays is not for most people an activity they will engage in in real life; but some people may like to do it; they may wish to contribute to some publication, even perhaps to earn money writing for local newspapers or magazines, and in some activities such as local history, it is an essential part of the overall task. If such a constructed activity is set before the learners, then they need to be able to see how the task contributes to the whole programme of learning, to the general goal. We do not want to pre-set precisely the behavioural objectives of our learning programmes; but it is useful to set a range of behavioural objectives jointly by the participants and the teacher.

Conditions

Learning objectives at all levels can therefore be expressed in terms of accompanying behavioural changes. But not just in simple words of action. We need to set out not only *what* the learners themselves hope to be able to do but also the contextual *conditions* under which the behaviour will need to be practised (how fast or slow, perhaps, or with or without help, and so on) and the *standards*, the level, of the activity – not just that they should be able to do something but as far as they can to do it to

a certain level of competence (Charnley and Jones 1979). Such performance indicators help to establish the criteria for evaluation of the learning achieved (see Chapter 12). Today many such criteria are set out in the
form of targets to be achieved. This is of course relatively easier for those
programmes designed to achieve a particular skill – courses such as crafts,
art or languages; but even in these cases we will need to spell out the
conditions under which we anticipate that the final task will need to be
performed. Academic courses have (often unstated) standards for work
done (within a set time frame, with a particular level of accuracy, covering an understood range of subject matter and avoiding irrelevancies,
without plagiarism, etc.).

The teacher in association with the participants, then, needs to set the
objectives of the programme of learning in terms of *multiple* observable
behavioural changes as well as in terms of the unique inner learning.
Both sets of objectives will be needed. We cannot afford to concentrate
on just the competencies arising from the learning without any concern
for changes in understanding and attitudes, or on the internal personal
changes in appreciation without any concern whether these express
themselves in changed patterns of behaviour or not. Of the two, the
inner learning changes are the more important. It is not a question of
what we as teachers expect the learners to be able to *do* after the course is
over; rather, it is what we and they hope they will *be* and how that will
express itself in action. Our aim is not simply a trained person but someone whose personal understanding and attitudes have been enhanced.
Equally, we want someone who reflects that enhancement in practice in
a way which they find most appropriate. Above all, we want to help them
to continue to learn purposefully after the end of the course. Developing
learning skills further needs to form part of every course for adults.

Activity 7.3

Is it possible to express the goals of your course in terms of:

- expressive objectives (private effects)?
- behavioural learning objectives (public effects), stating the conditions
  under which such achievements should be performed?

How do the teacher's goals relate to the student learners' intentions?

The teacher needs to give attention to the relationship between their
goals and the student participants' goals. Apart from their overall search

for increased adulthood in terms of greater maturity and full development, wider perspectives and increased autonomy (which are all cultural constructs of their own society), adult students come to achieve particular purposes. They bring goals with them, and they usually express these goals in behavioural rather than expressive terms. They are used to setting their own goals in their own learning episodes, although these may not always be expressed very clearly (see pp. 84–8). For some of them, their objectives will be concrete and immediate, for they will be thinking in terms of some learning change that they can recognise and use at once. They will want to be able to do something new or better at the end of the learning programme. But this is not always true, and the teacher will need to explore just what the students have in mind when they come to the course.

Further, they have usually selected themselves for the learning programme according to the expressed goals of the teacher-agent – the specific goals (Figure 7.2a) rather than either the immediate or the overall goals. They will tend to leave the setting of the immediate goals, the various stages of the learning process, to the expertise of the teacher, while the overall goals are, as we have seen, largely unspoken. The student participants have come in order to join in the stated activity of the group, to produce a particular product (a pot or a report), or to learn how to keep fit, how to market a new product or pass an exam.

Activity 7.4

Set out what specific goals you think your student participants will have come to your group for.

A number of caveats must be entered here.

First, there will almost always be a *wide range of student intentions*. And they will not always be very clear, even to the student learners themselves, or clearly expressed. In many adult learning programmes, some student participants will say that they have joined a group in order to achieve the same goals as the teacher-planner has set out, but in reality they are there for some other reason. Student participants come to classes from all sorts of motives and for all sorts of purposes, often unstated. And those which are clearer will often change as the course progresses.

Adult student groups contain a wide spectrum of differing intentions related directly to their individual situation (Figure 7.4a). At one end of the spectrum is the person who has come in out of the cold or whose regular night out is to attend some form (it does not much matter what) of adult class. At the other end is the person who wants to do just one

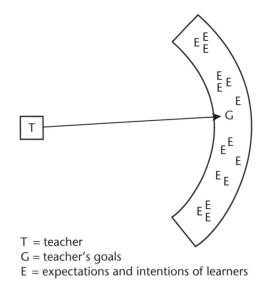

T = teacher
G = teacher's goals
E = expectations and intentions of learners

Figure 7.4a

part of the programme on offer. In a commercial subjects class, for example, we may have at one extreme the attender who seeks companionship and comfort without disturbance, who has no real goals of learning, and at the other extreme the participant who wants to learn how to use a particular word processor program and nothing more.

If the aim of education is to meet such 'needs' alone, the task of the teacher in these circumstances would be impossible. But we have seen that education is not just meeting needs, it is purposeful learning. So the teacher has a purpose, a goal. Those of the learners whose goals are closest to the teacher's goals will learn most quickly, most efficiently and most permanently; those who are further away will have greater difficulty in learning and may even prevent the other participants from learning. We will see later (Chapter 8) how a learning group can help to deal with this situation.

The range of student intentions is not evenly distributed throughout the spectrum; they will tend to come in clusters. Nor will the teacher's goal necessarily be at the centre, it may well be to one side. This can be explored only once the teacher has met with the learning group. If the preponderance of student intentions lies away from the teacher's goal, then it would make for more effective learning if the teacher were able to move his/her goal nearer to those of the majority of the student participants. If in a woodworking class we intended to focus on making bookcases, and the majority of the participants want to make garden

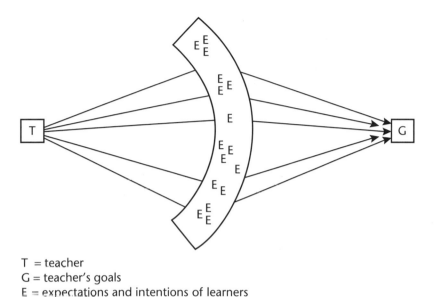

T = teacher
G = teacher's goals
E = expectations and intentions of learners

Figure 7.4b

furniture instead, it would be in the interest of all parties including our own to change our goal rather than expect the learners to change theirs. But this is not always possible.

But we need not change the *specific* goals, for these lie behind the immediate goals. It may be that the purpose of the class is not just to make one type of furniture but for the student participants to learn general approaches to woodworking. In this case, the teacher can accept and go through the widely varying goals of all (or at least most) of the student learners and still direct them to the goal of the course as a whole (Figure 7.4b). It will however be difficult to do this for those at the very edge of the spectrum, who frequently do not want to learn much or who are willing to learn only over a very narrow territory.

Activity 7.5

Write down some of the intentions and hopes of the student participants in your class; try to grade them on a scale of closeness to or distance from your own goal.

A second caveat is that some of the participants may see *a different picture* from the teacher. The table, the level of fitness, the type of writing to be arrived at may all be very different in the minds of the learners and of the teacher. Management development programmes often fall down over different views of management styles and relationships, teacher enhancement programmes over different views of the roles of teachers. It is a valuable exercise for us to spend some time exploring the minds of our student participants to discover their perception of the task in hand.

Nor should we assume that, once we have done this, the picture we possess will remain static or that the goals will remain unchanged. One of the main characteristics of goals is that, the nearer one comes to achieving them, not only does the picture of them change but they exert less and less pull on the learners who begin to look beyond that goal to the next one. We should listen and explore with our student participants what goals they have and how these are expressed; and we should continue to discuss this as time goes on to see how the students' goals are changing. We will learn much of misapprehension in our students and in ourselves as a result.

Activity 7.6

Try to write down some of the different pictures of the 'end product' of the course that you think your student participants may hold. How can you test if you are right?

To summarise: in order to create purposeful learning, the teacher will set a series of objectives for the learners and from them construct a programme for the student participants to arrive at the goal of the course. But the adult participants may have their own objectives or, even when they indicate that their goal is the same as the teacher's, the picture they may hold of that goal may be different. Only as the teacher and the student participants interact can these ambiguities become clearer and be removed.

The relationship of the various parties to the different goals may be set out as in Figure 7.5.

Widening the goals

So far we have concentrated on the 'How?' side in our discussion of setting the goals. A consideration of the 'Why?' aspect will also help us to be more effective in the programme we draw up for our student learners.

There is space for only one example, which is taken from woodworking, though it could just as easily be drawn from geology, health and nutrition,

	Teacher-agent	Student participant	How set out
1 Overall ultimate goals (aims)	Usually set by the programme organiser, but the teacher will possess own version of these goals	Students rarely directly interested in this level	Rarely spelled out, usually assumed; implicit in whole programme
2 Specific goals	The main purpose of the teaching–learning situation as the teacher sees it; usually devised by the teacher in association with or independent of the organiser	Usually what the learners will hold as their goals, the reason for attending the course; what they are most interested in	Usually set out more or less briefly in the course publicity or information sheet
3 Immediate goals (objectives)	The narrower goals of each learning task; usually determined by the teacher	Students will have an unformulated version of these goals, but this will usually become clearer as the course progresses	Sometimes set out in the syllabus or schedule of work, but often discussed class by class, task by task

Figure 7.5 Levels of goals: teacher–learner interaction

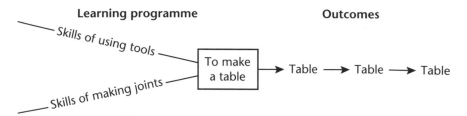

Figure 7.6a Scenario 1

music, computer studies or industrial training programmes. For here we consider the longer-term purposes of teaching adults. The purposeful learning opportunities that we plan for adults will, we hope, lead to permanent learning changes, which in turn will lead to changes in the way of life of the individual and thus contribute towards change in society at large.

Our goals may be narrow, specific and limited, measurable, or they may be wider, designed to extend and maximise the changes in the individual. We can express this in a series of scenarios.

Scenario 1

A class comes together to learn to make a table. The goal is limited: *to make a table* (specific goal). The programme is therefore also limited: to learn how to handle the wood and tools, and to make those joints which are needed to make a table (immediate goals). The achievement too is limited to the skill of making tables (overall goal). This is expressed in Figure 7.6a.

Scenario 2

We may widen the specific goal: *to make a range of furniture* beginning by making a table. The programme then is wider: to learn a wider use of wood, tools and joints, going beyond making a table. The achievement too is wider: the learner is encouraged to innovate with new tools and new joints, to make new furniture (Figure 7.6b).

Scenario 3

We can widen the goals still further, though still using the table. The goals will then be *to understand and appreciate furniture* through making a table. The programme in this case will be much wider: to learn how to design a table and make a comparison with other tables; to study and analyse wood and develop a feeling for it; to acquire a wider range of

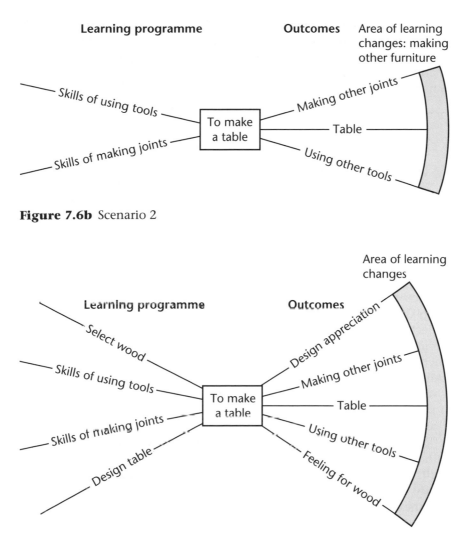

Figure 7.6b Scenario 2

Figure 7.6c Scenario 3

skills of using wood, tools and joints; a study of the history of furniture making and other kinds of furniture than commonly used. And the area of achievement, of learning changes, has also been widened so that the student participant is being encouraged to develop critical attitudes as well as technical skills (Figure 7.6c).

Goals, then, may be set on a narrow or a wider basis, and as a result of these goals, learning will tend to be either narrow in confine or wider. We must allow for the active involvement of the adult student participants.

Some will seek to use even the narrow goal-based teaching to learn over a wide front, but their task will not be easy. In any case, it is the intention of the teacher-planner that concerns us most at this point: whether we plan that our student participants should learn over a wide field or over a narrow field. This is our choice.

Activity 7.7

Taking your case study as an example, choose one of your goals and see if you can build on the learning programme and outcomes to widen it to take account of the 'areas of learning changes' as shown in Figure 7.6c.

The value of training

We saw on pages 58–60 the distinction between training, education and indoctrination. We suggested that the main purpose of education is to help the participants to become free to innovate, to develop critical reflection, to increase the range of choices before them. The increase of the ability to achieve in one field will contribute towards a sense of achievement in general. In this respect, training – the acquisition of a particular skill, the growth of knowing how to do something, the development of competence – has greater long-term benefits for the learner than has a process of 'informing' that may lead to a sense of dependency of the learner on the teacher.

In this we can see one of the distinctions between training and indoctrination. Training, that development of knowledge, understanding and skills leading to mastery over some narrowly defined area of activity or study, can become one of the steps towards education as freedom and may be used as a basis for a widening approach to learning. Indoctrination, in contrast, a confinement of ways of thinking and behaving, can never lead to freedom.

Elements of training will inform a good deal of what we do in teaching adults. A balanced view would suggest that some of the goals of the teacher will be narrow (the acquisition of particular skills or data), and some will be wider (building awareness, developing understanding of relationships, furthering a sense of appreciation and the like). It will help the learning task greatly if both the teacher and the student participants are able to distinguish the wider from the narrower goals. Both will be involved in our teaching. Training is an essential element of education. The use of training objectives, the development of specific skills, will contribute to widening the perspectives and increasing the confidence of the learners. But it is not education; more than this is needed. The pursuit of critical learning will not be achieved if teachers of adults confine their goals to specific narrow training goals such as 'learning outcomes'. Part of our aim in all forms of teaching adults is to widen the horizons before the individual participants, to encourage them to become more conscious and effective learners.

Should the teacher attempt to lead the student learners from the narrower to the wider goals in this way? Is not such an approach in itself indoctrination? This question has received a good deal of attention. We need to remind ourselves

- that as teachers we inevitably possess goals as we pursue with the student participants their purposeful learning – such goals are inescapable;
- that in treating the student participants as adults, the teacher will seek to make sure that they are aware of what these goals are, so that they may (a) opt in or out of the learning situation and (b) contribute to their formulation and reformulation.

Without this transparency, such teachers will be denying the adulthood of the learners. The continual modification of the teacher's set goals in the light of the changing goals, aspirations and intentions of the student participants is part of the dialectic of teaching adults. Setting and modifying goals is paradoxically a process by which the teacher may contribute towards the students' growth towards greater consciousness of learning; and equally the surrender of autonomy by the teacher in this area is part of the process of building up the autonomy of the learner.

Further reading

Davies, I.K. (1976) *Objectives in Curriculum Design*. London: McGraw-Hill.

Knowles, M.S. (1980) *The Modern Practice of Adult Education: From Pedagogy to Andragogy*. New York: Association Press.

Neary, M. (2002) *Curriculum Studies in Post-compulsory and Adult Education: A Teacher's and Student Teacher's Study Guide* (3rd edn). Cheltenham: Nelson Thornes.

Tennant, M. (2006 edn) *Psychology and Adult Learning*. London: Routledge (especially pages 99–106).

Walters, S. (ed.) (1997) *Globalization, Adult Education and Training*. Leicester: NIACE.

Youngman, F. (2000) *The Political Economy of Adult Education and Development*. London: Zed Books.

Chapter 8

The Adult Learning Group
How does it work...?

Adults learn naturally from others. The formation of a learning group is therefore a valuable tool for helping adults to become more conscious of and more effective in their learning. This chapter will look at the learning group and the various roles played in it. As we signalled earlier in the book (see p. 13), our focus is on face-to-face learning rather than an online environment. However, much of what follows we believe has relevance in an online learning environment. There is sometimes an assumption that online groups can be left to themselves or that online learning is an individual activity. However, both online student learners and tutors can benefit from considering group processes and methods.

The importance of groups in adult learning programmes

Learning is individual. Each person comes to claim for themselves something new and in the process changes their thought patterns, their competencies and their behaviour to a smaller or greater extent. Such learning changes come from direct interaction between the individual learners and their environment (including the subject matter and other people). Much of the teaching of adults, however, is done in groups. There are a number of one-to-one teaching–learning situations – in some adult literacy programmes, for instance. Work-based apprenticeship forms of adult learning are also spreading again; and the increasing use of libraries and teach-yourself manuals are signs of this trend; individual music lessons continue and there are the increasing distance and open learning activities which many adults engage in, and an emerging interest in individual learning through modern information and communication technologies (for the similarities and differences in working online see, for example, Jacques and Salmon 2007: 15–16, 20; Tennant 2006: 120–121). But the majority of the planned learning opportunities for adults are still undertaken in some form of group.

There are a number of reasons for this:

- Schooling has habitually structured itself in this way. We ourselves learned a great deal in groups (classes), and on the whole we expect and even prefer to teach in groups.
- The use of a learning group seems to be the most efficient way to use the resource of a single teacher.
- Most adult students seem to prefer groups as a context for learning. Much of their informal learning is undertaken through associating with others. A reaction against the newer forms of 'lone-ranger' education can often be seen in the continuing demands for face-to-face contact between teacher and taught and between the learners themselves. In joining a taught learning programme, the participant is deliberately constructing themselves as a 'student' (see p. 53) – and since being a student is (in our society) equated with 'education', part of this construct is an expectation of joining a class, a learning group.
- There are sound educational advantages in group learning. The learning group can often achieve more for its members than a one-to-one situation can.
- Whether the existence of learning–teaching groups is more a question of habit or economics or gregariousness or educational effectiveness, the fact remains that learning is individual even when the teaching is a group matter. Herein lies tension. The group may be a great help towards achieving learning; but equally it may on occasion inhibit the sort of individually determined learning changes we hope will be achieved. The teacher of adults needs to balance the usefulness of the group against the growth of individuation, discrimination, creativity and self-reliance which constitute the goals of so much of what we set out to do. It is another form of that tension between education as conformity and education as liberation.

Activity 8.1

Before we go on to explore the nature of learning groups, write down in your own words and from your own experience (a) some of the practical **values** of a group for your student participants and (b) some of the **hindrances** that the learner might find in a group.

   For example, one **value** of working in a group might be the opportunity to share the viewpoints of other participants in addition to the teacher. Conversely, it may be difficult for participants to share their viewpoint if they believe others are 'better' informed; the group then becomes a **hindrance**.

The nature of groups

Before we analyse groups in the context of teaching adults, we need to note two things about studies of groups and the way they work. First, much of the work done on groups during the last fifty years has concentrated on small informal (learning or therapy) groups, and in particular on group dynamics (Lewin 1947; Egan 1973; Hare 1976; Jacques 1991; Knowles and Knowles 1972; Shaw 1981; Banbury and Carter 1982). Much of this research concentrates on groups performing practical tasks rather than learning, and Jacques and Salmon (2007: 22) suggest that tutors need to test how relevant such evidence is to their own teaching.

Secondly, many of these discussions have generalised and decontextualised the groups. It is assumed in much that has been written that most groups function in certain ways in all circumstances. The diversity of groups; the diversity of responses within groups; the diversity of interactions within each group; the importance of the immediate and more general contexts in influencing the ways in which groups form and perform – these have been largely overlooked. It is possible that there is a similar tendency in what follows, but we need to identify the ways in which our learning groups are unique as well as the ways in which they conform to current understandings of how groups work. For each group exists in a particular social context which to a large extent determines the way its members see themselves, the group itself and the way they behave.

What is a group?

A group is more than a collection of individuals. It is an entity, something whole in itself. There is a continuum of groups: at one end, the tightly knit team, the integrated group where all the members have submerged their individuality; at the other, the loose-knit bundle. There are elements beyond each end of this continuum – the *folie à deux* at the integrated end and the collection of isolates such as a cinema audience at the other – but these lie outside most definitions of 'group'. The classes, 'circles' or other types of group we teach will be at some point along this continuum (Figure 8.1).

Figure 8.1 The continuum of approaches to teaching

For a group to exist, there must be some form of common identity, but of itself this is not enough. The group has to be distinguished from the 'set' (all redheads, for instance) which although possessing a common characteristic cannot be classified as a group because it has no interaction. So two features are essential to a group: a common sense of identity (usually a common interest or purpose), even if it is unspoken, for all of its members; and some interaction between the members allowing for the sharing of attitudes and feelings, some emotional involvement and the emergence of a minimum set of agreed values or standards. And it also shares a common 'discourse', a specific kind of language devoted to the common goal. However, groups are not static but dynamic. They grow, they develop within their specific context and to meet their specific tasks, they construct as well as use their common discourse. Successful groups are those which feel that they are moving forward in one way or another.

The term 'group' covers a wide array of social units, from very small working parties to large organisations. Even in the field of formal education, groups are not all the same. A lecture audience is frequently large and loose-knit. A class is usually rather smaller but at times it is equally loose-knit, closer to the 'collection of individuals' end of the spectrum as each of the members works on their own (the 'no-talking-in-class' syndrome). A discussion group/seminar is often smaller still and closer. A task-oriented group, such as a syndicate focused on problem-solving or producing a collaborative piece of work (as in a group project) may be even smaller and may generate a good deal of warmth, if not heat; while a 'buzz-group' is usually smaller still, but it is unlikely to be able to maintain its strength of interaction for any length of time.

And as we have seen, groups do not stay still. Any group may well pass through a number of stages at different times, changing its nature according to its function. Groups may move up and down the continuum continuously. Rather than ask, 'What is the essential nature of this group?', it is more useful for the teacher to ask at each stage, 'What is this group doing now?'

Activity 8.2

Before we go further, jot down one or two groups (not necessarily educational: they can include a committee, for example, or a band) with which you are associated, so that you can test the characteristics to be discussed against your own experiences. At this stage simply fill in the first two columns. We will return to the other columns later in the chapter.

	Name of group	Size (approx.)	(a)	(b)	(c)	(d)	Comments
1							
2							

Types of group

Some analyses of groups suggest that there are different types.

Formal groups

In these groups, the structure is set before any member joins, and the new recruit does not contribute materially (e.g. the army or the police). Sanctions may be brought to bear on the members, and the group is not altered in any way by its changing membership, only by outside influences. Such groups do not in general concern adult education – though it has been suggested that some schools and classes even in higher education on occasion display some of the characteristics of formal groups. Most forms of adult learning groups, being voluntary and participatory, are we feel more informal. We see formality and informality not as two separate categories but rather a continuum along which groups operate.

Informal groups

These are usually divided into primary and secondary groups. *Primary* groups are normally small face-to-face groups, a close-knit team based on mutual acceptance of roles. A family, a committee, a reading circle are usually primary groups. Each member is influenced by the others and a sense of loyalty exists, founded on regular contact. In this group, a member may have a strong sense of affiliation, but at the same time the individual will normally be very open to influence in the group.

Secondary groups are usually too large to have regular face-to-face relationships. It is even possible for them never to meet, despite the fact that the ties are clearly felt. The members of an order of monks, for example, or school teachers in general form secondary groups. More often, however, the secondary group will meet in some way or maintain some other means of contact (e.g. newsletter, etc.). This group will affect the behaviour, attitudes and outlook of its members, and although the individual will not be so exposed as in the primary group, the influence of the group will still be strong.

Primary and secondary groups are not two clearly distinguished forms; rather, once again there are shades of grey between black and white. Any group may be mobile, moving backwards and forwards along the continuum. A group may display at different times some of the characteristics of a primary group and some of a secondary group. Groups have a life of their own, to a large extent independent of the wills of the individual members. Also, primary and secondary groups overlap; they are not mutually exclusive. A Methodist will belong to her/his chapel and even to the choir within that chapel – two different primary groups – and also to the Methodist circuit, district and communion (secondary groups). All those who come to learn in adult education, teacher and student participant alike, bring with them many different and overlapping primary and secondary groups.

A general point concerning the members of groups may be helpful. Those who seek to use the group to defend themselves from the outside world can do so only by opening themselves more and more to influence inside the group. Those who reject the openness demanded by the group will find themselves unable to use membership of the group as a defence against the outside. It is not possible to belong fully to a group without being willing to expose oneself in some measure to its influence. This is an important point in connection with motivation.

Activity 8.3

Go back to the list you created in Activity 8.1 and try to determine how far your group is formal or informal [column (a)]. This may be hard to determine.

	Name of group	Size (approx.)	Formal/informal? (a)	(b)	(c)	(d)	Comments
1							
2							

Reference groups

There is a third 'level' of groups, the reference group. This is hardly a group at all, but it concerns us for the influence it exerts on us and our student participants. The reference group covers those people from whom we draw values, standards, aims and goals by our own sense of affiliation. The group itself doesn't know we belong to it (we may not even be official members of the group) but *we* know. The reference group of our Methodist friend is the Christian Church (or more likely the Protestant branch of the Christian Church). Other such reference groups might be trade unionists (or 'workers' in general), cricketers, farmers, teachers, clergymen – a sense of identity towards whom will help to determine the range of attitudes we possess and a willingness to identify with other members of the same reference group.

The teacher of adults will find him/herself a member of a number of different groups. One will of course relate to the course members. Another such group may be related to the subject being taught (e.g. counselling or literacy/language); another such group may relate to all the teachers of adults in the organisation which is providing or supporting the course, especially those in the same building, if there are any.

Our adult learning group, to begin with, may not be much of a group at all. Rather, it may consist of a collection of individual hopeful word processors, trainee hairdressers or French-language speakers. In many cases, however, especially in adult education contexts, it will quickly become a primary group with secondary and reference attachments. One secondary group to which the members may belong could consist of all the other adult students in the centre or institution where they are learning (e.g. 'mature students' in a university). Another may include those elsewhere who are engaged in the same sort of activity as that of the class. Participants in a trainee hairdressing group, for example, will relate to other similar students nearby, if there are any, and/or to other people interested in hairdressing in the region. They may also join a local branch of their professional association. Managers taking an advanced course will each bring with them to the primary learning group the other primary and secondary groups of their own businesses as well as the institution within which the course is being held. Beyond these, there is the reference group: the world of hairdressing as represented by journals and other publications, for instance, or all managers, or all adult education students (the 1980s Save Adult Education campaign in the UK for a short time brought a sense of coherence to this reference group, and Adult Learners' Week is currently doing something of the same on an international scale).

Activity 8.4

Go back to the list you created in Activity 8.1 and try to determine what
are the primary and secondary forms of each group [columns (b) and (c)].
The task may not be straightforward but have a try.

	Name of group	Size (approx.)	Formal/ informal (a)	Primary (b)	Secondary (c)	(d)	Comments
1							
2							

Most adult learning groups seem to work most effectively as small
primary groups (suggestions vary between 10 members as a minimum
and 30 as a maximum) that meet regularly (say, once or twice a week) or
for short intensive periods of a few days, and share common tasks
between each meeting. A larger group than this may prevent effective
interaction between all its members; a smaller group is often too vulnerable
to sickness and other causes of absence to ensure continuity of learning,
and this inhibits the growth of group coherence and performance.

Group structures

It has been suggested that any primary group will structure itself in a
number of different ways. The first is the *task group* – i.e. the way the group
members relate to each other in order to achieve the common aim. A
football team illustrates this. It has its own structure, and the members
play mutually recognised roles to fulfil the task. Task groups are usually
primary groups, only rarely secondary groups, and they are distinguished
by two features: a defined goal and a recognised leadership structure.

Task groups are made up of individuals who may be willing for a time
to submerge their own preferences in order to achieve the task but who
remain individuals and relate to each other independently of the task.
Some of them may dislike particular members with whom they work
closely, while they may interact with others at deeper levels. At some
distance from the task, then, the primary group may adopt another structure; its members may fill roles different from those they occupy in the
task group. Such a group has been called a *socio-emotional group*, and it
has its own rewards as well as its own structures. It is, for example, not

always the case that the football captain is the team's best public speaker; that leadership role off the field may belong to another member of the group.

An amateur dramatic society, to take another example, has a particular structure during rehearsals. The producer or director is the recognised, often tyrannical, leader of the task group. But after rehearsal in a more convivial atmosphere, he/she may as likely as not sink back exhausted and remain silent for long periods; the leadership role comes to be adopted by another member of the group. Many new roles emerge in a different social environment that are not displayed in the rehearsal room.

The task group and the socio-emotional group are the same group acting in different ways. The former stresses the function of the group, the latter its social relationships. Some groups have no task orientation or structure. The drinking partners who meet most evenings in the corner of the bar that we may frequent are there only to enjoy themselves and to exchange useful and useless pieces of information. It is clearly a socio-emotional group but hardly a task group. On the other hand, few if any task groups will fail to have socio-emotional aspects.

A primary group committed to a task at times swings in its activities and in its structures from one aspect to the other. It can rarely remain all the time in the task format alone. Such a switch is healthy. It helps to facilitate the task and to increase the strength of the bonds in the group by relaxing the tensions created by the task orientation.

Such changes seem to be most easily made when the task structure and the socio-emotional structure are not too far apart. If however the structure of the task group and the socio-emotional group become too distant, or if the socio-emotional structure becomes too strong – if for instance the leader of the socio-emotional group is expected to play a clearly subordinated role in the task group with no recognition of the position the rest of the group accords to them – then the performance of the task group can be damaged. If, in our example above, the producer or director of the play and the leader of the socio-emotional group clash over the task and their respective roles in the task (if, say, the leader of the socio-emotional group objects to some of the casting), then the whole production suffers. A group appears to work best when the two structures are different but not too different, and when the socio-emotional structure is subordinate, with everyone's consent, to the task.

When this happens, the socio-emotional group will serve as a *maintenance group*. It will seek to help the task group to attain its goals. A maintenance group and a socio-emotional group can at times be distinguished, for the maintenance group has the task before it and ceases to exist once the task has been completed, whereas the socio-emotional group seeks to keep itself in existence, perhaps by choosing another task. One example of this is the local WEA group who wish to stay together and either invite a new tutor in or the same tutor who introduces a different subject. In this case, the task comes to serve the ends of the socio-emotional group, whereas the maintenance group exists to serve the task.

Activity 8.5

Return to your two groups in Activities 8.2 and 8.3 and ask yourself whether your groups are predominantly task groups or socio-emotional groups; which of these two structures predominates. Note your thoughts in column (d). In some cases, it will be half and half, but in others, one type of group structure will stand out clearly.

	Name of group	Size (approx.)	Formal/ informal	Primary	Secondary	Task/socio- emotional	Comments
1							
2							

Groups in adult education

How can we adapt all of this to our adult courses and programmes? Apart from the important but often overlooked point that all of our student participants will bring with them a number of overlapping primary, secondary and reference groups of which they are members, what is the relevance of this discussion to our teaching? Do we need to convert a set of individual learners, whom most of us teach, into a primary group with both task and socio-emotional orientations; and if so, how do we go about it? What are the advantages of adults coming together into groups to learn? How can the presence of other learners help, and hinder, our student participants?

The discussion above will be helpful here. We have seen that part of the task of the teacher of adults is to build on the natural learning processes which all adults engage in, making these processes more conscious and more effective. In our informal learning episodes, we rely on the experience of others as much as on our own experience to engage in critical reflection, using 'search and select' techniques. Much learning is done with and from other people. Imitation, comparison of ourselves against others, and feedback are essential elements in our natural learning processes. The importance of 'communities of learners' in adult learning is increasingly recognised, as social learning theories point out.

Situated learning (see pp. 115–6) suggests that in many forms of learning we set ourselves, or are set, on the edges of 'communities of practice' from whom we learn and into which we are drawn. And Vygotsky's 'zone of proximal development' (see p. 143) is insistent that our major learning is accomplished through working with others. Human beings are social animals, and our learning, although individualised, is best achieved in association with others. Simply being a member of a community will bring about some learning.

This applies also to our adult learning groups. Belonging to such a group will bring some learning. Much of that learning will be informal learning – learning the discourse, values, practices and structures (roles) of the group usually subconsciously at the same time as we are learning its subject matter more formally and more consciously. Teaching adults is itself one form of socially embedded activity. Membership of the learning group (a class or discussion group) therefore carries with it the same kinds of informal learning as does membership of a community group, a church or mosque, a pub drinking set or a local dramatic group, *at the same time* as it carries more formalised learning of the subject matter which forms the focus of the learning programme.

Advantages and disadvantages of groups in formalised learning

Views differ about the advantages and disadvantages of groups in formalised learning. What will seem to some to be a help will be a cause of concern for others. Nevertheless, four main values appear to flow from the use of groups in teaching adults:

- they provide a *supportive* environment for learning;
- they provide a constant *challenge* to the learner;
- they provide resources to build richer and *more complex* structures for learning;
- they have a *life* of their own, which can assist the learning.

Each of these needs elaboration.

Advantages of groups for learning

1 *Supportive environment.* There is a sense of solidarity in a group in which the participants can undertake the task (in our case, a learning task) more easily. The social context is one where all the members of the group are engaged in the same activity. The individual will be supported by the group. For example:

- The group calls for conformity to its norms. In this way the group provides a measure of *suggestibility* and reinforces patterns of change. If others in the group can relate to the subject matter and cope with it, strong encouragement is given to individual members.
- The group can establish the *status* of the learner and thus provide encouragement. Endorsement of one's worth, acknowledgement of one's potential, recognition of the role one is capable of playing within the group (especially a task group) and which the group is willing to accept – all of these can enhance the learners' self-image and encourage them to greater effort.
- The group supports *experimentation*. The shared empathies that spring from the awareness of others in the same situation encourage each student participant to launch out and innovate. In this inner circle, ideas can be tested out first before their assertion in the outside world, skills can be practised prior to their demonstration before all and sundry. With a good many adult students, it is their vulnerability that is most touched upon in learning; and the group can provide the security needed for personal development.
- The group *rewards* success. The warmth of fellowship and other emotional interchanges help to overcome the anxiety over changes that some learners experience. The group gives confidence. It is even possible for fellow participants to criticise or to motivate one another at times when it is not possible for the teacher to do so. The group can provide much of the evaluation and reinforcement needed for learning.

All this depends on the members accepting and internalising the group goals and norms.

2 *Challenge*. The group provides an additional challenge to the learner. It creates a new setting calling for novelty in inter-relationships. 'Newness' is in the air from the start. Most of us are accustomed to changing groups and joining new ones – from our family to school we go on to work and leisure groups, new family groups and so on. We accept all of these, usually willingly, and build up new norms often with a sense of excitement. An adult teaching–learning group is another such group. We meet new ranges of views, prejudices and experiences, all of them calling for learning changes and widening horizons. Some adults come to educational programmes more for the experience of newness

than for anything else. Much of this acculturation learning is done informally. This is particularly true for changed attitudes; the existence of the group often provides the stimulus for change, for increased awareness and critical reflection, for the internalisation of values.

3   *Building complex structures.* The group, drawing upon the variety of experience possessed by its members, can build larger and more complex cognitive structures, can create more satisfying products, can present a wider range of possible solutions to problems, can bring into play more evaluative judgements than can any learning environment consisting of teacher and student only. Because all the participants have their own well-trusted learning styles, the methods available in the teaching–learning process are greatly multiplied. It has not been unknown for a student participant to teach another member of the group a particular skill or concept when the teacher's methods have failed. The resources that both student participant and teacher can call upon are greatly increased by the existence of the group.

4   *Dynamic.* The group has a life of its own, a momentum that carries the participant along, helps to create and maintain motivation, and sets joint goals and a pace of learning that is satisfying to most of its members. Loyalty to the group will often bring about greater effort at particular times than any demand the teacher can make. The teacher's task in these areas is greatly eased.

In this way, a learning group can become something of a community which draws all its members in.

Disadvantages of groups for learning

However, each of these same characteristics of learning groups may also act as a hindrance to learning in certain cases.

1   *Learning environment.* The pressure to conformity, the *suggestibility* that the group exerts on the individual member, can promote imitation, not the free exercise of experiment. The group may smother the individual. At times (this often happens in an adult learning group) pre-existing prejudices and expectations are confirmed and strengthened by the presence of other participants who share them. Thus conflict between some or all of the student participants on the one hand and the newer ideas and

ways of other student participants and of the teacher on the other may be generated and made more bitter. Trying to convince one student out of ten that his/her way of holding a chisel is inefficient and dangerous is relatively easy – until they are strengthened by the presence of even a few other people who share their idiosyncrasy. The group, in whole or in part, can thus become a new form of authority to which the individual is expected to conform.

The *status* offered to the individual member by the group may become restrictive. The individual may become typecast by the group into a set role and may thus find it hard to break out and adopt another role (see Chapter 9).

What is more, the success of the group in providing *reinforcement* for its members can lead to some of the participants experiencing anxiety and fear of isolation, of being an outcast from the group if any of them experiments with a new way of doing something or expresses a divergent point of view. Many a participant has refused to express an opinion because of the strength of opposing views held by other members of the group. The participant can so easily become dependent upon the group, and even come to fear the rivalry of other groups. Such dependency can lead to learning ceasing rather than continuing when the group disperses.

2   *Challenge*. The closeness of the group, as each member engages in the 'new' activity, can become a threat to some of the more individualistic learners. At times, the challenge of the group may be strong enough to deter experimentation and encourage conformity by those who are less confident.

3   *Building complex structures*. Some learners may find it difficult to cope with the wide range of experience and views that others see as the richness of the adult learning group. They may prefer the unified authoritative vision of the single teacher. The more elaborate structures that the group builds may in their case lack the necessary foundations for comprehension and acceptance.

4   *Dynamic*. The pace set by the group may not be that needed by the individual member, either too fast or too slow. Thus additional pressures can be created by the group. Some learning groups can be very intolerant of those who are felt to move unusually quickly or slowly. Again, the relationships within the group may be inimical to the personality traits of some individual learners.

Forming the group

Economics, educational considerations, student expectations and existing traditions of schooling all help to create a situation in which most of us find ourselves teaching a number of student participants at the same time. Each of us will have to weigh up how far in our particular circumstances a coherent learning group is necessary or whether we will teach our students without encouraging them to form themselves into a group, a cooperative for learning. A great deal will depend on the context within which our teaching is taking place and the aims of the programme. Learning programmes for adults which lead to some form of examination or which focus on enhanced work-related practices will tend to remain closer to the set than the group, as individualised and competitive rather than collaborative learning tasks form the staple of the learning activities. Courses which aim more at community development will tend to move quickly to group formation and collaborative tasks. Courses which concentrate on personal development (from keep fit or continuing professional development to music appreciation) will vary considerably according to the underlying beliefs of the teacher and the student participants as to whether adults learn best individually or collectively.

If we do decide that both the learning needs of the student participants and the objectives of the programme are best served by helping our disparate students to become a more cohesive group, what steps do we need to take to help turn these separate individuals into a group? Will it happen by itself?

There are several different models of how groups coalesce and develop. The one that has most currency would appear to be as follows. The first stage is when a collection of socialised individuals, seeing a common goal, come together and express their need and willingness to interact. There is a common bond. Then comes an exploration stage, during which the individual members debate and set goals, when their inner inclinations become aligned onto the agreed goal. During this stage, members interact because they see that others are looking towards the same (or similar) goals as their own. They express their mutual dependence and begin to explore other bonds they may share, such as common interests, concerns or acquaintances. Third, the group begins to structure itself. Its members start to adopt roles, and these – after a period of experimentation, jostling and even conflict – stabilise into the formation of agreed role identities and the acceptance of common rules for all members of the group. Finally, the organisation completes itself into a

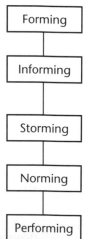

Forming

Informing

Storming

Norming

Performing

working group – dynamic, not static, with interlocking roles, specialisations and division of functions. In other words, the individual participants have become something of a team, dedicated to the achievement of commonly agreed goals.

(Some have added further stages to this structure, such as 'informing' when the group talks to the outside world, 'deforming' as it disperses and 'mourning' as the group ends its work. But these seem artificial.)

Not all groups, nor even all adult classes, pass through all of these stages, though many will. Perhaps the first lesson for us as teacher or leader of a group of adult learners is to watch what is going on in the group, not to be worried when conflicts arise, and to do all in our power to help the group achieve a measure of self-consciousness in identifying and achieving its goals. Nor must we assume that, once the group has begun to perform in relation to the common task, its structure will remain stable. As we shall see (Chapter 9), roles will constantly be changing in the group, and this will make some of the members feel uncomfortable. It does not harm most groups to get them to discuss from time to time the nature of the interrelationships within the group.

This becomes particularly true of the group that takes off on its own, that begins to move towards the formal end of the continuum. The mutual identification – in which the group meets the socio-emotional needs of the members as well as the task needs – can on occasion lead the members to join with each other against outsiders. Praise, good luck, blame and even persecution of individual members are shared, and the concept of 'we' becomes exclusive. Loyalty and solidarity are expressed in a group symbol (a name, headed notepaper, etc.), then a badge, insignia, tie, dress or uniform. It is not long before ranks and titles emerge; taboo behaviour is laid down and jargon encouraged. The group is still a group; standards, values, attitudes and customs are shared, and norms are learned. But it has become more formal.

This is a very powerful tool of conformist learning but it scarcely leads to self-development, to increasing the choices before the members or to critical learning. Formal groups of this kind have their uses and are especially effective in achieving some goals (e.g. political change), but they are hardly *education* making for individuation. Nevertheless, some long-running adult education groups seem to have gone a good way down the road to formality.

The teacher and the group

What can we as teachers of adults do within our own contexts positively to encourage effective learning in the group? First, we may be able to help the group to emerge from the collection of individual learners who have joined the class by encouraging the members to coalesce. Frequent face-to-face exchanges, together with some emotional involvement (for instance, collaboration on a shared immediate or short-term task) will help in this. People who have nothing to share will never become a group. Students who come to classes and sit saying nothing, waiting for the teacher to begin to teach, with a coldness that suggests a lack of emotional commitment to the exercise, will remain a collection of individual learners, not introducing each other to the combined riches of the group. Equally, dominance of the group by one or two individuals will not help at all. Without a shared ownership of the task and a sense of achievement arising from its completion ('*We* did it'), the learners will remain in loose affiliation.

Seating patterns can help. Figure 8.2 suggests that such arrangements can contribute to the interrelations between group members; but we must be careful not to be too deterministic in this.

Secondly, it may be possible to watch the balance between the personal self-development of each participant and the supportive/challenging role of the group. Both are desirable, but the needs of the student learner should perhaps take precedence. Each group member needs to be given opportunities to exercise their skills and express their views without fear of criticism, contradiction or exclusion by the group. As teachers, we will constantly try to be aware of the pressures the participants in our groups are exerting on each other. All of them can be enabled to experiment and practise, to play their own games and explore their own concepts. Each

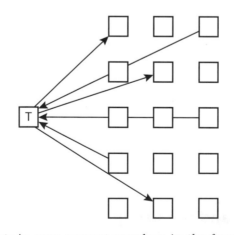

Figure 8.2a Seats in rows prevent members in the front from talking to those behind them, while the only face that all the learners can see is that of the teacher

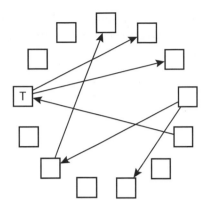

Figure 8.2b Circular seating helps all members to talk freely with each other as well as with the teacher. Even when engaged on individual tasks, such an arrangement allows for interaction (computer terminals can with advantage be set out in this rather than a more formal format, though often only with some difficulty)

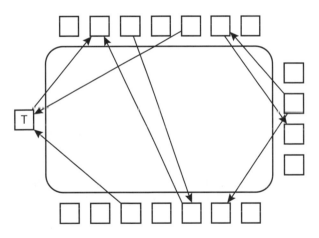

Figure 8.2c A large table doesn't always help. The members at the far end have formed their own group; watch out if the same people sit there every time

will have their particular contribution to add to the common pool. But equally, the capacity of each individual for affiliation varies, and no one ought to be pressed too hard.

Thirdly, we can pay attention to both the task structure of the group and its socio-emotional structure. It is not always necessary to discourage the emergence of informal, non-task related interactions (a short break from the task, such as for refreshments, is a great opportunity for this, as well as the periods at the start and end of each session). Nor is it necessary for the teacher to occupy the leading role in the socio-emotional group; indeed it may be helpful if a different leadership could be encouraged. But we do need to ensure that the socio-emotional structure is subordinate and contributory to the task group, that it helps with the work of the group as a 'maintenance group'. The task is, after all, learning, in whatever field of activity the class is concerned with. If both structures are contributing towards the task, the teacher will not be unduly worried when the group continually moves in and out of its different aspects, not even when the socio-emotional structure seems to predominate for a time ('What about our party this year?'). But it is not always easy to keep a balance, to keep the common goal before the group when so many of its members seem to wish to engage in anything except the learning task.

Sometimes it may be desirable to break up the group, to form sub-groups or create new roles and new structures, in order to encourage the learning task. The use of sub-groups inside any teaching programme is invaluable. They provide an opportunity for the student learners to engage directly with the material of the course and to supply their own experience, to discuss and come to their own conclusions. They enable some participants who may not be willing to participate in the full plenary to express their views more certainly and thus gain confidence. They develop the skills of note-taking and communication in reporting back from the sub-groups into plenary session. They encourage peer learning and demonstrate that not all learning will come from the teacher. The role of the teacher changes into one of facilitator, going round the sub-groups and assisting as problems arise. A balance between peer-group learning and whole-class teaching needs to be maintained in every adult learning programme.

But this can lead to the formation of cliques. When the participants appear to be reluctant to come back from their sub-groups into the full group, it may well be that the sub-groups are satisfying some need that the full group isn't meeting. If such a sub-group becomes permanent, especially if it gets between the group and the goal, conflicts will arise. In these cases, setting a closer subordinate goal, a short-term task with its own sense of achievement, will sometimes help to recreate the whole group and can also help to break up cliques or prevent cliques forming.

On occasion, however, it can be the teacher who wittingly or unwittingly encourages such a division in the group. An 'in-group' centred on the teacher (especially one who adjourns to a nearby bar with some of the members after each meeting) and a consequent 'out-group' frequently occur in adult education. The out-groupers may be willing to accept the role assigned to them, but they will not be as keen on the learning task as they were when the group was whole. The in-groupers for their part will often assert their role, either displaying a proprietary interest in the teacher (asking specialised questions, for instance) or preserving an attitude of aloofness during the class as if to keep their contributions until later when the out-groupers are excluded and they can have the teacher to themselves.

Throughout this minefield, we will need to tread carefully. The most important attribute for any teacher to develop is *sensitivity*: awareness for example of the group members' non-verbal as well as verbal interactions; awareness of group tension and its release symptoms (jokes, laughter, etc.); awareness of its signs of satisfaction. The way a group member sits on the edge of (or even outside) the group, the way they lean forward or draw a breath preparatory to taking the plunge into the common activity, anxious to make a point as soon as there is a reasonable break – these and other signals will be absorbed, often half-consciously, by the teacher. Some teachers are born; they seem to take to this naturally. But all of us can increase our awareness by understanding the ways groups operate and by learning to watch.

A learning group and sub-groups, then, are valuable tools for promoting adult learning. A group builds on the experience of all of the student participants in their own learning episodes, encouraging more participation in learning activities; it becomes a site for horizontal learning. It will form a community of learners, providing an immediate context for situated learning. All its members will engage in informal learning as they enter more fully into membership, while at the same time they are engaging in more formalised learning. It provides an arena in which the specific and the general are brought together (the dialectic of contextualised and decontextualised learning) which, it is claimed, is specifically adult. And it enables the power relationships inherent in taught learning to become more visible and to be challenged in a way appropriate to adults. All of these elements can be made conscious through the group.

Facing some problems in an adult learning group

We are all faced with many problems in the course of our teaching of adults, and with experience we learn how to solve most of them. The main point is to be sensitive to the existence of a problem. Once we are aware of this, the task of solution often becomes less difficult. Some people have this sensitivity from the start; others have to learn it the hard way. It would be a good thing, as a first step, if we can *decide where we stand on this issue of sensitivity*, whether we think we are or are not aware of how our group members are reacting to our teaching. But even if we are among those to whom such awareness comes easily, it will still be helpful for us to *arrange as many and as varied channels of feedback* as we can, so that we can keep ourselves informed of how well our student participants are doing and how they feel about aspects of the work.

A few of the more common situations that can arise are listed here, and some of the ways of dealing with them are suggested. The solution to any problem that works well on one occasion may not work equally well another time; each situation in adult education is unique. Thus the suggestions listed here are not meant to be prescriptive. In most cases there are several possible ways of coping with a problem, which need to be tested out at our discretion so that eventually we can evolve our own ways of meeting such situations.

The primary attribute of the teacher of adults, above all, is *tact*. What is stated here briefly and on occasion baldly could be disastrous unless the execution of it fits into the normal pattern of our relationships with our learner participants. An artificial reaction based on a set of instructions in a teaching manual, bringing with it an abrupt change of classroom climate, could be ruinous for the work of the group. We thus need to choose a tactic that suits our own teaching style and adapt it; we must take our time over it. We also need to balance the needs of the individual against those of the rest of the group.

Problems[1] involving individual student participants

Persistent talkers

There are occasions where one individual tries to monopolise the discussion, refusing to let go of the stick they are worrying. There are also occasions where two members of the group (or a very small group) insist on talking to each other to the exclusion of the other group members.

It is important not to let them wreck the group. Their behaviour can generate considerable irritation among the other members, and this will rebound onto us as teachers unless we are seen to take some steps to limit their impact on the group.

To begin with, a gentle approach may succeed: 'Let's hear what the others have to say first.' If that doesn't work, they may have to be taken

---

1 This section has been adapted from a paper prepared by Dr Sam Lilley formerly of the Department of Adult Education of the University of Nottingham for use in traditional adult education classes consisting mainly of discussion and included in that university's training pack for part-time tutors. However, it may be useful in other contexts including more formal courses for adults in educational institutions.

on one side and spoken to, either by ourselves or by one of the more respected participants.

If gentle tactics fail, slowly increasing firmness may be necessary. Take advice before going too far along this route. 'You really must give the others a fair chance' can lead on to a firm indication that, by monopolising the discussion, the over-talker is spoiling the enjoyment of everyone else. (We must not forget, however, that they may have a following in the group.) Such remarks could first be made privately, but after a time the group will expect us as teacher and group leader to adopt a firm line in public. We risk losing a group member, but this is usually a smaller risk than we think; and in any case ruining a learning group is worse than losing one member.

The monomaniac

The person who raises essentially the same issue in every session is fortunately relatively rare. A simple statement that they have already mentioned the point in question and an appeal to stop is worth trying but unlikely to succeed. Fairly harsh measures may become necessary at an earlier stage than with the persistent talker. We can try to pre-empt the particular contribution: when setting out the work to be done, we might end with the words that 'So-and-so will no doubt say that . . .', summarising their point in perhaps a quarter of the time they would take. We could even involve the person directly – 'That's how you would put it, isn't it?' – but allow them little or no time to develop the discussion by bringing in the rest of the group. One can go further and prime other members of the group to speak up: 'We've heard that often enough; let's talk of something else.' Sometimes we can even develop our own contract with a monomaniac – give them a set time to present their views on condition that they agree not to raise the point again. But they may not keep the bargain, and a firmer line may be necessary in the end.

The quiet participant

A reticent member may refuse to be drawn into any discussion or group activity. This needs great care and tact, for the causes of the reticence are rarely clear. Unlike the cases above, the loss of a shy person as a result of tactlessly applied pressure would deny the whole purpose of the adult group.

We could perhaps try to persuade the member to talk outside of the group session – before the meeting starts, after it ends or during refreshments – to ourselves or to another participant. It may be possible to find out some opinions they hold, some skill or experience they possess; we can then try to guide the work of the group into these fields so that eventually they can fittingly (but never easily) make some contribution. Even then the hoped-for participation may not be forthcoming, and we may have to put words into their mouth: 'I was impressed with what so-and-so was saying to me . . .' We could then repeat the point, perhaps not quite accurately or with doubt expressed about some aspect of it; this may at last provoke an interjection. And once the ice is broken . . .

An alternative is to increase the contribution such members can make to the group by getting them to prepare a particular piece of work. It may then turn out that at some point this person is the only one with the relevant skill or knowledge to help forward the group's work. In this case, still using caution so that they do not feel too exposed, we can ask them directly to join in. It is useful to keep an eye on them (but not too obviously) as the programme continues; a frown or raised eyebrow, a drawn breath or a change in posture may indicate the one moment in the session (even perhaps in the whole course) when something is ready to burst out. We need then to abandon all else to make this happen if the student is to be freed to become a full participant.

The use of sub-groups may help such a student to participate. But some group members are so reticent that even the most experienced teacher is unable to extract a contribution from them during the whole programme. Because of this, we can never be sure that any progress is being made at all. Yet the person may still benefit from the course. Active participation by all the members is a desirable goal of all learning situations, but ideals are never fully attained. Silence is not a sin. However, there may be occasions where the silence or non-participation of a group member becomes problematic, as they can occupy a position of power which in turn affects the rest of the group. This is particularly the case in groups in which disclosure of personal views or opinions is a core element of the course (e.g. a counselling course). On these occasions, the teacher will need to intervene by taking the student to one side and discussing it and pointing out the effect silence has on the group dynamic.

More serious is the case of a whole group of reticent members, who may even sit together in silent sympathy. They may think of themselves as less skilful, less knowledgeable or slower thinkers than the others. Equally it could be our own fault for concentrating our attention on a few more congenial learners. Such a group needs careful attention, as we shall see.

The alternative expert

One or more members may continually remind the group that they are more knowledgeable than the teacher in some part of the subject. We are often asked by our student participants to teach on the limits of our subject; indeed, on occasion we are challenged on aspects of the subject about which we know little or nothing. In these circumstances, a person who asserts publicly that they know a good deal about some part of the subject can be looked upon by us and/or the rest of the group as an alternative expert.

This person is exceptional only in degree. Every group member knows something relevant to the subject that the teacher doesn't know, and they must all be given the opportunity to teach the others what they know. It is not always easy to discover what that something is, but if we can find it, every student participant can have their own teaching moment.

But for this particular person, the expert, there is usually no such problem. They often parade their special knowledge at every possible moment, perhaps with a display of more or less deference to our role as teacher. They may even deny our right to teach. We could find this threatening. We need to accept the situation – indeed, we can make them feel welcome, for they can be valuable teaching assistance. They almost certainly respect our general position, our expertise or experience, or they would stop coming to the group. In return, we need to respect their expertise and involve them from time to time in the work of the group as teacher of either the whole or part of the group. Maybe they will show themselves knowledgeable but unskilled in teaching adults, in which case we can help them in this respect. In doing so, we too will learn. Watching others teaching, and talking to them about their teaching, is an instructive experience.

It may be that the alternative expert comes to the group because it provides them with an easy platform to demonstrate their knowledge and skills. They are less concerned with the rest of the members learning something than with showing off. It is not easy to cope with this, for these people tend to be thick-skinned. One possible strategy is to formalise the situation as they would wish it to be for a short time. We could give them the opportunity to take over from us formally for a while. They may then learn that their knowledge, although deep, is too limited to sustain them over a lengthy period face to face with the student participants. It may be that the rest of the group will indicate their preference for us as teacher. Equally, they may not!

The unruly participant

Sometimes we are faced by unacceptable behaviour on the part of a particular student learner.

What is 'unacceptable' is of course a huge matter of debate. So that most adult learning groups these days now start off by establishing (and agreeing) a set of 'rules' to govern the interactions: 'always to respect the views of others; not to speak while someone else is speaking; to maintain agreed times of starting and finishing, etc.' Sometimes the group may even agree internal penalties (often humorous) for breaches such as mobile phones going off during the group session. Identifying in a participatory way what is 'unacceptable' to the whole group may help all participants to avoid such behaviour.

Problems concerning the working group

The mixed group

This group contains members of varied abilities and/or experience and/or knowledge. Most adult learning groups will comprise a wide range in terms of age, existing knowledge, experience and willingness to learn from that experience, skills, attitudes and learning abilities. Some will see themselves as 'beginners', others as more 'advanced'. We may in time come to regard the mixed-ability nature of the group as an advantage, a widening of the teaching opportunities open to us. But for the moment:

1   We do not need to feel that we ourselves have to do all the work of teaching. On carefully chosen occasions, we can ask those who know most or have more verbal facility to explain a point to the ones who know less about the subject or are slower thinkers. We may be surprised how much the 'learned' will expose their own weaknesses – and set about remedying them; equally how much the less experienced members can flourish. The group will become more united as time goes on.
2   On the other hand, we could teach a sub-group of the class. No group objects to a teacher who spends time now and again on an explanation of some process or concept for those who need it, or another two or three minutes making a special point that only the most knowledgeable or skilled appreciate. It is surprising what can be done for the more advanced members of the group by means of a few well-chosen asides.
3   We may be able to satisfy the demands (or some of them) of the more advanced and well informed at some occasion outside of the group meeting. It is often possible to ask those who require some special 'bridging' provision to come a few minutes early or to stay behind for a short while.
4   Dividing the group into smaller groups in order to give each of them the attention they need – provided the other members are

engaged in meaningful tasks, either as individuals or in their own small group – is a useful strategy that paradoxically makes the entire group cohere more strongly. The use of sub-groups to maximise learning is a key element in the teacher's armoury. There are many kinds of sub-group, selected on different criteria: by ability (though the dangers of 'streaming' remain as true in adult education as in schooling), or mixed-ability groups working on different or the same assigned exercises. Sub-groups throw up their own structures, and we can help or hinder this by choosing or not choosing a leader/chairperson who may or may not be the same as the *rapporteur* (if one is needed). We need to experiment with various forms of sub-grouping.

5   Perhaps the most rewarding, but the most difficult, procedure is to adopt an unorthodox and original approach to the topic, to use materials that the knowledgeable have never seen before and that keep both beginner and more advanced interested. This requires a lot of time and resources, and it may be that the full-time adult teacher will be able to work out such approaches more fully than the part-time teacher. It would be useful for us to keep in touch with other subject specialists we may know; they will probably have teaching material and/or methods that are new to us, which they may be only too glad to share.

6   The class/group meetings are not the only times available for learning to take place. The use of differential tasks (not the same work set for all participants like school homework) to be done individually between sessions helps to overcome the problems of disparate learning groups. We need to structure these carefully and be prepared to give time to discussing this work with different participants.

In the end, however, all the members of the group start at different places and, using skills and aptitudes that vary markedly, end up at different places. Our objective is not to make all the learners alike, not to bring them all up to the same 'high' standard but to enable them to get the best out of themselves, each in their own way.

The duologue

A group may degenerate into a dialogue between the teacher and one member (or a very few). The danger is greatest when a participant has presented some piece of finished work for us or the group as a whole to evaluate. One possible answer is to get the fellow members to do their evaluation before we take part. But the teacher and the individual participant may be the only people present who have adequate knowledge of the subject under review, and it is natural for us to address our comments entirely to this one participant, which reinforces the exclusiveness of the situation. We need to remember that others are present also, to embrace them with our looks, to keep our eyes open for some slight change of expression or posture that will reveal the time when we can invite someone else to join in. Sometimes direct questions can be thrown out to the other members: 'What do you think about that?'

The mêlée

On occasion, two or three topics get mixed up. This arises (particularly in discussion groups) largely because members of the group, instead of listening to and addressing their attention to what has gone before, are anxious to deliver themselves of what they have prepared, while other group members may continue to concentrate on earlier subjects. We cannot afford to let this go on too long; the intermingling of different material causes confusion and mis-learning. We may have to turn martinet for a short period and insist that the issues be sorted out so that each can be dealt with separately. To prevent people thinking that they are being cheated of what is their concern, we can make a list (perhaps on the blackboard or flipchart for all to see) of the different topics to be covered and tick them off one by one. The chances are that the subjects turn out to have more in common with each other than appeared at first sight.

The irrelevant topic

A question may come up at the wrong time. We may be in the middle of a carefully prepared demonstration or presentation, intended to develop a clear logical sequence, when suddenly a participant interrupts with a question or comment that may divert attention away from the main point. Or it may be a question we intended to raise rather later on. Do we answer now or ask the participant to wait?

The art of teaching adults involves continual judgements on matters like this. Sometimes we get it right and sometimes wrong. We have to think on our feet.

The matter is relatively simple if the question reveals ignorance of something essential for the success of the demonstration or presentation; we should deal with that issue before going any further. We may feel inclined to do the same, even if the question is a hindrance to the group session, if the comment or question comes from one of the more retiring members who rarely makes a contribution. Sometimes the interruption will have less of an effect on our carefully prepared material than we think; at least there may be several strings to our answer that can lead back to the main topic.

On the other hand, we need not be too hesitant about asking members to wait until later for us to deal with their point. We can briefly explain at what stage in the session the matter will be handled and ask that it be postponed until then. Making a note of the matter or doing something to convince the questioner that the issue will not be evaded is useful. Many students have had experience of education that is designed to avoid answering difficult questions, and they may expect the same of us. We must be sure to deal with the matter in the end, perhaps with some recognition of the value of the participant having raised it at all.

The missing group

Sometimes only two people turn up – it happens to most of us occasionally. The first thing to do is to try to avoid it by persuading all members to indicate when they cannot be present. But it will still happen in groups of adult learners; bad weather, illness or a popular local event can interrupt even the most loyal attendance.

It may be possible to deal with some discrete topic that is not essential to the main line of the course that the two or three who are gathered together find useful and rewarding for their efforts but those who are absent will either not miss or can catch up on quickly. This is especially important if there is a high degree of continuity in the group's work, and to have a vital chunk of material missed by many of the participants would be harmful. One useful activity is to spend part of the time getting to know the participants better – their interests, experiences, abilities and intentions. We may learn a lot about how the course is going on these occasions.

The missing problem

It is impossible to compile a complete catalogue of concerns faced in teaching adults. New ones are always appearing and even the most experienced teacher never learns how to solve all of them. So we need not be discouraged. But some of the comments here may help us to identify such issues and to worry out some home-made ways to address them. In many cases, it will be useful, both for our own sake as teachers and for our students' sake, to find another teacher (or a supervisor/provider/organiser) or someone else to swap experiences and advice. It always helps to talk things over.

Activity 8.6

We have seen that a learning group is a valuable tool for promoting adult learning. How will you use the ideas in this chapter within your teaching? Will you divide the group into sub-groups at any stage? Can you foresee any difficulties in working as a group within your own situation?

Further reading

Barron, R.S., Kerr, N.L. and Miller, N. (1992) *Group Process, Group Decision, Group Action*. Buckingham: Open University Press.

Douglas, T. (1983) *Groups: Understanding People Gathered Together*. London: Tavistock.

Imel, S. (ed.) (1996) *Learning in Groups: Exploring Fundamental Principles, New Uses and Emerging Opportunities*. San Francisco, CA: Jossey Bass.

Jacques, D. and Salmon, G. (2007) *Learning in Groups – A Handbook for Face-to-face and Online Environments* 4th edn. London: Routledge.

Kasl, E. and Elias, D. (2008) www.transformativelearningtheory.com/groupLearning.html

Zander, A. (1982) *Making Groups Effective*. San Francisco, CA: Jossey Bass.

Chapter 9

Roles and the Teacher
What part shall we play . . . ?

In joining an adult learning programme, the participants are constructing themselves as 'student learners'. This chapter looks at the roles
members of a learning group may play, at the importance of helping
them to change roles, at the roles that the teacher of adults will play
and at the importance of the teacher changing roles. Again it is a matter
of making conscious what we do in natural learning.

Roles in adult learning groups

We have already seen (p. 53) that when pursuing an intentional piece
of learning, the adult deliberately constructs themselves culturally and
experientially as a 'student'. The basis for this personalised construction
is both general (the cultural climate of their social context) and individual
(their personal experience of other forms of education). For some, it will
mean adopting a 'pupil' status. For others, it will imply a willingness to
'study', to work under guidance. For all, the role seems to involve some
(temporary) abandonment of autonomy, a willingness to accept direction
in order to achieve a (normally self-set) goal.

And as we have seen (p. 187), being 'a student' carries with it, for
those who come to our taught programmes rather than go to distance or
open learning, a willingness to join a learning group, a class, and to play
whatever roles are implicit in being a member of that group. As we have
noticed, there is an increasing amount of 'blended learning' with adults,
the mixing of open/distance learning processes with face-to-face teaching.
This chapter however concentrates on the roles played by the student
learners and the adult teacher in face-to-face groups.

Just as adults seek different social settings for different activities they wish
to pursue (mosque, cinema, community hall etc.), so they put themselves
into a new environment in order to achieve a specific learning goal. They
are willing for a time to divorce themselves from their other environments
and join a special environment for the purpose of learning.

Roles and changing roles

Every group has a structure, and this fact implies roles. Groups rely on roles, mutually recognised and accepted, both to achieve a task and also to work effectively in their socio-emotional and maintenance aspects. In the learning group, all of the members (including the teacher) will play some part in its functioning. Such roles are fulfilled in meeting different situations, performing various activities and engaging in patterns of behaviour.

The way each of the members of the group views their role may differ from how others in the group see the same role. To ensure group coherence and performance, it is valuable if there can be a measure of agreement about, and acceptance of, roles. This will normally be achieved without being fully explicit, through the pressures of suggestibility and through conformity to and internalisation of the assigned place in the group – although, as we have seen, the capacity for affiliation that each member possesses will vary. The roles of student learner and of teacher have been socially constructed over many years, and their interpretation will vary according to the individuals and to the context of the learning programme.

Equally, engagement with the new material on which the learning changes will be based will call for each group member to adopt new roles – at first in relation to the new material and subsequently (and consequently) in relation to the other group members. Part of the learning process for each of the group members (including the teacher) is to change roles, to try out new situations and perspectives. Much of this is of course undertaken through informal learning – it is done subconsciously and derives from the community which is around the individual group member. Informal learning is going on in the learning group at the same time as formalised learning. Part of the teaching process is to encourage and help all members of the group (again including the teacher) to enter new roles and to interpret old roles in new ways. This is part of that process of making task-conscious learning more learning-conscious.

Group roles

There is a wide variety of roles that will exist in any one group. In Activity 9.1 is a list collected from a number of teachers of adults of some of the titles they have used to describe individual members of their learning groups. There is no particular significance in the order in which they are given, and in most cases the meaning of the epithet is clear.

A few comments on this list may be useful. First, such a list can never be complete; the roles are too diverse, and in any case we will each see them in different terms. To a large extent, the range of roles and the way they are defined will be set by the context within which the learning group is set. Secondly, titles like these describe a series of activities undertaken by the group members and depend on judgements made by other members of the group. Some of them will be adopted roles, some of them ascribed by other members. Thirdly, since these roles depend on reactions to different situations, all members of the group in their time will play several parts – roles in relation to the teacher (or group leader), to the subject matter and to the other members of the group. A given title must not imply that any person will adopt that role to the exclusion of all others. Fourthly, there are dangers in giving such labels (which some people will in any case see as patronising). They tend to be more negative than positive (although the value to the learning group of the 'jester' and the 'expert' is often substantial). Equally, they may lead to stereotyping and even to self-fulfilling prophecies. But such titles can help to point out the wide range of reactions within any one group of adults engaged in learning under our supervision. Finally, the *teacher* will be called upon to adopt some of these roles during the learning group.

Activity 9.1

This list contains 'titles' given to particular roles which some adult student participants have adopted. You can do three things with this list:

- Use each title to describe how you think such a student participant will behave both in and out of the group.
- Add to this list titles from your own experience.
- Note which of these roles the teacher will be called on to adopt and why.

Title	Description	Teacher role
Student leader	Speaks for the group	
Questioner	More interested in asking	
Queen/King	questions than in listening	
Jester	to answers	
Professional simpleton		
Leader of the opposition		
Expert		
Prefect/monitor		
Cynic		
Know-all		
Last-worder		
Eavesdropper		
Self-styled ignoramus		
Special disciple		
Deviator		
Arguer		
Add to the list		

Breaking roles

Each member of the adult learning group, be it class, lecture course, training group or voluntary body, will play a role in the group. All these roles need to be accepted by the group in some way if the person is to feel fully a member of that group. Rejection of the role is interpreted as rejection of the individual. However, the role may be tolerated only in so far as it helps in the achievement of the goal; and this fact can create tensions between those members who have set themselves roles that do not directly contribute to the task and those members who are committed to the group objective. It will be the teacher's task to try to identify and minimise these tensions. Part of our work is therefore to watch for the signs of these roles, to be sensitive to the cues that indicate the nature and strength of the role being played.

Perhaps the greatest problem with these roles, and with giving titles to them, is that they may quickly become fossilised. The 'talker' at the first meeting may remain for ever the 'talker' and thus stop the 'listener' from becoming for a time a talker. The 'show-off' will continue to demonstrate their skills to all and sundry, in the process not only limiting their own learning changes but undermining the confidence of other group members not so proficient. There is often considerable group pressure on members to keep to their roles, although equally it is sometimes surprising how much effort a group as a whole will expend in its attempts to limit troublesome roles (to quieten down the 'joker', for instance) and to encourage the 'quitter' ('I-know-I-can't-do-it-so-I'm-not-going-to-try') or the 'quiet one' to join in.

These actions of the group, when they occur, are valuable and show the contribution of the whole group towards the learning task. They will complement the efforts of the teacher to encourage changing roles in the course of learning. The teacher's main aim is to help the student participants to learn, both through the group and also independently of the group. Learning must not become dependent on the group or on the role played within the group. Role changes will be necessary if learning is to take place. So the teacher needs to resist any tendency for roles to fossilise, joining with the group when it seeks to urge some of its members to break roles, and even if necessary being willing to break up the group structure if it will help members to change their roles.

Although some of the student participants will change their roles willingly in a spirit of exploration and experimentation, others will be more hesitant. They may feel that their sense of identity in the group, their security, depends on the role they have acquired, which has been accepted by the other members. One useful way around this is the use of smaller subgroups, dedicated to achieving a significant part of the task, yet providing opportunities (even perhaps the necessity) for members to adopt roles different from those they possess in the full group. Those who are very quiet in the full group will often speak more easily in smaller syndicates. And some of those who are over-assertive within the full group may become less assertive in sub-groups. It is also possible to use the group itself, its loyalty and sympathy, to encourage such changes in individual members.

It will be desirable – indeed perhaps necessary – at times for the group as a whole to become more aware of what is happening within the group, to become critically reflective on the activities and roles within the group. Only in this way can the group change and grow as its members change and grow. Open discussion of this with the whole group from time to time will be useful.

The roles of the teacher of adults

Just as each of the student participants brings with them a package of experience, expectations and concerns, a self-image of being a 'learner' which does not exist to the same extent in informal learning, so too the teacher brings their own package – and this fact needs to be recognised and acknowledged. Every teacher is at the same time an adult learner, engaging in learning episodes with their own preferred learning style. All that is stated above about the adult learner applies to the teacher as a learner in their own life. However, making learning conscious will alter the nature of the self-image of the teacher; they will see themselves as 'teacher' in their own construct of that term. The way that the role of teacher is constructed in any context is one of the key elements in the teaching–learning situation.

Activity 9.2

Before moving on to look in detail at the role of the teacher, note down how you and the agency within which you work see your role as 'teacher'.

It has often been suggested that the teacher is the most important single element in creating the whole tone of the learning group. But if there is a tension inside the group between its coherence and the call for individual learning, so too there are a number of tensions within the role of the teacher in relation to the group. Teachers will have at least four main parts to play:

- as *acknowledged leader of the group*, whose purpose it is to keep the group together, to keep things going;
- as *teacher*, an agent of change;
- as a *member of the group*, equally subject to the pressures which the group itself exerts;
- as *audience*, outside the group, the person before whom the group members will perform their newly acquired learning in search of evaluation and reinforcement.

It is a daunting role and there will often be some clash between these different roles, but the rewards more than compensate for the difficulties.

1 . . . as group leader

The teacher is the group leader. Our role in this respect is clearly recognised and accepted by the group. We cease to be a teacher when we abandon this role. There have been many, and increasingly complicated, attempts to describe the role of the group leader. One way to discuss this subject is under the three subheadings of task, interaction and maintenance, as suggested by Ivor Davies (1971).

Task

The group leader identifies and clarifies the learning task ahead, whether it be improving skills, learning a subject or solving a problem. The leader – with the participants – also clarifies the goals that they set for themselves. The leader keeps the worthwhileness of the whole enterprise constantly before the group. The leader evaluates with the group, as the learning process goes on, what progress towards achieving these goals has been made and is being made. The leader proposes the courses of action and with the group makes decisions between alternatives.

Interaction

Although part of the group, nevertheless the teacher is the one person who can watch what is happening from a position of committed detachment, involved and yet an observer. The teacher, through participant observation:

- monitors the interactions within the group and the structures it builds for itself;
- sees the roles each of the group members adopts, and seeks to assert that all the individual members of the group count;

- acts as arbiter if necessary so as to ensure that monopolies or persecutions do not arise;
- watches out for special relationships that occur and seeks to use them creatively, so that in the end every member will contribute positively and meaningfully towards the achievement of the common task, the learning.

The teacher as group leader can, and often should, help the group to see for itself what is happening. This is part of the process of developing a learning-centred consciousness.

Maintenance

The teacher assists the group to identify the resources available to them and the constraints under which they operate. He/she will encourage and help the group to mobilise the necessary resources and materials (equipment, books, speakers, exercises) needed for learning. This may often include persuading individual group members to utilise the resources that are at their disposal.

Most of these functions can and often should be shared with the participants rather than kept to one person. But the person ultimately responsible for seeing that these tasks, necessary for the performance of the group, are carried out is the teacher acting as group leader.

Problems sometimes spring from the creation of dependency syndromes. The group as a whole may come to rely on us in direct proportion as we act effectively as its leader; and individuals in the group, especially those given special attention in the course of the group's activities, frequently develop an attitude of reliance on 'their' teacher. Some measure of dependency may be desirable, even necessary, in the production of a play, but in an adult learning class or group, it will in most cases inhibit real education. This danger exists even where the teacher is attempting to develop the self-sufficiency of the learners, for group members will often try to keep us in the role of group leader against our wishes. We need, as time goes on, to play a less dominant role as leader of the learning group, whatever pressures the group members may bring to bear on us.

At other times or in other situations, groups will strike out on their own. And some teachers of adults find a problem here. It is not always easy to accept – after a lengthy period of nurturing the group – the decision of the group that it does not want us to continue in that role, that they wish to pursue their own agenda, that they can manage without us. Some teachers of adults, subconsciously fearing such a situation, try to prevent such independent action being taken by the group members – 'in the interests of the group', we often argue. But the interests of the group will best be served when they have come to a large extent to control their own learning programme.

2 . . . as teacher

The teacher is the promoter of learning changes, the encourager of the learners. The term 'change-agent' has been used for the teacher in some circles. We aim to use the group to help bring about changes in knowledge, understanding, skills, attitudes and ultimately in behaviour. Teachers thus have to be 'stirrers', to achieve change without breaking up the group.

The teacher operates in two ways: as manager of the learning process and as instructor.

Manager of learning

In this role, four main types of activity may be identified: planner, organiser, leader and controller of the learning process for each of the members of the learning group.

- *Planner* – the teacher analyses the programme of learning, identifies the skills, knowledge and attitudes required, sets out the learning objectives and the individual learning tasks that need to be completed in order to achieve these goals, determines what resources will be necessary and constructs the learning sequences (the curriculum). Most or all of this can be done with the student learners.
- *Organiser* – the teacher organises the learning tasks, subject always to the context within which the learning takes place, the environment of the class or group, the conditions under which the student participants engage in their work. The end purpose is to make it easier for the participants to work and learn together. It is thus important that such organising should be done to meet the requirements of the learners rather than for administrative convenience or for an easy life for the teacher.
- *Leader* – the teacher encourages the student participants, selects and uses appropriate teaching–learning methods and materials. For this part of our work, we need the most effective social tools we can find.
- *Controller* – the teacher to a large extent determines the relevance of the activities and the material to the task in hand and to the ultimate objectives of the learning programme, revises the programme and changes direction when necessary. S/he rules out irrelevancies and helps to create and maintain the momentum of

the learning group. It is here that one of the key differences between adult learning programmes and those for younger persons can be seen. For in many programmes (although not all), adult participants exercise more control over the learning programme than do younger students. They will frequently determine what they want to learn, when and how – and they will reveal these decisions in their own study patterns. In the end, they will simply cease to participate fully when they feel that they have achieved their own learning goals.

It is worth noting here that some teachers of adults feel that their role as teacher has changed in recent years. They would argue that their role as planner has diminished, as syllabuses and curriculum have increasingly been set externally, particularly in accredited provision. This in turn means that the adult participants too have less control over what they learn and how.

We would argue, however, that despite this trend towards accredited courses with prescribed learning outcomes, the teacher of adults cannot hide behind such provisions to deny that they have roles as planners and organisers. Even within the restrictions of externally set learning programmes, the teacher will still take decisions about teaching (the route to achieve the goal). Many externally set programmes 'dictate' the learning outcomes and assessment tasks but will leave the teacher to make decisions about the order in which the programme is taught, the content, the materials used and the teaching methods. Thus the autonomy of the teacher is maintained in many areas.

Instructor

Several attempts have been made to categorise the different instructional styles teachers adopt in relation to their learners, ranging from what has been called the 'sheepdogging' approach to teaching (herding the flock by constantly snapping at them) to the opposite extreme – allowing the student learners to 'free-range'. Some writers have divided teachers in their personal approach to the student learners into different types such as 'lion-tamer', 'entertainer' or 'cultivator'; it is not difficult to see the force of these terms as they apply to teaching patterns. Others have reflected on the contrast in modes of relating to the group: the autocratic, the *laissez-faire* and the democratic, for example. Others again have spoken of those teachers who 'tell', those who 'sell', those who 'consult' and those who 'join' the group of learners. Such descriptions attempt to depict some of the different continua of approaches to teaching (Figure 9.1); they are not distinct categories.

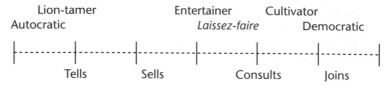

Figure 9.1 The continuum of approaches to teaching

Activity 9.3

Describe briefly the sort of activity each of these teachers engages in; you could perhaps mark those you feel you most nearly approximate to.

Lion-tamer	Autocratic	Tells	*Your own list*
Entertainer	*Laissez-faire*	Sells	
Cultivator	Democratic	Consults	
		Joins	

Others have spoken of the teacher's manner: of those who on the one hand are aloof and egocentric as opposed to those who are friendly and understanding; of those who are dull and routine as against those who are stimulating and imaginative; of those who are evasive and whose work is unplanned as against those who are engaging and highly organised. Such characteristics are major factors in creating the atmosphere within which we all have to work in a learning group.

Class climate

Teaching styles help to create a 'climate' for the adult class or learning group. The atmosphere of the learning group may be relaxed, warm and friendly, or it may be tense, cold and hostile. The responses of the student participants could be on the one hand apathetic, obstructive, uncertain and dependent, or on the other alert, responsible, confident and initiating. Attempts to assess the different elements to this climate have been made on the basis of four main characteristics:

- *Warmth* – the strength of emotions and identification between the teacher and the student participants; is the group welcoming, affirming, encouraging to the learner, not dismissive or exclusive?
- *Directness* – whether the interactions between the teacher and the student participants are direct or indirect, whether the teacher does all the work or whether the group stimulates the learners to do their own work.

- *Enthusiasm* – the way the teacher feels about the subject being taught, about the students and their learning; the commitment of both teacher and student participants to the learning task.
- *Organisation* – how far the teacher demonstrates competence in organising; the strength and efficiency of the process of managing the learning situation, devising carefully planned and purposeful exercises so that all involved feel they are not wasting time.

It is the teacher (as well as the learning programme setting) who to a large extent controls these elements and who helps to create the climate of the learning groups by his/her own styles. The concern of the teacher is both to promote the emotional well-being of the student participants and to ensure learning.

The climate of the class or learning group may be stable, with a consistent style used throughout; or it may fluctuate as the teacher swings from one style to another. Sudden and unexpected changes of climate may leave many of the participants uncertain of their roles and less able to cope with the learning tasks; but some modifications of climate are probably desirable for learning changes to take place. A static climate may not encourage the experimentation that is necessary to much learning.

Implications for the teacher

The fact that there are different ways of depicting the relationship between the teacher and the student participants prompts a number of thoughts. The first is that there can be no universal descriptions of the very complex series of relations that go on within a learning group. So much depends on the learning context, on the individual values of the teacher and on the student participants. Each of these may define these interactions in different ways. It is easier for us to describe and classify the relationship of other teachers to their students than it is to do so for ourselves. We are aware how far such categories fall short of the complexity of reality in our own case.

Figure 9.2 sets out a possible matrix of two of the main sets of factors controlled by the teacher and the sort of activity that may result from the varied teaching styles and class/learning group climates.

Activity 9.4

Where do you prefer to operate on the matrix in Figure 9.2? And why?

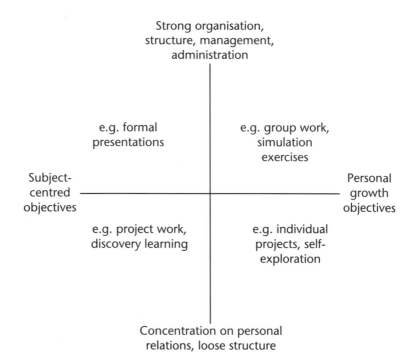

Strong organisation,
structure, management,
administration

e.g. formal
presentations

e.g. group work,
simulation
exercises

Subject-
centred
objectives

Personal
growth
objectives

e.g. project work,
discovery learning

e.g. individual
projects, self-
exploration

Concentration on personal
relations, loose structure

Figure 9.2 Matrix of class/learning group climate

Secondly, most of us as teachers do not adopt any one approach consistently. We move about throughout these styles as the need presents
itself. The effective teacher will probably use many of these different
ways of relating to the learners in the group during the course of teaching, just as the students also move about.

Thirdly, we will sometimes find ourselves torn between the style
adopted in relation to the whole group and the style needed for certain
individual learners. How for instance shall we handle the situation of the
slow learner who holds up the group? Or the very able who speed ahead
and thus begin to distance themselves from the group? Which comes first,
the welfare of the individual student participant or of the whole group?

And finally there may be – and often is – a tension between the role
which the teacher wishes to adopt in relation to the adult learning group
and the role which the student participants wish the teacher to adopt.
Many students want their teacher to teach formally, to present information; they sometimes regard discussions as a waste of time. But some
teachers find this a role which they cannot easily adopt. A conflict can
arise from the dissatisfaction felt by those teachers of adults who are unable to reconcile themselves to the teaching–learning approaches which
their student participants desire.

It is impossible to answer such questions with universal rules. Each teacher must think about them and answer them for themselves in the context of their own style of teaching and institutional framework. If each of the participants in our learning groups has their own learning style, which they have come to use effectively, it is also true that each of us as teachers has our own particular teaching style that we are happiest with, and this will to a large extent determine how we react in our learning groups. We need to recognise our own particular style for what it is; to improve it with practice; and to try to make sure that it accomplishes what it is intended to accomplish – student learning. We should also perhaps experiment with alternative styles at times.

The learning programme material

Being the main instructor of the learning programme will involve introducing the learner to the material comprising the learning task. One of the duties of the teacher is to encourage the student participants to engage directly with the subject matter for themselves. Here the triangle of learner, teacher and subject matter occurs again. In many cases, the subject matter is at first mediated through the teacher; then the teacher gradually withdraws, urging the learners to encounter the material face to face, until we have rendered ourselves to a large extent (ultimately completely) redundant to the learning process (see Figure 9.3). Unless we withdraw from this process of interaction between student participant and subject matter, learning will tend to cease when the class comes to an end or the group disperses.

3 . . . as group member

As teachers of adults, we are concerned with the learning needs of our student participants. Their learning styles need to be practised, their

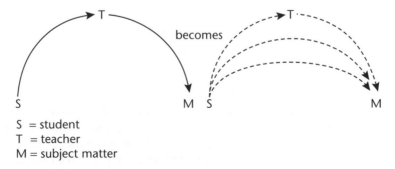

S = student
T = teacher
M = subject matter

Figure 9.3 The student learner (S) approaches the subject matter (M) at first 'through' the teacher (T) but later directly

learning skills strengthened and enriched. In this process, the teacher's third role, as member of the group, becomes important. Not only will it enable us to experience something of what the other group members will be experiencing, it will directly assist us in helping the various members to learn.

Some teachers of adults find being a group member difficult. But the teacher can become a model of learning for the student participants. It has been said that 'the most important attribute of the teacher [is that] he [*sic*] must be a learner himself. If he has lost his capacity for learning, he is not good enough to be in the company of those who have preserved theirs' (quoted in Kidd 1973: 303). The way we ourselves learn and engage with the subject matter can be used as an illustration of the way other learners in the group can relate to the subject matter. All of us in the group, including the teacher, are learners; and we can all learn from each other how to learn.

The teacher and the class session

If we approach our learning group in this way, the meetings begin to assume a different perspective. We will become conscious that we, as teachers, do most of our learning for this programme outside of the group meetings. So that, instead of seeing our students as 'attending classes', we, and they, will see all of us as engaged in a course of study, a programme of work that will occupy a good deal of our time as long as we remain committed to it. Just as teachers of adults need to learn between class/ group meetings – as they engage with the subject matter, prepare the material for the next learning step and evaluate progress made – so it is possible for them to encourage the other members of the learning group to learn in similar ways. It is odd that so many teachers of adults expect their students to learn in class only, while they themselves learn much outside the group. Those teachers who aim to make their students independent learners will seek ways to enable them to learn as much *between* class sessions as in the group meetings. The open and distance learning modes increasingly used in 'blended courses' have shown some of the ways to do this effectively.

There are two possible models of the face-to-face teaching session in relation to learning. Teachers will adopt either model to suit different sets of circumstances, or indeed mix them from time to time. In one, most of the learning activity is done during the class meeting: demonstration of a new method of working, for instance, reading and discussing a text, listening to a lecture, engaging in practical exercises, etc. The period between each class/meeting is spent by the learner reinforcing (by practice, reading, writing, etc.) the learning done in class (Figure 9.4a).

Part of each class session will then be spent in feedback, an assessment of how much and what sort of learning has gone on since the last meeting. This is not a waste of time. Indeed, to expect all learning to be confined to those times when we are face to face will not only create dependency, it will waste all the time between each meeting available for reinforcement and run the risk of learning changes being lost.

An alternative model moves the main learning process out of the class session to the period between each meeting. A task is thus set during the class, to be completed before the next session. In this case, the next meeting will be spent partly assessing and evaluating how well the task has been performed and the material learned, and partly setting another task (or an adaptation of the same task if it has been inadequately learned). Most of the new learning will take place outside the class/group meeting (Figure 9.4b).

Using the space between meetings for learning will not occur automatically. As long as we concentrate on the teacher teaching, we shall think of the learning session in isolation from the rest of the student learners' lives; we shall believe that all learning goes on during the

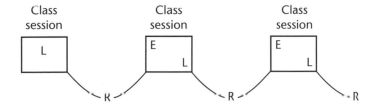

L = doing the learning exercise
R = exercises reinforcing the learning done in class
E = evaluating the reinforcement exercises

Figure 9.4a One model of using teaching and learning time

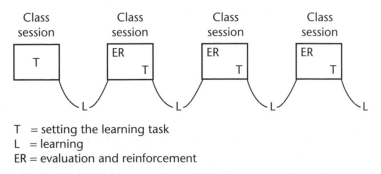

T = setting the learning task
L = learning
ER = evaluation and reinforcement

Figure 9.4b A different model of using teaching and learning time

face-to-face encounter. Even when we re-orientate ourselves and think more in terms of the students' learning as an ongoing process, continuing even when we are not present, there will be obstacles in the way of using to the best effect the time between each session. Many adult student participants tend to see the encounter between teacher and learner as the essential focus for learning. We need therefore to take conscious steps to ensure that continued learning occurs outside of the group meetings and to evaluate what learning is taking place.

4 . . . as 'audience'

The fourth main aspect of our task as teacher is that of evaluator. By creating the learning tasks and calling for them to be performed before us for our comments and evaluation, we remove ourselves to some extent from the group. We become the criteria by which our student participants' learning efforts are judged. In this respect, we are the expert, not just the instructor but the assessor of the learning which our students have done. In this again, the teacher will share the activity with the student participants so that they may become jointly reflective on their own learning. But in the end, the students, individually and collectively, have put themselves into a situation where they call for feedback from us as teachers. This is discussed at greater length in Chapter 12.

The student learners and the teacher: horizontal learning

At this point, the greatest change of role comes about in both teacher and student learner. In order to learn, the student participant needs to become for a time a teacher. The learner demonstrates the newly acquired skill or presents the newly learned material to the teacher, who in turn adopts the role of listener/learner. Adult (lifelong) education has been described as an activity in which all the participants 'alternate between the roles of student, teacher and person' (Thompson 1980: 67). Every adult learner needs to come to teach in some way or other. The teachers watch, listen, read and evaluate as they assess the student participants' work, just as the learner demonstrates, talks, writes and displays the new learning in other ways. The teacher–learner exchange of roles is the single most effective method of learning. (Formal institutions have long recognised this when they prescribe the writing of essays as a tool of learning, though there are many better ways of the student undertaking teaching functions than writing essays, and demonstration is not of course more appropriate for most skill-based learning programmes.)

In performing this role of evaluator, the teacher comes to make critical judgements about the work of the student participants. So it is essential that we come to know ourselves, become aware of those biases that influence the judgements we make. Such preferences include those between male and female, between white and black, between old and young, between professional and working class, between the law-abiding and the law-breaking, between the known and the unknown. We all possess such prejudices, and they affect all we do and think. We should try to be open with ourselves about such preferences.

Resistance to change

The teacher makes demands on the student participants as learners. We set tasks and call for them to be performed under our critical eye, until the stage has been reached when the subject matter makes its own demands on the learners. There will be times when we are faced with a measure of resistance on the part of some of the student participants. There will be several reasons for this:

- Some of the participants do not in fact want to change. They come to our learning programmes for many purposes (sometimes even believing that they want to learn), among which socio-emotional needs may be strongest – and these reasons often militate against change. Others may be there for career-related reasons rather than out of a desire for learning. They want to acquire the accolades that go with the completion of the pro-gramme of study but they do not want to learn, to change. Most groups of adult learners contain some members like this.
- Sometimes the roles played by the student participants establish their status in the group, and abandonment of those roles may be seen as damaging. Several adults find engaging in group learn-ing exercises embarrassing; they see such activities as damaging the picture they believe others have of them.
- Learning changes can be, as we have suggested, uncomfortable and even painful to make, the more so as the adult grows into a concept of self-maturity. To admit to learning needs is in itself challenging to some adults, while others resist the effort needed to change their views and attitudes. Where student participants are challenged to change their views or attitudes they may experi-ence what Atherton (2009) describes as 'learning as loss', that is, the student is asked to 'supplant' old learning with new ideas. The loss is not so much as a result of the learning itself but of the implications of the new learning, particularly where there is a high emotional cost.
- Perhaps most frequently, many student learners will object to the teacher who abandons what they see as the traditional role of instructor and expert, especially the teacher who on occasion

admits ignorance. Some students may become anxious when a teacher engages in participatory activities: they want authoritative guidance or reassurance, and even discipline from a 'superior' person. Many groups will go to considerable lengths to keep the teacher as teacher and the learners as learners.

Fight or flight

When faced with a request to engage in some learning activity, group resistance can take one of two main forms of reaction: fight or flight. In 'fight', open resistance ('We don't want to') is on the whole less common than the question, 'Why should we?' This is often not so much a genuine enquiry, an expression indicating that the participants are unconvinced of the necessity of the particular learning task, as a statement meaning – 'We won't' (although many adult students are too polite to say so). 'Flight' may be expressed in the form: 'We will, but later'; 'It's a good idea but we can't do it because/until . . .'; 'We must find the proper material (or do this or that) before we can begin.' An alternative form of flight is compensation, the substitution of some other task for that proposed.

We should recognise these tactics for what they are. One effective way of dealing with them is to help the group to become aware of them as avoidance techniques, as resistance to engaging in learning activities.

Expectations of the teacher

Most members of adult learning groups of all kinds expect the teacher to occupy the teaching role and the student participants to occupy the learning roles all the time. They see the teacher as both *an* authority (a specialist in the subject) and *in* authority (in command of the class/group). Many teachers see themselves in this way too; they collaborate with the pressures of the student participants. They feel safer being in charge of the whole process. They are often anxious about letting the student participants loose to experiment and learn by doing on their own – fearful that the learners will 'get it wrong'. They feel that they are not fulfilling their responsibilities as teachers, not fulfilling their students' expectations of them, even not 'earning their money'.

Just as the student roles are expressed non-verbally as well as verbally, so too are those of the anxious teacher. How often do we stand up before the class unnecessarily, rising to point out something to the rest of the group or to use the flipchart, especially when pressed with a question to which we are unsure of the answer? Standing above our students reasserts our authority both to them and to ourselves, like preaching from a pulpit, 'six feet above contradiction'. In non-verbal ways like this, we buttress our position when we feel challenged. We should try to become aware not just of how the roles of the learners are expressed but also of how we express the position we wish to occupy in the group.

This position is compounded of many different roles. The students call upon us to express many of these in the course of our encounter with them. In particular, many group members expect the teacher to be a performer, what Richard Hoggart (in J. Rogers 1969) has called 'a Pied Piper of Hamelin', leading our flock by our playing to a dreamland of success. Some students consciously exert pressure to keep a teacher in this performing role: 'I could listen to you all day'. And some teachers respond to this demand willingly, adding one more role to the many they are already playing: 'Even more than most teaching, adult education invites its tutors to a range of attractive . . . forms of role-playing'.

Some of these roles contradict each other. The list in Activity 5.9, selected from the descriptions compiled by different groups of teachers over the years, indicates some of these roles; you may wish to add to it from your own experience. It is no wonder that at the end of a discussion of these roles, one teacher in the tutor-training group exclaimed: 'We have just described God!'

Activity 9.5

Here is a list some of the roles that teachers adopt in relation to their student participants. You may find it helpful to write notes against each of them to say how you expect the teacher to behave in these circumstances. Add to this list from your own perceptions.

Expert: a resource, a source of knowledge	Expected to provide instant answers to all queries
Provider:	Gives access to resources
Explainer:	
Demonstrator	
Discipliner:	Especially against a disruptive group member
Organiser:	
Instructor:	
Motivator:	
Protector:	
Chairman: arbiter	
Examiner: evaluator	Assessor of the work done, the one who maintains standards, checks work, etc.
Counsellor:	The one who will help, advise, guide, reassure, support, encourage the individual learner
Others:	

This last remark provokes a few final comments about the role of the teacher.

First, expect a life of isolation. As teacher, it will rarely be possible for you to join the group fully. You will always have one foot outside the group, however much you join in. You will nearly always be the 'audience' before whom the participants will practise their newly acquired learning and who will be expected to evaluate and approve their performance. The teacher is 'in' but not always 'of' the group.

Clearly a thorough knowledge of one's subject is essential for teaching adults. Teaching adults is not low-level work, as some in other areas of education have suggested, for the student participants frequently push the teacher by their questions to the very limits of the subject. The teacher of adults needs to be fully acquainted with all aspects of the subject, for unlike the university lecturer we cannot always choose what we teach about; the student learners often determine that.

Equally, the teacher of adults must be prepared on occasion to say, 'I don't know'. We will usually have some idea of how to find out. It is very rare that an adult group will respect any teacher the less for admitting gaps in their knowledge. They are themselves aware that the amount that is not known is far greater than what is known, and they will rarely expect the teacher to be an expert across the whole of any field.

Expect on occasion to feel threatened by the students. Some of them know more about parts of the subject matter than their teacher. Some possess many of the social skills which the teacher may wish s/he possessed. In such circumstances, there is a danger of the teacher falling back onto authority – the claim to leadership which the role of teaching endows. The teacher of adults needs to allow and indeed encourage the group to be student-led without feeling that their role has been usurped.

This suggests that social skills may be more important in selecting teachers of adults than subject specialism. It is not always the best policy to get the most up-to-date expert or series of experts to talk to a group of adult learners. Continuity of contact may be more important to allow for growth over a period of time rather than a series of individual teaching sessions by specialists.

If our task as teachers of adults is so demanding, it follows that we should seek out all the help we can get. Most teachers of adults work in isolation from each other, and we rarely spend enough time searching for the resources available in the community to assist us in the task. We need support, and it is up to us to find it. Our employing agency, if we have one, should help; but if not, there *are* other teachers of adults in our neighbourhood. Joining and building networks of adult teachers is a most worthwhile activity.

And finally, faced with the multiple and very demanding roles which the teacher needs to fulfil, we must be realistic and agree that not many of us will achieve much of all this. We must not become too self-conscious about our roles, our methods and our relationships. It is useful now and again to check how we and the group are performing, and every so often something will pull us up and make us realise the nature of the group reactions. But provided we are sensitive to what is happening, we can let things flow naturally, helping just a little here and there to direct the current towards the goals.

In view of the superhuman range of expectations that both we and the group hold of the teacher's role, we cannot expect 100 per cent success. Most of our teaching sessions will have at least one blatant error, sometimes many more. The task of being a teacher needs to be learned, and that takes time.

Further reading

Brookfield, S. (ed.) (1988) *Training Educators of Adults*. London: Routledge.

Hillier, Y. (2002) *Reflective Teaching in Further and Adult Education*. London: Continuum.

Moore, A. (2004) *The Good Teacher: Dominant Discourses in Teaching and Teacher Education*. London: Routledge.

Ostervan, K. and Kottkamp, R. (1993) *Reflective Practice for Educators*. London: Sage.

Schön, D.A. (1995) *Educating the Reflective Practitioner*. San Francisco, CA: Jossey Bass.

Teaching Adults: there are some useful papers among those on the following site: http://honolulu.hawaii.edu/intranet/committees/FacDevCom/guidebk/teachtip/teachtip.htm

Chapter 10

Teaching: Content and Methods
How shall we do it . . . ?

> This chapter argues that the learning content chosen and the teaching–
> learning methods used in the process of promoting learning are inextric-
> ably linked. Here again we can build on the methods of informal learning
> which our student learners already employ.

We have seen that, in order to build on the natural learning process – the
informal learning which is based on our experience of and interaction
with our social and physical environment – we can utilise the learning
group and the various roles within it. Equally, in order to ensure that
each of the student participants in our groups can learn in their own
way, using their own learning practices and styles and at their own pace,
we can espouse a varied range of teaching–learning methods that will
involve the student participants in their own programme of work. It is
the purpose of this chapter to explore this second avenue.

Curriculum

Methods and content together make up the curriculum, and a word on
curriculum is thus necessary. There is relatively little material on curriculum
in adult or lifelong education, and what there is tends to focus on the
subject areas felt to be most appropriate to adult participants rather than
on curriculum as a whole (Egan 1986). Griffin's pioneering study (1983)
concentrates on socio-philosophical concepts of the adult curriculum,
and on the whole neglects more practical aspects which are more fully
explored in a short study by the Further Education Unit in 1984 *Curriculum
Development in the Education of Adults: A Manual for Practitioners*. Much
more work on curriculum has been done in relation to schools, and it is
therefore necessary to adapt what is known about curriculum in schools
(see Smith 2000).

Curriculum is often seen as a body of knowledge and skills, the content
of education to which the students need to be exposed. But curriculum is
much wider than a list of subjects to be studied; it is not only what you
say but how you say it! One view of curriculum is that it is 'all the planned

conditions and events to which the student is exposed for the purpose of promoting learning plus the framework of theory which gives these conditions and events a certain coherence' (Travers 1964: 42). The word 'curriculum' itself comes from a Latin word meaning 'racecourse', and this is a powerful reminder that what we are talking about here are the activities which the *students* will engage in to achieve their learning goals rather than a programme of actions which the teacher will fulfil. 'Curriculum' is the sum total of all the experiences, planned and un-planned, of the student learners during the learning programme.

Five elements have been seen as making up the curriculum, the philo-sophic framework, the context of the learning programme, the contents, the events and their sequencing, and the evaluation inherent throughout the programme.

Philosophical framework

Part of the curriculum which the student learners learn consists of those attitudes which underlie all of our teaching. Woodwork may be seen as a series of techniques or as part of a concern for good design and good living; family planning may be taught on its own, in isolation from all other subjects, or as part of a holistic approach to personal growth, family development and human sexuality; HIV/AIDS and other health education can be addressed as a medical issue controlled by drugs or as a socio-moral issue reflecting on patterns of behaviour. Sociology may be taught as an academic study or as a practical exploration of personal experiences. Natural history may be taught as a leisure pursuit or as part of socially concerned issues. In every case, the difference will show in the way the subject is taught. Continuing professional development or work-related training programmes can be taught as purely technical matters or in a much wider social framing. This philosophical framework and the discourse employed relate to those overall goals discussed on page 165. In particular, it will reflect our assumptions as to whether the education we are engaged in is designed to reproduce or transform existing social systems, whether it is aimed to lead to conformity or to liberation (see pp. 64–66).

Context

The student learners will also learn much from the way in which the learning programme is organised. There are two main aspects to this:

- The *setting* – the venue of the learning programme, the furniture, the lighting and heating, the levels of noise and other distractions in the immediate environment. The amount of attention the teacher gives to these factors forms part of the curriculum experience. But it goes further: the institutional setting and even the building within which the learning programme is located, whether formal or non-formal, the location of the course, the social and academic environment in which it is set, whether it is accessible, close to or distant from the learner's base, whether the student participant can reach the centre easily or only with difficulty, the timing of the learning programme – all of these are part of the learning experience and will teach the student learners much. They will not always, of course, be under the control of the teacher of adults, but the teacher needs to assess such features and take them into account when planning the teaching–learning experience.

- The *climate* – the atmosphere created in the class session by two sets of relationships: those between teacher and student learners and those between learner and learner. The climate, as we have seen, may be warm, informal and open or it may be cold, formal and closed (see pp. 224–5). In adult learning programmes in particular, the climate will reflect how seriously the organisers and teachers take the intentions of the student learners, what importance they attach to the expectations and hopes of the student participants. In particular, it will reveal how much the different expectations of the student learners about the formal or non-formal nature of learning and of the particular learning programme (see Chapter 4) have been taken into consideration by the teacher.

One important factor in creating the climate in any programme of adult and continuing education is the staffing of the learning programme. A series of lectures given by different experts may tend not only to create problems for the students in relating both to the teachers and also to the subject matter (problems of overlap or gaps or contradictions between the material of different sessions, or establishing the relationships between the different material in each lecture), but it will also arouse a number of (often subconscious) questions about the nature of knowledge itself and the relationship of the student learners to expertise. Are they all expected, for example, to know everything that each of their different lecturers know? If not, which parts are important and which not?

This raises other questions. To whom does knowledge belong – to the expert or the learner? Whose knowledge counts? Can the student learner ever become an expert, and how? More continuity of teacher–learner contact will reveal a care to help the student learner to learn. It will indicate a belief that learning is in many cases a continuous process, to be pursued persistently, not a spasmodic series of inputs; that learning goes on all the time, not just in the lectures.

Again, frequent and arbitrary changes of timetable to suit the demands of the organisers and/or teacher will teach the student learners the level of importance which the agent attaches to the programme – and the student learners may begin not to take the learning programme seriously themselves. A commitment to honour the contract to learn, clear indicators that the student learners come first in every case, will form part of the learning experiences of the course. These will teach the student learners much that is not discussed formally as part of the learning programme. They will form the 'hidden curriculum', the learning by subconscious assimilation that goes on inside every formalised learning programme.

Content

The subject matter to be covered clearly forms part of the curriculum. There are many different aspects to this area of our discussion. Apart from the *amount* of subject matter to be covered, there is the *sequence* in which it is handled, and the *conditions* attached to the learning. These are matters where formalised learning brings special insights to the teaching–learning process, for there is in informal learning less concern with sequencing or with conditions attached to the learning other than are required within the task to be performed. In formal learning programmes, the sequence is planned to facilitate learning; if then a change is introduced because a particular teacher or resource is not available, the participants will learn that the priorities of the teaching staff are higher than the priorities of the student learners. And the level of performance, the speed at which the task should be completed, the fluency of the use of the material, the measure of understanding which accompanies the performance, all form part of the curriculum. What is required of the student learner is as much part of the learning experience as the subject matter itself and needs to be made explicit.

Is there a specifically 'adult' curriculum? – some things which can *only* be learned as an adult (e.g. a mortgage) or which can *best* be learned as an adult (e.g. finances) rather than as children? Are there things which adults *need to* learn to function in today's society (e.g. computers) which they were not able to learn at a younger age – a catch-up curriculum? The *IFLL Report* sets an adult curriculum consisting of four areas: digital capabilities (best learned as a child); health capabilities (both children and adult); financial capabilities (mainly adult learning); and civic (community, national and global) capabilities – but the report admits this is not based on any theoretical basis but emerged from the submissions to the commission. Where does this leave creative or spiritual development? (the report tries to squeeze creativity in uncomfortably into civic capabilities, as it does global interdependence). This is a marginal matter for most teachers of adults who already have their subject area and whose concern for a curriculum lies within that subject area; but it does help to contextualise our teaching.

The content of a learning programme is often set out in a syllabus, especially in the increasing number of programmes based on credit accumulation and a modular system. But syllabuses normally omit to say much about the conditions attached to the learning. And they rarely indicate in any detail the teaching–learning *materials* which may be used. Here we can go to informal learning for some guidance. In informal learning, the materials for learning are what comes to hand, what is needed to achieve the task. They are directly relevant and usable materials, 'real' in the sense that they relate to the daily life task on which the student learner is engaged, rather than having been created specifically to promote learning. As well as specially prepared materials which involve sequencing and the conditions for the learning, we also need in our teaching of adults to use materials which are immediately relevant to the student learners, materials which they can often choose and provide. This calls for responsiveness and innovativeness on the part of the teacher of adults.

On the other hand, a syllabus will sometimes include elements of *methods* as well as subject matter. A management course syllabus may include not just a list of topics such as 'personnel recruitment; selection procedures; career development; staff training; promotion criteria', etc., but also a note of some activities such as 'workshops; syndicate work; group discussion with report back to plenary session'. A number of course outlines for adults now indicate the kind of in-class and out-of-class activities which the tutors expect of the students.

Events

The activities which the teacher plans and which the student learners experience, and the sequence in which they occur, are all part of the curriculum. The planned lectures, talks, discussions, small group work, reading, written exercises, student presentations, practical work; the materials used, visual and audio aids, handouts, reading lists and texts, websites; the educational technology used with varying levels of com-petence – all these and many other elements help to create the curriculum, the programme which the student learners are expected to follow. Some events of course occur which are not planned: the interruption of a learning programme because of the absence of a lecturer; the inter-ruption of a session by a visitor, an organiser or supervisor to make an announcement; or even in some cases the weather – all form part of the learning experiences of the student participants. Such unplanned events will either contribute to or distract from the learning, and one of the traits of an effective teacher is the ability to use such happenings as they occur to help forward the learning process, to direct even distractions towards the student learners' goals.

Processes of evaluation

Among the experiences of the student learners are those planned processes of evaluation – examinations and tests; assignments and other activities for feedback; criticism and assessment; ways in which the student learners can express their satisfactions and so on (see Chapter 12). These too form part of the curriculum.

All these five elements contribute to that pattern of experiences and the philosophy which embraces them which together go to make up the learning course. It is the curriculum that brings the content and methods of our learning programmes close together.

The relationship between content and methods

The link between the methods and the content of the teaching–learning encounter thus depends upon the approach which we as teachers adopt. An emphasis on content, a set amount of matter that must be covered, to a large extent prescribes the methods to be used in the class/group. It will normally lead to a concentration on 'transmission', on presentation methods of some sort and formal processes of evaluation. On the other hand, a concentration on the processes of learning will tend to mean that more time will be spent on the varied student learners and their needs; relatively less of the content will be dealt with, and it will normally be used as an example of how the rest of the material may be handled by the student learners on their own. The emphasis will thus vary according to whether the approach to learning is teacher-centred or learner-centred. This distinction corresponds to what Bruner (1966) describes as the *expository* approach to teaching–learning, in which 'the decisions concerning the mode and pace and style of exposition are principally determined by the teacher as expositor, the student as the listener', and the *hypothetical* approach, in which 'the teacher and the student are in a more co-operative position . . . The student is not a bench listener but is taking part in the formulation and at times may play the principal role . . . [through] acts of discovery'.

Others have made a distinction between decontextualised learning (the material being mastered is generalised) and contextualised learning (the material is drawn from, and related and adapted to the experience of the different student learners in the group). Contextualising the learning will not only affect the material chosen for study but also the teaching–learning methods used.

There is on the whole a close correlation between these two sets of approaches. A content-/subject-based decontextualised approach tends to emphasise the teacher's presentation methods, the sort of activity the teacher engages in in the group; whereas a process-/methods-based contextualised approach will be more learner-oriented, more concerned with what the student participants do than with what the teacher does. But this is not necessarily the case, and a matrix (Figure 10.1) would seem to be a better model. (It may be helpful for you to locate your own learning programme on this matrix.)

Most of us need to adopt varied approaches. Sometimes our work will need to be teacher-centred, sometimes learner-centred; sometimes it will be concerned with subject matter, sometimes with process. Both Bruner's expository and hypothetical approaches will be called upon at different times. Exposition is a valid tool of the teaching–learning situation, a necessary part of the process – it is one of the basic skills the teacher needs. Despite the protests of some adult educators, much learning by adults consists of acquiring and developing new knowledge. The student participants need to inform themselves, to learn new processes, to obtain new information and understanding from outside of themselves. They do not possess all the knowledge they need. They can of course do this in a variety of ways, and presentation is a valid and widely used method of teaching.

Nevertheless, in order to promote independence of learning, the student participants need to engage in acts of discovery for themselves and to construct the knowledge for themselves in ways which match their prior knowledge and experience. The decision as to the balance between presentation and discovery learning to be adopted will to a large extent

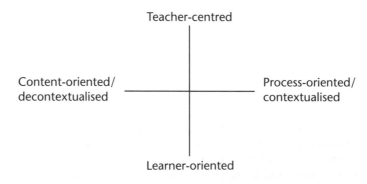

Figure 10.1 Matrix of methods/content in the adult learning process

be determined by our attitudes towards the balance between content and methods in our teaching programmes and by the learning styles of the participants.

Activity 10.1

Use the diagram above (Figure 10.1) to place some of the teaching you are doing or will be doing in each of the segments. You may, for example, place 'introducing a new topic' in the content-oriented/teacher-centred segment whilst 'learner-led research' may appear in the process-oriented/contextualised segment.

   What kind of balance is there between the segments? Is your teaching dominated by one or the other? Is this the right kind of balance or can you think of ways of re-balancing your teaching to provide a greater range of teaching methods and content?

Content

There are two parts to our discussion of the development of new knowledge: the amount of new knowledge needed to complete the learning task, and the ways that students can develop this new knowledge.

Amount

The amount of knowledge required for any specified learning task is almost always decided by the providing agency, organisers and teachers. The evidence suggests that teachers in lifelong education (as in other parts of the educational world) regularly overestimate the amount of such input. Many teachers try to insist on what they see as a complete coverage of a topic. There are, it is true, some programmes where the amount of new knowledge is *under*estimated: 'Learn this skill and don't bother with the theory' is sometimes the approach. But there are signs that many adults wish to learn something of the background to the particular process they are engaged in learning, some framework of understanding within which to locate the new material meaningfully. On the whole, however, most programmes are over- rather than under-loaded. Perhaps the reason for this is that teachers tend to take themselves and their own range of knowledge as the norm for their students. They often determine the amount of knowledge needed for the completion of the task by what they themselves know rather than by what the student learners need to know. They judge the speed at which the student participants will be able to move by how quickly they themselves can learn. They assess the student learners' ability to cope with new knowledge by their own ability, and they frequently choose the processes of learning by taking the way they learned in the past as the norm. None of this may be correct.

The result can be undue pressure on the student learner. The teachers set the pace of learning by judging the amount of material they feel they need to 'cover' against the time they have at their disposal, not by the abilities and commitments of the student learners. Teachers of adults often think that the time allotted to them amounts to more learning time than is in fact the case. But seen against competing pressures on the student learners, the time available is not great, especially when a significant number of adult student learners may have been away from formal learning for some considerable period. Developing skills and understanding takes time; and adults need to relate their new knowledge and understanding (present experience) to past experience, which also takes time. We may underestimate this and press on, bound by our material and the time available for the learning programme.

On the other hand, as teachers we need to recognise that we ourselves experience internal pressures. We have been asked to teach a subject for which we may possess considerable enthusiasm. We have in our minds the amount of material we think the student learners *ought* to cover. Even without the pressure of formal evaluation assessments, there is a compulsion on us to round off our subject matter, to bring the episode of learning to a satisfying conclusion. As in music, we may feel unresolved, incomplete, if only part of this matter is dealt with, if the material is 'broken off' before its 'natural end', if the syllabus is not finished.

This compulsion may encourage us to employ formal modes of presentation (lectures and the like). It is not inevitable that a concern for the comprehensive nature of the content of the learning programme and expository methods should go together. It is possible to combine a realistic assessment of the amount of new knowledge needed with formal methods of instruction, just as one can choose an excess of material to be covered when trying to use participatory methods.

But on the whole the pressure of trying to cover a good deal of subject matter in a limited time leads to a concentration by teachers on their own presentation of the material to more or less passive students. Such teachers tend to resist efforts to pursue anything other than the main line of the learning process. How many groups have heard a teacher say, 'I can't deal with that point now; I must get on'? Yet there is no reason why the teacher 'must get on'; it is the student learners who must 'get on'. It is likely that the majority of adult learning programmes now have externally set syllabuses to be covered and examinations to be passed, though there are still a number which are relatively free in what is taught and learned, which set out to 'explore' jointly (student learners and teacher) some field or other. But in both, it is more important that our student participants learn than that we teachers complete for our own satisfaction the whole of the content. Many of the student participants will expect us to cover the ground, to deal with most of the important topics of the subject matter, whether it be skills-related or knowledge-based. But if covering the whole of the material means going so fast that the student learner cannot learn deeply enough, with understanding and the ability to use the new learning, then the learning programme is not effective. What is the point in the teacher completing the syllabus if the student learner does not really learn?

In most cases, such pressure is not only harmful, it is unnecessary. The main aim of our work is to create more effective student learners, people who will carry on their own learning when our learning programme is over. They do not need to learn everything from us. A view claiming that complete coverage of the subject matter is desirable in a learning group is based on the assumption that the student learners cannot be trusted with their own learning, that they can learn only when a teacher is present, that if they don't learn it now they never will.

It is far better to help the students learn how to learn more effectively by concentrating on part of the syllabus and to let them do the rest for themselves than to try to teach them everything. A course on IT does not need to cover all aspects of the subject; as new software emerges, new understandings of computer tasks and new technologies continue to become available, the range of learning is constantly widening, and the student learners will need to cope with these for themselves. Similarly, an English or European history course that sets out to cover the entire range from the Romans through medieval and early modern to the twentieth century will make unrealistic demands on both teacher and student participants. To concentrate instead on part of this field, however much it may offend the susceptibilities of some academic authorities, may well provide the students with both a greater sense of satisfaction (intrinsic motivation) which will lead to a desire to pursue the learning further, and at the same time greater appreciation and further practice in the methods of continued learning to enable them to do so. By examining one or two shorter periods in depth, the student learners will learn more of how to study history than a teacher-presented overview will teach them. We are reminded of a former colleague who said (talking of another colleague), 'He wants his students to *know* history; I want my students to *like* history'. Part of the task of teaching adults is to help them to develop their motivation and their skills, knowledge and understanding so that they will continue learning, not to teach them all they need to know.

Ways of developing new knowledge

The adult learner needs to develop new knowledge: practical knowledge of processes (how to do something), factual knowledge (data) and theoretical knowledge (concepts). The teacher is there not to *impart* anything – skills, knowledge or information – to the student participants but to help the student learners to develop these for themselves. We cannot impart literacy or the skills to run a cooperative, a knowledge of politics or an understanding of healing; the student learners develop these for themselves. Our task is to help and encourage them to learn.

Research and experience suggest that the more active the student learners are, the more effective is the learning process; the more passive they are, the less deep will be the learning. Figure 10.2 indicates those processes that are seen to be most potent in achieving learning, ranked

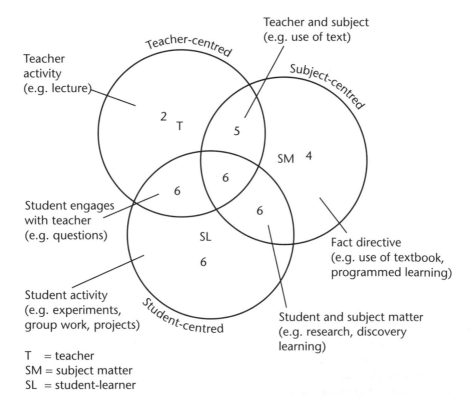

T   = teacher
SM = subject matter
SL = student-learner

Figure 10.2 The figures indicate the relative effectiveness of these methods – 6 being high, 2 being low

on a scale from 1 to 6. As may be seen, a high emphasis is placed on student-centred activities, especially those in which the student participant engages with the teacher and/or with the material directly.

Substantial amounts of teacher-centred activity may not advance the cause of greater student learning. The straight lecture is one of the least efficient methods of teaching (Bligh 1972). It calls for very advanced learning skills on the part of the listener (concentration over a long time, adaptation of the mental images, and the testing of the subject matter against experience *at the same time* as listening to yet further material, etc.), and the rate of forgetting the subject matter is high ('What I hear, I forget; what I see, I remember; what I do, I learn'). Too often the lecturers choose their own ground to discuss rather than the concerns of the students, and there is often little opportunity for feedback or further exploration, except perhaps at the end of the lecture. So the listeners have to retain in their minds the points they wish to make or questions to ask while still paying attention to the next points the lecturer is making.

There are occasions of course when a lecture has value – when summing up a previous complicated discussion, for instance, or when introducing an overview of a new area of study, or when as a part of the learning process one might say to the other participants, 'Allow me for a time without interruption to explore the implications of a particular argument to see where it leads us.' But these will need to be set within some other kind of learning context, because lectures call for special skills on the part of the participants, and they will thus be most appropriate to limited numbers of adult students. In every case, the teacher could well ask whether there are other, more active, more effective ways in which the student learners could develop the new knowledge: by reading a text, by discussion, by discovery methods and so on. There nearly always are better methods than direct exposition by the teacher.

Knowledge and authority

This combination of agency-chosen subject matter, an agency-determined amount of knowledge, an agency-fixed time frame, and teacher-presented material can create one of the greatest obstacles to effective adult learning: authoritarianism. Authoritarianism is not confined to the teacher; it can also attach itself to other statements such as a textbook or handout. There are several reasons for avoiding excessive reliance on such statements: the adulthood of the student learners, the fact that their well-established learning patterns are usually based on testing the validity of all statements against their experience, the fact that such statements normally lay new patterns of knowledge (authority) on top of older patterns without disturbing them. A different approach, which disturbs the existing pattern of understandings, is needed. This calls for a range of social skills and attitudes towards the student learner that the teacher of adults will come to only gradually (pp. 219–24).

The issue of authoritarianism has become increasingly important in adult learning programmes as the use of IT approaches to learning expand. Here the teacher and/or a specially favoured text are no longer regarded as the unchallenged source of all new knowledge. But searching the web can lead an adult to a variety of websites, not all of which carry the same level of authority. Wikipedia, for example, is often the first port of call for new searches; but – as the site itself recognises – it is often not the most accurate or comprehensive source. Developing judgements relating to discrimination of the relative value of websites – just as with textbooks which may contradict each other – is needed as new sources of information are accessed by student learners.

Once more, a balance is necessary. Examination courses may well call for the recognition of prescriptive texts, and only the teacher can provide this guidance. Equally in terms of process, while wishing to eschew exaggerated directiveness, there will be times when the dynamics of the situation will call for the teacher to be assertive – for instance, when constructing a learning exercise or perhaps in relation to a participant who persistently slows down the group (see pp. 205–6). The teacher will then want to be conscious of the reactions of the other participants if the work of the learning programme is being held up by one person. The sensitivity of the teacher to the needs and intentions of the participants will dictate the approach (i.e. methods and content) to be used.

The teachable moment

Teaching is not just a mechanical process and teachers are not made to a set recipe – a packet of this, a pinch of that. Each teaching–learning situation (especially with adults) is unique, calling for innovation on the part of the teacher, untried and individual responses to new circumstances, the courage and willingness to venture into new methods, to experiment, to dare. All the skills, knowledge, experience, attitudes, understanding and emotions of the teacher come to be focused onto the one moment in which the learning may be successful. Once past, the opportunity may be lost. That moment is not set by any textbook or manual of teaching; it will be spontaneous, often inspired. Teaching is an event, a fusion of enthusiasm, of adaptability, of reacting on the spur of the moment.

Learning too consists of the same sort of inspiration, the catching of enthusiasm. It comes from encounter, interaction – either person-to-person interaction or learner-and-material interaction. Some people have seen this engagement in terms of struggle; a learner struggles to 'master' a new skill, subject, tool or concept, and to use the new material. Others see it as a 'spark' between two poles which fires the imagination, illuminates new fields, motivates the learner, gives power and throws light on new ways of looking at reality.

Such interactive learning requires three contributions from the student learners: the use of their existing experience and knowledge; the exercise of their learning abilities (intelligence and learning skills); and effort (practice of the technique, reflection on the new material, collection of data, discrimination between the various elements of the learned matter). In determining the methods to be used in teaching, we should bear in mind these requirements on the part of the student learners and provide them with opportunities to:

- use *their* existing experience and knowledge;
- exercise *their* learning abilities;
- and practise.

Teachers may be reluctant to pursue these teachable moments in the pursuit of 'covering the curriculum' and moving onto the next topic. Pursuing the teachable moment may mean deviating from the 'session plan' so as to take advantage of that 'spark' to explore something not planned for that session or indeed at all. The teacher needs to develop confidence to follow such matters through, even if it means at times abandoning the tidy and cherished structure of the teaching session.

Activity 10.2

Think of an example when you have been part of a group where the teacher has gone with the 'teachable moment' or where you have gone with the teachable moment as a teacher.

- What happened?
- What did you learn or what did the student participants learn that they may not have learned without that moment?

Planning the schedule of learning

Does this emphasis on the practical and direct involvement of the student learner with the subject matter mean that the teacher has nothing to do other than to set the tasks and watch the student learners do them? Real learning can be going on in a group when everyone (especially the teacher) is silent, and perhaps we should try this more often. The existentialists have shown us that it is in silence that moments of crisis lie – moments of decision, of rearrangement, of change; and it is noteworthy that in some adult groups the student participants, rather than the teacher, try to avoid silence by any means.

But the role of the teacher is not just that of overseer and taskmaster. There are (at least) four main areas of activity in selecting the programme for learning:

- Determining *the general approach* – the goals of the learning, whether the programme will be curriculum- or process-oriented; whether the student participants are intended to learn something or to learn how to learn something (some may wish to do both at the same time). Our concern in this part of the task is with the end product: what the student learners will have achieved by the end of the learning programme. As we have seen (Chapter 7), we cannot avoid taking up some sort of attitude towards this; it underlies everything that we and our student participants do together. We make a decision on this even when we are not conscious of doing so. It is best if such decisions are taken with the student learners and certainly the approach needs to have been accepted by the participants; but in many cases, especially in accredited courses, these decisions are taken by the teachers and by the agencies/institutions (such as awarding bodies) in which they work in the course of planning the programme.

- Selecting *what will be learned* – choosing the material and the way it is marshalled in order for learning. The overall subject of the programme will have been agreed by all members, but the detailed content of a learning opportunity on computers, keep fit, geography, management or nutrition will be the concern of the teacher or the credit-awarding agency. Again much of this can be determined in association with the student learners, but the decision will normally rest with the agency.

- Deciding *how much of this material can be covered* in the time available – what will most help the learning process and what can be left to a later stage; phasing and sequencing the work of the group or the individual learner. As we have seen, most of us tend to overestimate the amount that adult student learners can cover. It would be better to underestimate and adjust later as we surprise ourselves and perhaps the student learners. Interaction with the students will be necessary to ensure that an appropriate balance is maintained. The pace of learning of different members of the learning group will be a major concern of the teacher of adults in order to meet the expectations of as many students as possible.

- Determining *how the student participants will engage with the material* – whether they will watch and exercise for themselves, whether they will listen, read, discuss, write, practise and so on. We will determine the steps the student learners will be asked to take in order to complete the task, to learn the process or the subject matter. As far as possible, close relations with the individual members of the learning group will be needed to ensure that the tasks set and the steps taken are the most useful for learning.

The learning steps

Some writers have suggested that such learning steps will normally be cumulative and sequential, combining to make a course for the student learners to engage in for themselves. They have analysed the stages by which a new skill or concept is learned. One such list is as follows:

- *Stage 1* – 'Play': this is the encounter stage, when the student learners meet the new elements, gain familiarity with them, lose their fears of the field of study and begin to experiment with one element in it – perhaps playing it backwards or asking 'Does it *always* work?', etc. A good deal of time is often needed for this stage.
- *Stage 2* – 'Structured play': trial-and-error exercises are planned as the field is explored systematically. The material and situations are so arranged to lead in a certain direction – i.e. to Stage 3. This stage too must not be rushed, it takes time.
- *Stage 3* – 'Grasping': the material 'falls into place'; it is related to other material, mostly by insightful learning; it 'clicks', makes sense, becomes 'real' or 'true'.
- *Stage 4* – 'Mastery': practice, not just learning but using, exploring the material or process further, discovering more relationships and properties, obtaining mastery over it. This in turn leads to an appreciation of further learning needs and intentions, new skills or concepts. The process is a dynamic and ongoing one.

Such steps call upon us to set for ourselves and for the participants clear signposts throughout the programme of learning, indicating the point reached and the relationship of what is being done to what has gone before and what will follow. Creating milestones is an important task for the teacher, often overlooked. Some student learners may not be able to see the overall structure that we have in our minds unless we make special efforts to clarify it as we go along. And the relevance of the particular learning activity to the final goal of the learning programme also needs to be understood by the student learner. An understanding of both the structure and the relevance of the learning process is required for effective learning to take place.

In this way the teacher sets the curriculum, the syllabus and the schedule of work for the group. This should as often as possible be done in discussion with the group, but in the end it is the teacher's responsibility. Such a task calls for a series of skills that are part of the essential equipment the teacher needs and which can be practised and learned:

- The skill of determining what is needed to achieve the goal – what basic concepts, facts and techniques are required to perform the task and how they relate to each other.
- The skill of selecting the tasks most suitable and of grading them in sequence. Again these will be related to each other, not isolated or compartmentalised. The relationship may be *vertical* (one task can be attempted only after another has been successfully mastered), *horizontal* (a parallel task at the same level of complexity) or *oblique* (a mixture of both of these). Several of these tasks will overlap with others.
- The skill of breaking down the subject matter and processes into steps for learning. For this activity we need to learn something of what goes on in the process of learning, based partly on theory and partly on experience of what works in practice.
- The skill of identifying and selecting the resources to be used – the equipment, materials, objects and texts, sequence of demonstrations, words of the teacher, discussions. We will devise some of this material for ourselves, other parts we will take from elsewhere. It is our task to choose, arrange and often present it; this is what the students will expect of us.

Methods

We have begun to see how the teacher, in selecting the content, also implicitly selects the methods of the learning group. We need now to look at this in more detail.

The choice of methods

Most teachers underestimate the number of different teaching–learning techniques available to choose from. We often tend to be unimaginative in this part of our work. In one group of teachers, we gathered a list of 49 different teaching–learning techniques by using a brainstorming session, and that did not exhaust the possibilities. But in fact we all use a very limited range of teaching–learning methods: just as we all have our preferred learning styles, so all teachers have their preferred teaching styles which we use often unconsciously. Some research suggests that when teachers feel unsure of themselves – threatened by inexperience, new material, a challenging group of student learners, lack of time or self-doubt – they frequently revert to using those teaching methods by which they were themselves taught; perhaps we should all watch for this and see it for what it is.

There are no generic teaching methods. We need to think about and identify different methods, to experiment with them and select those that seem to suit us and our student participants for each particular purpose. We should test whether this or that method does in fact fit the students' learning practices and, if not, choose another one. We need to practise too, until we can use these methods effectively. A new method may not always go well for the first few occasions it is employed, but that does not mean we should give it up. It is worth persisting with. We should also try out methods with which we are less familiar. In short, we should become 'reflective practitioners', thinking critically about our own teaching: we can learn much about teaching while we are teaching.

The basic range

Methods may be divided into four main categories (Rogers 1991b):

- *presentation* methods (teacher activities such as demonstration, exposition, use of whiteboard or flipchart, text or audio-visual media, Powerpoint);
- *participatory* methods (interaction between teacher and learner, or learner and learner, such as questions, discussion, group work);
- *discovery* methods (in which the student learners on their own or in groups work on tasks, exploring and discovering knowledge for themselves through practice, experiments, reading, writing);
- *evaluatory* methods (some of the techniques we adopt to evaluate the learning already done such as tests, quizzes, role play; these can be the means for further learning).

Activity 10.3

- List any teaching methods you can think of; you can add to it as time goes on and as new ideas or experiences present themselves.
- Indicate against each item whether it is *primarily* a teacher activity (T), a learner activity (L) or a group activity (G).
- Mark those that are more content-oriented (C) and those that are more process-oriented (P).

Which type of method predominates in your own teaching?

Some examples:

- discussion (G)
- use of AVA
- seminar
- field visits
- (C) test
- lecture (T)
- quiz
- handouts
- tutorial
- role play (L)
- (P) buzz group

Many programmes of taught learning concentrate more on presentation methods than on the others. But informal learning employs the other three sets of methods, seeking out presentation methods less frequently. In informal learning, we use discovery, play, trial and error and role play; we discuss and ask questions; we use our learning to see if it works and test it out on other people. If the goal of our teaching is to build on the natural informal learning process which we all engage in, often unconsciously, and make it more conscious, to take it further, we need to use these other teaching–learning methods more consciously (see Stephens and Roderick 1971; Belbin 1980; Sork 1984; Christensen and Hansen 1987; Ramsden 1992).

And not in isolation. They can be built up into a complex range of activities. Thus exploratory methods may be accompanied by interaction methods as the student learners present the results of their exploration to the group or to the teacher for evaluation. Not all of these take place in the classroom; field visits and excursions, practical work on the shop floor or in the lab frequently partake of all four kinds of learning methods during the course of the programme.

The different methods can be divided in other ways. There are those, such as demonstrations, the use of texts, lectures and handouts, that are more concerned with the subject matter of the learning programme. Others, like simulation exercises and projects, are more concerned with the process of learning. Equally they may be divided into those that are primarily teacher activity, student activity or group activity (Activity 10.4).

Activity 10.4

Looking again at the learning programme you have chosen, which group of teaching–learning methods predominates in your planning?
Presentation?
Participatory?
Discovery?
Evaluatory?

The basis for selecting the methods

The determination of the approach most appropriate to the particular teaching–learning situation depends on a number of factors – for example, the area(s) of learning involved: whether it is *primarily* skills, knowledge, understanding or attitudes; the need to get the student learner actively engaged in the process of learning; the learning styles of the student participants – what they prefer and what they are able to do; the experience which the student learners bring to the programme; the demands of the subject itself, especially in accredited courses; the availability of resources. Decisions on all these matters can often be taken jointly by teacher and students, not by the teacher alone.

Student engagement

Many adult students seem to expect and even prefer teacher-centred and content-oriented methods. Some studies have suggested that for goal-oriented programmes (for example, those directed towards an examination), where the student learners feel the speed of learning is more important than the depth of learning and thus a leisurely pace is felt to be irksome, the students achieve more of their intentions in a teacher-centred environment. Even outside these contexts, it is often urged that active learning methods are slow, that the material can be dealt with more quickly if the teacher instructs and expounds and the student learners watch or listen. This is true. Much more ground can be 'covered' by expository methods than by participatory methods. But 'covering the ground' is not the purpose of the exercise; the goal is learning. The student learners may listen but in listening they may not learn what the teacher intends.

It is argued that such varied methods are not appropriate to some subjects or in some contexts. For example, in examination-led programmes, it is suggested that active methods are inappropriate because they are too time-consuming. Equally, some teachers of adults find it difficult to accept interactive methods. How can they be applied, for instance, to music appreciation which tends to involve listening to recordings often over long periods? But a little imagination will quickly suggest a variety of methods, all appropriate to the subject matter, apart from 'discussion' – so ubiquitous in many adult learning programmes. Other tutors have encouraged their student participants to write their own programme notes, record-sleeve introductions or reviews of particular recordings, or to present to other group members in a structured way a concert programme – why one piece of music 'goes' or does not 'go' with another. The student participants can in fact do most of the tasks that we as teachers reserve for ourselves.

It is not however just a case of the teacher devising situations in which the student learners can use their new learning. Rather, it is a question of approaching the student learners in a new way. Too often we treat the student participants as if they are totally incompetent or ignorant and have to be taught everything (see p. 68). As with other self-fulfilling prophecies, many of the students will therefore cast themselves in the role of ignoramuses – 'you must teach us everything' (see p. 85). It will be hard for the teacher to encourage these persons to *learn by doing*, by reflecting critically on what they already know and what they can already do, when they wish instead to *learn by preparing for doing*, when they seek to learn what they think they do not know or cannot do.

Nor can we encourage such student engagement during those periods *between* each group meeting or class session while at the same time treating the student learners as passive listeners *during* the class meeting (see p. 229). The way we treat the student participants in class and the methods of learning we select for them to use at other times should be consistent in approach. Student activity begins in class.

Critical teaching and learning

The learning cycle (see Chapter 5) can be adapted to provide a framework for the choice of different teaching–learning methods (Figure 10.3). A major concern of adult learning programmes, even work-based training programmes, is with the promotion of critical reflection on experience to be fulfilled in action (see p. 119). In this process it may be helpful to remind ourselves:

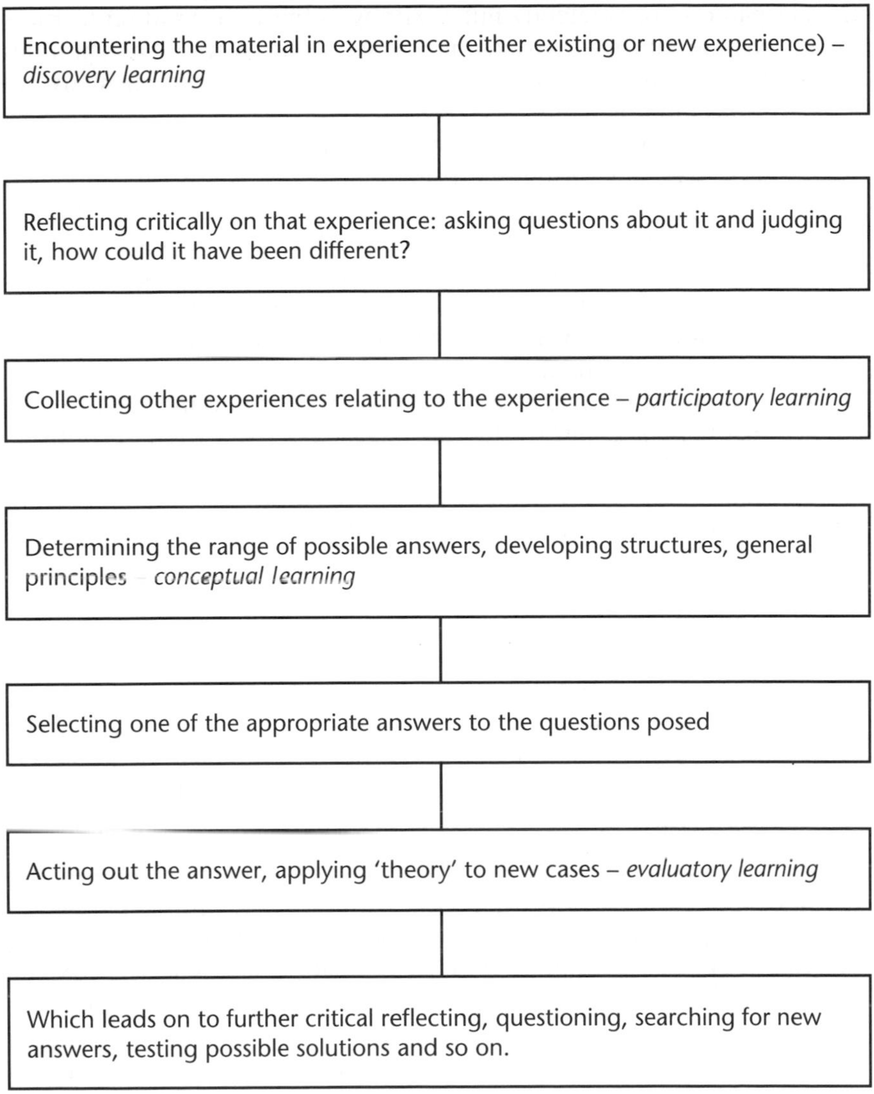

| Encountering the material in experience (either existing or new experience) – *discovery learning* |

| Reflecting critically on that experience: asking questions about it and judging it, how could it have been different? |

| Collecting other experiences relating to the experience – *participatory learning* |

| Determining the range of possible answers, developing structures, general principles – *conceptual learning* |

| Selecting one of the appropriate answers to the questions posed |

| Acting out the answer, applying 'theory' to new cases – *evaluatory learning* |

| Which leads on to further critical reflecting, questioning, searching for new answers, testing possible solutions and so on. |

Figure 10.3 Applying the learning cycle to teaching adults

- that the student learners need to experience the material directly for themselves. If the material is embodied in the teacher alone, this may make for a transmission model of teaching and learning, and thus to dependency. The material needs to be separated from the means of conveyance, be that teacher, film, book or website. This can be done by using more than one conveyance for the same material (which incidentally reinforces the teaching–learning material), by helping the student learners to draw on their own experience, and/or by creating opportunities for the participants to have a new direct relationship with the subject matter.

- that the student learners' activities should be *productive* – mastering processes, answering questions as actively as possible and even posing questions themselves; not just watching or listening but doing, reading, writing, talking, etc. Only if the student learners are engaged in activities which they see as meaningful and relevant will they learn and change. New skills will thus be grasped, new knowledge be developed permanently, new understandings and concepts be formed.

- that the student participants need to become more conscious that *learning is the task* they are engaged in. They need to continue to learn how to learn, with encouragement. They should spend the maximum amount of time on this process.

- that the student participants should come to realise that learning is *not a matter of rote memorising* of processes and facts but a complicated matter of asking and answering questions, finding solutions, practising skills, spotting relationships and linkages, constructing explanations and making 'maps' in the mind. They also need to realise that this is done by producing their own work in written or spoken words, both for an immediate check by themselves and for a more considered check by others. This is the 'questioning, thinking and testing' of which Handy spoke (see p. 127).

Such considerations as these help us to choose the most appropriate methods of learning – not just a demonstration (of computer program writing or piano piece performance, say) by an expert but a fumbling practice by the learner, followed by an evaluation by the learner, by the teacher and even on occasion by other student participants as well; not just a lecture (on psychology, say) but a series of carefully constructed observational analyses and role plays; not just a slide show (on architecture) but the development of a new sense of awareness by looking at buildings in the neighbourhood; not just reading a text but the construction of an argument on the basis of the material contained in it.

Teaching – choosing content and methods

If, then, our classes and groups are really to promote learning, four things seem to be necessary, as Dewey (1933) pointed out:

- An *experience* on the part of the learner. The learning group is itself an experience that ought to be maximised: 'All genuine education comes about through experience'.
- A *climate* in which the student learners play their part in structuring the learning process, where there is 'a concern for the development of persons . . . [where] the growth of people has precedence over the accomplishment of things'.
- *Continuity* of encounter. The process of learning builds on what is already there. The present experience of the learning group needs to be related in the learner's mind to past experience; the latter can be used by the teacher, not left passive: 'Continuity of experience means that every experience both takes up something from those which have gone before and modifies in some way the quality of those which come after'.
- *Interaction* between the student learner and the new material, either through the teacher, or directly by practice; interaction between what is outside and what is inside the learner.

Choosing content and methods

The function of the teacher of adults is thus wider than just that of a demonstrator, lecturer or presenter of information. Rather, the teacher (on his/her own or with the agency providing the learning programme) constructs a sequence of learning activities for the student participants to engage in. But this does not mean that the traditional instructional activities are inappropriate to a teacher; we need both types of skill.

What, then, makes a good teacher of adults? A number of different skills and attitudes appear to be necessary:

First, a series of *attitudes towards the student learners* – concern, sensitivity and support; attitudes of flexibility and innovativeness; a willingness to experiment, to adapt the material to meet the specific needs of the learning group, not just be stuck with one set of teaching–learning methods and content – and *towards the subject matter*, an enthusiasm for the material and its philosophy.

Secondly, *a clear understanding of the philosophy of adult teaching*. The effectiveness of what we do depends to a very large extent on the clarity with which we hold the logic frame of our activity. We need to know and understand the concepts of adult learning and adult teaching. The aim of our work is to help make learning conscious.

Thirdly, we need to develop *the skills of teaching*:

- *Planning skills* – selection of teaching–learning strategies and the effective use of learning resources.

- *Communication skills* – the development of means of communication and a sensitivity to how effective these are, an awareness of when (for example) the wrong message may have been received from the presentation. It is surprising how few teachers can place themselves in the position of the receiver of their messages, how often they use vocabulary, concepts and sentence construction outside the field of experience of some of the participants.
- *Caring-guidance skills* – counselling the participants, adjusting the learning tasks to the needs, intentions and capabilities of the individual learner.
- *Evaluation skills* – identifying the goals, monitoring progress and evaluating the usefulness of the learning process, presenting such evaluations to the participants.
- *Subject skills* – competencies in the subject matter of the learning programme, and continuing learning in this area.

But above all, we need to possess a measure of *self-confidence and self-respect* based on a belief in our own competence – a feeling that will quickly communicate itself to the student learners. Adult participants will come to respect us as teachers and accept willingly the learning tasks we set for them in so far as we display confidence in ourselves and trust in them. This respect comes about only when we respect ourselves.

Working at teaching

We must not become too confident, however, nor confident without the skills and attitudes to go with that confidence. It has been said that in lifelong education, as elsewhere in the educational world, there are no bad students; that if there is a failure to learn, or if attendance falls off, this is because the teacher has not prepared an adequate programme of learning or adopted appropriate teaching–learning methods. This is of course not always true; there are many factors outside the control of the teacher of adults which will affect the effectiveness of our teaching, so that the failure of our programmes may not always lie with ourselves.

Nevertheless, there is much truth in the adage that there are no bad students, only bad teachers! We must not expect our task to be an easy one. It is difficult, lengthy and at times tedious. We may have to prepare our own teaching material, adapted to the needs and intentions of the particular group of adult learners we are helping, which may be equivalent to writing and experimenting with a good-sized textbook with exercises. Even when we are able to use material prepared by others, we still need to fit it in with each situation, with each student group, and this too can be a challenging and time-consuming process. As teachers of adults, we cannot rush into teaching without preparation, relying on our experience and expertise to help us flannel our way through. Preparation and choice between alternatives lie at the heart of the process.

And we must not become too hidebound in approaching the issue of teaching–learning methods. We need to be flexible. There will be occasions when we find we need to adopt methods with which we are in general out of sympathy (e.g. lecturing to some student learners because that is what they feel they need). Imposing discussion on student participants may not always be conducive to effective learning. Equally, there may be times when we wish 'to get on' but are being held up by the student learners engaging in what seems to us to be futile and time-wasting discussion. But this may be part of the process by which they are relating the new material of the course to their own experience and perceptions.

Preparation and choice between alternatives lie at the heart of the process. We ourselves need to learn that we cannot be doctrinaire in the teaching of adults. And much of this learning how to teach adults will be task-related learning, and much of it will be unconscious learning. Part of the aim of this book is to help us all to become more conscious of this process. We need as teachers to continue to learn deliberately in many ways – by personal study, by experimenting and evaluating our experiments and by meeting with others. Through networking with other teachers of adults, we can form or join communities of practice; we can learn from and with our peers. The task of learning to teach is never finished. And, while setting our own standards high, we must not expect too much of ourselves.

Activity 10.5

At this point it is worth thinking about the teaching methods and the content you use or plan to use. What will you change as a result of your reading?

- Does your teaching need to become more learner-focused?
- Are the teaching methods you employ appropriate to your subject?
- How much autonomy do you allow your learners?
- Do you need to engage your student learners in more active forms of learning?
- How far are you prepared to deviate from your teaching plans in order to capture those 'teachable moments'?

You may find it helpful at this stage of the book to reflect on what you have learned so far and to formulate an action plan for your own continued learning. It is a useful exercise to do.

Further reading

Daines, J., Daines, C. and Graham, B. (1993) *Adult Learning, Adult Teaching*, 3rd edn. Nottingham: University of Nottingham.

Galbraith, M.W. (ed.) (1991) *Adult Learning Methods: A Guide for Effective Instruction*. Malabar, FL: Krieger.

Griffin, C. (1983) *Curriculum Theory in Adult and Continuing Education*. Beckenham: Croom Helm.

Moore, A. (2004) *The Good Teacher: Dominant Discourses in Teacher Education*. London: Routledge.

Stephens, M.D. and Roderick, G.W. (1971) *Teaching Techniques in Adult Education*. Newton Abbot: David & Charles.

Smith, M.K. (2000) 'Curriculum theory and practice', *The Encyclopaedia of Informal Education,* www.infed.org/biblio/b-curric.htm

Pause for More Thought

In the first part of this book we looked at the nature of learning. We have seen it as a natural and largely subconscious process (like breathing), using informal 'acquisition learning' processes, or what we have called 'task-conscious learning' because the student learners are not conscious of learning but only of a task they wish to fulfil. We have seen that taught learning (education) uses a different process, 'formalised learning' or 'learning-conscious learning' because the task of which the student learners are conscious is learning. We have suggested that our teaching of adults should build on both processes, making the task-conscious learning more learning-conscious and building tasks into the learning-conscious learning.

We also identified two major problems for the teacher of adults:

- the wide range of experience, learning abilities, styles and intentions that the members of the adult learning group possess;
- the tension between the need to define learning objectives clearly in order to achieve learning on the one hand, and the desire to be open to, respect and encourage the autonomy of the mature adult on the other.

In the second part of the book we saw that there are at least three ways in which these problems may be addressed:

- by negotiating the goals and objectives with the participants as far as the context of our learning programme admits;
- by the encouragement and use of the learning group;
- by the use of a wide range of varied and active teaching–learning methods and materials.

The remaining chapters are devoted to making our work of teaching adults more effective – making their learning more conscious, overcoming obstacles to learning, testing the value of our work and encouraging the student learners to take more and more control over their own learning processes.

Chapter 11

Blocks to Learning
What is stopping us . . . ?

This chapter examines some of the barriers to learning and suggests that, although some of these may spring from pre-existing knowledge and psychological factors, others come from socio-cultural factors, including the learning programme itself. These blocks do not exist in the same way in the natural (informal) learning process. It may be that we are creating barriers for our participants[1].

Identifying the problem

At different times, everyone who has taught adults has come across the person who seems unable to learn something they say that they wish to learn. A serious block appears to exist. We have all experienced this in ourselves as well, a failure to comprehend or master some aspect of the subject under consideration.

This chapter sets out to discuss the nature of these blocks to learning. Two introductory points are needed. First, all we can try to do here is to assess what appears to be happening and, if possible, why. What is not always so easy to see is how to cope with each situation as it arises.

The second point is that when we as teachers of adults come across these blocks, we will lack firm evidence for an analysis of the situation under review. We will be trying to draw a picture of what is 'really' happening rather than what the student participant *says* is happening. On occasion, the two may be the same. But more often, even when the student learners are able to describe why they find themselves unable to learn something (and that is on the whole rare), they may be unwilling to give the reason for this.

One way of bridging this gap is for us to use our own experience to describe and explain the situation. This is a useful tool, provided we recognise the limitations of this process. Those who teach adults are likely

---

1 We wish to acknowledge the work of Gordon Douglas formerly of the Department of Adult Education in the University of Nottingham with this chapter. But he is not responsible for the version here.

to be people who have been successful in their approach to the subject, not a failure. We are therefore unlikely to understand fully the problems that some of the student learners will feel. Nevertheless, it is necessary for us to draw upon our own insights in this field; and throughout this chapter, as elsewhere in the book, you will find the material of greater value when you test it against your own experience. To be an effective teacher of adults, we must learn to know ourselves.

It is important for us to remember that we are discussing here the blocks to *learning*. Patricia Cross in her study of *Adults as Learners* (1981) identified three main sets of barriers which adults face: barriers which arise from the *situation* in which they find themselves; barriers which spring from the *learning programmes* themselves; and barriers which lie within the student learners themselves, the *attitudes* which the adults may possess towards themselves or the programme. She was talking about 'barriers to participation' in planned learning activities rather than barriers to learning once one is participating in adult learning programmes. Although her three categories can be applied to the blocks to learning, the primary focus to our discussion of barriers to learning will be the personality barriers which prevent some adult student participants – people who attend classes regularly and who want to learn – from learning. What is it that is stopping them from learning effectively within our programmes?

The scope of the problem

Blocks to learning exist, and there are many reasons for them, the most important of which are personality factors. At one end is the 'I-don't-want-to-learn-this-thing' participant – not the wholly unmotivated but those who, although still attending, find the difficulties of some particular part of the learning programme so great that they withdraw from learning. At the other end is the learner who tries most anxiously to grasp a particular process or idea but just cannot make it fit, remember it or understand how the various pieces of the subject go together. For the first, self-perception prevents the development of new skills or the assimilation and creation of new knowledge; they think that the problem lies with themselves. For the second, something perceived to be within the subject matter itself or the way the new material relates to existing patterns of knowledge gets in the way; they think the problem lies in the subject.

It is of course possible that some of the blame falls upon us as teachers. But this is not always clear-cut. How many of us have struggled through the first few pages of Stephen Hawking's *Brief History of Time*? We want to learn from it but find we simply cannot make progress. We are not sure whether to blame the author or the subject matter; we have been assured by so much press coverage that if anyone can explain the concepts clearly, it is Hawking – so we feel hesitant to blame the author/teacher. The problem must lie either in us as readers or in the subject matter. So we give up – some more quickly than others – and feel more inadequate because of the experience.

There are other reasons for the failure to learn, and we can discuss these briefly first. Some blocks to learning new skills and new concepts arise from *physical changes*: for example, declining dexterity or failing eyesight or hearing account for many futile learning experiments. More important and frequent are those immediate, and on occasion temporary, *situational* causes: physical or contextual factors such as hunger, poor health, tiredness or other preoccupations (money, family needs, work, shopping, etc.) which may weigh on the minds of the student learners. How many adult classes have been ruined for the teacher or the student participants because one of them has just recalled some errand left unfulfilled, some commitment uncompleted, and their mind is engaged in concocting excuses with which to meet the offended party? Other situational factors more specifically related to our *programmes* include the room being too hot or too cold, too bright or too dark, over-crowded, smoky or poorly equipped (for instance, with uncomfortable seating), or where there are too many distractions that prevent concentration. There are also those frequent blocks that spring from bad relations between the teacher and the learner or between learner and learner, or from the teacher's failure to communicate properly with the learner.

All of these, although not unimportant or rare, may be relatively easily remedied, once identified. And the evidence is that these physical and contextual factors are hindrances rather than blocks. They seldom operate on their own but rather provide material for the other mechanisms to work on. Distractions alone rarely form a block to learning but come into play when other blocks begin to exert themselves. They are used by the learner to prevent learning, rather than preventing learning by themselves.

This is not of course to say that these situational barriers to learning are not significant. They are. It is most important that we recognise that our adult participants are part of a particular socio-cultural context, and that their knowledge and values are rooted in and are continually being created by them in interaction with their physical and social environment. Our student learners are not psychological isolates divorced from a specific context; they are social beings. And this context will be at one and the same time a help and a hindrance. It will often provide the cause of the learning intention, but it will also provide many barriers to learning changes. It is from this context that our student participants will bring to the purposeful learning episode which we are building for and with them the knowledge and experience which they have accumulated over many years and the values attached to that knowledge and experience.

Hindrances which arise from this context will thus reinforce personality blocks, those blocks to learning that exist for the alert motivated student participant even in a context conducive to learning. Learning is not simply a matter of reason; it also involves the emotions and the physical well-being of the learner, questions of identity and status in a social setting, recognition by oneself and by others.

Activity 11.1

Before we go further, try to identify two 'blockages' that you have experienced, either as teacher or as learner. Alan and Naomi have both identified learning to draw and knowing what goes on under the bonnet of a car amongst our blockages. We know we can't learn either.

1
2

It will be useful to distinguish between those blocks to learning which are more concerned with pre-existent knowledge and those arising from social or personality factors. In the former, the new knowledge challenges the existing knowledge (tacit or conscious) which has been built up from experience or from some prior educational activity. The learner cannot see how it will 'fit'; it does not 'ring true'; and it leads to resistance, to 'fight'. In the latter, the learner makes a generally negative assessment of themselves in relation to the learning compared with other people; 'I couldn't do that' even if other members of the learning group can; this normally leads to 'flight'.

Activity 11.2

Indicate how far you think the blocks to learning you have experienced spring from pre-existing knowledge and how far from your own picture of yourself as a learner.

1
2

Pre-existing knowledge

We have seen that adult student participants know a good deal about what they are studying, often more than they think they know (see pp. 81–3). Students in a learning programme on medieval English history frequently assert that they know nothing about the subject, but it is not very difficult to elicit from them a series of names such as Robin Hood and Sherwood Forest, the Black Prince, Wat Tyler, Chaucer and Wycliffe, the Black Death, as well as the clear markers of Domesday Book, the Crusades and the Wars of the Roses. Most of them will have visited a medieval parish church, if not a castle or monastery and learned much unconsciously from such visits. Any view of medieval history that omits to deal with these, to make sense of them in an overall context, may prove unsatisfying to the participants. Indeed, these topics provided by the group members can become hooks onto which most aspects of the course of study can be hung. The student learners can see that they have helped to construct the syllabus. The same is true of woodworking, keep fit, management courses, academic subjects and literacy classes. The student learners will already have some knowledge and experience, direct or indirect, of these fields of study, some perception about the subject matter, much of it unconscious and obtained through informal learning from their socio-cultural context.

Adult student participants have already invested emotional capital in acquiring this knowledge and experience. They will expend much more in defending the integrity of this knowledge, so new learning changes will sometimes be strenuously resisted. Thus a blockage arises from the *emotional investment in knowledge* that we make.

And there are social factors involved: we all learn from some 'significant other', some outside authority such as a person or a book, etc. Any challenge to this learned material implies either a challenge to our significant other (it may be mother, father, teacher or some other respected authority), or a challenge to our self-judgement (we chose to rely on that person, book, magazine or newspaper; it seemed reasonable to us at the time), or to both.

In both cases, a sense of loss may be felt (see Atherton 2008). Two reactions may then be created. In the first, by the use of 'withdrawal mechanisms', the challenged student learners will seek to defend their existing knowledge. In the second, through the employment of 'ego-defence mechanisms', the learners will seek to defend their self-image to themselves and to others. We will discuss both of these in a moment.

A second cause of such blockages is existing *prejudices*. These may be defined as strongly held beliefs, perhaps based in part on knowledge, that we are reluctant to examine in detail. Often this is because we suspect that they are not firmly founded, but equally there are social factors involved: it may also be that the fear of others, loss of face, prevents us from exposing our prejudices to analysis, for we may be forced to abandon stances we have taken up in public. Prejudices are one form of what is called 'over-certainty', a state that results in stereotyped reactions. Racial, religious or ideological hostilities are perhaps the most conspicuous forms of prejudices; sexual, social or cultural preferences perhaps the most insidious.

A third cause of such blockages arises in those who are *habit-bound*. They have traditional patterns of thinking or ways of doing things, not merely from their search for security but also from an undue reverence for the past. Similarly, some people's *conformity needs* are very strong. Such people cling to existing ways and understandings as long as they perceive them to be the ways and views of the majority. Once more, social and emotional investments lie at the base of these reactions.

All these factors lead some of our student participants to resist learning changes. They cling to pre-existent knowledge and attitudes and they find it difficult to assimilate new material, to make it harmonise with what is already there. So they adopt mechanisms, most commonly of withdrawal, in an attempt to preserve what they already possess.

Withdrawal mechanisms

There are many ways of withdrawing from a situation. The most obvious (not necessarily the most common) is physical withdrawal, what many educators call (with unconscious bias) 'drop-out', a term to be avoided because of its pejorative overtones. The student participant deliberately stops coming to the group. More common however are the following:

- *Compartmentalism* – the student learners keep their knowledge in separate boxes; they create distinct patterns that don't touch each other but are drawn upon in different circumstances. This is a particular favourite of people who have been exposed for a long time to a formal educational system with its separate 'schools' of history, geography, maths, etc.; but others too engage in it.
- *Authority-ism* – the quotation of and excessive reverence for authorities. Some student learners fall back on books (the *Encyclopedia Britannica* syndrome) and just seeing something in print or on the web leads them to conclude that 'It must be true'. New knowledge is challenged if it lacks such authority. Others cite trusted people as the ultimate source of wisdom: 'If they say so, we can believe it'.

- *Reality-evasion* – i.e. daydreaming and lack of attention. This is more likely to be a withdrawal mechanism than anything else. This can be tested, for the withdrawal mechanism is highly selective in its attention and perception. The student participants will notice everything that supports their existing patterns and just not hear whatever contradicts them.

Perceptive teachers will come to recognise these and other withdrawal mechanisms. But teachers are also selective in what they notice. We ourselves often ignore those things that contradict the views we hold about our adult students as well-meaning, highly motivated and intelligent friends – or alternatively as dull, reluctant student learners. We should constantly examine ourselves to see what we are perceiving and what we are missing.

Unlearning

To grapple with this problem of the pre-existent knowledge, habits or attitudes of our student participants, we need to explore the notion of unlearning. It is sometimes said that for adults the process of unlearning is as important as the process of learning; that all participants in adult learning activities have much to unlearn as well as new material to learn. It is not possible for us to know in the case of every individual participant precisely where the new material conflicts with pre-existing patterns, but an awareness of the reactions of the student learners to such situations reveals much to the sensitive teacher.

The new material, to be properly learned, needs to be enmeshed with the older knowledge and not be left lying 'on top of' the existing patterns, leaving them unchanged. This may mean not merely an exploration of the pre-existing knowledge itself but also of the way it was acquired. This is particularly important when dealing with the many long-standing myths with which all subjects, both skill-oriented and understanding-oriented, abound. Authoritative denials of traditional practices or other knowledge will be weighed against existing beliefs in which considerable emotional investment may have been made.

Unlearning: an illustration

In any church training course which involves the narratives of the Christian Nativity, we will run up against the traditional stories of those who came to bring gifts to the infant Jesus. The existing information held by most of the student participants (i.e. that there were 'three kings') will be seen to be 'incorrect'. We can pursue a number of strategies:

- We can *tell* the student learners (authoritatively) that they were not kings and that there were probably not three of them. Such a statement will be assessed and may even be accepted out of respect for our expertise, but it will lie uneasily on top of the earlier acquired knowledge because it has not challenged the source of that information. Within three or four minutes, the participants will be talking of 'three kings' again.
- We can *show* them the narrative accounts in the New Testament that speak of 'certain wise men' (soothsayers or fortune tellers), not 'three' and not 'kings'. Such a reference will give cause for more serious reflection, and some will be convinced. Nevertheless, most of the student participants will within a relatively short time be talking once more in terms of 'three' and 'kings'. We will not have challenged the weight of tradition and the emotional atmosphere of childhood, families, Christmas festivities and the constant reinforcement by Christmas cards, carols and the like, all of which have created an *attachment* to the idea of three kings.
- The only successful way to bring about the new learning will be through a process of *unlearning*. This will involve seeing how the two ideas ('three' and 'kings') arose in the first place – how the statement in the Psalms that 'kings from the East shall bring gifts' was quoted in the primitive Christian Church; how the early representations of the magi in pictures and mosaics with tall headdresses were taken by later interpreters to indicate royal imagery; how the fact that there were three gifts led to an assumption that there were three travellers, etc. The students will thus understand the processes involved in the transformation of these stories, and their traditionally held views will become readjusted. They will see the constant reinforcement of incorrect knowledge for what it is, and when they themselves join again in references to 'three kings', they will hold a part of themselves back with an inner assertion that now they know better. Only as the learner comes to see *how* the description of the visitors in these narratives was altered will there be a major change in knowledge and attitudes. The story will be seen to be a later myth making an important theological statement, rather than historical truth.

The above case study is a trivial example, not one to be pressed too hard. It is not perhaps important to bring about this particular item of unlearning, any more than the correction of the traditional tales of Robin Hood and the Sheriff of Nottingham may be important. But each of us at some stage will run across an area where an unlearning process will be necessary – where some traditional but ineffective or harmful process, skill or knowledge (for example, in health matters) needs to be corrected. It is not enough to make authoritative statements of facts or to give orders, for neither will overcome the attachment given to the weight of tradition combined with the practice of contemporaries. Rather, the process is in most cases much the same as above. The most unsatisfactory and impermanent method of dealing with such views is one of authority, laying new knowledge on top of the older learning without disturbing it or relating the new to the old. A better way is to examine the basis of the old (incorrect or undesired) knowledge and the newer (desired) knowledge; but this too will lead to conflict, setting authority against authority. The most effective unlearning process is not straight contradiction but the lengthier activity of helping the learner to examine how the incorrect pattern came about and has been reinforced through long acceptance and use and a good deal of emotional attachment. Unlearning is part of the process of critical reflection; it is often a difficult and lengthy process, but an essential part of teaching adults.

Self-perception factors

Sometimes (as with *The Brief History of Time*) there is no great range of existing knowledge to impede new learning, but still an inability or a refusal to learn exists. In these cases, another set of factors comes into play: emotional manifestations of negative self-concepts, some of them enduring (in which case they may be seen as long-term personality traits), others situationally controlled (which we may term emotional variables). The most important and the most common of these, especially for adults, is *anxiety*.

Anxiety

Anxiety is a characteristic of many adult learners. And it is not in itself an undesirable feature of adult learning. As we have noticed, we can welcome anxiety as useful for motivation for certain tasks (see p. 87), especially for those calling for persistence of application and the less difficult kinds of 'reception' learning. Anxiety can *help* performance, especially in a task where traditional answers are adequate; after all, the anxiety in most cases could not have been too strong or the adult would never have come to the learning group. But we do need to distinguish such anxiety from over-anxiety. Over-anxiety tends to interfere with and inhibit original thought. It can impede the mastery of new motor skills. Over-anxiety in many people tends often to be higher when the learner is faced with intellectual or creative exercises, lower when faced with physical tasks. Tasks requiring some degree of personal judgement are thus harder for the over-anxious student participant than tasks demanding conformity to rules. Such anxiety inhibits complex learning tasks that are more dependent on improvised skills than on persistence.

Most teachers of adults will face it in their student participants at some stage. It is a diverse phenomenon. It seems to consist of three main elements:

- a fear of externally imposed requirements that are seen as a threat – the difficulty of the subject matter itself;
- worries about the self, the capacity to cope; issues of self-esteem, an awareness of the process of ageing, of physical tiredness and declining powers of memory and concentration, or a negative self-image, promoting too high a sense of need;
- concern about self-image – what others will think of them, a fear of public failure and humiliation.

We must be careful of attributing such attitudes to all student participants in adult groups. But they do exist. Social factors play a part here. A too low assessment of one's abilities, judgements and resources in comparison with one's peers, or a lack of trust in oneself may be elements in anxiety-creation. A sense that to admit need at all means that one is less than adult, or that by becoming a student learner one is rejecting the company of adults, even denying one's adult identity (based on the view that 'education' is for children, a process of initiation) can play a part in creating over-anxiety. On the whole, these persons see the cause of their 'failure' as themselves. They do not see the cruel judgements of their peers as the cause of their distress. 'Far from regarding themselves as casualties of an inadequate and ramshackle system, they see themselves as educational failures' (Rogers 1977: 50). Thus for some, adult education is seen to be for failures, those who did poorly at school or who never took advantage of the initial education system and who must return to a system built on pupilage and dependency, opposed to adulthood and responsibility.

Such anxiety is not confined to 'second-chance' adult learners. It can exist in many other forms of adult learning, in both the formal and the non-formal sectors. Teachers selected to engage in learning programmes on IT or educational management, hospital administrators required to learn new skills or new approaches to their task, community workers coming to grips with new social trends, adults entering full-time certificated courses and so on – all of these can experience a concern as to whether they can cope with what is required of them: 'I opted to go on a special course for chief executives. The publicity emphasized that it would be very stretching – it was being run by a university business school. I know it was silly, but I felt that there was a severe risk of being out of my depth' (quoted in Rogers 2001: 8–9).

Anxiety may not take the extreme form of over-anxiety as described above, but it may well be present in some form. In many cases, anxiety becomes highest at times of evaluation: tests or examinations, submitting work to the judgement of the teacher or other members of the group. At such times, consciousness of what is perceived as the lack of educational skills is at its greatest: 'I can discuss but I can't write'; 'I can talk in the small group but not in the large group'. Uncertainty about the standards to be used for assessing work done will add to such anxiety. For those who see education as instrumental in achieving a set goal beyond the learning itself, there will be pressure against 'wasting time'.

What seems to be happening is that the change from a task-focused learning situation (using the natural informal learning which rarely generates anxiety) to a learning-focused situation (with all that conscious learning implies in contemporary constructions) is creating the anxiety. It is the idea of 'learning' that is making these student participants worry about whether they can cope or not.

Over-anxious adult learners tend not to trust themselves and thus turn to authority for guidance. But such anxiety may be expressed in a number of ways. Sometimes there are physical reactions – sweating, shaking and other signs of distress. More usually it will be confined to inner emotions which the learner seeks to hide. The individual is more likely to take refuge in 'flight': attempts to avoid the testing situation by either absenting themselves physically (non-attendance) or mentally (daydreaming), but there are occasions when they 'fight' by, for example, refusing to join in (see p. 232).

What can we do about it?

Because there are so many different causes of anxiety, there are no simple answers. It may be tackled by trying to reduce the anxiety itself or by trying to reduce opposition to the learning tasks.

Some strategies will help. Perhaps we can cultivate an atmosphere in which the fact that one dares even to the point of looking foolish becomes acceptable. The use of the group is helpful here. On the other hand, sarcasm and ridicule will be counter-productive: 'The adult tutor is there not to correct what the student says, because this denies his [sic] previous experience, views and beliefs, but to build up ways in which the students can evaluate their own opinions against those of the teacher and the rest of the group' (Rogers, J. 1977: 39–40). This is as true of skill-based learning programmes as it is of information-processing courses. The student learners need to be encouraged to experiment with new techniques and to evaluate the older practices against the new. Criticism, poor evaluations, signs of disapproval (the so-called 'chain-anxiety-producing sequence') will increase anxiety.

We can do more than just try to prevent the anxiety from growing. By managing the learning situation, we can help to reduce anxiety. The learning tasks can be broken up into smaller units to build up a sense of achievement. Carefully tailored rewards and reinforcements will be needed. The use of sub-groups may help, especially if the anxiety includes fear of failing before other members of the learning group. Something of the fear-inducing 'novelty' of the new learning can be lessened, although some sense of novelty is often needed to key the learner up, to create expectations and awareness. The pace of work should be monitored and adjusted if necessary.

Above all, we should seek to build up a sense of confidence in the student learner. We have already seen (p. 104) that (along with motivation) confidence is one of the twin pillars of learning; it is an essential component for all learning; without confidence, there can be no learning. Building confidence is therefore the primary task of the teacher of adults. Student participants who see in the teacher a sense of confidence and an encouragement to confidence, and who thus come to trust the teacher, in time also come to accept the teacher's assessment of their own ability to learn. If we believe that our student learners with our help *can* cope with learning tasks put clearly before them, and if we command their respect, most of the participants themselves will come to believe that they too can cope. It takes time but it can be done.

Positive aspects of anxiety

As we have seen, a certain amount of anxiety is desirable, for it will often motivate the learner; it is over-anxiety that creates the problem. A series of graphs that appear in a number of books on education and learning illustrates this point. Figure 11.1a shows that maximum learning is achieved by a steady but relatively slow arousal of interest until high motivation is attained; but excessive arousal so as to create too much anxiety will prevent learning.

Figure 11.1b suggests that too-quick arousal can achieve high performance in the short term, but performance will soon fall off. It will prove impossible to maintain the level of interest and therefore the level of performance.

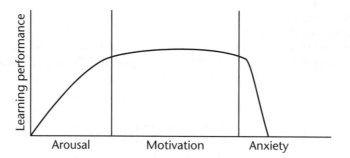

Figure 11.1a Maximum learning achieved by steady but slow arousal of interest; excessive arousal will prevent learning

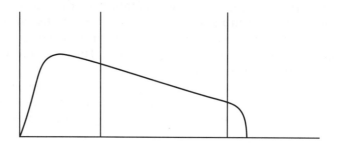

Figure 11.1b Too-quick arousal can achieve high performance in the short term, but the subject will be under-learned and performance will soon fall off

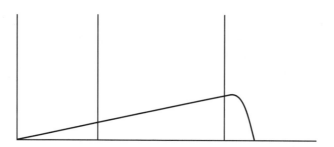

Figure 11.1c Failure to arouse a student's interest will result in the material apparently never being learned properly

On the other hand, Figure 11.1c indicates that failure to arouse a student's interest will result in the material apparently never being learned properly.

In all three cases, once arousal has passed through the motivated stage to the stage of excessive anxiety, learning falls off sharply and a block to learning occurs at this point.

Some sources of emotional difficulty

Emotional blocks other than anxiety may present themselves. The *fear of failing*, in the eyes of the group or the teacher (either as friend or as authority figure), or indeed in one's own eyes, causing possible pain or shame, is one of these. The pictures we have created of ourselves and of others spring in large part from our personal experiences, and these may exert real pressure on us: 'We were told we were going to have a free discussion and that we were all going to be expected to speak. That was all right for those who'd been at school more recently than me, but I'd been a mere housewife only a week before, and I made up my mind on the spot that wild horses wouldn't drag any discussion out of me. I *knew* I'd say something silly' (quoted in Rogers, J. 1977: 34). Such an individual will refuse to take risks. This is particularly characteristic of people who preserve a 'stiff upper lip', who consistently undervalue or hide feelings and who use their emotional energies to hold back spontaneous reaction.

Another such block may arise from a *reluctance to join in the methods of learning*. This may be due to an unwillingness to 'play' on the part of someone who is too serious, too academic in their approach, who fears to seem foolish. Activities such as ice-breakers, buzz-groups and role plays are anathema; they are not willing to play around with problems or with concepts, to imagine, to experiment with the unusual. Or it may spring from an 'impoverished fantasy life'. Such an individual asserts that the world of the senses is the real world; fantasies or play are unreal. They won't pretend, won't say, 'What if . . . ?' They cannot work out the implications of a hypothesis because they are wondering all the time whether the hypothesis is true or not.

On the other hand, student participants who refuse to engage in the methods of learning may be running away from what they are sure will be inevitable frustration. Their thresholds are too low. They give up quickly in the face of obstacles. They try as hard as they can to avoid pain, discomfort or uncertainty. They will not practise or memorise, asserting that they know it will not be worth the effort.

A third and frequent block to learning comes from the individual taking too low a view of themselves; their *'self-horizon' is too narrow*: 'I can't do it, I know I can't'. 'I know I can't remember all that'. Experience has taught them what they can and cannot do; and they feel that they are incapable of change. These people suffer from resource myopia, the failure to see resources to help them, either in their environment or in themselves; they undervalue both, especially themselves. Sometimes this may be due to sensory dullness. The would-be student learners make only partial contact with themselves and with their environment. The result is that their capacity and desire to explore the world become atrophied.

A further block can be seen in those who *fear the ambiguous*. These people avoid situations that lack clarity or where the probability of success is unknown. They will not 'try this' to see if it works, for they are convinced that, even if it does work, the reasons for success will remain unknown. They over-emphasise the unknown against the known, and so they won't set out to explore any part of the unknown.

Similar to these individuals are those who *fear disorder*, who dislike confusion and complexity, who have an excessive need for balance, order and symmetry. We all like to know where we are in any subject, to have signposts; but with these people it goes further than this. Their fear often leads to over-polarisation into opposites. They see everything in terms of black and white, good and evil. They thus fail to integrate the best from both sides of an argument. Role play for such student participants could become dangerous, for they may identify too closely with the case they are presenting.

Some student participants *fear to seem to influence others*. They don't want to appear too pushy or aggressive, and thus they hesitate to identify with new points of view.

There are other blocks to learning, but those listed above are probably the most common. Some of them can lead to other forms of blockage. Anxiety or too narrow a self-horizon can result in a failure to make any effort (most of us have met the student participant who sits on the edge of the group looking on with admiration as the other members master step after step of the subject), or conversely in trying to push too hard. In the latter case, the learner makes a more or less desperate attempt to keep up, to arrive at a solution. They become unwilling to let things 'incubate' or happen naturally. Too much effort sometimes springs from the same cause as too little effort.

There is a danger of exaggeration here. With all these various types of blockage present in every group of adult learners, and since we all to some extent share these characteristics, it may be wondered how any learning is done at all. But a good deal of learning does take place. The reason for itemising these blocks is not to deter the teacher but to remind ourselves that, when we meet a block to learning, it may well be caused by one of these factors.

Ego-defence mechanisms

Faced with a challenging situation like a lifelong education group, student participants with one of the above characteristics tend to employ a range of defence mechanisms to preserve their self-image. Such ego-defence mechanisms may be defined as unwitting devices, unconscious distortions, subterfuges or self-deceptions that we all practise to some extent to maintain our conscious psychological equilibrium, to avoid mental pain, to keep up appearances to ourselves as well as to others in the learning group when threatened by frustration, conflict or painful emotion.

There are a large number of such mechanisms. Some are aggressive in nature, others involve compromise or substitution. What follows is a brief annotated list intended for the teacher who wants to know what is going on in the group. Most of them involve some form of interaction with other members of the group. Those who wish to learn more about the subject can turn to the standard works on psychology.

- *Fantasy* – not just random idling or daydreaming but escape from the situation in imagination even though physically the person remains present. In fantasy, the participant gains alternative satisfaction; they fulfil themselves in imagination.
- *Compensation* – the group member turns to alternative activities (such as bizarre behaviour or costume) to make up for real or imagined inadequacies. If this leads to perpetual evasion of present problems and responsibilities, it will be over-compensation.
- *Identification* with others – the vicarious achievement of goals. This often happens in an adult learning group. One participant will join with another more successful one and bask in the reflection of the latter's glory though making little or no effort themselves. Sometimes identification can be with an imaginary 'hero' but normally it is with a real character, whether acquainted or not.
- *Projection* onto others of our own impulses and traits – we observe them in others or we attribute them to others. This usually takes the form of criticism; we blame others for the faults that lie in us. Most adult groups which engage in participatory learning methods end up having a scapegoat. Sometimes it is possible to imagine that others are more critical than in fact they are. Those who adopt this mechanism are often on the defensive against imaginary criticisms, noticing slights and innuendoes, and hence constantly taking offence.
- *Rationalisation* – the spontaneous giving of 'good' reasons. We find arguments to justify what we want to do or believe and even convince ourselves that these are the 'real' motives behind our actions or beliefs.
- *Repression* – selective forgetting according to the level of interest or displeasure associated with the technique or idea. Here again is a mental device that may prevent learning.
- *Sublimation* – a form of release, the diversion of frustrated energies into other (normal) channels of activity. In this, it differs from compensation. For an adult student participant, it may take the form of being particularly helpful in the group, performing certain

chores and so on, in an attempt to avoid the more distasteful (i.e. active learning) work of the programme.

There are others. *Displacement* is a process by which frustration or some other such emotion is turned away from the object that caused it and is vented on someone else. Supervisors reprimanded by their superiors have been known to 'take it out' on the people under their control; these in turn may express anger towards their families or other groups. Some teachers may vent the irritation caused by their student groups on others close to them, while others bring outside frustrations into the learning group. *Negativism* sees every request as a threat that will ultimately lead to trouble and blame, and thus sees the appropriate response as 'No'. It is an extreme form of an uncooperative attitude designed to avoid difficulties. *Reaction formation* is another mechanism by which we concentrate on the opposite of what we really want to do but are rather ashamed that we want to do it.

We are likely to meet most of these ego-defence mechanisms at some stage or other. If you look again at your own blockages (see p. 267), you will probably be able to determine what withdrawal and/or defence mechanisms are employed in each case. In our own cases (drawing and car repair) there is withdrawal; probably we set our horizons too low for both skills (we have been told so by colleagues who teach these subjects to adults; a certain art teacher used to insist that *everyone* can learn to draw). In the case of the car Alan employs displacement, turning his frustration at his own failure and helplessness against the garage or the AA or anyone else in sight when the car won't work and he can't do a thing about it. Still he refuses to learn! Naomi withdraws and contacts the garage!

It is easier to describe 'blocks to learning' than to know what to do about them. Knowing what is happening is usually more than half the battle, and lines of approach may suggest themselves. But it is not always easy, when faced with student participants who persistently fail to learn, especially when this distresses them, to identify which of the many causes underlie the failure and precisely why the student learners are seeking to defend themselves. It must be left to the individual judgement of each teacher in each setting to determine what to do about it. As with so much in lifelong education, there are no answers for universal application by all teachers, just a series of options to choose from, alternatives to try out.

Activity 11.3

In relation to the blocks you identified in Activity 11.1, can you identify any of the strategies which you have adopted?

Learning attitudes

The introduction of learning changes into the area of attitudes is perhaps the most difficult task that faces the teacher of adults. In an oral rehydration therapy project in India, it was possible to teach mothers in certain villages that children plagued with diarrhoea should not be starved, the traditional remedy, as they would suffer from dehydration and die, but instead should be fed with the rehydration mixture of water, sugar and salt. By the end of the learning programme, the knowledge and skill levels which the mothers possessed were demonstrably quite adequate for the change to take place. But it was not so easy to persuade them to follow this in practice. It went against their family and community traditions, what they had learned from the past and what others around them were doing and expected all members of the village to do. There was a block to learning new attitudes, not new knowledge or skills. The experience over many years of Alcoholics Anonymous, anti-smoking campaigns and drug programmes have shown that it is not lack of knowledge which inhibits effective behavioural learning but inadequately learned attitudes.

Modifications of attitude are the hardest change of all. The following suggestions may point to some strategies:

- Identify as clearly as possible precisely what the existing attitude is that is preventing learning changes and what are the most important pressures against making such changes, not just what the student learner says they are.
- An adequate basis of new or revised knowledge is necessary for any attitudinal change. Later threats to the new attitudes will be resisted in proportion as the new knowledge is firmly based and internalised.
- The amount of change called for should not be so great that the learner rejects it outright as calling for too radical a reappraisal of thinking and behaving. It should build on existing life patterns, not oppose them. (But equally it should not be presented as insignificant or trivial; no effort to change will then be made.)
- The student learners should be encouraged to draw their own conclusions from the material learned in this context, not exhorted to change their attitudes and practice.
- The new material should come from a source regarded as trustworthy and attractive (this will reflect on the teacher). The main mode of learning is what is often called 'human modelling'.
- The use of a learning group to create a climate in which such changes can be brought about is often effective. A public display

of new attitudes helps to promote more permanent changes. It is largely a matter of commitment to new ways of thinking and behaving, and commitment within a smaller group can assist in this before more public display (in the Indian village mentioned above, some of the mothers formed themselves into an oral rehydration therapy group with a badge and soon others came to join them).

- Role play, through which the participants play out the parts of those who hold the new desired attitudes and perhaps also those who hold in an extreme form the undesired negative attitude, can also be useful, though it needs to be used with great care.

Each teacher of adults needs to face every situation as a unique event, requiring a new assessment and perhaps new methods. What will work with one group may not work with another.

Most of these blocks seem to come from the way the student learners are constructing themselves as students in relation to themselves, to others and to the subject matter. They spring from their conception of what is involved in 'learning'. They do not exist when these same persons engage in the natural informal learning, for their attention there is concentrated on the task they intend to perform. It is up to us as teachers to help the participants to reconstruct their perceptions of what it means to be a student so as to reduce these blocks.

In summary, we do not wish to exaggerate the blocks to learning. There are many adult student learners who are keen to learn, to innovate, to experiment; who delight in new knowledge and positively seek it out, who welcome challenge. But there will always be some for whom innovation appears to be a risk, who do not welcome challenge.

We have suggested that these student participants put a good deal of emotional investment into defending their existing patterns of knowledge, attitudes and behaviour. In addition, most adult learners have built up a self-perception which they will often be reluctant to change. Attempts to build up new patterns, to encourage changes in their self-perception, may result in strong emotional reactions. The teacher must therefore tread carefully.

We have also suggested that all our student participants are part of a specific socio-cultural context. They are not psychological isolates but have created and are constantly recreating themselves in interaction with that context. We need to help them to identify and to build upon the motivators and resources, and the support networks and mechanisms in that environment, just as we need with them to identify the demotivators and to take action to weaken their effect (see p. 111). 'Start where they are' is a useful rule of thumb for all adult educators: and that means that the teacher of adults needs to find out as much as possible about the participants in the programme and their background – the teacher needs to become a researcher, using ethnographic approaches (see Brice Heath and Street 2008).

Further reading

Alexander, C. and Langer, E. (eds) (1990) *Higher Stages of Human Development: Perspectives on Human Growth*. Oxford: Oxford University Press.

Atherton, J.S. (2008) Doceo: Learning as Loss 1: http://www.doceo.co.uk/original/learnloss_1.htm

Birren, J.E. and Schaie, K.W. (eds) (1990) *Handbook of the Psychology of Aging*, 3rd edn. San Diego, CA: Academic Press.

Gibbs, G., Morgan, A. and Taylor, E. (1982) Why students don't learn, *Institutional Research Review*, 1(10).

Gross, R.D. (1987) *Psychology: The Science of Mind and Behaviour*. London: Hodder and Stoughton.

Storant, M. and van den Bos, G.R. (eds) (1989) *The Adult Years: Continuity and Change*. Washington DC: American Psychological Association.

Tennant, M. (2006) *Psychology and Adult Learning*, 3rd edn. London: Routledge.

Chapter 12

Evaluation
How can we tell . . . ?

> The criteria used for evaluation in informal learning are different from those in formalised learning. The evaluation of task-conscious learning is based on the successful completion of the task (does it work?); it therefore goes wider than the learning. In taught learning, the criterion tends to be whether the subject matter and skills have been learned as revealed by an artificial test of some form or other. This chapter argues that it is necessary to use both kinds of criteria when evaluating our teaching of adults – assessing not simply what the student learners *can* do (capabilities) but what they *do* do (practices).

The subject of evaluation in the teaching of adults is both a huge topic and an important one.

It is huge because much has been written about evaluation, and many people outside of the immediate teaching–learning context are involved in it. Providers, government, employers all are involved in and use evaluations of adult learning as well as those inside the learning programme, the teachers and those adults who study and use the results of their studies in their lives. Distinctions can thus be seen between on the one hand formal and public evaluations and on the other hand informal and immediate classroom evaluations, between generalised, standardised forms of evaluation and case-specific evaluations, between descriptive and judgemental, and between holistic and analytical evaluations.

It is not our intention here to engage in a full study of all aspects of evaluation in adult learning programmes (for work on adult education and evaluation, see, for example, Ruddock 1981; Rowntree 1987; Andrews 1991). Our focus is on the teacher and his/her uses of evaluation with his/her group of adult learners. But the wide-ranging literature on evaluation has led us to the view that we must beware of over-systematising this chapter (see, for example, Guba and Lincoln 1981; Eisner 1985). Any discussion of evaluation (with its concepts of assessment, certification, accountability and other concerns) will always be a mess. This chapter then makes no attempt to be completely coherent; 'managing messes' is what we are about. We are likely to raise as many questions as we answer.

The importance of evaluation

But at the same time, evaluation is important for teachers of adults, for it goes to the very heart of their task. As we have pointed out already (see Chapter 1), many of those who teach adults today are faced with a changed context. 'Adult basic education has come under a microscope in the last fifteen years, with policy makers demanding clearer evidence of the impact of adult . . . programming . . . What starts as a process of creating a learner-centred program that can flexibly adapt to the changing needs and interests of a learner becomes hampered by requirements for extensive documentation requiring clear goals, measures and outcomes as defined by government officials' (Campbell 2007: 123, 128). 'Strong political and social pressures pull the mindset and practices of practitioners and learners towards assessment that certificates achievement on behalf of external agencies . . . Assessment and formal processes to recognise and certificate achievements now dominate all the diverse sectors that comprise post-compulsory education and training'. Evaluation systems have become more standardised and are based on 'easily quantifiable outcomes . . . The formalisation of assessment and quality-assurance systems . . . blurs the distinction between assessment systems for 16 to 19 year olds and adult returners', resulting in a chaotic system which is 'enormously complicated for practitioners and awarding body officials to understand and use effectively' (Ecclestone 2005: 25, 1, 4, 46).

It is these newer processes of evaluation that create pressures on adult teachers today to move away from an older model of adult and continuing education, seen as a programme designed to help adults to learn what *they* want, when and how *they* want and to what level *they* want, towards standardised courses where the individual responses to learning are of less importance than the uniform performance of certain standard tests. The challenge for many teachers is how to retain some of the unique features of adult learning programmes while adhering to the processes of evaluation required today.

Evaluation and adult learning

We start from the position that evaluation is not something separate from the teaching. Despite the position of this chapter towards the end of the book, we believe that evaluation is not something to be bolted on to a programme after it has been designed or indeed started to be implemented, but is a process integral to all our activities. Planning evaluation commences with the start of planning the programme. The key questions we face as teachers of adults right from the beginning of our programme are: What are we trying to do? How do we know we are being successful? What are our measures of success?

For evaluation is integral to the whole process. Teachers of adults are already evaluating their student learners as part of their teaching. And the student learners too are engaging in evaluation – not just in their formal and non-formal adult learning programmes but also in their informal learning. So the aim of this chapter is to attempt to demystify evaluation, to help teachers of adults to keep under review and to critique their existing practices, to become more aware of what they are doing, often unconsciously, and of the constraints they have to this area of their work; in other words, to understand evaluation more fully and to engage in it more effectively. Despite appearances, it is possible for teachers to critique the processes of evaluation which are often required of adult educators today; and it is possible for them to have some choice in the measures of success and in the strategies – in the 'what' and the 'how' of evaluation.

Here it may be worth drawing a distinction between 'evaluation' and 'assessment', terms which are often used very loosely, even at times interchangeably. One possible definition suggests that *assessment* is the collection of data on which we base our evaluation. It tends to be quantitative, descriptive and objective. *Evaluation* on the other hand goes beyond the assessment; it is a process of making personalised judge-ments – decisions about achievements, about expectations, not just the effectiveness but (as the word 'evaluation' implies) also the *value* of what we are doing. It involves notions of worth, of 'good' and 'bad' teaching and learning and outcomes of learning programmes.

Activity 12.1

Before going further, look at the course which you are taking as your case study and try to determine how it is or will be evaluated – what indicators are being sought and how will they be collected? Write them down.

Everyday evaluation

Evaluation is an everyday activity, something we all do in our daily lives. We are all assessing, measuring. There is often an aura of mystery around 'evaluation' which is unnecessary. For example, we all make judgements about ourselves and others all the time: Can I do this or that activity (for example, run the marathon; cook a meal for visitors; ride my bicycle in heavy traffic, etc.)? Do I need to add to my skills and knowledge to do this and how good am I or will I be? We make judgements of what we can do and what not as we plan ahead; we evaluate our activities as well as those of others. We collect – often unconsciously – data to help us to make such judgements. In our work as teachers of adults, we need to build on these processes: evaluation in our adult learning programmes can be seen as 'an extension into the everyday work of educators of those continuous appraisals of conditions and events on the basis of which humans act and interrelate' (Adelman and Alexander 1983).

Thus just as learning (often unconscious learning) is integral to living, so evaluation is an integral (and again often unconscious) part of the process of learning, a tool for developing new skills, knowledge and understanding. To see how assessment and evaluation are integral to learning, we can take as an example a skills-based nursing course and a knowledge-based course on English literature. One model of learning suggests that

- the learner engages in an activity (with help from the teacher and/or peers) – e.g. bandaging a wound or discussing a passage of a Shakespeare play;
- the learner reflects on this activity and assesses it critically, again with the help of the teacher and of peers;
- the learner considers the feedback from teacher and peers;
- the learner makes a judgement, an evaluation;
- the learner makes alterations, often but not always at the suggestion of teacher and/or peers;
- the learner re-does the activity in a changed form and starts whole process over again.

The process of learning to bandage a wound or to engage with others in an analysis of Shakespeare is then based on assessment and evaluation; and the judgements and alterations made during that process is learning. And it goes on all the time; it is an essential ingredient in the process of learning.

Evaluation, then, is already a major part of both formal and informal learning, conscious and unconscious. Our student learners are well accustomed and indeed expert in evaluating their own learning episodes. Unthinkingly hitting a ball against a line on a wall in a tennis practice session brings about no learning changes by itself (though it may strengthen the muscles). What is needed is a series of assessments and judgements: 'That was above the line' – assessment; 'That was too high' – judgement, i.e. evaluation; 'That was too low' – modification; 'That was about right' – repetition; 'That was good . . . now again'; and so on. Without such an evaluative process, learning changes would not be made.

The difference between the everyday informal (task-conscious) and the more specific formal (learning-conscious) learning can be seen very clearly in evaluation. The former evaluates whether the learner performs the task, while the latter evaluates whether learning has been achieved, not whether it is being used. Evaluation in task-conscious learning is not a clear-cut process, not linear from simple to complex, but messy, using any criteria to hand. Like informal learning itself, it is a largely subconscious process, or when conscious, it is related to the task rather than to the learning. Much of it is self-judged, relying on a sense that the newly learned material 'fits', 'rings true' or 'works'. In this, the learner uses a number of different sources for assessment and a range of different criteria for evaluation, both chosen by the learner. And the outcomes of the learning will express themselves in multiple ways, rather than just one set of performance indicators.

Evaluation and education

Formalised learning, even in lifelong learning programmes, denies most of this. On the whole, education views evaluation as an external process using criteria chosen by the education-provider and undertaken in a format and at a time chosen by the learning programme rather than by the student learner. And it relates to the learning: it asks, 'Has the material been learned?', not, 'Does the material work?'

And, as we have seen, most teachers of adults today are part of this formalised educational culture, and have learned attitudes towards, and processes of, evaluation from this context. The increasing concern of government and other agencies for 'getting over messages', for using formal educational tools to address social issues has given a boost to the transmission model of learning; and the attempts to measure the success of these programmes lead us away from learner control of the learning outcomes. So instead of testing learning, adult courses are often now learning testing: students are being taught what they will need to pass the test.

Now we must be careful of exaggerating these developments. First, it is still true that some students resent this pressure, particularly those 'for whom career advancement and the development of employability skills are less important than their own personal development'; an adult learning programme for them is 'a way of opening horizons and a form of relaxation and socialising' (Longcroft 2008). There are still some open-ended contexts where adult is teaching adults without the constraints of formal externally prescribed assessments – art and reading circles, church and other religious groups, local history and environmental societies, study days run by museums, record offices and libraries. These are not subject to external validation processes – they set their own goals and evaluate themselves, often informally. The ideology of learner control is not yet dead, even though it is not so dominant. You may care to explore such opportunities which are still available in your area.

Secondly, while some adult education practitioners see the growing accreditation of adult learning programmes as increasing equality of educational opportunities, others are resisting them in their own way as representing an unhealthy 'commodification' of learning, the destruction of the 'free spaces' of learning. For example, the adult literacy field 'has resisted this narrowing of purpose. Practitioners continue to emphasize the need to include the broader purposes of adult literacy such as personal development, community participation, supporting children's education and social change'. Thus, 'affective factors (e.g. self-esteem, self-awareness, and the ability to reflect on one's self and one's actions) are beginning to be incorporated into assessment frameworks and systems of documenting progress' (Campbell 2007: 126, 145, 148; see RARPA and Wider Benefits of Learning in Further Reading). Some programmes are making their assessments more flexible, giving greater learner choice: the personalisation of learning trajectories, the increase in continuous assessment or individual portfolios are some of the ways in which learner-centredness is retained in evaluation to some degree (although the modularisation of courses does not always lead to increased learner-centredness).

At the same time, however, we recognise that some (perhaps many) of the newer students in adult learning programmes today do want to have learning objectives/outcomes set and tested by some outside agency. Recent surveys suggest that an increasing number of adult students are willing to participate in such assessment procedures. Many have had prior formal education at an advanced level, though for some that experience was a number of years ago. They are accustomed to formal assessments; they are willing to accept greater direction in their learning; they welcome the challenge of formal assessments. Our bandage learner is keen to be shown how to do it and then replicate it rather than work it out for himself; our Shakespearean reader is open to new ways of looking at the text provided by the teacher perhaps more than by her peers or her own new insights.

In such a situation, the teacher of adults needs to explore how much choice s/he really does have, and how much the student learners have. How can each of these be increased? (see Chapter 13 on participation). A distinction can be drawn between the *external* and occasional evaluation, practised by the organiser of the programme or by an external validating body, and the *internal*, more regular evaluation, practised by the teacher and the student learners in the course of the teaching programme. While accepting external measures and the processes of assessment, teachers of adults are not limited to such measures. They can set their own additional measures and devise their own processes for collecting data on which to make their evaluation. 'When you see a student walking in, standing straight, shoulders back, head up, after two months of tutoring, you know that you are succeeding' (Arneson 1999 cited in Campbell 2007: vii). Happiness and joy at achievement are visible, but not measurable; and measures like these can be added to the measures prescribed by the course organisers.

There is a temptation here to confuse the internal and external evaluations with the distinction which has often been drawn between *formative* evaluation – seen as the ongoing evaluation that is inherent in the learning process itself, which the teacher controls and which leads to learning change – and *summative* evaluation – seen as that evaluation which takes place at different times, particularly at the end of the programme of learning, to assess how far we have got, often (but not always) controlled by external bodies. But these are not in fact two distinct processes; there is an inevitable blurring between formative and summative evaluation. If a summative evaluation undertaken at the end of a course (a teacher's report, for instance) is used to plan new programmes and new approaches, if the results of an end-of-course examination are used to help develop a student's progression, then they are being used in a formative way. It is the way evaluation is used that distinguishes it. If it looks only backwards and reviews what has been done, it is summative; if in addition it looks forward to, and influences, new procedures, it is formative. The latter is more productive; evaluation judgements should lead to change. But there is also a time for the former, especially when issues of accountability come to the fore. (We are aware that this sounds 'messy', but then we agreed that any discussion of assessment and evaluation will be messy.)

Some people have distinguished formative evaluation from what they call *developmental* evaluation – where the student learners rather than external bodies are involved in their own evaluation as part of their learning process. Learning the processes of self-evaluation is a major part of developing further the skills of learning so that the student learners can continue with their own conscious and purposeful learning.

The role of the teacher in evaluation

Teachers of adults have a number of roles to play in evaluation. They (with the student learners) are evaluating all the time for learning; they are assessing the learning; they are often implementing outside evaluation. And they also evaluate their own work – they are concerned with whether they are being effective as teachers; whether the objectives they have set are the right ones and at the right level, as well as whether they are being met. They will be making (sometimes half-consciously but sometimes more formally) assessments of their student learners at the beginning of the programme (we need to distinguish this ongoing process from the 'initial' assessments made by many adult education organisations using formal tools such as the assessment of prior experiential learning (APEL) (see Evans 1992b) and the even more formal use of 'diagnostic assessments' by experts). During the course, teachers will assess progress of both individuals and the whole group, and the match between intentions (objectives) and outcomes (the results) of the teaching–learning process. They will be seeking to measure change, appraise efforts and identify new needs, strengths and weaknesses. They will wish to learn whether the short-term goals and the tasks they have laid before the learning group have been achieved and whether they are of the kind that will contribute towards the desired longer-term learning changes. They need to test whether the student learners are ready to move on to the next stage or not. They will want to see clearly the *intended* programme of learning, the *implemented* programme (which may be different from what was intended for various reasons) and whether that again differs from the *received* programme.

And they will need to try to understand the evaluation system which they are called upon to implement – for this will affect their teaching. The organiser and/or awarding body through inspectors and examiners together with those to whom they are accountable (governments, funders, clients, etc.) will be assessing how far the programme objectives are being met. Are we getting in our groups the right kind of student learners, the ones the programme is primarily intended for, those we feel to be in most need? Are they learning the right things? Are the courses meeting the needs and intentions of the participants? Are the programmes on offer reflecting the selectivity-, competitiveness- and competency-based criteria of the formal educational system, or are they offering a different ethos (non-selective, non-competitive and effort-based)? They will be concerned with quality control, whether the resources are being used most effectively and, in certain circumstances, to establish priorities. To do all this, they will need criteria to determine whether some courses are 'better' than others and to plan accordingly.

'. . . making the important measurable'

The climate which surrounds evaluation in many adult learning programmes today is one which denies to the non-quantitative much of its validity. It tends to stress what can be counted and to omit what cannot be counted (the ambiguity in the words 'to be counted', as meaning (a) 'to be enumerated' and (b) 'to be considered important' is no accident in educational evaluation). Traditional educational evaluation 'makes the measurable important'; that is, what can be counted and measured such as participation and contact hours, or the results of tests and examinations, come to dominate the teaching–learning programme, and they then become the goal of the programme, valued above all the other outcomes. What cannot be counted is ignored or demeaned.

But most teachers of adults will be aware that there will be multiple outcomes of new learning that go beyond the uniform pre-set learning outcomes. Their task will be to 'make the important measurable', that is, to find techniques by which the many different ways in which adult learners will express their new learning can be measured and if possible converted into statistical form that can be used as the basis for comparative evaluation. The problem is how to make each of the many varied ways in which the new learning will be used assessable, measurable and comparable. This inevitably raises issues of value judgements on the part of the evaluators. How the new learning is employed will not always satisfy the educator. But it is inevitable that adult participants who each have their own agenda will express their learning in quite different ways.

Whose criteria?

Thinking about the evaluation you are being asked to implement in your adult learning programme or which you are devising for your own programme raises the question as to how far the student learners can and should be involved in establishing the criteria for the evaluation. If they have their own agendas, their own purposes in coming to our learning programmes, should we not evaluate the success of the programme by how far *these* goals have been met rather than by whether the goals of the programme itself have been met?

Criteria can be either imposed or negotiated with the participants. In addition, they can be either closed, pre-set, standardised and fixed, or they can be more open, multiple in expression and flexible. Every evaluation of lifelong learning will thus be characterised by activities in which

- the criteria being used will be either closed (i.e. uniform and pre-set) or open (i.e. allowing for multiple expressions);
- the criteria being used will be either imposed (external to the programme) or negotiated (i.e. internal to the programme).

A useful matrix of these issues has been produced which will cause many of us to think more deeply about the evaluation of our programmes (see Figure 12.1).

Figure 12.1 Matrix of evaluation (based on Thomas 1987: 386)

Activity 12.2

See if you can determine where the evaluation of your case study fits into the matrix shown in Figure 12.1, if at all.

Evaluate what?

Despite the fact that, in many forms of adult learning programmes today, the measures of success are already prescribed by the agency or the awarding body, we would argue that there is still a choice for the teacher of adults. And the selection of what should be included and (by implication) what should be excluded is a 'political' decision; it reflects the ideology of the teacher.

The most common approaches to evaluation in taught learning programmes appear to focus on three main areas: the *outcomes* (both intended and unintended), the *structures* and the *processes*. But the last two are assessed by whether they contribute to the intended outcomes; there are no independent criteria for judging structures or processes.

We can look at these areas in more detail.

The intended learning outcomes

The first area of any evaluation will be the planned goals and objectives of the learning programme. Normally evaluation concentrates on how far these intended learning outcomes have been achieved, without asking first whether these are given or negotiated goals, whether they are clear to ourselves as well as to the student learners, and how they relate to the (often changing) goals of the participants (see Chapter 7). That the intended learning outcomes today are most commonly given by some outside agency may be welcomed by the teacher and student learners or accepted reluctantly. It is important for any teacher of adults to enquire as to how far their goals and learning outcomes are given, and how much choice the teachers and student learners have.

Activity 12.3

Try to determine for yourself how much freedom you have in setting goals and assessing progress in your own teaching–learning activity.

Nor is there much consideration given as to whether these are the right goals. We often take for granted that the goals of our courses are self-justifying, but these assumptions need to be examined. What values do they imply? Are they in fact the most appropriate goals for this particular set of student learners? What criteria shall we use to assess this? Is the learning primarily concerned with personal growth, or with socialisation and/or social change, or with vocational advancement? Are they open or closed goals? (see pp. 14, 292).

There is also the question as to whether the goal of the learning programme lies within the programme itself or beyond it – and this will affect the evaluation. For example, is the goal of the creative writing course that the student learners will produce work satisfactory to the teacher by the end of the course or is it that they will write creatively after the course finishes? If a student produces acceptable work during the course but never writes again, is that success or failure? If a literacy learner is able to read and write to the satisfaction of the teacher by the end of the course but never reads or writes after the course, is this success or failure? If a training course is intended to help the participant to get a job but s/he does not gain employment despite obtaining the certificate, is that success or failure? Is the goal of the bandage course for the student nurse to pass the certificate or to practise effective bandaging for many years to come? Such questions determine much relating to evaluation.

Here the distinction between what are sometimes called 'hard' and 'soft' (or sometimes 'tangible' and 'intangible') outcomes will prove useful. The measures which are usually prescribed by outside agencies in most adult learning programmes are indicators which can be measured – the performance of certain tasks, for example. These are often expressed in terms of *competences* – the ability to complete specified activities to a certain level which may be carefully graded. These are felt to be universally valid and transferable from context to context. Such competences have been modified in recent studies by looking at *capabilities* which take into account the contextual factors which may affect the exercise of competences; but capabilities too are thought to be testable and transferable. These are called 'hard' outcomes – they are thought to be uniform across all the varied body of adult student learners, and they can be tested and measured.

The problem with adult learning programmes, however, is that the student group is very varied; they come with varied intentions, and express their learning changes in multiple ways rather than in the one specified way. Adult students wish to explore, to develop, change in unspecified ways; they make their own meanings, engage in critical reflection, create their own research approaches, grow in communication skills. Such learning gains are harder to measure although they can often be seen clearly enough. An increase in individual confidence, changes in self-perception and identity, even status – these are the so-called 'soft' outcomes of learning – although as we have seen they are often the outcomes of 'participation in adult learning programmes' rather than of 'learning' (see p. 9).

An essential part of evaluation in adult learning programmes, then, will be concerned with the attitudinal development of the student participants – with how much additional confidence, how much increased motivation have arisen from the teaching–learning programme. This aspect is often omitted from evaluation processes, which concentrate more on 'value-added outcomes' – on increased knowledge and more highly developed skills. But the assurance and enhanced self-image of the students, their willingness to continue to study, their increased interest, their 'walking tall' are all outcomes which need to be evaluated and acknowledged.

Such soft outcomes are important in adult learning programmes, for, when asked for their own assessments of learning achievements and to express the learning changes that they have experienced, many adult learners 'tend to describe changes in themselves and in their activities as much as, or more than, they talk about changes in their reading and writing skills' (Campbell 2007: 136). But assessing such personal learning outcomes is not easy: as has been pointed out, programmes which are specifically designed to 'promote freedom, initiative, self-mastery, social co-operation, planning, organization and judgement' find it difficult to identify 'suitable measures to determine learning gains' (Campbell 2007: 95).

Teachers of adults who find themselves faced with the implementation of specified 'hard outcomes' can add to their list of learning outcomes 'soft' outcomes – signs which indicate to them that the student learners have changed in ways which the student learners themselves feel are important. Such outcomes also need to be assessed and evaluated, although this is not as straightforward as assessing hard outcomes (for some contemporary work in this area, see http://www.rarpatoolkit.com/en/default.asp).

Learning achievements

A key element of any evaluation will be an assessment of whether the programme of learning is proving effective. This will need an agreement as to what signs and/or products will reveal whether the participants have learned what they were intended to learn. At the heart of the evaluation process lies the question of how much and what are they learning, whether it is product or process, to handle tools or to produce a table to a set standard (see pp. 180–3). What is the quality and level of their learning? How well is the material learned? These and many other similar questions occur in the process of thinking about the evaluation of student learning.

One of the issues here lies with the concept of progress in learning. Those who concentrate on the acquisition of new skills, knowledge, understanding and attitudes will see progress as advancement along a straight line of development, more knowledge and skills building on existing knowledge and skills. Those who concentrate more on attitudinal development, increased confidence and greater awareness, will be aware that there is not always a straight line of progress in learning. Most desired outcomes are both multi-tasked and multi-skilled; progress can mean accomplishing one life task after another, where the later task may not be more difficult than the earlier task.

Learning structures

So far, the concentration has been on the evaluation of the student learner(s) rather than the programme or system. But since a large part of the aim of the evaluation is to change our teaching so as to become more effective, we also need to identify what is most successful in what circumstances (although it is important to remember that other factors will influence the effectiveness of any teaching programme). Thus issues such as contact hours and the quality and supply of materials will impact on the programme. The way the programme has been developed and is resourced, the climate created, the methods and materials used will all need to be analysed and valued.

Among the factors that contribute towards the effectiveness of the learning process are those relating to the context within which the teaching takes place. The concern of evaluation by both organiser and teacher includes the identification of the positive and negative influences that affect our teaching, such as the *setting* (the room, furniture, temperature, lighting, teaching aids) and the *emotional climate* and *management controls*, both of the institution within which the course is set and of the learning group itself (see pp. 222–3), to see how far these are conducive to the participants' learning and to remedy any hindrances they may contain. These do not necessarily reveal whether learning is taking place, but they do contribute to the criteria by which we can assess teaching–learning effectiveness. For example, there is little hope of creating effective learning changes in the direction of greater self-confidence and self-determination if the class denies to the student learner any opportunity to exercise such qualities. Overt and covert pressures for or against the goals are important elements in the process of teaching adults and need evaluation.

Some approaches to programme evaluation have adopted tools such as the appropriately named SWOT approach: to assess the *strengths* and the *weaknesses* of the programme or class; to assess the *opportunities* which it opens and which may or may not have been taken up; and to assess the *threats* (or obstacles) which will hamper the effectiveness of the programme and which need to be addressed if the goals of the programme are to be achieved. This approach has specific advantages in that it encourages us to look beyond the normal assessment of outcomes and achievements to explore other possibilities and the risks faced in the programme.

Learning processes

The processes of the learning programme also need to be evaluated. Once again the concern is more with learning than with teaching; for the purpose of teaching is student learning. Regular ongoing evaluation includes the process of feedback which is a form of evaluation.

In this context, there are two aspects to 'self-evaluation'. As many writers have pointed out, the professional teacher will be reflective on his/her own teaching. Brookfield (1995) suggests using autobiography, student assessments, colleague assessments, and adult learning theory as tools for such professional reflexivity; others like the Hay McBer report (2000) concentrate on such things as a teacher's professional characteristics, teaching skills and class climate.

Certainly, there is a need for the evaluation of the teaching–learning process. The range and nature of student activity is a part of the evaluative process. Formal research into classroom interactivity that has been conducted by some scholars (see, for example, Flanders 1970) may well be beyond the resources of most teachers of adults, but informally it is possible for teachers to assess such things as the nature of the group, the kinds of interaction between members, the range of expectations and intentions they declare and the clarity of their goals, the kind of work they do in each session and between sessions, the questions they ask (as signs that they are grappling with the new material), the involvement of the student learners in evaluating themselves – for positive recordings in each of these areas are thought to be indicators that learning is taking place. At each stage, judgements need to be made: for example, as to whether the activity in which the participant is engaged really aims 'at the *improvement* and *development* of knowledge, understanding and skill and not merely at its *exercise*' (NICCE 1980: 10). In the end, a description of the programme of work is not in itself an adequate means of assessing effectiveness, but a programme in which the student learners are active is more likely to lead to learning changes than one in which they appear to be passive recipients of information and instruction.

Learning impact

Finally we will need to look for the unexpected outcomes, the impact of our teaching–learning programmes – what is sometimes called 'the ripple effect'. There will be many of these, and not all of them will be life-enhancing for the student participants, although many will (a tutor once asked a group of students for those 'other outcomes', and one person replied that she got married!). One member of a photography-for-leisure class determined almost at the end of the class to set up a small business for wedding photographs; this was not his intention or the course's intention at the start of the programme, but it was a clear *outcome of* the programme. Some of this evaluation may have to be done some time after the course has finished – what is sometimes called *post hoc* or postscript evaluation. Experience indicates that at times, whereas the learning objectives of a programme may have been achieved and the learning outcomes were positive, the longer-term impact of the programme could be negative (see, for an example, Rogers 1992: 216–25). Although much of this will be beyond the influence of the teacher, it is important for the teacher to be aware of it.

Activity 12.4

Write down under each heading ways in which you are able in your course to evaluate:

- the intended learning goals
- the learning achievements
- the learning structures
- the learning processes
- the impact of the programme.

How to evaluate

Although in many cases, the tools of evaluation will have been specified in the programme, we would argue that the teacher should also identify and create other ways (both formal and informal) by which to assess the learning achievements and to evaluate the learning changes of the students.

Activity 12.5

In relation to the course you have identified, we suggest that, before you read further, you list here some of the tools you (would wish to) use to assess whether you were being successful in promoting learning.

There are three basic forms of evaluation processes – observation, performance testing and student feedback.

Observation should be the main tool of evaluation for any teacher of adults. Observation of the way student learners undertake tasks, of their conversation and activities, of their approaches to the work of the learning group will reveal much. But involvement by the student learners in the learning activities does not always reveal the *kind* of learning taking place, even if it can be relied upon to indicate that some form of learning changes are taking place. We noted in Chapter 7 the difference between the private (inner) learning and the public (behavioural) expressions of that learning, and the debate as to whether all 'private' outcomes can and should express themselves in behavioural (performance) terms. The major problem with the evaluation of learning is to identify appropriate ways in which the inner learning changes are expressed publicly. What are the signs, what products can provide evidence of both hard and soft outcomes? Behavioural changes are easier to assess than inner changes in understanding, values and attitudes; part of the process of evaluation is to interpret behavioural patterns in order to see how the more private learning changes are expressed. Analytical observation is the process by which such assessments can be made.

But secondly, the teacher should also *provide opportunities* for the student learners to demonstrate to the teacher and to others the learning that is taking and has taken place. Some teachers do not provide such opportunities, preferring their teaching to be one-way.

Such opportunities could be a piece of writing, a series of exercises, a fabricated article or role-play exercise. The range available is very wide and is now being adapted to the personalisation of learning: it includes 'portfolios; demonstrations; presentations; written responses; projects; oral retellings; . . . self-assessments and reports; peer assessments; and where appropriate, tests' (Campbell 2007: 255).

Peer assessment is growing widely in many forms of adult learning as an appropriate tool for evaluation – moving away from a monopoly of teacher-led evaluation. But it will still fall to the teacher – in association with the participants – to develop the formats within which those opportunities for demonstration of learning will take place.

When devising such opportunities, teachers of adults need to remind themselves of a number of features:

- the primary purpose is to evaluate the hidden depths (expressive objectives) that lie beneath these competency-based activities, not just the surface competences;
- outside influences may hinder or prevent the exercise of the desired function. Activities (including words) do not always reflect inner learning changes or their nature, but they may be at times the only way we can evaluate the learning changes.

Such opportunities for the demonstration of learning as are designed are often artificial activities intended to be performed in the classroom – artificial in an artificial context – such as tests, quizzes and exercises. These have a certain value as indicators of competences. Increased value can be obtained from the use of 'real' tasks, even if these are conducted in the classroom – real in an artificial context; here monitoring of the performance and immediate corrections can be made.

Examinations or testing

Despite the hesitations of many of those who teach adults, examinations are increasingly being used to evaluate adult learning. The variety of so-called 'objective testing' (both subject-based and/or skill-based: many governments are currently preoccupied with assessing key skills rather than subject-based knowledge) is also increasing. Coursework (assignments serving both as part of the learning process and also as a form of assessment) is normal now, not only in distance learning programmes but also in many face-to-face adult learning programmes. End-of-course assessments now range from the very formal (standardised testing) to the very informal: written examinations (unseen, open-book, pre-set or home-based), tests, essays (whether structured or subjective – i.e. devoted to whatever the student learner wishes to write about), practicals, observation of exercises, oral tests, questions, discussion, projects and so on. Some are group-based, more are individual. They attempt to test the competences attained.

The problems of marking examinations, such as norm and criterion referencing (i.e. whether each exam is to be marked against a 'normal' distribution pattern of success and failure, say 5 per cent top grade, 20 per cent second, 50 per cent third, etc., which is apparently less popular now than it used to be, or against an 'objective' standard of competence that is supposed to exist somewhere outside of the examiner as in key-skills or key-competences assessments), are well known and well rehearsed. Also well known are their accompaniments – the prejudices of the examiners in relation to particular student learners or academic practices, the problem of extrinsic rewards rather than intrinsic motivation, the increase in competitiveness and selectivity, enhanced feelings of anxiety, failure and injustice, the distortion of the curriculum and of the pace of learning, the fact that many exams are set and marked by people unknown to the student learners so that the aim comes to be to defeat the examiner by guesswork rather than to learn. All examinations and tests are of course culturally bound; and those student learners who come from within that cultural framework are at a considerable advantage against others who come from other cultural backgrounds. A one-size-fits-all approach to testing is now widely recognised as inadequate for adult learners, but it still persists.

Such concerns have led to a search for ways to replace élitist and selective examinations with other forms of evaluation; to replace prizes with goals that all may achieve (the distinction that we noticed on pp. 5–6 between the athletics match and the marathon). Through negotiated forms of criteria-setting, some modern approaches to evaluation are seeking ways of helping student participants to assess their own learning progress through self- and peer assessment (see Boud 1995). This chimes in well with the informal ways of learning, for self-assessment is the primary mode of evaluation in the natural learning process, with self-initiated peer evaluation also a feature; and it suggests that formative and summative assessment are coming closer together.

Nevertheless, we should not dismiss such formal methods of evaluation entirely, for they can be formative as well as summative in their nature. Internal tests may be as much a means of new learning as of assessment – many a new insight has been developed during an examination. Sometimes they are intended to be solely summative, leading to the determination of attainment levels and the award of certificates of competency. There is clearly a place (and a good deal of demand) for these in some adult teaching programmes, but a number of factors limit their usefulness:

- The problem of how to evaluate *progress* made in the learner journey as distinct from *levels of attainment*. Most teachers of adults will be only too aware that some student learners, starting from a base lower than that of others in their group, make more rapid progress but remain well behind the attainment levels of the rest. The wide range of the participants in adult learning programmes makes this issue more acute, especially in institution-bound education. The way to reward such effort and advances while retaining the prescribed or desired attainment levels is problematic.

- Adult learners not only start at very different points; they also choose different goals for themselves. The ends and intentions of adult learners are not always homogeneous.
- There are no age-related criteria for adult learners as have been agreed for younger people (for example, standard reading ages or age-related key stage assessments). After all, what is the 'appropriate' level for a 47-year-old?

Certification

Where there are examinations, there are almost always certificates. It is often assumed that the public recognition of achievement calls for such certificates. But other forms of public demonstration of learning may be equally valid. For example, the creation of individual portfolios, exhibitions of students' works, the development by groups of students of radio programmes, videos, even television programmes and publications, the public activities of environmental groups and local history classes, the writings of creative literature circles – these public demonstrations are sometimes felt to be of more value than a certificate. Existing official policies on the accreditation of adult learning programmes seem to us to be inadequate, too limited, unimaginative and unrewarding for many adult student learners – there are wider options available if some flexibility can be tolerated.

Nevertheless, some adult student learners themselves are 'keen to gain a recognized qualification as evidence of their achievement which gives them a portable certificate to take on to further education, training or employment' (Campbell 2007: 276). Certificates now take many forms, with in some cases notes being attached elaborating on the achievements represented by the certificate. But they still in the public mind represent some form of objective truth; and their agreed transferability leads to a common belief in the standardisation of these certificates. The search is on everywhere for that most elusive of all holy grails, commonalities between different disciplines and levels in a National Qualifications Framework – almost impossible in an adult learning programme. How does one compare learning bandaging with understanding Shakespeare?

Every certificate, then, has its limits. In particular, it only acknowledges what a person *can* do, their competences. It cannot accredit what any one person *will* do in the future. It asserts that one can bandage 'correctly' but it does not indicate that the individual may not do it correctly in future if s/he is always in a hurry. It will affirm that a person can read and understand Shakespeare but it cannot reveal that s/he very rarely does so because other things are more important and s/he has no time for such reading. The assumed predictive function of certification, that the learner can behave now and 'will be able to apply the skill or attribute being tested . . . in future situations' (Ecclestone 2005: 35) is illusory. Behind all certificates are a range of assumptions – that performance in a test will mean performance in daily life, for example; that activities done once in the classroom can be transferred to the workplace or the community, that what is done today will always be done in future. Such assumptions need to be tested regularly.

Despite all its difficulties, however, standardised public recognition is for many adults more than an instrument of progression; it can be for them life-affirming, part of their newly assumed identities, conferring status.

Satisfaction indicators

In view of these issues, it is not surprising that many teachers (and providers) of learning programmes for adults tend to rely on the third option for the evaluation of learning, student satisfaction indicators. It is worth listing some of these in order to indicate that there are other ways of assessing adult learning than formal assignments and examinations:

- *indicated demand* – requests from prospective student participants, individually or through organisations, on which the programme is built and which are taken to indicate that it must be 'meeting needs' (exactly what those 'needs' are is often left unexamined: they may simply be for a pleasant and relatively cheap evening out!);
- *effective demand* – the numbers of student learners attracted to particular classes (the size of the group is sometimes taken as a means of assessing the value of a course);
- *follow-on* – whether an extension of the learning situation is requested and taken up (a course is deemed successful if the student learners request more of the same);
- *follow-up* – similarly whether the student learners continue to study or pass into new programmes;
- *attendance figures* – in terms of both regularity of attendance and low numbers of withdrawals;

- *verbal or written comments by the student participants* – both approval and complaints, indicating the student learners' sense of success or dissatisfaction; end-of-course student evaluation schedules (sometimes called 'happy sheets'!) are being used regularly.

Participant feedback (which is not the same as peer evaluation) is perhaps the most common form of evaluation in most adult learning programmes. Teachers and organisers frequently use such popularity indicators to evaluate their work. And with some justification, for such criteria are closer to those used in our personalised learning episodes: we judge if we have succeeded by a sense of satisfaction that 'it works' or 'it feels good'. But it is not always clear that these truly signal that effective learning is taking place. Indeed, in some courses, a number of 'happy sheets' taken at regular intervals throughout a course reveal little or nothing about the learning of the group. For one thing, most of them simply record immediate uncritical sentiments; and those who distribute such forms assume that the participants have the skills and experience to make such judgements about the value of the teaching. More useful are tools which require the participants to indicate issues or events (such as critical incidents) which may have arisen or occurred during or soon after the learning programme (Brookfield 1995). In any case, ethnographic studies indicate clearly that participant statements always need triangulation by observation, for participants are not always conscious of the full implications of the processes of which they are a part.

Encourage learner self- and peer-evaluation

But that is not to suggest that such statements are valueless. Indeed, such 'happy sheets' can become instruments for encouraging our student participants themselves to evaluate their own learning. In fact, many adult student learners do make such judgements. The participants engage in a conversation with the teacher, their peers and the subject matter of the course in formative evaluation in order to learn. They also from time to time pursue summative self-evaluation for motivation: assessing their own progress and performance, determining how far they have progressed and whether it is in the 'right' direction, thus diminishing or rekindling their enthusiasm for the learning goals in the light of their achievements (what is called *ipsative evaluation*). Many are the adult student learners who decide they are not making enough progress and therefore they withdraw (they do not 'drop-out' – they actively withdraw). And such participant evaluation includes some judgement about the 'relevance' of the learning programme to their own purposes. Again many adult students judge that what they are learning is not what they planned or wished to learn: they also withdraw. But often they make such judgements subconsciously; and it is part of the role of the teacher of adults to help them to make the subconscious conscious. Discussion among the group of such issues is a vital part of adult learning; filling in 'happy sheets' in collaboration can be a useful tool if it leads to peer-evaluation. The development of the attributes of self- and peer-evaluation should be a key component of adult learning programmes; 'being professional' is in large part a matter of being self-critical based on adequate processes of self- and peer-assessment.

Practices

In the end, the only fully satisfactory mode of assessment as to whether the student learners have learned is their performance *after* the end of each stage of the learning programme. Do they act in such a way as to *reveal* increased confidence, in whatever field of learning they are engaged in? Can they be seen to exercise new or enhanced skills more often? Does the student nurse regularly bandage 'properly' (i.e. to an acceptable level); does the literature student go to the theatre more often, watch more classical drama programmes on TV and video, join a theatre or poetry group or demonstrate in some other visible way the new learning? In what ways do they reveal new understandings and new knowledge in what they say and do? Are they continuing to learn in directions of their own choice? Do they show signs of being satisfied with their own performance in their chosen field or of striving towards further improvement? In other words, is the learning *used* in some way to improve the quality of life of the student? The ultimate evaluation of the success or failure of all adult teaching will be seen in the *exercise* by the participants of new skills, knowledge and understandings and of new attitudes towards themselves and the world around them.

Such *post hoc* evaluation is not easy, especially as most teachers of adults lose contact with their student participants soon after the end of the course or programme. The possibility of delayed learning (we know that it takes time for feelings, creative approaches and understandings to emerge) means that we can never be sure, in the case of seeming failures, that our work will not eventually bear fruit. Nor can we be sure that the learning of those with whom we seem to have been most successful will be permanent. The student participants may have learned enough to get a certificate in bandaging or a degree in literature; but whether they have really learned anything which will change their practices and in which directions will often remain unclear.

Some teachers of adults will find this unsatisfactory, but we will often have to be content to cast our bread upon the waters in the expectation

that it will (may?) return to us after many days. Perhaps the most rewarding aspect of the evaluation of adult learning are those signs of satisfaction (and not just in words) that so many adults reveal in their relations
with their teachers. The student participants are after all the best judges
of whether they are getting what they feel they need, for this is how they
evaluate their own informal learning.

Teacher self-evaluation

Which brings us back to the teacher's own goals. Why are we teaching?
What are *our* goals? Can we evaluate these goals? How can we assess
whether we are achieving them? What signs shall we look for (walking
tall?)? How can we improve, fulfil our goals more fully? And how can we
demonstrate publicly our capabilities?

One part of this analysis relates to our *performance* as teacher, centred
both upon our subject expertise and upon our skills of presentation and
communication. Evidence of preparation, both of the subject matter and
of the modes of teaching; awareness of the student learners; the clarity
with which the goals of learning are defined; the structure of the learning
programme – its level, pace of learning, relevance to the student learner
and to the task in hand; the clear signposting of each step of the learning
process; the number and nature of the teaching–learning materials used
and teaching–learning activities devised – all these are capable of assessment. Our personal style of teaching (self-projection, confidence, voice
level, powers of organisation, the rapport built up with the student learners, the development of interaction and feedback), the range of methods
used, the involvement of the student learners in the processes and the
creation of feedback and evaluation procedures can all be recorded on a
positive–negative scale. Positive recordings are those which it is believed
will produce an occasion conducive to learning.

It will be useful for teachers of adults to undertake such self-appraisal
from time to time, for many will be faced with some form of external
evaluation such as staff appraisals. Learning how to cope with external
evaluations of your teaching–learning programme is a large part of learning to teach adults today for many tutors.

The wider significance of evaluation

Such external assessments reveal that evaluation in all forms of education, including adult learning programmes, frequently has a wider
application. As we have already noticed above, other people will often

take the information provided by your assessments and use it for various conclusions which are based on a wide range of untested assumptions. For example, the fact that an individual performed a task within the classroom to a level 'satisfactory' to the examiner (whatever that might mean) is taken by others without any justification to imply that this individual will replicate that performance time and again over a long period of time outside the classroom where conditions may be very different. Employers assume that passing an examination means that the student learner will make a good employee – but in fact passing an examination actually demonstrates very little except an ability to pass examinations and that is a doubtful indicator of future performance. Again, educational administrators assume that attendance figures above or below a certain (arbitrarily determined) level mean that teaching and learning in that course are satisfactory or inadequate, and take decisions about resources on that basis. Judgements are made about progress from the data provided by assessments. Untested assumptions underpin almost every evaluation which is undertaken in adult learning programmes – for example, that knowing about something in itself will lead to changes in patterns of behaviour (which experience demonstrates time and again is simply not true). It is necessary to unpack the assumptions being made and test them.

For evaluation in adult learning programmes today, especially in its summative form, has social as well as individual roles to play. It is not just for teacher and student learner alone. Issues of accountability, cost-effectiveness, social inclusion and cohesion, quality assurance, public recognition of learning all play their part. It is a part of our role as teachers to which we need to give much more attention.

Further reading

Campbell, P. (2007) *Measures of Success: Assessment and Accountability in Adult Basic Education.* Edmonton, Alberta: Grass Roots Press.

Ecclestone, K. (2005) *Understanding Assessment and Qualifications in Post-compulsory Education and Training: Principles, Politics and Practice,* 2nd edn. Leicester: NIACE.

Gardner, J. (2006) *Assessment and Learning.* London: Sage.

Race, Phil: Assessment, Learning and Teaching in Higher Education: www.phil-race.co.uk

RARPA: Recording and Recognition of Progress and Achievement (RARPA) in Non-accredited learning: www.rarpatoolkit.com/en/default.asp

Wider Benefits of Learning: www.learningbenefits.net

Chapter 13

Participation
Can we all join in . . . ?

All adults are natural learners; they learn in a self-directed way. They are accustomed to determine for themselves what they want to learn, when and how, and are free to decide when they have achieved their own goals. This chapter argues that in our teaching of adults we should as far as possible encourage the student learners to exercise these freedoms within the learning programme rather than deny them. But it points out that many adults, coming into educational encounters, especially those with accreditation, expect to abandon this self-determination in their desire for learning assistance; and this expectation is strengthened in many cases by the increasing control of adult learning programmes by the providers, including the government. This tension faces all of us who teach adults.

Participation is a word and a concept which has many different interpretations and values attached to it. It is not our purpose here to unravel all of these, for there are many detailed works on participation. Rather, we shall pick out three which have direct implications for our work as teachers of adults:

- participation as active involvement in the learning process (participation as practice);
- participation as control over the teaching–learning process (participation as power);
- participation as attendance at teaching–learning programmes (participation as presence).

We will look at each of these in turn.

Participation as involvement in the process (active learning)

We have seen that informal learning (which is the way we all learn naturally) is active learning, initiated and controlled by the student learner. This implies that, for learning in our taught programmes to be effective, the student participants in our groups need to be active, fully involved in the learning activities. Although the teacher 'teaches' (whatever that may mean), it is the student learners who do the learning. It has been said that for teachers to say that 'we taught but the students didn't learn' is as ridiculous as saying, 'I sold him a car but he didn't buy it'. Teaching adults is a matter of setting up a programme of activities, study and practice, and encouraging and enabling the student participants to engage in it. They run the length of the 'course', they engage in the activities, they do the work and arrive at the goals. The teacher cannot make the learning changes; only the student learners can do this. (This is rather different from – although sometimes confused with – the current interest in the 'personalisation' of learning; see Chapter 10 on curriculum; see also websites at end of chapter.) It is possible to envisage personalised learning plans which do not include active learning methods, just as it is possible to have standardised active learning programmes.

It is surprising how often we forget this simple truth, that learning is what the student learners do. As teachers, we often concentrate on what *we* are doing rather than on what the student participants are doing, often think that learning is dependent for its effectiveness on our teaching activities (the way we present knowledge or processes, our skills of communication, our demonstrations and visual aids and so on). Naturally, any book that deals with teaching adults runs the danger of compounding this error by concentrating upon the activities of the teacher rather than on those of the student learners. So right at the end, especially when we have just been considering evaluation, a task most teachers see as theirs alone, it is necessary to spell out once more that informal learning is a natural and essential human activity, undertaken in a specific human context via a conscious or more or less subconscious process (see pp. 143–4). Within the more formalised learning programmes which are implicit in our task of 'teaching adults', we need to build on this active learning process. Learning is what the student learners do.

This is important for a number of reasons. First for motivation. Students can 'make their own meaning' more effectively when engaged in active learning (see Petty 2008). Engaging in activities such as working together on practising in a given situation or evaluating a text develops thinking, problem-solving skills and evaluation processes. Secondly for learning itself – the internalising of the learning changes. These activities may be formative activities, their own assessments as to whether they see themselves as being on the right lines, trying out whether this is or is not a useful way of going about it, reflecting critically if these are the right processes for themselves or not – all of these activities and judgements are involved in the process of learning. Some activities will be summative activities, assessments as to how much has been completed, how far the learners feel that they have got and how much further they feel they need to go to approach the goal; such assessments are essential for keeping going at the learning tasks.

Continuing learning

It is often argued that a further reason why the student learners should be active is the need to encourage them to continue learning once our particular programme is over. But as we have seen, learning will continue throughout life (see pp. 130–2); it is a necessary part of life itself, not just a preparation for life. We all need to continue to learn because we cannot learn at the start all that we shall need during our uncertain path through life. Not only is there not enough time, but also many things will be unforeseen. In any case, many things will not make sense until we are actively engaged with them. To give an example: with changed social attitudes, alternative therapies are now a regular part of many medical practices but most GPs who find themselves faced with this subject have had to learn about these from scratch; their initial training made little or no contribution to their understanding in this area. Even if the subject had been included in the curriculum of their medical training programmes, it would not have made as much sense or been treated with the same regard as it is now that these doctors are faced with the question in real life. The same is true in other fields. For many positions, there is no initial training programme available – no one can take a course specifically to become a bishop, for example, an MP, or a trade union leader. What we want to promote is not lifelong learning, for that will go on anyway. We want to help our adult participants to engage in *purposeful and structured planned learning* in the form of learning episodes.

Much the same is true of teaching adults. While there are courses which can help prepare for this role, we need to learn how to do it while we do it. However much training we may have received in advance, however many books we read about it, it will not make sense until it is put into practice for real – and that is when the real learning begins.

But apart from such structured and purposeful learning, our learning episodes, there is all that continuing incidental learning which occurs throughout the whole of life. Our experiences will challenge us into learning. Such continued learning will come upon all of us at the most unexpected moments in our lives. As we have seen (see pp. 51–2), we shall find ourselves learning as our occupations change, as we enter new social roles and relationships or reinterpret existing ones, and as we enter new phases of self-development, develop new interests or discover new talents within ourselves.

In many parts of Western societies, it is agreed that the ultimate objective of all this learning is enhanced adulthood within our particular social context – i.e. the drive towards greater maturity and self-development, the search for meaning and a fuller sense of perspective, and the impulse towards increased autonomy: responsibility for ourselves and perhaps for others within that context. In this sense, the final aim of learning is liberation, self-determination, freedom, individuation, all making full use of the social context which we inhabit. But these highly personalised aims are not universally accepted today; they contrast sharply with other perspectives which are increasingly being promoted, especially by governmental bodies, which put the well-being of (economic) society before private gains as the main outcome of lifelong learning. Other cultures see the main purpose of continued learning throughout life as greater and greater consolidation within communities of interest, finding self-fulfilment in the welfare of the group rather than in individuation.

Most adult student learners engage in our programmes as part of their ongoing purposeful structured life-related learning activities. This means that the way we conduct our adult learning should contribute towards the goal of their learning, whether that be self-fulfilment, social commitment or occupational advancement. Our aim is to enable the student learners to achieve *their own* goals. These goals may coincide with our own goals; but again, they may be markedly different. For some, this will be to enhance their own sense of adulthood, to maximise the range of choices before them, to increase their control over aspects of their own lives, environment and their own learning. For others, it will be to improve their occupational prospects or to fulfil their social goals.

Teaching for freedom

It has been argued throughout this book that the most effective means of helping adults to learn is to understand and then build our teaching–learning programmes upon these natural lifelong learning episodes, their formats and their processes. The taught learning opportunities we create for the student learners should *utilise* these more structured natural learning episodes rather than *contradict* them or *deny* their existence or relevance. We need to make them more conscious, enhance their processes, make them more effective.

Such an approach will help us to determine not only the goals of our teaching of adults but also our subject matter and our methods. Both the selection of the content of our programmes and the methods we use should foster the adulthood of the student learners, however that is constructed. Our work with adult student learners needs to contribute to continued learning and strengthen the collaborative learning practices of the participants.

This means breaking the traditional dependency lying beneath so much current education: 'To build a safe atmosphere where people can trust one another across divisive social differences, we must begin to name the inequalities in the classroom and devise ground rules for communication' (Campbell and Burnaby 2001: 3). Anything we do that leads to the student learners becoming dependent upon ourselves or others as teachers will be denying their adulthood. We teachers need to work to make ourselves redundant in the process of creating self-directed, self-managing and discriminating but collaborative student learners. This can be achieved only through active learning methods in our adult learning groups. If we want our student learners to use active learning methods in their own learning *after* our programmes have ended, we must use such methods *inside* our programmes.

The dangers of directive participation

There is however a dilemma here – what if our student participants do not wish to join in the activities we have so carefully planned for them? Many adult learning programmes have failed because the teachers have employed what can be called 'directive participation': marching to another's drum. They tell the students that they *must* engage in this or that active learning process when the student participants do not wish to join in ice-breakers or role plays or simulation games. What if they do not wish to exercise responsibility for their own learning? For many adults do not expect their *taught* learning to be like this. They often expect and indeed wish for it to be more formal (see p. 89), for the teacher to 'teach' and for themselves to be more or less passive recipients of wisdom. To employ participatory approaches when the students want formality; to employ discussion when the students feel they need information from an expert leading to a page of notes; to try to share power when the students want hierarchy; to ask the students to tell the teacher when the students want the teacher to tell them – all of these would be to court disaster. Strong emotions become involved.

For some student participants, then, participation seen as active learning processes can be felt as a threat. As a tutor has written:

> Some of my student learners come from such chaotic backgrounds and families that they actually welcome and thrive in a structured, formal learning environment . . . I'm finding that the majority of my students don't function well in [a participatory] environment . . . many need more structure and expectations from me in order to feel 'committed' and to persevere . . .
>
> (personal communication)

We believe that it is important that all teachers of adults 'start where the students are' and not expect them to join us on our own starting line. It is important that we help the students to learn in whatever way they wish, even if that is formal and we wish to be non-formal. However, experience suggests that even in the more formal adult classes, after some time during which the student learners have been treated not as peers but as pupils and more or less ignorant student learners, they will themselves begin to challenge, to ask questions, to indicate points at which the things they are learning do not correspond with their own experience. Although it is true that some compartmentalise what they are learning into 'safe' areas, remote from their experiences, most adults test what they are learning against their own accumulated experience, they assess whether 'it rings true'. When they begin to feel that it does not is the moment when they start to become critically reflective of the learning programme, when they begin to engage actively rather than passively with the learning process. Such moments need to be carefully looked for and, when they occur, seized, cherished, built on. But this may not come quickly. Teaching adults is not always a matter which can be rushed; it will often take a lot of time. Starting off with too active participation will – in some cases – alienate some of the student learners.

Sharing, not serving

Does this mean that the teacher of adults is simply a facilitator of someone else's learning? We want to suggest that, if 'the arrogance of the learned' (see p. 8), the 'deficit and input' model of learning is to be eschewed, we must equally avoid the opposite extreme, what may be called the 'pooling of ignorance', the rejection of the help of any teacher, the refusal to admit that the experience of the qualified teacher has its own worth. Some new insights, some introduction to the processes of finding out, some available new experience for the student learners to 'search and select' (see pp. 120–1) are necessary to achieve effective learning programmes. Just as adult students have much to bring to the teaching–learning programme, so too adult teachers have valuable experience, insights, knowledge and skills; just as the teacher needs to take the student seriously, so too the students need to take the agendas and experience of the teacher seriously. Teaching adults is a meeting between a number of parties, all with valuable experience and insights; it is a sharing of knowledge, skills, perspectives, values, attitudes, horizons, 'teaching' on more or less equal terms – horizontal learning rather than vertical learning. Teaching adults is 'a pooling of differences'.

Any process of teaching adults that introduces unequal divisions and despises the views and activities of some is unacceptable. Teachers must not only be able to admit that they have much to learn from their students, they must seek to strengthen rather than weaken the different elements brought into the learning situation by all the participants. It is a process of sharing, of valuing each other, of increasing diversity, of 'celebrating the other'. So the student participants – within their own expectations and willingness – can and need to play a full part in that sharing, not simply be passive recipients of what the teacher has on offer.

Activity 13.1

Return for a moment to Activity 10.3 in Chapter 10: Contents and methods. In that Activity, you listed a number of methods you might use in your teaching. Using that list, think about some of the actual activities you are planning for your student learners to engage in during your course. Make a list of them.

Participation as increasing control over the process

'Participation as involvement in' does not imply any real control over the processes used; the teacher can and often does control the contents and determines the active processes to be used in the learning programme. But adult student learners are more likely to learn effectively if they have become involved in the creation of the teaching–learning programme; if they feel that (in part at least) they 'own' it: 'Learning will be enhanced as control over and responsibility for learning is concentrated in the hands of the learners, or at least shared between learners and resource people' (Campbell and Burnaby 2001: 318). They need to participate in determining what they should be able to do and what they should know about:

> It is now coming to be widely accepted that the best and most secure learning occurs when students are centrally involved in controlling, directing and monitoring their own learning progress, in ways and according to particular modes of proceeding that they select for themselves, in accordance with their own characteristic mode of cognitive operation and their awareness of how best to proceed in mastering new concepts, information and skills.
>
> (Aspin et al 2001: 21)

As Albert Mansbridge put it long ago (1920): 'The initiative must lie with the students. They must say how, why, what or when they wish to study'.

Now we have to be careful here. Some programmes in a non-formal context have said that they have given a large amount of control to the student learners; but a closer examination of these claims reveals that such matters are all on the periphery of the programme, for example, the location of the course or the timing the session starts, or the breaks needed during the course. Very rarely do these matters of control extend to the length of the course, the contents, the teaching–learning materials and methods and the processes of the evaluation of the programme. These are matters which are kept strongly under the control of the providers. The more adult education comes to resemble schooling, the more adult participants are denied control over the programme contents and methods – as are children – and indeed the more most adult participants do not expect to have any say in these matters.

In an attempt to increase such control, there are currently many moves towards personalised learning programmes, learning contracts and other forms of programme, where individual student learners are encouraged to help plan their own learning – provided these plans fall within the constraints of funding, external assessment and often classroom settings. But, even apart from such personalised learning plans, groups of adult student learners can join more generally in the planning of the learning programme, helping to determine the stages of learning, the steps by which the skills and knowledge are developed – areas that most providing bodies and teachers guard carefully to themselves. Adult student learners can contribute to setting the goals, for they have their own intentions in joining our learning groups, and it is best, if we wish to encourage autonomy and independence, to start from these intentions rather than to impose our own. Student learners can help in constructing the learning schedule, the methods/content part of the learning programme, the sequence of events and activities, for they all have their own skills of learning. They can provide some of the teaching–learning materials. They can (and should) determine how long the course should be. They can (and again should) also share in the process of evaluation; they will often watch more closely than the teacher what is happening in the group; and they will determine for themselves whether they have reached their own goals. Adult student learners can contribute to *all* parts of the teaching–learning process. The problem today is that most learning programmes for adults do not allow space for such contributions to be made.

Activity 13.2

You have made a list of activities based on some of the methods of teaching you have chosen. How involved have the student learners been in making those choices? Are there ways that you can think of to involve them more in the decision-making process?

Learning for freedom

All this implies that education, especially the education of adults, consists of 'two-way learning'. Teaching seen as 'informing' will be one-way and dependency-creating; it will not be liberating education. Clearly some information-gathering is necessary as part of the learning process, but the new knowledge does not need to be provided by the teacher alone. Compared with 'informing', training in the skills of locating and mastering knowledge for themselves can make the student learners free to exercise their newly-won learning as and when they wish. But training on its own can also be binding, especially when it sets out to demonstrate the 'right' way to do something without considering that there are likely to be circumstances in which the 'right' way might well be wrong! It is not enough to teach people how to do something or other without encouraging them to consider the social and political factors involved in this activity and the structures of society that control access to these resources. Only by undertaking this wider task of helping the students to consider critically the power implications of what they are studying will the participants be able to grow towards a freer way of life.

How do we do this? It is easier said than done. We can talk about 'teaching on equal terms', and we can see how it applies in some contexts. Social action groups that choose their own leader, women's studies circles and community development programmes will be able to operate on such a basis more easily than will certificated courses in dressmaking, advanced engineering or computing (although management training programmes have followed this route for a long time). But even in these contexts it is not always plain sailing, for 'voices are never equal, even in a democracy', and participation in this sense can 'increase the learners' sense of powerlessness because they do not speak the language of the educators' (Campbell and Burnaby 2001: 223, 229).

New relationships

We each need to explore these attitudes and the changed relationships between student learner, teacher and subject matter for ourselves. Perhaps the key, when we have come to put the student learner first rather than the teacher, is the need to listen more and to talk less. This book is, as we saw early on, not a good example of what we mean. It is by nature one-way, though we have tried to encourage you to use your experience on the material it contains and to test the views it expresses for yourself. Throughout, we have sought to promote the development of a listening society rather than the talking (or even shouting) society in which so many of us live. The maintenance of pluralism rather than uniformity, the valuing of the experience, knowledge and insights of others, and the search to strengthen these rather than weaken them, are, it seems to us, basic to all approaches to teaching adults, if we truly respect their adulthood. Participatory education 'will act as a catalyst to begin addressing the power dynamics outside of the educational environment' as well as within it (Campbell and Burnaby 2001: 3).

Such insights have led providers and teachers of adults to experiment with different forms of learning groups for adults. Some of these are very exciting – experiential learning programmes, confidence-building, self-exploration and self-programming groups such as those with unemployed workers, immigrant women, local community groups, shelter residents, parents' groups and young men who have been prevented from benefiting from traditional education (see e.g. *Adults Learning* 2001). Many other types of participants, such as weight-watchers, Alcoholics Anonymous, group therapy and self-awareness programmes, writing circles, social action groups (especially local community and residents' groups engaged in self-directed conservation and environmental enhancement activities) and quality circles have emerged from such concerns. The variety of groups is great and the range of activities wide. Even in more traditional programmes, whether based in the community or in an educational institution, where the presence of a recognised teacher figure is accepted, experiments with different forms of student learner involvement in the control of all the stages of constructing the activities have been conducted. Deciding what shall be learned, how it will be studied and what shall be done with the learning changes at the end of the programme are all matters for the group and not for the teacher or provider alone.

The student learners and knowledge

But it can go further than this. Adult learning groups can create knowledge. This truth has come to be recognised in some forms of teaching adults that have sprung up: self-learning groups, community action, research study groups and project study groups which publish their findings (Rogers 1995; Thornton and Stephens 1977). The archaeology group that under supervision explores an area and excavates new sites; the natural history members who record the flora and fauna or survey the geology of a region; the residents' group that investigates the schooling, housing or development needs of its own community; the village community that conducts its own needs survey; the literature course that engages in creative writing – all of these create knowledge. Many of them seek to give that new knowledge back to the community from whence it came, through exhibitions, publications, radio programmes, videos and films, websites and other media. In the process, new insights into the varied kinds of knowing have been produced and a new relationship between student learner and knowledge has come about (Unwin 1994).

It is important for us as teachers of adults to appreciate this. Knowledge is not the preserve of the few, the educated, to be doled out in small parcels to our student participants so that they in their turn can become 'experts'. It is something all of us can share in creating and discovering, and disseminate to others; something which we will all view from our own particular perspective (Barr 1999).

The teacher and knowledge

This calls for a radical change in the role of the teacher. Teachers and organisers nearly always do too much for their students; they work too much on their own. They exclude (often without realising it) the student learners from many parts of the task. It is the teacher and/or the provider who determines the length of the learning programme, the subject and the content matter. It is the teacher or provider who selects the goals, the pace of learning, the level of the learning programme. It is the teacher who chooses the materials, the methods and who usually evaluates the results.

All of this is done naturally, for it springs from a deep-rooted set of attitudes towards the student learners. Some of us tend to see the student learners as deprived of skills and knowledge, in which case those who possess the ability and the knowledge should give them; the student learners need 'input'. Some of us also tend to believe that the student learners are not capable of taking control of their own learning, that they cannot act on their own; they need to learn first before they can participate. There is a sense of the superiority of the teacher arising from the traditional world of education, a world that sees being 'learned' as the desired goal of all education, a state of attainment that the student learner might, by great effort, ultimately reach. There is often in this hierarchical attitude a view of education as a one-way process, the transfer of knowledge and expertise, the imparting of some good. Education (teaching) has become separated from life, from the kind of learning we use in our own natural learning episodes. Formalised learning has become separated from informal learning and has come to regard itself as superior to informal learning.

A reappraisal of the roles of both teacher and student learners will affect all parts of the teaching–learning encounter. If the teacher abandons the attitude of 'I know and I'll tell you' and instead says, 'I'll help you to work it out', the whole curriculum will change. If the teacher abandons the attitude of 'I'll communicate with you' and instead says, 'I'll help you to engage in a series of learning activities', the whole body of teaching methods will change.

Such a reorientation of the relationships between teacher, student learner and subject matter will seek to cast aside attitudes based on 'the arrogance of the learned'. There will be no more room for saying 'I know what you should learn'. We will move away from a view of education based on a hierarchy of knowledge: there will be no more placing of theoretical knowledge higher than practical or experiential knowledge. Such attitudes demean experience and lay unhealthy stress on accumulated practice or book knowledge. A view of teaching based on informal learning as well as on formalised learning will give value to all views (not just those of the academic), will see the application as well as the general principle, and will admit on occasion that 'I don't know' or 'I don't see it like that'.

Participation as presence in teaching–learning programmes

There is a third meaning of the word 'participation', one which is used more often than either of the other two meanings, 'participation as *process*' and 'participation as *power*': and that is 'participation as *presence*'. Published studies of 'participation in adult education' almost always mean studies of who attends or not. They say nothing about the programmes these people are being invited to join; they do not say what these 'participants' will do when they are in the programmes; they say nothing about whether the 'participants' have any say in determining the programme or not. They are simply interested in attendance – who comes and who does not, and what can be done to increase participation from different social classes, residential areas, gender groups, social communities, etc.

Here the issues of access and accessibility become important. Put briefly, 'access' normally means encouraging those who are not yet in our existing programmes to come in – through better advertisements or communication, persuasion and motivational projects – without necessarily changing the programmes. 'Accessibility' on the other hand means changing the programmes themselves – their location, their length, their timing, etc. – so that those who find it hard to attend can join. The provision of travel costs and/or of child-minding facilities are all part of accessibility (see Rogers 1980; Wright 1991).

Those outside and those inside?

Both of these approaches, access and accessibility, set out to help more people to attend programmes of adult learning.

But a view that teaching adults is not a process of instructing others but of enabling them to get a voice; not a process of bringing them from a position of exclusion 'into society' (our society) through our learning programmes but of helping them to play a fuller and more equal part in the society of which they are already full members, may lead us to question such appeals. We hear much today of 'social inclusion', especially in educational matters – a concept which is frequently used without deconstructing it to see precisely what it means and what attitudes it reveals (or hides). For example, in a country where those who are functionally non-literate form nearly 60 per cent of the total population, a view of literacy that speaks of 'bringing the illiterates into society' treats the majority as inferior and the minority alone as having true value. The concept of social exclusion assumes that the elites are always right; it does not critique the 'core' into which those who are defined as 'excluded' are urged to enter. The same goes for other social and cultural contexts where those who have been defined by the dominant groups as 'excluded' may not be majorities but minorities.

But the so-called 'excluded' are already part of society, and it can be argued that our task is to help them to lead a fuller life in their own terms, not necessarily to join *our* life pattern. It may well be to encourage and enable them to share in the work of controlling what is already their part of society.

If we see our work as part of this process, if we seek to share with equals rather than to instruct our inferiors or to persuade the excluded to become included into a core which they did not help to create, if we seek to help those who live in the slum to change the slum and improve their way of life in their own way, then we will be concerned about those who are *not* in our learning groups as much as with those who are. If we teach gardening, it will concern us that there are some who have potentially productive gardens who apparently do not wish to learn more about this aspect of life (we are not speaking here of the many skilled gardeners who already have rewarding gardens); it will also be important for us to consider why some people have no gardens at all. If we teach health studies, we shall be concerned that those who are not in reach of our programmes have opportunities for their needs to be met as well. If we teach adults in university degree courses, we will have some concern for those who wish to participate but are prevented from participating in such programmes.

Barriers to participation

The question of participation, then, is not just a matter of what the student learners in our classes and learning groups do in the process of learning. It is not just a matter of persuading the students to share in the planning and evaluation of the programme. It is also about encouraging others to take advantage of the learning opportunities. This will lead us to experiment with new formats of learning groups, with new timings, with new approaches to the subject matter that will be more appropriate to different groups of student learners, with restructuring our contents and methods to try to overcome the barriers that still exist in all societies.

Three things will try to work against our involving our student learners more effectively in managing their own learning programmes. First, there will be the pressures exerted by the increasing outside control and accountability which tends to focus on the teacher rather than on the student learners. Secondly, the trend to increasing personalisation of learning will reduce the influence of the learning group as a whole. And thirdly, we will all face some measure of participant reluctance – and indeed teacher reluctance – to share in power. But the effectiveness of our teaching depends not on our teaching but on the direct involvement of the student learners in the learning programme. This should be our main aim.

There are two parts to this. On the one hand, there is the provision of programmes to meet the needs of existing and new participants. In the course of this, we will become more aware of the barriers we ourselves put up to full participation – not only to those not in our learning groups but also to those who are – and seek to reduce them. We can play our part in increasing provision, creating new learning opportunities to meet the needs of those who do not attend. (Archbishop William Temple is reputed to have said that the Christian Church is an organisation that exists for the sake of those who are *not* its members; teachers of adults will often share much of the same concern.)

On the other hand, simply increasing provision does not always lead to greatly increased participation. The barriers of attitudes (the 'it's-not-for-me' syndrome) remain among many potential participants. And formal education remains the bastion of privilege:

> A participatory model [of learning] is welcome in few workplace settings. Practitioners are often only able to weave it in, intermittently, with more traditional approaches. But this is true outside of workplace education as well, even though the language of 'empowerment' and 'student directedness' is everywhere. Adult education is generally oriented to preparing people to uncritically participate in current work, school, and political systems. Many argue this is what adults say they want. Participatory education will continue to ask deeper questions to find out if this is *all* they want.
>
> (Campbell and Burnaby 2001: 194)

It is up to us as privileged people who are also teachers to address ourselves to the problem of working to overcome any sense of exclusion that we have created in many of our fellow human beings. Then we shall be truly concerned for participation.

Activity 13.3

Do you think that there are student learners who may be excluded from your learning programme? Who might they be and why do you think they may be excluded? Can you think of steps you or your provider organisation could take to increase participation in your programme?

The invisible teacher of adults

Participation in our dealings with our adult student learners will involve us in working with them to adopt an appropriate range of teaching–learning activities – not just the ones *we* feel they should do to be active, but the ones which fit *their* own perception of what it means to be a student.

Participation will also mean working with our student learners, sharing all our hopes and plans with them just as they share their hopes and plans with us. In addition, it will mean not just concern about those who are not in our programmes but taking what steps we can to ensure that the doors are at least open.

It is unlikely that we shall be hymned for all this. For if we really help our student participants to become more conscious and more effective learners on their own, we shall have made ourselves redundant. The following verses, which have been attributed to many different persons, say it all:

> Go to the people
> Live among them
> Learn from them
> Love them
> Start with what they know
> Build on what they have.
> But of the best leaders [read: teachers]
> When their task is accomplished
>   Their work is done
> The people all remark,
> 'We have done it ourselves'.

Further reading

Campbell, P. and Burnaby, B. (2001) *Participatory Practices in Adult Education*. London: Erlbaum.

Imel, S. (1999) *How Emancipatory is Adult Learning? Myths and Realities*. Columbus, OH: ERIC.

Participation in learning projects and programmes: www.infed.org/biblio/b-partln.htm

Personalising Learning: http://www.ssat-inet.net/whatwedo/personalis-inglearning.aspx

Petty, G. (2008) http://www.geoffpetty.com/activelearning.html

Rogers, J. (1976) *Right to Learn: The Case for Adult Equality*. London: Arrow.

Thompson, J.L. (ed.) (1980) *Adult Education for a Change*. London: Hutchinson.

Walters, S. (1996) *Gender in Popular Education*. London: Zed.

Conclusion
The learning and teaching of adults

This book about teaching adults has been concerned with two main themes. First, all of us, both teachers of adults and our student participants, construct ourselves and our learning programmes. We construct:

- the role of being an adult;
- the meaning of education (formalised learning);
- the role of being a 'student learner' and the role of being a teacher';
- the contract to learn between the teacher and the student participants.

These constructs are built on our diverse prior experience and on our socio-cultural context. Over the years, we and they have learned (mostly subconsciously but sometimes more formally) how to be an adult, a student and a teacher of adults. We do not always agree on what these roles should be, but in every case we construct such identities for ourselves and for others.

Secondly, there are different kinds of learning. We have seen two main kinds: the natural learning process which (like breathing) all persons engage in all the time, which we have called 'informal learning'; and the more planned and purposeful formalised learning. Informal learning continues throughout life. It is largely subconscious, or rather it is 'task-conscious' – the learning takes place within, and relates to, some lifeworld task. It is highly contextualised, limited to the specific task of which it forms a part. Formalised learning on the other hand is conscious learning. It includes decontextualised generalisations, basic principles and standardised meanings which enable knowledge to be used in more than one context. The task here is learning, mainly (but again not exclusively) for some future activity rather than for an immediate one.

Informal learning takes place within and is derived from our experience within our immediate socio-cultural context. It helps us to become inducted into, and yet help to shape, a particular culture or set of practices. Although critical reflection is a part of much informal learning, on its own informal learning will not normally help the learner to become critically reflective. Only if the learner is engaged with other critical reflectors will informal learning help them to become critically reflective on experience. We are suggesting that this is the key role of formalised learning – to help the adult learner to move beyond the limits of informal learning.

This book suggests that when we help adults to learn, we will be most effective if we can bring together both informal learning and formalised learning, for they both have much to offer. This will mean:

- making the sub-conscious informal learning more learning-conscious and critically reflective;
- making formalised learning more contextualised, more task-conscious.

The aim of teaching adults is to do both – to explore consciously how general rules can be applied to particular situations (and indeed, how they may have to be broken by specific contexts). Teaching adults in this way is to engage in a dialectic of contextualised and decontextualised learning. Neither is more important than the other; they need to be brought together.

But the sequencing of these two may be important. To start with the formal and move towards contextualised examples of application may in some circumstances be appropriate; this may be what the student learners expect and want. But in many cases of teaching adults, on the principle of 'starting where they are', it may be more helpful to start with the local and specific, and to widen out to the more general. Best of all is a cyclic approach: re-visiting both the formal and the informal in ever-increasing circles, gathering in new material as the programme progresses.

Teaching adults, then, is helping our student participants to become more conscious of who they are – and what they know and do not know, what they can do and what they cannot do, and above all of *how* they learn and how they can learn more effectively. This book itself is part of that process. We will already have learned much about teaching adults subconsciously through the informal learning of our experience, direct or mediated. And this process is most important – for the gap between theory and practice in the teaching of adults is wide, between what this book advocates and what sometimes happens in the learning group.

The aim of this book is to help you the reader to make your own learning about teaching adults more conscious; to help you to reflect critically on your perceptions of yourself as adult and as teacher, on your history, your roles and practices. It seeks to explore generalities but at the same time to help you to relate these generalities to your own specific situations. While this book may challenge you, it is equally for you to challenge this book from your own experience.

As we have already said, this book is not the end of the process. For some, it may be a beginning, for others, a step on the road towards improved practice. For the real learning starts when we act, when we practise and reflect critically on that practice; when we become conscious of how much we all have learned about teaching through informal processes, and plan to make that learning more conscious by using it in real situations and reflecting critically on that use. That is the task before us now.

Final Activity:

You may care to write down one or two of the changes you now plan to make in your teaching programme as a result of the reading of this book.

Bibliography

ACACE (1979) *Towards Continuing Education*. Leicester: ACACE.

Ackoff, R.L. (1978) *The Art of Problem-Solving*. New York: Wiley.

Action Research: http://ear.findingavoice.org/intro/index.html

Adelman, C. and Alexander, R. (1983) Evaluation, validation and accountability, in O. Boyd-Barrett et al (eds) *Approaches to Post-School Management*. London: Harper & Row.

Adey, P. et al (1999) *Learning Styles and Strategies: A Review of the Research*. London: King's College London.

Adults Learning (2001) 13(1). Leicester: NIACE.

Alexander, C. and Langer, E. (eds) (1990) *Higher Stages of Human Development: Perspectives on Human Growth*. Oxford: Oxford University Press.

Alexander, W. (1975) *Adult Education and the Challenge of Change*. Edinburgh: Scottish Education Department.

Alpine website: http://www.qub.ac.uk/alpine/ALPINE/2.htm

Andrews, G.J. (ed.) (1991) *Practical Handbook for Assessing Learning Outcomes in Continuing Education and Training*. Washington, DC: International Association for Continuing Education and Training (IACET).

APEL: The Higher Education Academy: UK Centre for Materials Education. http://www.materials.ac.uk/resources/library/apelintro.asp

Apps, J.W. (1985) *Improving Practice in Continuing Education*. San Francisco, CA: Jossey Bass.

Aspin, D., Chapman, J., Hatton, M. and Sawano, Y. (eds) (2001) *International Handbook of Lifelong Learning*. London: Kluwer.

Atherton, J.S. (2008) Doceo: Learning as Loss 1. www.doceo.co.uk/original/learnloss_1.htm

Atherton, J.S. (2009) *Learning and Teaching; Angles on Learning, Particularly after the Schooling Years*. www.learningandteaching.info/learning/ (accessed 18 September 2009).

Ball, C. (1991) *Learning Pays: The Role of Post-compulsory Education and Training*. London: Royal Society of Arts.

Banbury, J. and Carter, G. (1982) *Teaching Groups: A Basic Education Handbook*. London: Adult Literacy and Basic Skills Unit.

Barr, J. (1999) *Liberating Knowledge: Research, Feminism and Adult Education*. Leicester: NIACE.

Barron, R.S., Kerr, N.L. and Miller, N. (1992) *Group Process, Group Decision, Group Action.* Buckingham: Open University Press.

Belbin, R.M. (1980) *The Discovery Method in Training.* Sheffield: Manpower Services Commission.

Belenky, M., Clinchy, B.M., Goldberger, N.R. and Tarule, J.M. (1986) *Women's Ways of Knowing: The Development of Self, Voice and Mind.* New York: Basic Books.

Benei, V. (2008) *Schooling Passions: Nation, History and Language in Contemporary Western India.* Stanford, CA: Stanford University Press.

Bentley, T. (1998) *Learning Beyond the Classroom.* London: Routledge.

Berne, E. (1970) *Games People Play.* Harmondsworth: Penguin.

Birren, J.E. and Schaie, K.W. (eds) (1990) *Handbook of the Psychology of Aging,* 3rd edn. San Diego, CA: Academic Press.

Bligh, D.R. (1972) *What's the Use of Lectures?* Harmondsworth: Penguin.

Bloom, B.S. (ed.) (1956, 1964) *Taxonomy of Educational Objectives,* 2 vols. London: Longman.

Blumberg, A. and Gloembiewski, R.T. (1976) *Learning and Change in Groups.* Harmondsworth: Penguin.

Boshier, R. (1989) Participant motivation, in C. Titmus (ed.) *Lifelong Education for Adults: An International Handbook.* Oxford: Pergamon.

Boud, D., Cohen, R. and Walker, D. (1993) *Using Experience for Learning.* Buckingham: Open University Press.

Boud, D. (1988) *Developing Student Autonomy in Learning.* London: Kogan Page.

Boud, D. (1995) *Enhancing Learning through Self-Assessment.* London: Kogan Page.

Boud, D. and Miller, N. (1996) *Working with Experience: Animating Learning.* London: Routledge.

Boud, D., Keogh, R. and Walker, D. (eds) (1985) *Reflection: Turning Experience into Learning.* London: Kogan Page.

Boyd, D. and Bee, H. (2008) *Lifespan Development.* New York: Pearson.

Brice Heath, S. and Street, B.V. (2008) *On Ethnography: Approaches to Language and Literacy Research.* New York: Teachers College, Columbia.

Brookfield, S. (1983) *Adult Learners, Adult Education and the Community.* Milton Keynes: Open University Press.

Brookfield, S.D. (ed.) (1985) *Self-Directed Learning: From Theory to Practice.* San Francisco, CA: Jossey Bass.

Brookfield, S.D. (1986) *Understanding and Facilitating Adult Learning.* Milton Keynes: Open University Press.

Brookfield, S. (ed.) (1988) *Training Educators of Adults.* London: Routledge.

Brookfield, S. (1995) *Becoming a Critically Reflective Teacher.* San Francisco, CA: Jossey Bass.

Brookfield, S.D. (2000) Adult cognition as a dimension of lifelong learning, in J. Field and M. Leicester (eds) *Lifelong Learning: Education Across the Lifespan*, pp. 89–101. London: Taylor & Francis.

Brundage, D. and Mackeracher, D. (1980) *Adult Learning Principles and their Application to Program Planning.* Toronto: OISE.

Bruner, J.S. (1966) *Toward a Theory of Instruction.* Cambridge, MA: Harvard University Press.

Bruner, J.S. (1983) *In Search of Mind: Essays in Autobiography.* New York: Harper & Row.

Cairns, T. (2001) Acquiring basic skills as part of everyday life, *Adults Learning*, 13(3): 20–2.

Campbell, P. (ed.) (2007) *Measures of Success: Assessment and Accountability in Adult Basic Education.* Edmonton: Grass Roots Press.

Campbell, P. and Burnaby, B. (2001) *Participatory Practices in Adult Education.* London: Erlbaum.

Carr, W. and Kemmis, S. (1983) *Becoming Critical: Education, Knowledge and Action Research.* Victoria, Australia: Deakin University.

Cattell, R.B. (1987) *Intelligence: Its Structure, Growth and Action.* Amsterdam: North-Holland.

Cenoz, J. and Genesee, F. (eds) (1998) *Beyond Bilingualism: Multilingualism and Multilingual Education.* Clevedon: Multilingual Matters.

Charnley, A.H. and Jones, H.A. (1979) *Concept of Success in Adult Literacy.* Cambridge: Huntington.

Chickering, A.W. (ed.) (1981) *The Modern American College: Responding to the New Realities of Diverse Students and a Changing Society.* San Francisco, CA: Jossey Bass.

Christensen, R. and Hansen, A.T. (eds) (1987) *Teaching and the Case Method.* Boston, MA: Harvard Business School.

Claxton, G. (1984) *Live and Learn.* London: Harper & Row.

Coben, D. (1998) *Radical Heroes: Gramsci, Freire and the Politics of Adult Education.* New York: Garland.

Code, L. (1991) *What Can She Know? Feminist Theory and the Construction of Knowledge.* Ithaca, NY: Cornell University Press.

Coffield, F. (ed.) (2000) *The Necessity of Informal Learning.* Bristol: Policy Press.

Coffield, F., Moseley, D., Hall, E. and Ecclestone, K. (2004) *Should We be Using Learning Styles? What Research has to Say to Practice.* London: Learning and Skills Development Agency.

Colley, H., Hodkinson, P. and Malcom, J. (2003) *Informality and Formality in Learning: A Report for the Learning and Skills Research Centre.* www.LSRC.ac.uk

Corbett, M. (2007) *Learning to Leave: The Irony of Schooling in a Coastal Community.* Halifax: Fernwood Publishing.

Corder, N. (2002) *Learning to Teach Adults: An Introduction.* London: Routledge.

Cranton, P. (1994) *Understanding and Promoting Transformative Learning.* San Francisco, CA: Jossey Bass.

Cross, K.P. (1981) *Adults as Learners: Increasing Participation and Facilitating Learning.* San Francisco, CA: Jossey Bass.

Daines, J., Daines, C. and Graham, B. (1993) *Adult Learning, Adult Teaching,* 3rd edn. Nottingham: Department of Adult Education, University of Nottingham.

Davies, I.K. (1971) *The Management of Learning.* London: McGraw-Hill.

Davies, I.K. (1976) *Objectives in Curriculum Design.* London: McGraw-Hill.

Davies, P. (ed.) (1995) *Adults in Higher Education: International Perspectives in Access and Participation.* London: Jessica Kingsley.

Department of Education, Ireland (1984) *Lifelong Learning: Report of the Adult Education Commission for the Republic of Ireland* (the Kenny report). Dublin: Department of Education.

Dewey, J. (1933) *How We Think.* London: D.C. Heath.

Dewey, J. (1938) *Experience and Education.* New York: Macmillan.

DIUS (2008) Department of Innovation, Universities and Skills, *Informal Adult Learning: Shaping the way Ahead.* London: DIUS.

Douglas, T. (1983) *Groups: Understanding People Gathered Together.* London: Tavistock.

Duckworth, K., Akerman, R., MacGregor, A., Salter, E. and Vorhaus, J. (2009) *Self-regulated Learning: A Literature Review.* London: Centre for Wider Benefits of Learning, Institute of Education, University of London.

Duke, C. (2001) Lifelong learning and tertiary education: the learning university, in D. Aspin, J. Chapman, M. Hatton and Y. Sawano (eds) *International Handbook of Lifelong Learning,* pp. 501–28. London: Kluwer.

Duke, C. (2008) Trapped in a local history: why did extramural fail to engage in the era of engagement?, *Ad-Lib Journal for Continuing Liberal Adult Education,* 36: 3–19.

Easton, P. (1996) *Sharpening the Tools: Improving Evaluation in Adult and Nonformal Education.* Hamburg: UNESCO Institute of Education.

Ecclestone, K. (2005) *Understanding Assessment and Qualifications in Post-Compulsory Education and Training: Principles, Politics and Practice,* 2nd edn. Leicester: NIACE.

Edwards, A. and Protheroe, L. (2003) Learning to see in classrooms: what are student teachers learning about teaching and learning while learning to teach in schools?, *British Educational Research Journal,* 29(2): 227–42.

Edwards, R., Sieminski, S. and Zeldin, D. (eds) (1993) *Adult Learners, Education and Training*. London: Routledge.

Edwards, R., Hanson, A. and Raggatt, P. (eds) (1996) *Boundaries of Adult Learning*. London: Routledge.

Egan, G. (1973) *Face to Face: The Small Group Experience and Interpersonal Growth*. Montercy, CA: Brooks/Cole.

Egan, K. (1986) *Individual Development and the Curriculum*. London: Hutchinson.

Eisner, E.W. (1985) *The Art of Educational Evaluation*. London: Falmer.

Elsdon, K.T. (1975) *Training for Adult Education*. Nottingham: University of Nottingham.

Elsdon, K.T. (1984) *The Training of Trainers*. Cambridge: Huntington.

Eraut, M. (2000) Non-formal learning, implicit learning and tacit knowledge in professional work, in F. Coffield (ed.) *The Necessity of Informal Learning*. Bristol: Policy Press.

Erikson, E. (1965) *Childhood and Society*. Harmondsworth: Penguin.

Evans, K., Kersh, N. and Sakamoto, A. (2004) Learner biographies: exploring tacit dimensions of knowledge and skills, in H. Rainbird, A. Fuller, and A. Munro (eds) (2004) *Workplace Learning in Context*. London: Routledge.

Evans, N. (1992a) *Experiential Learning: Assessment and Accreditation*. London: Routledge.

Evans, N. (1992b) Linking Personal Learning and Public Recognition, in J. Mulligan and C. Griffin (eds) (1992) *Empowerment through Experiential Learning: Explorations of Good Practice*. London: Kogan Page.

Evans, N. (1994) *Experiential Learning for All*. London: Cassell.

Evans, N. (2000) *Experiential Learning around the World: Employability and the Global Economy*. London: Jessica Kingsley.

Explorations in Learning & Instruction: the Theory Into Practice Database, http://tip.psychology.org/

Fenwick, T.J. (2001) *Experiential Learning: A Theoretical Critique*. Columbus, OH: ERIC.

Field, J. and Leicester, M. (eds) (2000) *Lifelong Learning: Education Across the Lifespan*. London: Taylor & Francis.

Fieldhouse, R. (1996) *A History of Modern British Adult Education*. Leicester: NIACE.

Flanders, N.A. (1970) *Analyzing Teaching Behavior*. Reading, MA: Addison-Wesley.

Foley, G. (1999) *Learning in Social Action*. London: Zed.

Fraser, W. (1995) *Learning from Experience: Empowerment or Incorporation?* Leicester: NIACE.

Freire, P. (1972) *Pedagogy of the Oppressed*. Harmondsworth: Penguin.

Friedmann, E.A. (1977) *The Meaning of Work and Retirement*. New York: Arno Press.

Further Education Unit (1984) *Curriculum Development in the Education of Adults: A Manual for Practitioners*. Bristol: FEU.

Gagné, R.M. (1972) Domains of learning, *Interchange*, 3(1): 1–8.

Gagné, R.M. (1975) *The Conditions of Learning*. New York: Holt, Rinehart & Winston.

Galbraith, M.W. (ed.) (1991) *Adult Learning Methods: A Guide for Effective Instruction*. Malabar, FA: Krieger.

Gardner, H. (1993) *Multiple Intelligences: The Theory in Practice*. New York: Basic Books.

Gebre, A.H., Openjuru, G.L., Rogers, A. and Street, B.V. (2009) *Everyday Literacies in Africa: Ethnographic Studies of Literacy and Numeracy Practices in Ethiopia*. Kampala: Fountains Press.

Gibbs, G., Morgan, A. and Taylor, E. (1982) Why students don't learn, *Institutional Research Review*, 1(10).

Giles, K. (1981) *Personal Change in Adults*. Milton Keynes: Open University Press.

Giroux, H.A. (1983) *Theory and Resistance in Education: A Pedagogy for the Oppressed*. South Hadley, MA: Bergin & Garvey.

Griffin, C. (1987) *Adult Education as Social Policy*. London: Croom Helm.

Griffin, C. (1983) *Curriculum Theory in Adult and Continuing Education*. Beckenham: Croom Helm.

Gross, R.D. (1987) *Psychology: The Science of Mind and Behaviour*. London: Hodder & Stoughton.

Guba, E. and Lincoln, E.S. (1981) *Effective Evaluation*. San Francisco, CA: Jossey Bass.

Habermas, J. (1978) *Knowledge and Human Interest*. London: Heinemann.

Hager, P. (2001) Lifelong learning and the contribution of informal learning, in D. Aspin, J. Chapman, M. Hatton and Y. Sawano (eds) *International Handbook of Lifelong Learning*, pp. 79–92. London: Kluwer.

Hager, P. and Halliday, J. 2009 *Recovering Informal Learning: Wisdom, Judgement and Community*. Dordrecht: Springer.

Hall, S. (ed.) (1997) *Representation: Cultural Representations and Signifying Practices*. London: Sage/Open University Press.

Hanson, A. (1996) The search for a separate theory of adult learning: does anyone really need andragogy?, in R. Edwards, A. Hanson and P. Raggatt (eds) *Boundaries of Adult Learning*. London: Routledge.

Hare, A.P. (1976) *Handbook of Small Group Research*. Glencoe, NY: The Free Press.

Havighurst, R.J. (1952) *Development Tasks and Education*. New York: McKay.

Hay McBer Report (2000) *A Model of Teacher Effectiveness*. Report by Hay McBer to the Department for Education and Employment June 2000. www.teachernet.gov.uk/_doc/1487/haymcber.doc

Held, D. (1980) *Introduction to Critical Theory: From Horkheimer to Habermas*. Berkeley, CA: University of California Press.

Henriques, J. (1984) *Changing the Subject: Psychology, Social Regulation and Subjectivity*. London: Methuen.

Herzberg, F. (1972) *The Motivation to Work*. Chichester: Wiley.

Hillier, Y. (2002) *Reflective Teaching in Further and Adult Education*. London: Continuum.

Honey, P. and Mumford, A. (1992) *Manual of Learning Styles*, revised edn. Maidenhead: Peter Honey.

Houle, C.O. (1961) *The Inquiring Mind: A Study of the Adult who Continues to Learn*. Madison, WI: University of Wisconsin Press.

Hudson, L. (1966) *Contrary Imaginations*. London: Methuen.

Hudson, F. (1991) *The Adult Years*. San Francisco, CA: Jossey Bass.

Hughes, J.A. and Graham, S.W. (1990) Adult life roles: a new approach to adult development, *Journal of Continuing Higher Education*, 38(2): 2–8.

Illeris, K. (2002) *The Three Dimensions of Learning*. Roskilde: Roskilde University Press.

Imel, S. (ed.) (1996) *Learning in Groups: Exploring Fundamental Principles, New Uses and Emerging Opportunities*. San Francisco, CA: Jossey Bass.

Imel, S. (1998) *Teaching Critical Reflection: Trends and Issues Alert*. Columbus, OH: ERIC.

Imel, S. (1999) *How Emancipatory is Adult Learning? Myths and Realities*. Columbus, OH: ERIC.

ISCED (1975) *International Standard Classification of Educational Data*. Paris: UNESCO.

Jacques, D. (1991) *Learning in Groups*, 2nd edn. London: Kogan Page.

Jacques, D. and Salmon, G. (2007) *Learning in Groups – A Handbook for Face-to-face and Online Environments*, 4th edn. London: Routledge.

Jarvis, P. (1987) *Adult Learning in a Social Context*. London: Croom Helm.

Jarvis, P. (1995) *Adult and Continuing Education: Theory and Practice*. London: Routledge.

Jarvis, P. (ed.) (2001a) *The Age of Learning*. London: Kogan Page.

Jarvis, P. (2001b) *Learning in the Third Age*. London: Kogan Page.

Jarvis, P., Holford, J. and Griffin, C. (1998) *Theory and Practice of Learning*. London: Kogan Page.

Johnstone, J.W.C. and Rivera, R.J. (1965) *Volunteers for Learning: A Study of the Educational Pursuits of Adults*. Hawthorne, NY: Aldine Press.

Kasl, E. and Elias, D. 2008: www.transformativelearningtheory.com/groupLearning.html

Kelly, G.A. (1955) *Psychology of Personal Constructs*, vols 1 & 2. New York: McGraw-Hill.

Kidd, J.R. (1973) *How Adults Learn*. New York: Association Press.

King, P.M. and Kitchener, K.S. (1994) *Developing Reflective Judgment*. San Francisco, CA: Jossey Bass.

Knowles, M. and Knowles, H. (1972) *Introduction to Group Dynamics*. New York: Association Press.

Knowles, M.S. (1980) *The Modern Practice of Adult Education: From Pedagogy to Andragogy*. New York: Association Press.

Knowles, M.S. (1990) *The Adult Learner: A Neglected Species*. Houston, TX: Gulf.

Knox, A.B. (1977) *Adult Development and Learning*. San Francisco, CA: Jossey Bass.

Kolb, D.A. (1976) *Learning Style Inventory Technical Manual*. Boston, MA: McBer.

Kolb, D.A. (1984) *Experiential Learning: Experience as the Source of Learning and Development*. Englewood Cliffs, NJ: Prentice-Hall.

Krashen, S. (1982) *Principles and Practice of Second Language Acquisition*. Oxford: Pergamon.

Laing, R.D. (1972) *Knots*. Harmondsworth: Penguin.

Lave, J. and Wenger, E. (1991) *Situated Learning: Legitimate Peripheral Participation*. Cambridge: Cambridge University Press.

Leagans, P. (1971) *Behavioral Change in Agriculture*. Ithaca, NY: Cornell University Press.

LEIF (1990) Erno Lehtinen: From superficial learning to true expertise – education challenge of the future, *Life and Education in Finland*, 2(90): 14.

Levinson, D. (1979) *The Seasons of a Man's Life*. New York: Ballantine.

Lewin, K. (1935) *A Dynamic Theory of Personality*. New York: McGraw-Hill.

Lewin, K. (1947) Frontiers in group dynamics: concept, method and reality in social science, *Human Relations*, 1(2): 5–41.

Lovell, R.B. (1980) *Adult Learning*. London: Croom Helm.

Lovett, T. (1982) *Adult Education, Community Development and the Working Class*. Nottingham: University of Nottingham.

Lucas, A.M. (1983) Scientific literacy and informal learning, *Studies in Science Education*, 10: 7–36.

Mahiri, J. (ed.) (2003) *What They Don't Learn in School: Literacy in the Lives of Urban Youth*. New York: Peter Lang.

McClelland, D.C., Atkinson, J.W., Clark, R.A. and Lovell, E.L. (1953) *The Achievement Motive*. New York: Appleton-Century-Crofts.

McClintock, C.G. (1972) *Experimental Social Psychology*. New York: Holt, Rinehart & Winston.

McGregor, D. (1960) *The Human Side of Enterprise*. New York: McGraw-Hill.

Mager, R. (1991) *Preparing Instructional Objectives*, 2nd edn. London: Kogan Page.

Mahiri, J. (ed.) (2008) *What They Don't Learn in School: Literacy in the Lives of Urban Youth*. New York: Lang.

Mansbridge, A. (1920) *Adventure in Working Class Education*. London: Longmans Green.

Maslow, A.H. (1968) *Towards a Psychology of Being*. New York: Van Nostrand.

Mayo, M. (1997) *Imagining Tomorrow: Adult Education for Transformation*. Leicester: NIACE.

Merriam, S. and Cafarella, R. (1999 edition) *Learning in Adulthood*. San Francisco, CA: Jossey Bass.

Mezirow, J. et al (2000) *Learning as Transformation*. San Francisco, CA: Jossey Bass.

Mezirow, J. (1981) A critical theory of adult learning and education, *Adult Education*, 32: 3–24.

Moll, L., Amanti, C., Neff, D. and Gonzalez, N. (1992) Funds of knowledge for teaching: using a qualitative approach to connect homes and classrooms, *Theory into Practice*, 31(2): 3–9.

Moore, A. (2004) *The Good Teacher: Dominant Discourses in Teacher Education*. London: Routledge.

Neary, M. (2002) *Curriculum Studies in Post-Compulsory and Adult Education: A Teachers' and Student Teachers' Study Guide*, 3rd edn. Cheltenham: Nelson Thornes.

Neugarten, B.L. (1977) Personality and aging, in J.E. Birren and K.W. Schaie (eds) *Handbook of the Psychology of Aging*. New York: Van Nostrand Reinhold.

NIACE (National Institute of Adult (Continuing) Education) (1970) *Survey of Provision*. Leicester: NIACE.

NICCE (Northern Ireland Council for Continuing Education) (1980) *Continuing Education in Northern Ireland: Strategy for Development*. Belfast: NICCE.

Nirantar (2007) *Exploring the Everyday: Ethnographic Approaches to Literacy and Numeracy Practices*. New Delhi: Nirantar. www.nirantar.net

OECD (Organisation for Economic Cooperation and Development) (1977) *Learning Opportunities for Adults*. Paris: OECD.

Ostervan, K. and Kottkamp, R. (1993) *Reflective Practice for Educators*. London: Sage.

Pahl, K. (2008) Tracing habitus in texts and practices, in A. Luke and J. Albright (eds) *Pierre Bourdieu and Literacy Education*, pp. 187–208. London: Routledge.

Papalia, D.E., Sterns, H.L., Feldman, R.D. and Camp, C.J. (2007) *Adult Development and Aging*. New York: McGraw-Hill.

Paterson, K.W. (1979) *Values, Education and the Adult.* London: Routledge.

Paulston, R.G. (1996) *Social Cartography: Mapping Ways of Seeing Social and Educational Change.* London: Garland.

Petty, G. (2008) www.geoffpetty.com/activelearning.html

Phillips, D.C. and Soltis, J.F. (2003) *Perspectives on Learning.* New York: Teachers College Press.

Pratt, D.D. (1991) Conceptions of the self in China and the US: contrasting foundations for adult development, *International Journal of Intercultural Relations,* 15(3): 285–310.

Prenzel, M., Kramer, K. and Dreschel, B. (2001) Self-interested and interested learning in vocational education, in K. Beck (ed.) *Teaching–Learning Processes in Initial Business Education.* Dordrecht: Kluwer.

Prinsloo, M. and Breier, M. (eds) (1997) *Social Uses of Literacy.* Amsterdam: Benjamins.

Rahman, M.A. (1993) *People's Self-Development: Perspectives on Participatory Action Research.* London: Zed.

Ramsden, P. (1992) *Learning to Teach in Higher Education.* London: Routledge.

RARPA: Recording and Recognition of Progress and Achievement (RARPA) in Non-accredited learning: http://www.rarpatoolkit.com/en/default.asp

Reid, C. (1969) *Groups Alive – Church Alive: The Effective Use of Small Groups in the Local Church.* New York: Harper & Row.

Resnick, L. (1987) Learning in school and out, *Educational Researcher,* 16(9): 13–20.

Rogers, A. (ed.) (1977) *The Spirit and the Form: Essays by and in Honour of Harold Wiltshire.* Nottingham: University of Nottingham.

Rogers, A. (1980) *Knowledge and the People: The Role of the University in Adult and Continuing Education.* Londonderry: New University of Ulster.

Rogers, A. (1991a) *Teaching Adults in Extension.* Reading: Education for Development.

Rogers, A. (1991b) *Teaching Methods in Extension.* Reading: Education for Development.

Rogers, A. (1992) *Adults Learning for Development.* London: Cassell.

Rogers, A. (1993) Adult learning maps and the teaching process, *Studies in the Education of Adults,* 22(2): 199–220.

Rogers, A. (1995) Participatory research in local history, *Journal of Regional and Local Studies,* 15(1): 1–14.

Rogers, A. (1997) Learning: can we change the discourse?, *Adult Learning,* 8(5): 116–17.

Rogers, A. (2003) *What is the Difference? A New Critique of Adult Learning and Teaching.* Leicester: NIACE.

Rogers, A. (2004) *Nonformal Education: Flexible Schooling or Participatory Education*. Hong Kong: Hong Kong University Press and Dordrecht: Kluwer.

Rogers, A. (2006) Escaping the slums or changing the slums? Lifelong learning and social transformation, *International Journal of Lifelong Education*, 25(2): 125–37.

Rogers, C.R. (1974) *On Becoming a Person*. London: Constable.

Rogers, C.R. (1983) *Freedom to Learn for the 80s*. Columbus, OH: Merrill.

Rogers, J. (1969) *Teaching on Equal Terms*. London: BBC Publications.

Rogers, J. (1976) *Right to Learn: The Case for Adult Equality*. London: Arrow.

Rogers, J. (1977) *Adults Learning*. Milton Keynes: Open University Press.

Rogers, J. (1984) *Adults in Education*. London: BBC Publications.

Rogers, J. (1989) *Adults Learning*, 2nd edn. Buckingham: Open University Press.

Rogers, J. (2001) *Adults Learning*, 4th edn. Buckingham: Open University Press.

Rotter, J.B. (1982) *The Development and Applications of Social Learning Theory*. New York: Praeger.

Rowntree, D. (1987) *Assessing Students*. London: Kogan Page.

Ruddock, R. (1981) *Evaluation: A Consideration of Principles and Methods*. Manchester: Manchester University Press.

Rundle, S. and Dunn, R. (1999) *The Building Excellence Adult Learning Style Inventory*. New York: Performance Concepts International.

Ryan, A.B. (2001) *Feminist Ways of Knowing: Towards Theorising the Person for Radical Adult Education*. Leicester: NIACE.

Rychen, D.S. and Salganik, L.H. (2001) *Defining and Selecting Key Competencies*. Seattle, WA: Hogrefe and Huber.

Ryle, G. (1949) *The Concept of Mind*. London: Hutchinson.

Sallis, E. and Jones, G. (2002) *Knowledge Management in Education: Enhancing Learning and Education*. London: Kogan Page.

Schein, E.H. and Kommers, D.W. (1972) *Professional Education*. New York: McGraw-Hill.

Schön, D.A. (1983) *The Reflective Practitioner: How Professionals Think in Action*. New York: Basic Books.

Schön, D.A. (1995) *Educating the Reflective Practitioner*. San Francisco, CA: Jossey Bass.

Schuller, T. and Watson, D. (eds) *IFLL Report* (2009) Inquiry into the Future of Lifelong Learning. *Learning Through Life*. Leicester: NIACE.

Scribner, S. (1988) *Head and Hand: An Action Approach to Thinking*. Columbus, OH: ERIC.

Shaw, M.E. (1981) *Group Dynamics: Psychology of Small Group Behavior*. New York: McGraw-Hill.

Sheehy, G. (1976) *Passages: Predictable Crises of Adult Life.* New York: Dutton.

Sigelman, C.K. and Rider, E.A. (2008) *Lifespan Human Development.* Belmont, CA: Wadsworth.

Sork, T.J. (ed.) (1984) *Designing and Implementing Effective Workshops.* San Francisco, CA: Jossey Bass.

Smith, M.K. (2000) Curriculum theory and practice, *The Encyclopaedia of Informal Education*, www.infed.org/biblio/b-curric.htm.

Stephens, M.D. (1990) *Adult Education.* London: Cassell.

Stephens, M.D. and Roderick, G.N. (1971) *Teaching Techniques in Adult Education.* Newton Abbot: David & Charles.

Storant, M. and van den Bos, G.R. (eds) (1989) *The Adult Years: Continuity and Change.* Washington, DC: American Psychological Association.

Stromquist, N.P. (1997) *Literacy for Citizenship.* New York: State University of New York.

Sugarman, L. (1986) *Lifespan Development: Concepts, Theories and Interventions.* New York: Methuen.

Sutherland, P. (ed.) (1997) *Adult Learning: A Reader.* London: Kogan Page.

Taylor, E.W. (1998) *Theory and Practice of Transformative Learning: A Critical Review.* Columbus, OH: ERIC.

Teaching Adults: there are some useful papers among those on the following site: http://honolulu.hawaii.edu/intranet/committees/FacDevCom/guidebk/teachtip/teachtip.htm

Tennant, M. (2006) *Psychology and Adult Learning*, 3rd edn. London: Routledge.

Thomas, H. (1987) Perspectives on evaluation, in M. Hughes, P. Robbins and H. Thomas (eds) *Managing Education: The System and the Institution*, pp. 373–93. London: Cassell.

Thompson, J.L. (ed.) (1980) *Adult Education for a Change.* London: Hutchinson.

Thornton, A. and Stephens, M.D. (1977) *The University in its Region: The Extramural Contribution.* Nottingham: University of Nottingham.

Thorpe, M., Edwards, R. and Hanson, A. (1993) *Culture and Processes of Adult Learning.* London: Routledge.

Tight, M. (ed.) (1983) *Education for Adults*, vol. 1, *Adult Learning and Education*; vol. 2, *Opportunities for Adult Education.* Beckenham: Croom Helm.

Tough, A. (1979) *The Adult's Learning Projects: A Fresh Approach to Theory and Practice of Adult Learning*, 2nd edn. Toronto: OISE.

Travers, R.M.W. (1964) *Introduction to Educational Research.* New York: Macmillan.

Tuijnman, A. and van der Kamp, M. (eds) (1992) *Learning Across the Lifespan: Theories, Research, Policies.* Oxford: Pergamon.

UNESCO (United Nations Educational, Scientific, and Cultural Organization) (1975a) *ISCED: International Standard Classification of Educational Data*. Paris: UNESCO.

UNESCO (United Nations Educational, Scientific, and Cultural Organization)(1975b) *Educational Radio and Television*. Paris: UNESCO.

UNESCO (United Nations Educational, Scientific, and Cultural Organization) (1976) *Nairobi: Recommendations on the Development of Adult Education: Declaration of Nairobi Conference*. Paris: UNESCO.

Unwin, P. (1994) *Group Research Projects in Adult Education*. Sheffield: University of Sheffield.

Valsiner, J. (ed.) (1995) *Child Development in Culturally Structured Environments*. Norwood, NJ: Ablex.

Van der Kamp, M. (1992) Effective adult learning, in A.C. Tuijnman and M. Van der Kamp (eds) (1992) *Learning Across the Lifespan: Theories, Research, Policies*. Oxford: Pergamon.

Verduin, J.R. (1983) *Adults Teaching Adults: Principles and Strategies*. Mansfield: University Associates.

Verma, J. (1995) Transformation of women's social roles in India, in J. Valsiner (ed.) *Child Development in Culturally Structured Environments*. Norwood, NJ: Ablex.

Vosniadou, S. (2001) *How Children Learn*. Paris: UNESCO.

Vygotsky, L.S. (1962) *Thought and Language*. Cambridge, MA: MIT Press.

Vygotsky, L.S. (1978) *Mind in Society: The Development of Higher Psychological Processes*. Cambridge, MA: Harvard University Press.

Wallis, J. (ed.) (1996) *Liberal Adult Education: The End of an Era?* Nottingham: Continuing Education Press.

Walters, S. (1996) *Gender in Popular Education*. London: Zed.

Walters, S. (ed.) (1997) *Globalization, Adult Education and Training*. Leicester: NIACE.

Welton, M. (1995) *In Defense of the Lifeworld*. New York: SUNY.

Whitehead, A.N. (1959) *The Aims of Education*. New York: Macmillan.

Wider Benefits of Learning: www.learningbenefits.net

Wiltshire, H. (1976) The great tradition in university adult education, in A. Rogers (ed.) *The Spirit and the Form: Essays in Adult Education by and in Honour of Professor Harold Wiltshire*, pp. 31–8. Nottingham: University of Nottingham.

Wood, J. (1974) *How Do You Feel?* Englewood Cliffs, NJ: Prentice-Hall.

Wright, P. (1991) Access or accessibility, *Journal of Access Studies*, 6(1): 6–15.

Youngman, F. (2000) *The Political Economy of Adult Education and Development*. London: Zed.

Zander, A. (1982) *Making Groups Effective*. San Francisco, CA: Jossey Bass.

Index of authors cited

Index of subjects